AF324005

EDI - Hundredth Volume

India's Economy

A JOURNEY IN TIME AND SPACE

--- Editors ---

RAJ KAPILA
Director & Chief Editor,
Academic Foundation, New Delhi

UMA KAPILA
Senior Editor, Academic Foundation
Former Reader (retd.), Deptt. of Economics,
Miranda House, University of Delhi

EDI - Hundredth Volume

India's Econ⊚my

A JOURNEY IN TIME AND SPACE

Editors: Raj Kapila and Uma Kapila

ACADEMIC FOUNDATION
NEW DELHI

www.academicfoundation.com

Published in 2006
by :

ACADEMIC FOUNDATION
4772-73 / 23 Bharat Ram Road, (23 Ansari Road),
Darya Ganj, New Delhi - 110 002 (India).
Phones : 23245001 / 02 / 03 / 04.
Fax : +91-11-23245005.
E-mail : academic@vsnl.com
www : academicfoundation.com

Cataloging in Publication Data--DK
        Courtesy: D.K. Agencies (P) Ltd. <docinfo@dkagencies.com>

    India's economy : a journey in time and space /
    editors, Raj Kapila and Uma Kapila.
        p.   cm.
    Contributed articles.
    "EDI hundredth volume."
    Includes bibliographical references.
    Includes index.
    ISBN 81-7188-581-0

    1. India--Economic conditions--1947-   2. India--Economic
    policy--1991-   3. Poverty--Government policy--India.
    4. Globalization--Economic aspects--India. 5. Agriculture
    --Economic aspects--India. 6. Finance--India.
    I. Kapila, Raj. II. Kapila, Uma.

    DDC 330.954   22

Designed and typeset by Italics India, New Delhi.
Printed and bound in India.

CONTENTS

LIST OF FIGURES AND TABLES 8

CONTRIBUTORS 11

MESSAGE FROM THE PRIME MINISTER OF INDIA, DR. MANMOHAN SINGH ... 13

FOREWORD BY DR. C. RANGARAJAN 15

ACKNOWLEDGEMENTS 17

INTRODUCTION 19

Section I

Economy: Growth, Poverty and Reforms

1. **India: On the Growth Turnpike**
   VIJAY L. KELKAR 35

2. **Towards a New Development Paradigm**
   ARVIND VIRMANI 67

3. **Growth, Poverty and Reforms**
   JAGDISH BHAGWATI 81

4. **Redefining the Approach to Poverty Reduction and Development**
   N.A. MUJUMDAR 89

...CONTD. ...

5. **Poverty and Development Policy**
    A. VAIDYANATHAN 99

6. **Fifty Years of India: A Journey in Time**
    ASHOK V. DESAI 143

7. **Public Governance**
    N.R. NARAYANA MURTHY 155

Section II

Globalisation

8. **India in a Globalising World**
    MONTEK S. AHLUWALIA 169

9. **Indian Economy in the Global Setting**
    RAKESH MOHAN 185

10. **India and Globalisation**
    BIMAL JALAN 199

11. **Half-hearted Globalisation**
    SHANKAR ACHARYA 205

Section III

Sectoral Development: Agriculture, Industry, Financial and External Sector

12. **Reshaping Indian Food and Agricultural Policy to Meet the Challenges and Opportunities of Globalisation**
    PER PINSTRUP-ANDERSEN .211

13. Food Security in India: Towards Elimination
of Hunger and Malnutrition

V.S. Vyas 231

14. Sustainable Use of Water for Irrigation
in Indian Agriculture

C.H. Hanumantha Rao 247

15. Mission 2007: Every Village a Knowledge Centre

M.S. Swaminathan 259

16. Unshackling India's Manufacturing—
The Ingredients of a Strategy

Bibek Debroy 263

17. Foreign Direct Investment in India:
Trends and Issues

R. Nagaraj 297

18. Financial Stability: Some Analytical Issues

C. Rangarajan 331

19. The Emerging Configuration in the
Financial Sector

S.S. Tarapore 353

20. Managing India's External Sector:
Overcoming Challenges in a Globalising Economy

Y.V. Reddy 361

Index 371

List of Figures and Tables

FIGURES

1.1   India's GDP Growth 36

17.1   FDI into India, 1992-2000 303

17.2   India's Share in World FDI 307

17.3   Actual FDI by Different Routes 307

17.4   FDI in Selected Asian Economies, 1991-2000 312

17.5   FDI in India and China 312

17.6   Decline in Technical Collaborations Agreements 322

TABLES

1.1   GDP Growth and Per-capita GDP 37

1.2   Structure of Tax Revenues from 1990 to 2001 51

1.3   Per-capita SDP and Population 53

1.4   Changes in Per-capita Investment in
      Different States 59

11.1   Indicators of Globalisation 207

14.1   Productivity of Irrigation for Foodgrains
       in Indian Agriculture (Growth Rates) 250

16.1   Industrial Classification and the 2-digit Codes
       and Discriptions 269

16.2   Share of the Manufacturing Sector in GDP
       (Per Cent) 275

...CONTD. ...

16.3   Seventeen Industry Groups at the 2-digit Level
          of Classification 277

17.1   Top 10 Investing Countries in India, 1991-2000 304

17.2   Sectoral Distribution of FDI Approvals,
          1991-2000 304

17.3   Distribution of FDI by Size of Investment,
          1991-1997 305

17.4   Top Five Destinations of Approved FDI among
          the Indian States 305

17.5   Alternative Estimates of the Actual FDI,
          1991-2000 306

17.6   An Illustrative List of Foreign Firms Not Listed
          in the Domestic Stock Market 308

17.7(i)   Share of M and A as in FDI Inflows in India 309

17.7(ii) Foreign Firms Related M and A in India 309

17.8   An Illustrative List of Units/Divisions Transferred
          to Foreign Firms 310

17.9   An Illustrative List of Foreign Firms Moving to
          De-list from Domestic Bourses 311

17.10   An Illustrative List of Foreign Companies that
          Issued to Themselves Shares at a Concession 318

Appendix Table

A-4.1   Prices of Rice Sold by Food Corporation
          of India (FCI) 98

Contributors

Vijay L. Kelkar .... *Chairman, IDFC Private Equity Company Limited, Mumbai; formerly Adviser to Finance Minister, Government of India, New Delhi*

Arvind Virmani .... *Principal Adviser, Planning Commission, Government of India*

Jagdish Bhagwati .... *Professor of Economics, International Economics Research Centre, Columbia University, New York*

N.A. Mujumdar .... *Editor, Indian Journal of Agricultural Economics, Mumbai; formerly Principal Adviser, Reserve Bank of India, Mumbai*

A. Vaidyanathan .... *Distinguished Economist; Formerly Professor, Madras Institute of Development Studies, Chennai; Ex-Member, Planning Commission, Government of India*

Ashok V. Desai .... *Consultant Editor, The Telegraph and Businessworld, New Delhi*

N.R. Narayana Murthy .... *Chairman and Chief Mentor, Infosys Technologies Ltd., Bangalore*

Montek S. Ahluwalia .... *Deputy Chairman, Planning Commission, Government of India; formerly Director (EvO), International Monetary Fund (IMF), Washington D.C.; Ex-Finance Secretary, Government of India*

Rakesh Mohan .... *Deputy Governor, Reserve Bank of India, Mumbai; Ex-Director General, National Council for Applied Economic Research (NCAER), New Delhi*

Bimal Jalan .... *Member of Parliament (Rajya Sabha), New Delhi; Ex-Governor, Reserve Bank of India, Mumbai*

Shankar Acharya .... *Honorary Professor, Indian Council for Research in International Economic Relations (ICRIER), New Delhi; formerly Chief Economic Adviser, Ministry of Finance, Government of India*

Per Pinstrup-Andersen .... *H.E. Babcock Professor of Food, Nutrition and Public Policy at Cornell University, NY; World Food Prize Laureate 2001; formerly Director General, International Food Policy Research Institute (IFPRI), Washington D.C.*

V.S. Vyas .... *Professor Emeritus, Institute of Development Studies, Jaipur, Rajasthan*

C.H. Hanumantha Rao .... *Chairman, Institute of Economic Growth, Delhi; Centre for Economic and Social Studies, (CESS), Hyderabad; Member, National Advisory Council, Government of India*

M.S. Swaminathan .... *World Food Prize Laureate 1987; Chairman, National Commission on Farmers, New Delhi; Chairman, M S Swaminathan Research Foundation, Chennai*

Bibek Debroy........................ *Secretary General, PHD Chamber of Commerce & Industry, New Delhi; formerly Director, Rajiv Gandhi Institute of Contemporary Studies, (RGICS), New Delhi*

R. Nagaraj............................. *Professor, Indira Gandhi Institute of Development Research (IGIDR), Mumbai*

C. Rangarajan .... *Chairman, Prime Minister's Economic Advisor Council, New Delhi; Ex-Governor, Reserve Bank of India, Mumbai*

S.S. Tarapore .... *Ex-Deputy Governor, Reserve Bank of India, Mumbai*

Y.V. Reddy............................. *Governor, Reserve Bank of India, Mumbai*

प्रधान मंत्री

Prime Minister

MESSAGE

I am delighted to learn that Academic Foundation is publishing the centenary volume of its extremely popular book "Economic Developments in India". The list of contributors includes some of our most distinguished and eminent economists. Each one of them has contributed immensely to the analysis of India's economic condition and to policy formulation in their respective areas of expertise. The theoretical and empirical work of the authors is recognised internationally as having contributed to the development of the discipline of economics.

Students of economics as well as policy makers have benefited immensely from this rich body of literature. I am, delighted that Raj Kapila and Uma Kapila have, over the years, put together this body of published literature in a series of volumes. The books have helped successive generations of economists to access widely dispersed literature published by some of our best economists. I am, therefore, not surprised that there is so much demand for these books. The fact that the 100th volume of "Economic Developments in India" is being published is a testimony to the popularity of this volume. I hope these essays will continue to educate and illuminate our thinking on economic policy in India.

I congratulate the Academic Foundation, for bringing out this volume and for the high quality of their published work.

(Manmohan Singh)

New Delhi
June 5, 2006

अध्यक्ष
प्रधानमंत्री की आर्थिक सलाहकार परिषद्
विज्ञान भवन सौंध 'ई' हाल
मौलाना आज़ाद रोड
नई दिल्ली–110 011

CHAIRMAN
Economic Advisory Council to the Prime Minister
Vigyan Bhavan Annexe, 'E' Hall
Maulana Azad Road
New Delhi-110 011

डॉ. सी. रंगाराजन
Dr. C. RANGARAJAN

Foreword

It gives me great pleasure in writing the FOREWORD to the Centenary volume of *Economic Developments in India* edited by Raj Kapila and Uma Kapila.

Launched in 1998, *Economic Developments in India* (EDI) is brought out every month and covers the latest developments in Indian economy, including analytical articles by economists, policy makers and researchers, as well as the latest reports, documents and discussion papers, and current statistics. The dual format (hard copy + digital) adds to the utility of this publication.

I find EDI extremely handy and useful as practically everything latest on Indian economy is covered in this publication. You name any report/document/policy statement on any aspect of Indian economy, you will find them in this handy volume. EDI is truly unique. Volume after volume, month after month, it has contributed immensely towards disseminating high quality academic writings and other important literature on various aspects of India's economy.

Over a period of time there have been numerous instances when I have picked up and referred to one volume or the other while looking for some Report or a piece of writing by a distinguished scholar.

Despite the deep impact of the Internet on our work culture, and given the fact that there is no dearth of available material, both in terms of views and research presentations through various forms of print and electronic media, a publication like the EDI continues to be a precious resource for providing at one place, some of the best pieces of academic writing and also important reports and policy documents on different aspects of our country's economy. It will not be an exaggeration if I say, I cannot find any parallel to this publication. It is indeed a unique ready reference resource.

The Centenary volume of EDI is a selection from over 500 articles published during the period 1998 to December 2005. The Volume, in three sections, includes articles by a galaxy of economists, on the most vital issues relating to growth, poverty, reforms, globalisation and the challenges facing the agricultural, industrial, financial and the external sectors.

I congratulate the editors, Raj Kapila and Uma Kapila, and the publishers, Academic Foundation, for bringing out this Centenary volume, as well as for their commendable efforts in academic publishing of high quality.

(C. Rangarajan)

Acknowledgements

We are profoundly grateful to all our authors who have been contributing to our monthly publication *Economic Developments in India* which has already run into 99 volumes, the present being the 100th volume.

The idea for the title of this volume *India's Economy: A Journey in Time and Space*—specially the subtitle—came from Dr. Ashok Desai's article (included in this volume). We owe our special thanks to Dr. Desai who has always been a big support to EDI.

The selected 20 articles for this Centenary volume, relating to growth, poverty, reforms, globalisation and the sectoral developments of Indian economy, very well reflect the journey of India's economic development through time and space. Our heartfelt thanks to the writers of these 20 articles.

We must express our deep sense of gratitude to our *Economist* Prime Minister, Dr. Manmohan Singh for graciously sending a very encouraging message for this special volume. We also wish to express our special gratitude to Dr. C. Rangarajan for writing an equally encouraging *Foreword* for this volume.

We take this opportunity to thank all our subscribers/readers for their support and encouragement which made it possible for us to bring out EDI month after month.

— Editors

Introduction

The present book entitled *India's Economy: A Journey in Time and Space* (The Centenary volume of Economic Developments in India) is a selection from over 500 articles published since its inception in 1998 up to December 2005. The 20 articles selected are arranged under three sections: (i) Growth, Poverty and Reforms, (ii) Globalisation, and (iii) Sectoral Development: Agriculture, Industry, Financial and External Sector.

In Section I, the first six articles (chs. 1-6) by Vijay L. Kelkar, Arvind Virmani, Jagdish Bhagwati, N.A. Mujumdar, A. Vaidyanathan and Ashok Desai provide rare insights into the growth process, the appropriateness of development policies, particularly with regard to poverty reduction. The seventh article (ch. 7) by N.R. Narayana Murthy deals with the vital issue of public governance.

The volume begins with Kelkar's article: *India: On the Growth Turnpike* where the author has very forcefully presented the logic and evidence which suggest that economic growth in India will considerably accelerate further in the coming decade. The author believes that India is at the threshold of 'golden age of growth' with India's democratic framework being a key growth fundamental and that over time India has paid the fixed cost of democracy in terms of creation of institutional infrastructure, tradition and conventions. Thus, India—riding the wave of growth fundamentals such as demographic transition, human capital accumulation, improved incentive structures, diffusion of new technologies such as IT, total factor productivity accelerators through 'network industries', and an improved security environment—will be growing at growth rates which can be above 10 per cent per annum i.e. double digit growth rates.

Arvind Virmani (ch. 2) advocates the need for a new development paradigm that recognises that 'government failure' is a much more severe problem than 'market failure'. The new paradigm must be based on a clear and non-ideological recognition of the strengths and the weakness of the state and the people. A democratic society has enormous potential for entrepreneurship, innovation and creative development. The people, their diverse forms of activity and association, such as companies, cooperatives, societies, trusts and other NGOs must be allowed and encouraged to play their due role. The state must focus on what only it can do best and shed all activities that the people can do as well or better. The heavy hand of government in the form of incentive distorting laws, rules, regulations, procedures and red tape, have corrupted industry and business and other organised interest groups. These must be removed so as to release the energy of the people. The state should confine itself to managing the economy so as to accelerate employment and income growth in a self-sustaining manner, ensure that all citizens receive their basic entitlements of basic public goods and services and empower the poor so that they have equal rights (and responsibilities) as the better-off citizens.

This requires, according to Virmani, right-sizing of government, shedding of activities that can be performed by others, decentralisation of governmental functions to lower levels based on the principle of subsidiarity, the creation of countervailing power, transfer of regulatory functions to independent professional regulators, empowerment of citizens and civic groups, giving voice to the under-employed and creation of checks and balances.

The next three articles by Jagdish Bhagwati, Mujumdar and Vaidyanathan discuss the issue of poverty and reforms. According to Jagdish Bhagwati (ch. 3): "Central to our economic strategy of alleviating poverty was the acceleration of growth and the creation of jobs for the poor. This requires, of course, that our policies promote growth, else the expected benefits in alleviating poverty will not materialise but the growth strategy itself was undermined because of our policy framework. However, what we need to remember is that growth requires complementary policies, where necessary, to prevent hurtful outcomes as and when they materialise. It is not only poverty that will fall with sustained growth but also, we will improve literacy and health, even other social agendas because a growing economy will generate resources, at given tax rates, for the government to spend on schools and public health. In short, growth improves incomes, pulls up people out of poverty, improves literacy, helps spend more on public health, and does much more along these lines. Economic reforms, aimed at a reversal of the anti-globalisation, anti-market, pro-public-enterprise attitudes and policies that produced our dismal growth performance, are therefore the most important thing that we need to do."

According to N.A. Mujumdar (ch. 4), although India has been in the business of poverty reduction for more than 50 years, since the inception of planning in 1950-51, yet more than a quarter of the total population continues to live below the poverty line even today. If China could reduce the magnitude of its poverty to a mere 3 per cent of the population in a span of two decades, what went wrong with India? Even assuming that the Indian economy would manage to remain in high growth trajectory of 8 per cent of GDP growth in the coming years, it would take perhaps another two decades to eliminate poverty.

Without waiting for two decades or so to eliminate poverty through the conventional route, Mujumdar asserts, it makes sense to redefine our immediate development objective in terms of eliminating hunger here and now, by utilising what contemporary Indian policy makers consider as 'surplus foodgrains'. To be able to achieve this objective in the short-run, decentralised and broad-based growth of the economy needs to be promoted. Microcredit institutions, micro-enterprises, self-help groups (SHGs) and NGOs and the private sector on the one hand; establishing and strengthening links and cooperation between government and *panchayat raj* institutions, NGOs and the private sector on the other hand. Such networking needs to be institutionalised taking into account the state-specific circumstances. Such institutionalisation also can facilitate decentralised and broad-based growth.

Vaidyanathan's comprehensive article (ch. 5) covers practically all issues related to poverty. He reviews the evolution and acceptance of minimum living standard among the objectives of policy in the agenda of political parties as well as governments since and even before independence. He has also discussed and analysed in detail, some important issues concerning concepts and measurement of poverty as well as the design and implementation of policies to tackle the problem of poverty.

The next article by Ashok Desai (ch. 6) provides an interesting account of Fifty Years of India: A Journey in Time. He traces the developments in Indian economy right from the period of the Second World War and the Bengal famine of 1943, the Independent India and then the period of Nehruvian Socialism i.e. the period of 50s and 60s, the turning point in the 70s; the oil crisis, the emergency; the rapid turnaround in BoP, the 80s, economically speaking a golden period, growth rate rising to five and a half per cent from the Hindu growth rate of 3.5 per cent but 80s also created the conditions for the payment crisis that followed—the crisis of 1991 and then the reforms that followed after 1991.

According to Ashok Desai, in spite of the obstructions, the little reforms we managed to implement worked beautifully, bringing out magnificent industrial boom and diversification of consumption habits, industry becoming more competitive and balance of payment improved year after year.

Now that business has been freed from shackles, our CEOs and managers should no longer confine themselves to their own businesses. They must make the business of the nation their own.

Ashok Desai also makes interesting points about Indian democracy. He says: "India is a peculiar democracy; it is the only functional democracy in which political parties have no stable, legitimate, established sources of income. Most democratic countries have a leftist party supported by trade unions, and a rightist party supported by businessmen; some nowadays have a green party supported by an environmental offshoot of the left. All these parties have loyal supporters, who vote for them, support them and when necessary, fund them. In effect, therefore, they are voluntary organisations funded by members. Out of the contributions they maintain offices and support leaders.

In India, however, it is just the other way round: it is not supporters who fund parties, it is parties that reward members. Hence, it is important for parties to get into government, and to siphon off government funds. Politics based on the capture and sale of state power is expensive and unstable. It is expensive because there are too many political forums and hence too many politicians in our country."

The last article in this section by N.R. Narayana Murthy (ch. 7) deals with the most vital issue of public governance. The fact that our nation of a billion people is still far off from achieving many of the goals that our founding fathers set for this nation compels us to make sure that we have a more efficient public governance in this country. This would require accountability, fairness and transperancy. Narayana Murthy strongly believes and rightly so that the aim of democracy is to realise the aspirations of people in a transparent and fair manner with full accountability to the people. This requires an effective governing system and this is where we have failed.

In a democracy, development has to be the main focus of the electorate and the election commission should make sure that all political parties fight on the basis of what they have contributed to the people rather than the issue of caste, religion or language that are not really important. If this could be done, this country will go a long way in redeeming the pledge that our founding fathers made and we can wipe the tears of the eyes of the poorest and the weakest, says Narayana Murthy.

The next four articles in Section II (chs. 8-11) by Montek S. Ahluwalia, Rakesh Mohan, Bimal Jalan and Shankar Acharya analyse the state and impact of globalisation on Indian economy.

Montek Ahluwalia in his well researched article 'India in a Globalising World' provides the reader a crisp background in which India the world's largest democracy has been charting her course in a globalising world. Based on India's experience, he says, there is no fear that globalisation will hurt India's growth prospects. On the contrary, India has experienced a distinct improvement in growth in the period when its policies reflected the compulsions of globalisation, compared with the 1960s and 1970s, when the Indian economy grew relatively slowly at an average of around 3.5 per cent per year. Growth accelerated to an average of around 5.8 per cent per year in the 1980s and 1990s and the economy is currently growing at about 6.5 per cent.

International agencies and independent scholars agree that the economy can achieve growth rates of 8 per cent or so provided supportive steps are taken. A much quoted recent study by Goldman Sachs identified Brazil, Russia, India and China as the set of large emerging market countries projected to grow rapidly over the next 30 years. Within the group, India's potential growth rate was projected to be the fastest—around 8 per cent per year—faster even than China which is currently, and has been for many years, the fastest growing economy but is expected to slow down in future. According to this study, by 2040 India will become the third largest economy after the USA and China.

What is required is the general strategy of pushing forward with economic reforms involving action on many fronts. The process of opening up the economy by reducing customs duties, reducing bureaucratic hurdles which make the investment climate less attractive, continuing with the process of reducing the list of items reserved for production by the small scale sector, and continuing with financial sector reforms. A sensitive area which is important for promoting expansion in labour intensive sectors, but where it is necessary to build a consensus, is the need for greater flexibility in labour laws.

According to Rakesh Mohan (ch. 9), globalisation throws both opportunities and challenges for benefit of societies. Opportunities offered by forces of globalisation offer India scope to improve the quality of life of its people, provided appropriate policies are put in place.

India's rank in terms of human development index and gender development index continues to be low compared to many developing countries. There is a need for linking growth with development and filling the gap between macroeconomic performance and social sector development.

While the economic integration of India with the global economy will continue to take place, a successful integration, with due regard to the interests of a vast majority, particularly, the poor in our country, would be possible only through sound public policies—evolved and redesigned from time to time. Given India's demographic advantages, the quality of labour force (in terms of relevant skills which need to be sustained, reoriented and upgraded in a globally competitive era) and the physical health of the workforce become crucial. Education and health, therefore, provide the link between supply and demand for labour through increases in productivity.

Bimal Jalan in his article *India and Globalisation* (ch. 10) points out that despite all the talk, we are nowhere even close to being globalised in terms of any commonly used indicator of globalisation. In fact, we are still one of the least globalised among major countries—however we look at it.

Transition from a closed to a vibrant, open and a more globally dominant economy will certainly take time and will not be painless. As of now, we have much greater tolerance for waste, non-work and survival of the inefficient, and the self-seeking than other fast growing countries. The real challenge of globalisation is to make this transition—from a less productive and less challenging economy to a more work-oriented and competitive economy. Our public policies have to respond to our own requirements rather than to any fixed global ideology or a pre-determined and internationally prescribed model of economic progress.

According to Shankar Acharya (ch. 11) we Indians have done a lot more talking on globalisation than action. A growing number of analysts have linked the fate of globalisation to its impact on the two populous giants (China and India) with billion plus population throughout the 21st century. While China has (for the last quarter century) decisively embraced global economic integration as a crucial plank of her dash to superpower status, we are no where.

"Three decades ago, in 1970, both China and India were rather closed economies, with the share of exports (goods and services) accounting for less than 4 per cent of GDP, compared to 12 per cent for developing countries as a whole. Interestingly, India's share at 3.5 per cent was almost double that of

China's at 1.8 per cent. When China opened up her economy in the late seventies, she did so with remarkable strategic decisiveness and determination. By 1982 her merchandise exports at $ 21 billion were already more than double India's at about $ 9 billion. By 1990 the gap had widened as China's goods exports almost tripled to $ 62 billion, while India's increased only to $ 18 billion. But China's truly astonishing export surge has come in the nineties with merchandise exports touching $ 250 billion in 2000, compared to India's $ 43 billion. As players in international trade, the two countries are now in different leagues."

According to Shankar Acharya, India is far lagging behind China in terms of globalisation. He strongly feels, it is not that we do not know what should India do to get greater gains from globalisation? The list of policies has been listed many times by many people, including, the recent Tenth Five Year Plan. "The problem is not with knowing what's to be done... but to do it. Until we DO sensible economic policies, half-hearted globalisation will continue to yield half-baked results!" says Shankar Acharya.

Section III analyses the sectoral development relating to agriculture, industry, financial sector and external sector. While chs. 12-15 including articles by Per Pinstrup-Andersen, V.S. Vyas, C.H.H Rao and M.S. Swaminathan are devoted to food and agricultural policy, food security and rural development, the next two articles (chs. 16 and 17) by Bibek Debroy and R. Nagaraj examine India's manufacturing strategy and issues relating to foreign direct investment. Financial sector and financial stability is covered in articles by C. Rangarajan and S.S. Tarapore (chs. 18 and 19) and the article by Y.V. Reddy (ch. 20) looks into India's external sector and challenges in a globalising economy.

Even though food availability in India might be described today as a state of plenty, India has to grapple with the paradox of persistent hunger. Food and Agriculture Organization of the United Nations (FAO) has estimated that over 225 million Indians remain chronically undernourished.

According to Per-Pinstrup Andersen although a number of factors contribute to food insecurity, it is widely recognised that poverty is the primary cause. In a country like India that produces large surpluses of basic foodgrains, it is clear that large numbers of people remain hungry because they have insufficient resources to purchase all the food they need. Improvements in India's already extensive safety net programmes could only help over the short- and medium-term. The long-run solution is investment in human resources (assuring access to health care and education for all), empowerment of poor people to better articulate and pursue their interests, and programmes and policies that assure poor people access to productive resources and employment opportunities.

Agriculture will remain an important source of livelihood for large numbers of Indians, either directly or indirectly, for a long time to come, as a majority of the workforce remains engaged in farming and related work. Moreover, most poor Indians live in rural areas. Therefore, broad-based agricultural growth must be at the centre of strategies to reduce poverty and achieve food security.

In order to achieve this, food and agricultural policy must shift from poorly targeted subsidies to a focus on investment—with an emphasis on human resources, public goods, and meeting the needs of poor people and regions. Key investment targets include less favoured areas, agricultural research, infrastructure (especially roads and storage), and education, for girls and boys alike. Alongside these public investments, agricultural policy also needs to shift from the heavy emphasis of the past on foodgrains to more diversified and higher value added activities. Much greater attention must also be paid to sustainable use of natural resources.

There is unanimity of opinion in our country, as in most other countries of the world now, that every person in a civilised society deserves to be food secure. India is also a signatory to international convents to abolish hunger and malnutrition at the World Food Conference convened by FAO, and the Conference on Millennium Goals convened by the United Nations. It has been endorsed as an important objective in our successive Five Year Plans.

According to V.S. Vyas while we have made significant progress in eliminating hunger, seasonal hunger is still rampant, and its incidence on some sections is very serious. We have not however made much notable progress, in filling in the calorie gap. The nutritional status in large parts of the country is probably deteriorating. If the objective of ensuring a healthy and productive life to all households is to be fulfilled, a time-bound programme to meet four critical requirements for Food Security have to be met i.e. (a) adequate availability, (b) reasonable stability in terms of quantity and price, (c) purchasing power to access food, and (d) desired nutritional intake.

With concerted efforts we have transformed a heavily import-dependent agricultural economy into one of food self-sufficiency, in fact one with exportable surpluses. "With the growth record of past decade which is likely to continue if not improve, availability of necessary institutions, and requisite experience, neither dearth of resources nor lack of expertise can be cited as reasons for further delaying the task of ensuring a food secure India. It can not now be considered an elusive goal or a distant dream," says Vyas.

The next article by C.H.H. Rao (ch. 14) is devoted to the vital issues of sustainable use of water for irrigation in Indian agriculture. According to Rao, water resources are becoming extremely scarce. As per the projections made by the National Commission for Integrated Water Resource Development Plan, the requirement of water for irrigation in India will grow by more than 50 per cent in the next 50 years. The water requirements for household consumption and for industry would rise even faster. In view of this, even after fully exploiting the usable water resources, the balance between the supply and demand for irrigation water can be achieved only by improving the level of irrigation efficiency in a big way from about 36 per cent efficiency in 1993-94 to 60 per cent in the year 2050 (Government of India, 1999).

In the last two decades, Rao states, we have been faltering in our efforts to augment water resources, even as the use of the available water resources has become increasingly unsustainable. Public investment in major and medium irrigation schemes has been declining, in real terms, throughout the 1980s and the 1990s, even though as much as 40 per cent of the potential still remains to be exploited. We have not taken significant steps so far for improving water-use-efficiency through modernisation/renovation of existing systems which have deteriorated over the years.

In this context, one may ask whether privatisation of irrigation can provide the necessary correctives. According to Rao market failure is as endemic in irrigation and water management as government failure.

Irrigation Management Transfer (IMT) to the user-farmers is being increasingly advocated and practised the world over to provide correctives to the distortions arising from the failure of the market as well as the state. India has embarked upon Participatory Irrigation Management (PIM), under which the management of some of the systems is being turned over to the Water Users' Associations (WUAs).

The next article by M.S. Swaminathan (ch. 15) is about Mission 2007: Every Village a Knowledge Centre. Following the launching of Mission 2007 over two years ago as well as the recommendation of the National Commission on Farmers that village knowledge centres (VKCs) should be established as soon as possible for the knowledge and skill empowerment of rural families, some developments have taken place that give hope that the urban-rural digital divide can be substantially ended by August 15, 2007.

M.S. Swaminathan has traced the developments that have taken place since the programme was launched two years ago and what needs to be done to make the programme pro-poor, pro-women and pro-livelihood in both design and implementation. He strongly feels that if we can achieve convergence and synergy among the numerous on-going as well as emerging programmes, the goal of achieving a rural knowledge revolution by August 15, 2007, can become a reality. While the green revolution helped us to improve the productivity and production of rice, wheat and other crops, the knowledge revolution will help to enhance human productivity and entrepreneurship in every sphere of human activity. The VKC is based on the principle of an integrated and appropriate use of the Internet, cable TV, cell phone, community radio and the vernacular press.

The article provides a glimpse of the road map for the success of Mission 2007: Every Village a Knowledge Centre which according to Swaminathan is very important for human security and well-being of our country.

In his article *Unshackling India's Manufacturing—The Ingredients of a Strategy* (ch. 16) Bibek Debroy talks about the labour cost advantages and the demographic dividend that India enjoys in comparison to other countries. According to Goldman Sachs, BRIC (Brazil, Russia, India, China) Report, India alone among the BRIC countries is unlikely to face a labour constraint. A labour shortage in developed countries means scope for immigration or for outsourcing manufacturing activities.

There are estimates that off-shoring of manufacturing activities to low cost countries can be significant and that India can reap part of this dividend. Outsourcing to India has happened. But that has been for services. In the 1970s, 1980s and even the 1990s, India missed opportunities in off-shoring of manufacturing. There is no reason why that should happen in the next two decades also, says Bibek Debroy.

Looking at sectoral composition of GDP, in 2003-04, at constant prices, the primary sector accounted for 24.4 per cent of GDP, the secondary sector accounted for 24.6 per cent and the tertiary sector accounted for 51 per cent. There is often euphoria about tertiary sector growth. However, in the history of economic development, no country has developed riding on service sector growth alone. The transition has been from the primary to the secondary and thereafter to the tertiary. That apart, such sectoral growth rates are not independent of one another. Tertiary sector growth requires secondary sector growth and in India's growth experience, the two have always gone together. In the 1990s, however, there has been an aberration from the trend. For achieving the desired rate of growth of GDP of above 8 per cent, the manufacturing sector, according to Bibek Debroy, has to have a growth rate of abour 12 per cent. To achieve this rate of growth, we have to identify the constraints in pushing manufacturing growth and the constraints themselves suggest the solutions. Debroy has clearly analysed these contraints and also the solutions.

R. Nagaraj in his article *Foreign Direct Investment in India: Trends and Issues* (ch. 17) points out that there is little evidence that greater FDI inflow ensures faster output and export growth. Such simplistic associations, usually based on cross-country analysis, seem to have support neither in principle nor in comparative experience.

What is needed is a strategic view of foreign investment as a means of enhancing domestic production and technological capability, and so also to access the external market for labour-intensive manufactures—as China has precisely done.

The next two articles (chs. 18 and 19) are devoted to financial stability and reforms in India's financial sector.

Serious financial crises that have gripped several countries in the last two decades have brought to the fore the issue of financial stability. The key element of a financial crisis is the disruption that is caused to the financial system and the consequent loss in real output. Stability applies to both institutions and markets.

C. Rangarajan (ch. 18) has highlighted some of the analytical issues relating to financial stability. The objective of banking sector reform in this country has been to improve the productivity of the system. In the period since 1991, there have been a number of disruptions to the financial system in India. These episodes of financial distress point to the need for: (a) enlarging the legal framework of regulation to include all segments of the financial system, (b) moving towards internationally accepted prudential norms and other standards of transparency and disclosure, and (c) strengthening the supervisory system to take effective preventive actions. A number of significant steps have been taken in all these areas. Worldwide also, these have been the trends. While the regulatory system lays down the rules, it is the supervisory system that ensures their implementation. A regulatory system is only as good as its implementation. What is needed is to evolve a system that will improve the ability to detect sources of vulnerability and to take timely corrective measures. That will pave the way for financial stability.

While Rangarajan talks about financial stability, S.S. Tarapore (ch. 19) undertakes a transparent and realistic stocktaking essentially to ensure enduring and sustainable reforms. He says, "It would only be fair to acknowledge that a lot has been achieved over the past decade and if the visible problems of the financial sector today appear more daunting than a decade ago, it is not as if nothing has been achieved. All that has happened is that the regulatory standards have been made more exacting and the system is revealing more of the truth. Banks and non-bank financial intermediaries are facing challenges in that competition is intensifying while barriers between different segments of the financial system are breaking down. In this context, all segments have to recognise that there is a paradigm shift which is putting into trail certain basic and irreversible changes. The watchword is going to be efficiency of operations and the bottom line would be the ultimate test of performance".

Tarapore's presentation focusing largely on problem areas and issues which have defied solutions should not be viewed as a negative approach. Identifying the problems in an open and transparent manner would contribute to their resolution. We cannot move forward unless we take decisive action to tackle the present problems, says Tarapore.

In the last chapter (ch. 20) Y.V. Reddy looks into the challenges facing India's external sector. Over the years, India's commercial and financial linkages with the rest of the world have been increasing with trade liberalisation and openness on the capital account. According to Y.V. Reddy this is reflected in the transmission of international impulses to the real sector and domestic financial markets. Trends in international prices have now significant influence on domestic prices. Indian corporates and institutions are increasingly accessing international markets with consequent diversification benefits. While this process has provided important opportunities, it has also brought in new challenges and risks, necessitating fine-tuning of macro policies in a much broader canvass and context. India is, thus, moving from a focus on managing external sector to implementing an optimal integration of domestic and external sectors, with the global economy.

To sum up, in this brief introduction we have attempted to give only a glimpse of the wide-ranging issues discussed in this volume, reflecting the journey of India's economic development through time and space. We may conclude this introduction on an optimistic note by quoting from Kelkar's article (ch. 1) "Thanks to the painstaking policy reforms initiated over the last two decades by successive Governments, India is at the threshold of 'a golden age of growth' .... In the coming decade or two, growth rate in India may surpass the 'miracle growth' rates achieved by other Asian countries. This is not surprising as India, compared to Japan, China and other high growth economies of Asia, will have the advantage of an access to productivity enhancing information technology, which was not available in earlier decades. This way, we will be cashing in on the 'late comer's advantage'."

We do hope that this volume will prove handy and useful to students, researchers and policy makers in this country.

— Editors

Section I

Economy: Growth, Poverty and Reforms

1

India: On the Growth Turnpike

VIJAY L. KELKAR

The term 'turnpike'—which is typically North American—refers to an expressway, and I propose to present logic and evidence which suggest that economic growth in India will considerably accelerate further in the coming decade.

Macroeconomic Trends and the Setting

A lot has been said and written about India's exciting growth story, which can be dated to the beginning of the 1980s. Let me start with the most interesting and important facts about India's growth experience.

From the early 1980s onwards, India got strong GDP growth, averaging 5.7 per cent over the last 24 years. This year, in 2003-04, GDP growth is expected to be 8.2 per cent, and GDP is expected to reach $ 625 billion. India's high GDP growth is sharply visible when GDP comparisons are done on a purchasing power parity basis. As of 2001, India came in at 4th place, with output of $ 3 trillion. It is likely that by 2004, India will reach 3rd place, displacing Japan. That will give us a global ranking of US, China, and India in that order.

Looking back, it seems to me that we had two broad phases in our growth experience: before 1980, and after. Before 1980, GDP growth had a mean of 3.5 per cent with a standard deviation of 3.5 per cent. In the 24 years after 1980, the mean rose to 5.7 per cent, and the standard deviation dropped to 1.9 per cent.

Many people have noticed India's high sustained growth over the last 24 years. But the low volatility of GDP growth is equally striking. For a

The views in this lecture are mine and not of my employers. It draws heavily upon the collaborative work in progress with Arbind Modi, Ajay Shah and Arvind Subramanian. I am grateful to Centre for Monitoring Indian Economy (CMIE) and National Council of Applied Economic Research (NCAER) for access to their databases.

comparison, over 1960-1999, the median value for industrial countries was 2.18. For developing countries, it was 4.28. So we have had two big changes around 1980 as a breakpoint: mean GDP growth went up, and GDP growth volatility went down.

I find it useful to look at the acceleration of growth in India using the tool of 'rolling window' growth rates, where at each point, we compute the average growth over the last decade. A decade is a broad enough window, which allows us to smooth out the fluctuations caused by an unusual monsoon or two. So every year, we look back at the last 10 years, and compute the mean and standard deviation of GDP growth over that decade.

This graph gives us new insights into familiar facts about the acceleration in India's GDP growth.[1] We departed from the 'Hindu rate of growth' of 3.5 per cent in 1982, and reached levels like 6 per cent from 1996 onwards. In this lecture, I am going to argue that we will go further up to substantially higher growth rates in the years to come.

Figure 1.1

India's GDP Growth

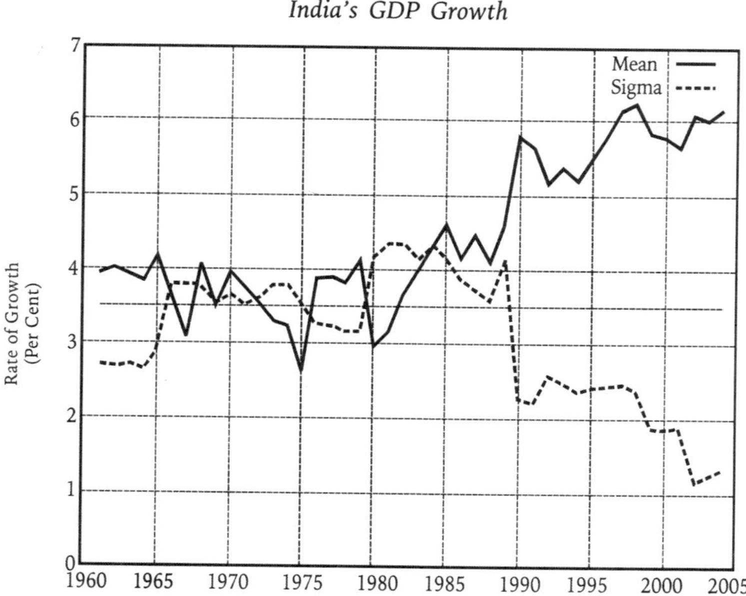

---

1. Delong, J. Bradford (2001). "India Since Independence: An Analytic Growth Narrative", July; Rodrik, Dani and Arvind Subramanian (2004). "From Hindu Growth to Productivity Surge: The Mystery of the Indian Growth Transition", *NBER Working Paper* No. 10376.

We have also obtained a sharp reduction in GDP growth volatility. Along with this, inflation and interest rates have also come down sharply. We seem to have thus created an extremely benign macroeconomic environment, with low inflation, low interest rates and high GDP growth.

Table 1.1

GDP Growth and Per-capita GDP

	GDP Growth (Per Cent)		Years to Double
Period	Aggregate	Per Capita	Per Capita GDP
1972-1982	3.5	1.2	57
1982-1992	5.2	3.0	23
1992-2002	6.0	3.9	18

Let me talk about this in a different way—as growth of per capita GDP. While GDP growth has accelerated, population growth rates have gone down slightly. These have combined to give an even sharper acceleration of GDP growth per capita. In the 1970s, this was 1.2 per cent and it went up to 3.9 per cent in the 1990s.

I want to emphasise that 1.2 per cent and 3.9 per cent both sound like small numbers, but there is a huge difference between the two in terms of their human impact. At 1.2 per cent a year, per capita GDP takes 57 years to double. A man sees one doubling in his adult life. At 3.9 per cent a year, per capita GDP takes 18 years to double. A man who lives to 72 sees three doublings as compared with the standard of living that he saw at age 18. This is an enormous difference!

Why did India Exhibit Resilience to Shocks?

A remarkable feature of India's growth experience has been its resilience to shocks. In many countries, short periods of high growth appear to be punctuated by years of poor growth.[2] Largely speaking, this has not been the case in India over the last 25 years. This is reflected in the figure above, which shows a sustained increase in average GDP growth rates, coupled with a sharp decline in GDP growth volatility from the decade 1980-1990 onwards.

---

2. Easterly, William (2001). "The Lost Decades: Developing Countries' Stagnation in spite of Policy Reform 1980-1998", World Bank, February.

This resilience of growth in recent decades is an important change when compared with preceding decades. In 1973 and 1979, growth in India was adversely affected by oil shocks. In the later period, this vulnerability appears to have been greatly reduced.

This aspect is important in understanding India's growth experience. It is important to address the questions: Why has India's growth been so consistent? Why has growth accelerated from decade to decade, without encountering the difficulties which are observed in many other developing countries? Why has India exhibited such resilience to shocks?

One could maintain a hypothesis that the Indian economy was exposed to smaller external shocks in the period after 1980; that this drop in volatility is an artefact of a benign external environment. However, this is just not true. In these years, the economy has faced many shocks, including international financial crises, security tensions, international sanctions, etc. From roughly 1995 onwards, the world has emphatically not been a quieter place. Hence, the drop in GDP growth volatility seems to reflect a genuine improvement in macro-stability and not a lack of shocks.

Another possible hypothesis is rooted in currency flexibility. A broad consensus that appears to be emerging in the literature suggests that greater flexibility in exchange rates is conducive to enhanced macro-stability. A recent paper[3] by Edwards and Yeyati finds that terms of trade shocks are exacerbated in countries with more rigid exchange rate systems. In their empirical work, under flexible exchange rates, the effects of terms-of-trade shocks on growth are approximately one half of those under pegged regimes. They also find that under inflexible exchange rate regimes, output growth is more sensitive to negative than to positive shocks.

If the economic reforms in recent decades had moved towards greater currency flexibility, then this could have been pointed to as a key source of improved resilience. However, a series of recent papers[4] have demonstrated that in India's case, currency flexibility has been broadly unchanged since 1979. Hence, a change in the currency regime does not constitute a feasible explanation for this decline in GDP growth volatility.

---

3. Edwards, Sebastian and Yeyati, Eduardo Levy (2003). "Flexible Exchange Rates as Shock Absorbers", *NBER Working Paper* No. 9867, July.

4. Reinhart, Carmen and Kenneth S. Rogoff (2002). "The Modern History of Exchange Rate Arrangements: A Reinterpretation", *NBER Working Paper* No. 8963, June; Patnaik, Ila (2003). "India's Policy Stance on Reserves and the Currency", *ICRIER Working Paper* No.108, September; Calvo, A. Guillermo and Carmen M. Reinhart (2002). "Fear of Floating", *Quarterly Journal of Economics*, Vol. 117, Issue 2, May.

One element of an explanation appears to be the improvement in price flexibility that took place in many other areas of the Indian economy. While price flexibility on two important markets—currency and foodgrains—did not go up, price flexibility rose sharply in the 1990s in myriad other areas such as interest rates, steel, cement, etc. In these areas, price volatility had been stifled in the traditional command-and-control paradigm of economic policy, and prices were freed up in the 1990s. This is expected to have improved the ability of the economy to adjust to shocks through changes in prices. A second explanation that we offer relates to the maturing processes of democracy, which I will come to later.

Globalisation

One of the most important phenomena about the Indian economy in the 1990s was the growth of international trade. We see striking changes in the one-decade period following 1991-92. India has engaged in unilateral removals of barriers to trade, and this process has been assisted by our WTO obligations.[5]

Through these, gross trade flows almost tripled over this period from $ 56.7 billion in 1991-92 to $ 155.5 billion in 2001-02. Expressed as a fraction of GDP, the trade-GDP ratio went up from 21.3 per cent to 33.1 per cent over this 10-year period. This was a fairly rapid pace of change for a structural parameter like the trade/GDP ratio.

A key feature of India's experience with trade has been the rapid growth of services exports. Over this decade, merchandise exports grew by 145 per cent but services exports grew by 275 per cent.

This high growth of services exports has been based on two distinct components. In the earlier period, invisibles revenues were primarily obtained through remittances from Indians working outside India. In recent years, improvements in telecommunications have implied that many services, which were previously non-tradable, could now be produced in India as part of global production chains. Export-oriented services production in India ranges from high volume production of low-end services like accounting, all the way to services that require highly specialised and highwage staff, like research and development. For example, research laboratories located in India by major US companies have filed for over 1,000 patents with the US Patent and Trademark Office.

---

5. Panagariya, Arvind (2004). "India's Trade Reform: Progress, Impact and Future Strategy", *India Policy Forum*, NCAER, March.

The high degree of public awareness about India's success in these IT-enabled services exports has led to a widespread perception that India is faring extremely well in services exports but has failed in obtaining growth in manufacturing exports. This perception is inconsistent with the high growth which is also seen with merchandise exports. Particularly in the last five years, growth rates of manufacturing and services exports have been rather alike.

India's success on exports growth has made a big difference to the overall outlook on the external sector. We began the decade of the 1990s with a BoP crisis. Today, India is widely seen as having an extremely strong position on the external sector. This was achieved through several elements: currency depreciation, export buoyancy, and policies of avoiding foreign currency debt. Our foreign currency reserves are now roughly as big as our external debt, so there can be little question of a BoP crisis shaping up.

Political Economy of Growth

One of the most interesting features about India's growth is the way it has been achieved under a democratic framework. There is a view that democracy impedes economic growth and India would eliminate poverty faster if we are willing to sacrifice freedom and democracy.

I quite disagree with this perspective. I believe that democracy is a 'growth fundamental', that we have come where we have come because of democracy, and not despite it. I found one insightful way of thinking about this in a 1988 paper[6] by Dani Rodrik, which offered an interesting framework for understanding resilience of output growth, when faced with external shocks.

$$\Delta \text{growth} = -\text{external shocks} \times \frac{\text{latent social conflict}}{\text{Institutions of conflict management}}$$

This 'equation' seeks to explain the impact on GDP growth of a given external shock. This is linked to three explanations:

1. The size of the external shock matters—bigger external shocks should obviously give a bigger impact on growth,

2. The extent of 'latent social conflict'. Rodrik defines this in terms of ethnic and religious heterogeneity.

---

6. Rodrik, Dani (1999). "Where did all the Growth Go? External Shocks, Social Conflict, and Growth Collapses", *Journal of Economic Growth*, Vol. 4, December, pp. 358-412.

3.   Rodrik focuses on 'institutions of conflict management' as the tool through which countries are better able to absorb external shocks.

Going by his definition, India has substantial 'latent social conflict', given the ethnic and religious diversity present in the country. Yet, we know that the output loss associated with shocks in India was small. How did this happen?

By Rodrik's argument, this suggests the high quality of the institutions of conflict management in the country. This is achieved through political institutions, and the functioning of democracy. As is well known, India is the world's largest democracy. Freedom of speech, regular elections, and an independent judiciary have characterised India's 57-year post-independence experience.

While India started out with very strong majorities for a single party (the Congress) in Parliament, over the decades, the political system has learnt how to obtain consensus through coalition governments. For example, in recent years, bipartisan support was essential for every piece of legislation. Milestones in economic legislation, such as the Electricity Act, the Foreclosure law, or the Fiscal Responsibility and Budget Management Act, would not have been possible without bipartisan support.

In many countries, the introduction of market-oriented reforms has been highly unpopular with the larger populace. This appears to have not been a constraint in India. One litmus test of this problem is found in the labour market. One revealing statistic about this is the number of strikes and the man days lost through strikes in 1992 and 2002. Major changes in economic policy have been actually accompanied by a sharp diminution in the incidence of unrest on the part of organised labour.

How was such a consensus in favour of market-oriented reforms forged? In the early period, market-oriented reforms may have appeared relatively novel and required consensus building to support embarking on relatively unknown territory. These innovations in policy were better accepted in India, as compared with the experience of many other countries, since they were crafted through the processes of a participatory democracy. In recent years, the consensus in favour of market-oriented reforms has been cemented by the results which better economic policy has delivered. One of the reasons for this has been the better sequencing of reforms which enabled 'early harvest' of the benefits.

The most important area of progress is that of poverty reduction. A shocking fact, embedded in Indian history, is the stagnation of the headcount of the poor at 320 million for the two-decade period from 1973 to 1993. From 1993 to 1999, in a short six-year period alone, the headcount of the poor dropped by 60 million. Taking into account various factors, it can be said that 100 million people have been brought out of poverty by the growth process of the last decade. This is an astonishing achievement, and it has had a positive impact on the political acceptance of economic reforms.[7]

As mentioned before, per capita GDP now shows three doublings in an adult life, as compared with one doubling in an adult life that used to be observed earlier. These changes have been accompanied by a reduction in the volatility of GDP growth, which has helped alleviate fears about the vagaries of the free market. All these changes have been manifestly visible in the political system and public discourse, and have helped cement the consensus in favour of economic reforms.

While democratic institutions are very valuable things to have, this is not to say that it is easy for a country to learn how to operate democratic institutions. Many countries have lost high GDP growth rates for a decade or more, in learning to make the transition from dictatorship to democracy. By now, India appears to have absorbed the costs of learning to operate vibrant democratic institutions.

Recent Themes in Reforms

A lot has been written about the economic reforms process in India. I would like to once again be brief and selective, and talk about a few big things that are going on.

I think the general principles that are driving the reforms process may be summarised as follows. We are trying to focus on incentives, and give the right people the right incentives to do the right things. We are trying to reduce frictions and transactions costs, so as to enable more transactions and more trading. We are trying to harness network externalities and obtain increasing returns to scale. Finally, we are trying to emphasise the 'meso-economic reforms', to put a focus on that in-between space between the macro and the micro, which consists of major institutions and 'rules of the game'.

---

7. Bhalla, Surjit S. (2003). "Not as Poor, nor as Unequal, As you Think—Poverty, Inequality and Growth in India, 1950-2000", Final Report of a research project undertaken for the Planning Commission, Government of India, December 4.

Deepening Globalisation

Let me start with globalisation. As emphasised above, our trade/GDP ratio went up sharply from 22 per cent of GDP to 33 per cent of GDP over a 10-year period. India has digested the lessons of the 1960s and 1970s, about the enormous distortions and harmful political economy that is induced by protectionism. So we have made much progress in doing unilateral trade liberalisation, and in exploiting the WTO process. We have eliminated quantitative restrictions, and brought down the peak customs rate on manufactured goods from over 150 per cent to a present level of 20 per cent.

What is particularly striking is that this year, with elections impending, we were able to sharply cut tariffs, and this was criticised by some observers as a 'populist' thing to do! This highlights the sea change that has taken place in India's attitude towards trade integration with the world economy. India, which was once described as a 'hesitant globaliser', has become a 'willing globaliser'!

The elimination of QRs, and the drop in the peak rate from 150 per cent to 20 per cent, was obviously costly for many firms and individuals. There are real costs that have to be paid in terms of obsolete business plans, and factors of production had to shift into areas where India has a comparative advantage. In my view, this is a subtle reason behind the upsurge of bad loans in the banking industry in the mid-1990s.

However, the difficult part of our adjustment to eliminating tariffs and QRs now seems to be behind us, and we are well on our way to single digit tariffs. It is striking to observe that while the multilateral discussions about trade reforms are still talking in terms of multi-decade horizons for adjustment, India has been able to move much faster, and unilaterally make progress on trade reforms.

Going from the current account to the capital account, there is now a broad consensus that capital controls are ineffective when there is a large and free current account. There are simply too many opportunities for moving capital across the globe by over invoicing, under invoicing, transfer pricing by multinational corporations, and trade in gold. Hence, India has steadily made progress on freeing up the capital account, particularly in the last five years. For foreign institutional investors, we are 100 per cent convertible. Indian firms can take up to 100 per cent of their net worth out of the country. Domestic citizens can take up to $ 25,000 out of the country, which is a lot when compared with the per capita income. The opening up of the capital account has enormous implications for the conduct of Indian macro policy. The impossible trinity is now with us, so that a restrictive currency policy comes at the price of monetary price autonomy. Hence, this is a new and exciting phase for Indian macroeconomics.

As an aside, I want to highlight some non-economic factors which have been at the foundation of India's success in rapid integration into the world economy. These consist of: our strong IT and telecom sectors, our use of english, and our vibrant democracy. Our strengths in IT and telecom have helped us to exploit the Internet, which is an important highway of globalisation today. Our use of English has meant lower transaction costs in interacting with the global economy. Our democracy has helped us avoid the difficulties and hindrances that come into the picture when repressive regimes try to block ideas from flowing in through the Internet. For example, we in India have multiple competing private sector Internet service providers, with high speed lines that reach into the outside world, with no large government effort at censorship or selective blocking of content.

Infrastructure Sector: Unfolding Meso-economic Reforms

Let me turn to infrastructure. In the early 1990s, infrastructure was high on our minds. The public goods of transportation and communications were clearly a bottleneck to efficiency, and to internal and international trade. In the presence of those constraints, our ability to harness gains from trade was limited, owing to the high transactions costs of engaging in trade. Our inefficiencies in transport and communications ultimately filtered into the exchange rate, where the rupee had to devalue enough to obtain rough parity on the current account.

India chose to go down the path of moving towards competitive markets in infrastructure, with private sector production, under a framework of sound regulation. I believe that this was the right path to go down. But as we all know, this is a difficult path to take. There are truly subtle difficulties in finding the right policy mix, the right 'rules of the game' which provide sound incentives to private firms to produce adequate quantities of these goods, while at the same time avoiding monopolistic profit rates. I look at the difficulties in California on electricity, and in the US on broadband telecom, and I sympathise with the problems that they are facing.

For many years, all economists, including myself, used to be somewhat pessimistic about the way things were going on in infrastructure sector in India. From 1991 onwards, the State ceased to invest in infrastructure, but the new policy framework had not fallen into place! So we were stranded between the two stools.

Today, it increasingly looks like the light is at the end of the tunnel on our infrastructure problems.[8] I believe we have made good progress on telecom, roads, ports, electricity and aviation. The big piece where we have yet to obtain real progress is railways.

In telecom, we have obtained a revolution by having competition between multiple, private telephone companies. We are now at 40 million mobile phones, and are growing at the rate of 2 million mobile phones every month. Little shops offering internet access are now all over the country. Every visiting card that I encounter has an e-mail address on it. We are one of the world's first countries to shift to a 'unified licensing', where the licensing is neutral to telecom technology. I believe we are the only market in the world where the two major technologies for mobile telephony—GSM and CDMA—are locked in grim competitive battle, with customers reaping the rewards of this competition. Total phone subscribers are at 71 million, and what was once thought to be an ambitious target for teledensity that should be achieved by March 2005 was actually achieved in December 2003. Given the existing pace of hectic growth, it looks rather likely that an additional 100 million lines will be added over 2004-05 and 2005-06. This would take teledensity from 7 per cent today to 17 per cent by March 2006.

In roads, we have embarked on an enormous project to build new highways, which will take the sustained mean velocity up from 30 kph to 80 kph. I believe these new roads will generate a new phase of growth in India, by harnessing what I call 'internal gains from trade'. I believe this is the classical gains-from-trade story, being repeated within the country, when firms 1000 km apart are able to trade for the first time, thanks to the lowered transaction costs. I think the full impact of these roads on investment, and the geographical distribution of production, will play out in the next five years.

We have yet to make the leap to 8-lane expressways, where we will get sustained mean velocities of 160 kph. But we have a big step forward in terms of learning new institutions, revenue sources, and contracting mechanisms, through which 4-lane highways are now very much in our grasp.

In the area of ports, we have made progress by contracting out the operations of ports to international firms who have specialised expertise on this subject. Remarkably enough, we find that when a public sector terminal

---

8. *Economic Survey* (2003-04). Chapter 9, p. 206.

competes with an international operator in the same port, the performance of this public sector terminal also improves! The turnaround time at ports dropped by half, from 7.5 days in 1996-97 to 3.5 days in 2001-02. These new ideas in contracting are being steadily applied across the country, giving a revolution in how the ports sector works.

These improvements in ports, roads and telecom sound nice. But are they large enough to make a material difference? Or are they high rates of growth on a very bad base? It is important to focus on the end-result of better infrastructure, which should be more efficient firms. Using the CMIE Prowess database, we observe the 4000 largest manufacturing companies in India. For these firms, working capital as per cent of sales went down dramatically from 13 per cent in 1996 to a level of 3.5 per cent today. This is a striking change, which reflects both the opportunities of being more efficient using the new infrastructure, and the competitive forces which are pushing firms to think more carefully about how they manage inventories.

In the area of electricity, the big change is the Electricity Act, which has setup a path-breaking pro-competitive framework whereby producers and consumers of electricity can interact in an unfettered market. We are already seeing myriad changes in the electricity sector in India as a consequence of this simple fact: that producers and consumers of power are now free to contract with each other across the country. Once again, I see this as a story of going from stifled markets to gains from trade.

Financial Sector Reforms: A Quiet Revolution

A major area of focus in the economic reforms has been the financial sector. Joseph Stiglitz has observed that finance is 'the brain of the economy'. The financial sector controls the efficiency with which incremental capital formation is converted into incremental GDP.

India has made good progress in building a sound regulatory framework for banking, insurance and the securities market. Many countries, all over the world, have experienced problems with banking. Obtaining safe and sound banking is genuinely difficult, given the extreme leverage of banks, the opacity of their assets, and the moral hazard induced by a safety net. Difficulties in banking escalate into major macroeconomic problems when the banking system is itself large, when compared with GDP. In India today, bank deposits are just 48 per cent of GDP, and net non-performing assets are just 2.3 per cent of assets. Hence, there is little possibility of difficulties in banking derailing the economy.

In recent years, much detailed work has taken place on strengthening the banking system. Banking has become more competitive through a steady pace of entry by domestic and foreign banks, and has been steadily transformed by the introduction of new technology such as Real-time Gross Settlement System (RTGS). Banking has also benefited, as all creditors have, from the strengthening of creditors' rights which began in 2001. This continues to be an active area for new work in developing legal structures and institutional mechanisms.

India's financial system differs from that of many developing countries and it is more in line with the Anglo-Saxon model, with large and liquid public securities market, and with bank deposits being relatively small when compared with GDP. There has been a particularly remarkable revolution in the stock exchanges in terms of a completely new design replacing traditional notions about how the market should be organised.[9] India's NSE and BSE are the 3rd largest and 6th largest exchanges of the world, measured by the number of trades in 2001 and given the present trends, it is likely that in 2004, NSE will surpass NYSE in terms of the number of trades or transactions. India was a pioneer in shifting to T+2 settlement. India is unique by world standards in the extent to which non-transparent transactions have been proscribed: all trades match on the transparent order-matching screen on the equity market.

Equity derivatives trading was launched in India in June 2000, and now has a daily turnover of $ 4 billion. This was one of the most successful launches of equity derivatives trading in the world.[10] India's success on the stock exchanges is a poster child of our ability to overcome difficult problems of political economy and entrenched interests, to obtain revolutionary change, and rise to the front ranks of the world. These institutions are precious assets today, and will be key building blocks in the next steps of modernising the financial sector, and improving transparency and competition, in the years to come.

In coming decades, enormous flows of savings are going to be intermediated through the financial sector. It is extremely important that the financial sector should be thoughtful and effective in delivering equity and debt capital into those firms in India which convert it into the highest possible

---

9. Shah, Ajay (1999). "Institutional Change on India's Capital Markets", *Economic and Political Weekly*, XXXIV (3-4), pp. 183-194, January; Shah, Ajay and Susan Thomas (2000). "David and Goliath: Displacing a Primary Market", *Journal of Global Financial Markets*, 1(1), pp. 14-21, Spring.

10. Thomas, Susan (2003). "Derivatives Markets in India 2003", Invest India—Tata McGraw Hill.

GDP growth. This is particularly important because, as we will argue ahead, there is a good likelihood that the savings rate in India will grow significantly in the coming decade. The financial sector is of crucial importance in converting these vast flows of savings into a maximal impact upon GDP growth.

We know, from the experience of other countries, that this process can go wrong. We need to continue to work on carrying through the reforms in the financial sector. We have many strengths in what has taken place in finance, particularly on the equity market, but a lot remains to be done in banking and the debt market.

A new frontier in financial sector development lies in pension sector reforms. From 1998 to 2003, an intensive effort took place in India to think about alternative strategies in pension reforms, and to design an institutional architecture that would be well suited to solve the unique problems of the Indian setting.[11] This led to important cabinet decisions in 2003 which are now being implemented.

The basic thrust of these reforms is to build a defined contribution pension system where workers would get a range of investment choices and fund managers. Centralised record-keeping infrastructure is envisaged, which gives scale economies, keeps down transactions costs, and maximises the contestability of the market for fund management services. This new pension system has been mandatory for all new recruits to the central government from January 1, 2004 onwards. It marks the dawn of a new breed of sophisticated institutional investors in the country, who will be sources of investment into debt and equity issued by the projects of the future.

Accelerating Privatisation

Privatisation has been a major new theme of reforms in recent years. Major successes, where control of a company has been sold off, include VSNL, BALCO, CMC and Maruti. The true significance of privatisation lies not in the proceeds, but in the impact upon productivity. There are 276 public sector companies at the central level. They contributed Rs. 2.28 trillion of 'value added' in 2001-02. Of these, there are 47 companies with negative value added; i.e., GDP would go up if these firms ceased to exist. Each 1 per cent

---

11. Bordia, Anand and Gautam Bhardwaj (2003). "Rethinking Pension Provision for India", Invest India–Tata McGraw Hill Series; Shah, Ajay (2004). "Issues in Pension System Reform in India" in Priya Basu and Marilou Uy (eds.) *India's Financial Sector: Trading Efficiency for Stability?*, Oxford University Press, forthcoming.

of increase in value added by these PSUs amounts to Rs.22.8 billion of additional GDP. The international experience suggests that the value added could go up by 20 per cent to 40 per cent after privatisation. Thus privatisation alone could generate a direct impact worth 2 per cent to 4 per cent increase in GDP. In addition, there would be many positive indirect effects of privatisation. Interestingly enough, considerable privatisation efforts are now taking place at the level of state governments also. Of the 919 companies owned by state governments, 33 have been privatised and 69 have been closed down in recent years.

Link to Productivity Growth

In my discussion about recent themes in reforms, I have highlighted four big areas: globalisation, infrastructure, privatisation, and the financial sector. It is important to reflect on the consequences of success in these four areas: these successes will give improvements in productivity. For a given level of labour and capital, progress in each of these areas will give higher output growth.

Areas of Concern

There are two major areas of concern in this happy picture. The first is the problem of successful resolution of fiscal consolidation issues, and the second is that of regional disparities.

Fiscal Consolidation[12]

As you all know, one of the biggest problems faced in India is the fiscal deficit. The consolidated fiscal deficit, of the centre and the states, has been at stubbornly high levels for around twenty years now.

The essence of this problem has been a stagnation in the tax/GDP ratio. From 1990-91 to 2003-04, we did obtain progress on direct taxes, which went up from 1.9 per cent of GDP to 3.5 per cent. The phasing out of customs duties has inevitably given poor growth in indirect taxes, which went from 7.9 per cent of GDP to 5.7 per cent. The fiscal difficulties at the states have given a fresh impetus to state level tax efforts, which have yielded some progress, with growth from 5.3 per cent of GDP to 6.3 per cent of GDP. However, the overall picture has been unchanged, with the tax/GDP ratio being stable at

---

12. *Report of the Task Force on Direct Taxes*, Government of India, December, 2002; *Report of the Task Force on Indirect Taxes*, Government of India, December, 2002; Shome, Partho (2002). *India's Fiscal Matters*, Oxford University Press.

15.5 per cent of GDP in 2003-04 and in 1990-91. The combination of large fiscal deficits with a stagnant tax/GDP ratio has given sharp growth in the debt/GDP ratio. From 1992 to 1998, the debt/GDP ratio was stable at 60 per cent of GDP, and that might have given some comfort. But after that, it has resumed an extremely rapid climb to the present level of 80 per cent of GDP. This has fuelled concerns about the possibility of India facing the problem of debt trap as interest payments have steadily become a bigger fraction of tax revenues.

Sometimes, India's fiscal problem is seen narrowly in terms of debt sustainability or a debt trap. I think this is a narrow perspective. The fiscal problem can be damaging to growth in coming years, even if it does not come to a debt trap. The reasons for this need to be reiterated :

- The high fiscal deficit has eliminated the room for manoeuvre in terms of counter-cyclical fiscal policy.

- It has sharply circumscribed the ability of the state to initiate new spending programmes which could produce highly beneficial public goods.

- It has served to crowd out private investment, and thus reduce GDP growth.

- It has generated incentives for many distorted policies in the financial sector, where it has helped inhibit banking reform and the development of liquid markets for interest rates.

It is important to observe that the fiscal problems would have had an exacerbated impact on growth, by 'crowding out' private investment, if it had not been for the growth in household savings that was discussed earlier. Roughly speaking, government has taken 10 per cent of GDP in 1990 and in 2003. However, household savings grew from 18 per cent to 23 per cent, thus supplying an additional five percentage points of GDP to non-government investment in the country.

In many countries, 'downsizing government', i.e. cutting government expenses, has been central to fiscal adjustment. In the case of India, central government expenses dropped from 18.9 per cent of GDP in 1986 to 15.6 per cent of GDP in 2001. These values do not appear to be particularly out of line by international standards, and are broadly consistent with the level of expenses that are required to produce public goods of the required quality and quantity.

Three difficult items of expenditure, i.e. interest payments, defence expenditures and subsidies make up near 100 per cent of tax revenues. In addition, there are highly inflexible expenses such as pensions, transfers to states, etc. Hence, it appears that there is little flexibility in obtaining a fiscal adjustment by compressing expenditures. There is a great deal that can be gained in terms of improving the extent to which existing expenditures are refocused away from subsidies towards providing public goods, and improving the efficiency of provision of public goods. However, it is hard to visualise a drop in expenses which would be large enough to significantly contribute to the required fiscal adjustment.

This leads us to focus on improving tax revenues as the central policy instrument in the required fiscal adjustment. Hence, efforts towards the fiscal consolidation, that have been undertaken, are focused on the following elements:

- Enlarging the tax base by rationalising exemptions and expanding service tax.

- Process engineering of the tax system.

- Achieving a simple and rational tax system.

- Reduction in transactions costs; improved taxpayer services.

- Reduction in subsidies, with better targeting.

Table 1.2

Structure of Tax Revenues from 1990 to 2001

Source	1990		2001	
	Collections	Per Cent	Collections	Per Cent
Income Tax (Individual)	5,010	9.7	31,764	16.8
Income Tax (Firms)	4,729	9.2	35,696	18.9
Customs	18,036	34.9	47,542	25.2
Excise	22,406	43.4	68,526	36.3
Service Tax			2,613	1.4
Others	1,455	2.8	2,463	1.3
Total Tax Collections	51636	100.0	188,604	100.0

Note: The table summarises changes in the structure of tax revenues from 1990 to 2001.

Have these efforts borne fruit? Many observers have pointed out that the tax to GDP ratio is still below the levels found in the late 1980s. This observation, taken in isolation, is sometimes interpreted in India. However, this aggregative fact masks important accomplishments in terms of obtaining change.

The most important accomplishment was in the area of direct taxes, which grew by almost 7 times over these 11 years. Direct taxes hence improved sharply from 18.9 per cent of collections to 35.7 per cent. This may be interpreted as a striking 'Laffer curve' outcome, where a sharp reduction in rates was accompanied by a sharp improvement in tax collections, by influencing incentives towards tax evasion and labour supply. Customs collections have lost ground, and will drop further, as India shifts away from protectionist policies. Taxing the services sector has now begun, in a small way.

These reforms anchor the fiscal consolidation envisaged in the Fiscal Responsibility Act,[13] and the commitments of state governments, which require elimination of the revenue deficit: from 5.83 per cent in 2002-03 to 0 by 2007-08. It is important to envision what the sources of a 5.83 per cent improvement could be. One example of a feasible combination could be as follows:

1. An increase in direct taxes to GDP ratio of 1.5 percentage points.

2. An increase in union excise duty (including services) to GDP ratio of 2 percentage points.

3. State VAT will be implemented in the near future. It will replace many existing taxes, but across the entire transition, it is expected that this will yield an additional 1 percentage point of GDP.

4. Reduction in subsidies and enforcement of user charges will yield 1 percentage point of GDP.

5. A reduction in interest payments to GDP ratio of 0.5 percentage point is expected, as new debt, at contemporary low interest rates, replaced old, high-cost debt.

The Interim Budget presented in February this year indicates that fiscal consolidation is proceeding on this line, as the revenue deficit for the year 2003-2004 has been projected to decline by 0.5 per cent. This has been due to combination of higher tax/GDP ratio and lower current expenditure.

---

13. Fiscal Responsibility and Budget Management Act (2003). No. 39 of 2003, *The Gazette of India Extraordinary*, Part II, Section 1, No. 43, August.

This fiscal consolidation will assist GDP growth in many indirect ways, including:

- Reduction in the cost of capital.

- Enhanced equity.

- Improved allocative efficiency.

- Increased administrative efficiency.

- Reduced transactions costs.

- Enhanced transparency and accountability.

A successful implementation of this transformation of the tax system, and an elimination of the revenue deficit by 2007-08, is perhaps the most important single issue in public policy in India today. The tax reforms that are currently underway will enable the economy to meet the objective of fiscal consolidation. Successful fiscal consolidation will enable the economy to achieve other important social goals such as better environment protection, greater investment in health infrastructure, research and development and the agriculture sectors.

Table 1.3

Per-capita SDP and Population

States	Per-capita SDP 1999-2000 (Thousand Rupees)	Population 2001 (Per Cent of India)
Bihar	6.3	10.7
Orissa	9.2	3.6
Assam	9.6	2.6
Uttar Pradesh	9.8	17.0
Sum of the above Four		33.9
India	15.6	100.0

Regional Disparities

A major problem that India faces is the large cross-sectional dispersion in economic development. There is a roughly 3:1 ratio in the per capita GDP, when we compare the richest states to the poorest states. Much attention has been focused on the 'BIMARU' states (Bihar, Madhya Pradesh, Rajasthan, Uttar Pradesh) which have high population density and low per capita output. The term 'BIMARU' is catchy because the word *bimaar* means 'sick' in Hindi. The table above identifies the four large states where per capita SDP was over 33 per cent below the national average. These four states make up 33.9 per cent of India's population.

Regional disparities in India have been present for at least a century, if not more. Under normal circumstances, the processes of the market economy should generate 'equalising differences', whereby firms move to low-wage areas in the quest for reduced costs thus equalising differences in wages and land prices. Similarly, individuals migrate to high-wage areas, thus equalising wages, and increasing the land per capita in poor areas. These processes are expected to generate convergence of per capita GDP in the normal framework of growth theory.

It is important to emphasise that the forces of convergence depicted here are based on factor mobility. They operate over and above the conventional notions of convergence through trade, which are based on technological catch-up and trade in goods, without factor mobility. This worldview has faced a challenge from the empirical evidence of the 1990s, where there is some evidence of a lack of convergence. Some states, particularly the states of the West and the South, seem to have excelled in harnessing the opportunities of globalisation and the market economy. In other states, weaknesses in human capital and governance have generated reduced growth rates in the post-1990 period.

This has been a source of much concern on the part of many observers, from two points of view. First, it is argued that if the economic reforms of the 1980s and 1990s failed to ignite growth in Bihar, then there is a need to find a new policy mix which can achieve high growth in Bihar. Second, there are fears of mounting political stress that might come about if income disparities between rich and poor states widen further. There is a remarkable similarity between these problems in India and those that have been observed in China, where coastal provinces have progressed enormously compared with the interior.

These problems are undoubtedly important, and are going to be a central issue in Indian economics and politics in the years to come. While the above difficulties are real, there are also many forces at work which are steadily having an ameliorating effect.

Flexibility of the labour market: Factor mobility is a fundamental element of the process of equalising differences. As of today, roughly 90 per cent of India's labour force is in the unorganised sector, which is a classical labour market, undistorted by labour law. In addition, unlike China, India has no government restrictions on inter-state or rural-to-urban migration.

This innate flexibility of the labour market will assist the process of convergence. In the historical data, migration flows do not (as yet) account for substantial movements of the population. The reforms of the 1990s ignited high growth rates in some states. It is likely that migration flows have a lagged response to high wage differentials. By this logic, the 2011 census may be expected to show larger migration flows than were observed in the 2001 census.

ii. Impact of new infrastructure on 'equalising differences': The development economics literature has emphasised the problems of landlocked states, which are unable to harness gains from trade through high costs of transportation.[14]

India's growth experience suggests that geography is important. At the same time, there are exceptions. Coastal states in India have fared well; however, Orissa is a coastal state. Land-locked states have fared poorly; however, Punjab and Haryana are land-locked.

Gains from internal trade are clearly an important mechanism through which poor states can obtain economic growth. This is critically related to costs of transportation. This suggests that the recent successes in infrastructure policy—particularly in roads, ports, airports, and telecom—are highly significant in thinking about regional disparities. The new roads being built by NHAI imply that vegetables produced in Bihar or Orissa can find markets in Calcutta. This constitutes a new impetus for the forces of convergence, as compared with the preceding post-independence experience.

iii. Fiscal transfers: India has a well-developed system of fiscal transfers, through which taxes collected in rich states are transferred to poor states. This constitutes an important channel for convergence: one that is perhaps reminiscent of the 60-year story of North Italy and South Italy.

While these rules have always been with us, the economic significance of these transfers improves in line with growth in GDP and in the tax/ GDP ratio. Holding the fiscal rules intact, when the size of the pie goes

---

14. Gallup, John Luke, Jeffrey D. Sachs, and Andrew D. Mellinger (1998). "Geography and Economic Development", *NBER Working Paper* No. 6849, December.

up, larger per-capita flows are being sent into poor states. In the decade of the 1990s, India's GDP was roughly $ 350 billion and the tax/GDP ratio was roughly 12 per cent. GDP has already risen to $ 620 billion, giving a quantum leap in the expenditures of government. Looking forward, in a few years, if we envision GDP of $1 trillion and a tax/GDP ratio of 15 per cent, then there will be enormously larger resource flows through existing fiscal institutions, which will generate much larger spending in poor states.

iv. Policy innovations: One important insight derived from the experience of economic growth in East Asia is the importance of 'regional role models'.[15] East Asian countries learned from each other. Across these countries, there was a significant amount of experimentation and real-world trials of alternative ideas, including choices of effective institutions, policies, and technologies. There was a contagion effect within this region with countries learning from each other's success stories.

In the decade of the 1990s, a similar phenomenon has begun with the states of India. States are now increasingly conscious of the importance of local public goods. The political leadership of many states is increasingly conscious of the need to find policy innovations which would improve the quality and quantity of local public goods.

The 1990s began with a certain heterogeneity of governance procedures in the states. The economic reforms of the 1990s have inevitably had a differential impact on various states; some states had policies which were more conducive to harnessing these opportunities. When the gap in per capita income widens, the political system has incentives to search for policy responses which would close the gap. Andhra Pradesh, Madhya Pradesh, West Bengal, and Kerala are all examples of states where there has been a distinct learning from the regional role models, and consequent changes in governance.

In parallel to this learning from regional role models, there are two important policy innovations which are going to fully play out in the coming decade. The first is the move towards smaller states. It is widely conjectured that smaller states are more effective at catering to local variation in preferences and technology, and at ensuring greater

---

15. World Bank (1993). *The East Asian Miracle: Economic Growth and Public Policy*, Oxford University Press, September.

accountability for public goods outcomes. Uttaranchal, Bihar, Jharkhand and Chhattisgarh are important experiments in this regard. It is, as yet, too early to tell whether the outcomes play out in line with the conjecture. If governance does prove to be superior in smaller states, then (a) it will generate convergence, given that these four states are all below the national average, and (b) it suggests one policy avenue for improving governance in other large states in the future.

The second innovation is the devolution to local governments, as a consequence of the 73rd and 74th constitutional amendment. The underlying premise of *Panchayati Raj* is that when local citizens control public expenditures, there will be a greater likelihood of obtaining good outcomes in terms of producing public goods. There are three key elements of local autonomy: (a) Transfer of functions and schemes, (b) Transfer of staff, and (c) Transfer of funds, and autonomous financial decision making. As of yet, different states have made different degrees of progress on these three fronts. It is, as yet, too early to tell whether the outcomes play out in line with the underlying premise. If we do obtain improvements in governance by empowering local governments, then this would constitute one channel for convergence.

Empirical Evidence

How are we faring? There is some evidence that these effects are already at work and are reshaping the nature of regional inequalities in India. There are two striking illustrations which show the changes which are taking place:

- In a deliciously ironic development, the very phrase 'BIMARU', which symbolised backward states as of 1990, has become out of touch with the location of poverty traps! This symbolises the dynamism of regional economics in India. Rajasthan and Madhya Pradesh have made significant progress in the 1990s. Chhattisgarh, Uttaranchal and western parts of Uttar Pradesh have lower poverty. The most difficult areas are now no longer the BIMARU states, but the eastern region comprising Orissa, Jharkhand, Bihar, and eastern parts of Uttar Pradesh. This illustrates the mutability of poverty traps in India, and suggests that there are forces at work through which poor regions can obtain convergence.

- The second illustration concerns the BPO industry. If the idea of exploiting IT for services exports, in areas like call centres and accounting, had been described to an impartial observer in 1993, the prediction which would have been squarely made is that this would flourish in southern states, owing to the superior quality of local public goods. This would include issues such as education, reliable electricity, law and order and gender issues. Questions of law and order, and empowerment of women, are extremely important in this field, given the need for women to work the night shift. The impartial observer would have solemnly argued that North India was innately and deeply hamstrung when it came to women obtaining high education, participating in the labour force, and working at night.

The actual outcomes, from 1993 to 2003, have been inconsistent with the prediction that IT-enabled services would primarily be located in the peninsula. When we look back at the last 10 years, it is an undeniable fact that Gurgaon, Noida and Chandigarh have also emerged as the major centres of IT-enabled services exports. While locations like Bangalore, Madras, Hyderabad, Poona and Bombay have all also succeeded in this area, Gurgaon and Noida are probably the largest centres. This suggests that issues such as low labour cost dominated issues such as poor production of local public goods, which suggests that forces of convergence were effective.

The most interesting evidence about the question of convergence is found in data for investment projects outstanding.[16]

The table below exploits the CMIE database which tracks investment projects at hand as of a point in time. It juxtaposes the projects under implementation as of April 1995 (the first point in the CMIE database) *versus* October 2003 (the most-recent date available). All values are expressed as rupees per capita.

This data is interesting from two points of view. Focusing on levels, we see states like Gujarat, which have above-mean output and above-mean investment. At the same, there also appear to be equilibrating forces at work. High growth in investment is seen in backward states like Kerala, Madhya Pradesh, Chhattisgarh and Bihar. In a striking display of convergence, of the 10 states with above-average growth in per-capita investment, 8 had a below-average level of per capita investment as of 1995. In addition, Punjab shows the opposite phenomenon. Low growth in investment is found in high income states like Punjab and Gujarat.

---

16. Ahluwalia, Montek S. (2002). "State Level Performance under Economic Reforms in India" in Anne O. Krueger (ed.), *Economic Policy Reforms and the Indian Economy*.

Table 1.4

Changes in Per-capita Investment in Different States

State	4/1995	10/2003	Change (Per Cent)
Delhi	313	5966	1804.8
Kerala	991	5579	462.8
Chhattisgarh	1097	4525	312.5
Madhya Pradesh	1846	6889	273.3
Tamil Nadu	2491	6941	178.6
Karnataka	3528	8265	134.2
Haryana	3021	6820	125.7
Maharashtra	4409	8957	103.1
Bihar	799	1560	95.3
Andhra Pradesh	3740	7083	89.4
Rajasthan	1852	2771	49.6
Punjab	3662	5148	40.6
Orissa	6073	7432	22.4
Uttar Pradesh	1302	1544	18.6
West Bengal	2408	2686	11.5
Gujarat	12531	11950	-4.6
Jharkhand	3908	3643	-6.8
India	**3258**	**5510**	**69.1**

These trends are indicative of the possibility of meeting the objective of regional equity with well defined policies at the central level and at the state level. Regional equity is going to be perhaps one of the most important issues for the political economy of growth in a federal system like India. We will need to be continuously mindful of this aspect and keep policies under review so as to achieve equity in outcomes across the states of our union.

Growth Outlook: Contributions from Labour, Capital and Productivity

Let me now shift gears considerably. So far I have talked about the reform efforts, repeatedly alluding to the impact of reforms on efficiency, productivity and improved resource allocation.

But what about the perspective for the growth of inputs? Ever since Krugman's 1994 article[17] in *Foreign Affairs,* about the extent to which East

---

17. Krugman, Paul (1994). "The Myth of Asia's Miracle—A Cautionary Fable", *Foreign Affairs*, November/ December.

Asian growth was 'merely' caused by a high flow of inputs in terms of labour and capital, all of us have had a heightened consciousness about both (a) the power of additional inputs in delivering high growth rates, and (b) the importance of asking whether there is productivity growth over and above this.

Labour

Let me start with labour. It is conventional to focus on citizens between age 15 and 64 as 'the working population'. The fascinating thing about India is that we will be one of the last large countries in the world to experience our demographic transition. Current projections show that from 2010 or so, the fraction of Chinese and of Koreans in the age group of 15-64 will start dropping. In the case of Japan, this fraction has been dropping from 1995 onwards.

In the case of India, we will experience 'demographic dividend' as the ratio of working population to the total population will grow all the way till 2050. In particular, a sharp drop in the dependency ratio from 59 per cent to 50 per cent is projected between 2005 and 2020. The dependency ratio is projected to drop to 47 per cent in 2040. It is only from 2040 onwards that India's dependency ratio is projected to go up. This will give robust fuel to the process of economic growth. This forecast for India reflects the existing young population structure, coupled with a deceleration of fertility, so that a large number of children are not expected to be added.

A second change that is taking place on the labour force is equally significant for economic growth. This concerns the quality of the labour force. Every year, the human capital of the stock of labour goes up, through gains in education and gains in experience. Hence, we are likely to obtain improvements in the labour inputs to economic growth from three, distinct directions: (a) Incremental workers, (b) Incremental education, and (c) Incremental experience of the existing stock of workers. All this is potent fuel for economic growth. The experience of Asia shows that the 'growth miracles' in Japan or in 'Tiger' economies of South East Asia or in China occurred at the similar stage of demographic transition when the share of working population in total population grew sharply.

Capital

What about capital? One element flows directly from demographics. Children and old people tend to save less; saving is the highest in the working years. Using NCAER survey data,[18] we find that in 1994-95, while the overall savings rate was 20.3 per cent, this dropped to 16.9 per cent when the head of household was below 30.

The highest savings rate, of 23 per cent, was found when the head of the household was in the fifties. In the case of urban households, these effects were more pronounced, with a savings rate of just 7.8 per cent when the head of household was below 30. So the demographic projections which clearly point out that India will have a bigger fraction of the population in the age group from 15 to 64 simultaneously predict a higher savings rate in the future. Further, holding household characteristics identical, a larger number of children would induce higher consumption, so declining fertility is likely to induce higher saving.

A second factor that is at work is the sheer GDP growth. NCAER data shows that there are extremely low savings rates for low income households. Remarkably enough, as of 1994-95, only 1.9 per cent of all saving was done by households with income below the then-prevalent median income. In 1994-95, the poorest 80 per cent of the population accounted for half the income, and this group accounted for 23.9 per cent of total savings. As a rough approximation, we may say that significant savings behaviour only took place in the top quartile of the income distribution of 1994-95. Households in the top decile had a much higher savings rate, of 35.8 per cent, as compared with the general population.

Economic growth steadily pushes households above the absolute income threshold required to be in the top quartile by the income distribution as of 1994-95. Thus, every year, a large number of households graduate into the income group where saving will commence. The bottom 30 per cent of the 1994-95 income distribution has near-zero or negative saving. GDP growth shrinks this set of zero-savings households. The top quartile of the 1994-95 income distribution had high savings rates. GDP growth pushes more households into this set of high-savings households. Through this process, holding other aspects of the stochastic environment of the household constant, the high GDP growth rates that India has been experiencing are likely to generate a steady escalation of the savings rate.

The two arguments suggested above—about the impact of income growth, and about the changing dependency ratio—have been at work for some time.

---

18. Pradhan, Basanta K., P.K. Roy, M.R. Saluja and S.L. Shetty (2003). *Household Savings and Investment Behaviour in India*, National Council of Applied Economic Research, September.

If these arguments are on track, then it should have been the case that the savings rate in India should have been going up in recent years. The empirical evidence is consistent with this prediction, for household savings grew from 18 per cent to 23 per cent over the period after 1990. Looking forward, our arguments suggest that household savings will grow further in the coming 15 years. In addition, growing openness of capital account would mean greater inflow of foreign capital as the country becomes a 'willing globaliser' i.e. more open to trade and investement. This means that in the coming decade, the supply of both domestic and foreign savings are going to sharply increase leading to a much higher rate of capital accumulation compared to the last two decades.

Outlook on Productivity

Paul Krugman noticed that East Asian growth had weak foundations in terms of productivity increases; that the high growth rates were primarily a combination of demographics (an increase in the working population) and capital being brought to bear on production. This is disappointing. The essence of development is improved technology; it is all about new ways of organising production, of injecting new scientific knowledge and new institutions into the economy. We expect that when economic development takes place, productivity should be transformed.

It is important to point out that many studies have taken place on productivity in India, and the consensus suggests that there has been significant TFP growth in India. The definitive measurement is by Bosworth and Collins in 2003,[19] who find that in the period after 1980, 2 per cent of the growth (out of a total of 5.73 per cent) was accounted for by productivity changes. This suggests that India's reforms process has been able to obtain results in terms of better incentives and competition, coupled with better public goods, inducing improvements in productivity.

The outlook for the acceleration in the TFP growth in the coming decade or two is very promising. This is for several reasons. The first is the impact of information technology. In the coming decade, the rate of diffusion of IT is going to be greater due to increased availability of hardware, telecom infrastructure and human capital. In the US and other countries, the diffusion of IT has had a well documented positive impact on productivity growth. The

---

19. Bosworth, Barry and Susan Collins (2003). "The Empirics of Growth: An Update", *Brookings Paper on Economic Activity* 2, pp. 113-79.

second reason is the beneficial impact of meso-economic reforms and privatisation of the infrastructure sector on productivity. The international experience has been that such meso-economic reforms have led to an all-round increase in productivity. The third element is the engines of increasing returns which will be accruing from network industries due to network externalities.[20] The new highway network and telecom networks are two prime examples of new network industries. In the US, both these network industries have had profound impact in accelerating growth in total factor productivity.

When we look back at the experience with growth across various countries over the last 200 years, each experience with rapid growth has been caused by accumulation of capital, coupled with a catching-up of scientific knowledge. Over the years, the technologies of information processing and dissemination have steadily improved. This suggests that the diffusion of knowledge takes place faster and faster. This is consistent with the fact that the more recent growth episodes, like those of China, Korea and Taiwan, have experienced higher growth rates when compared with the older growth episodes, like those of Russia, Japan and the US. Looking forward, India will benefit strongly from the great technological improvements in the diffusion of knowledge which have taken place in the last 25 years. When Korea was integrating into the world economy, and catching up with global scientific knowledge, the process of knowledge acquisition was slower than that found today in India, given the greater extent of information access through the Internet, voice calls, international travel, etc. This suggests that the speed of productivity change in India, in the next 20 years, could be higher than that seen in any experience with rapid economic growth in the last 200 years.

These arguments suggest that in the coming decade, it is not difficult to envisage a sharp increase of more than 50 per cent in the annual TFP growth a doubling of the TFP growth from the present trend of 2 per cent per annum. Such an increase would be in line with the international experience of dynamic economies.

On the Growth Turnpike

This brings me to my main thesis: that India may be about to embark on a new golden age of high economic growth. The key argument runs in these steps:

---

20. Shy, Oz (2001). "The Economics of Network Industries", February.

- There is a near inevitability that there will be a bulge in the working population, particularly till 2020. This effect will be further multiplied due to enhanced levels of skills i.e. accumulation of human capital.

- It is likely that this demographic dividend, coupled with strong GDP growth, will fuel an increase in the savings rate.

- Thus India is likely to fare better than it did over the 1980-2000 period, in terms of putting factor inputs into the growth process.

- The policies of the recent years—particularly in infrastructure, reductions of protectionism, and building modern securities markets—will continue to fuel TFP growth.

- Being a 'willing globaliser' will attract greater flow of FDI and technology.

- In addition, India has already shown a track record for obtaining TFP growth over the 1980-2000 period. TFP growth will show further acceleration, thanks to the impact of information and communication technologies upon the speed of knowledge diffusion and to the network externalities.

- These elements add up to a scenario where GDP growth in India over 2004-2024 will be much higher than that seen over 1980-2004. In the coming decade or two, growth rate in India may surpass the 'miracle growth' rates achieved by other Asian countries. This is not surprising as India, compared to Japan, China and other high growth economies of Asia, will have advantage of an access to productivity enhancing IT, which was not available in earlier decades. This way, we will be cashing in on the 'late comer's advantage'.

Concluding Remarks

Now, I would like to sum up. Thanks to painstaking policy reforms initiated over the last two decades by successive Governments, I believe that India is at the threshold of 'a golden age of growth', with India's democratic framework being a key growth fundamental. It seems to me that, over time, India has paid the 'fixed costs' of democracy in terms of the creation of institutional infrastructure, traditions and conventions. Further, India's democratic system has also internalised what Prime Minister Vajpayee calls "Coalition Dharma", showing that coalitions can provide stable government and push economic reforms. This means that in the future, the economy can reap the dividends from the resultant systemic stability. Thus, India—riding the wave of growth fundamentals such as demographic transition, human capital accumulation, improved incentive structures, diffusion of new technologies such as IT, total factor productivity accelerators through 'network industries', and an improved security environment—will be growing at growth rates which can be above 10 per cent per annum i.e. double digit growth rates. There is an ineffable sense of joy for me personally, and professionally, to see India embark on this growth odyssey, a journey that I call "India: On the growth turnpike".

2004 Narayanan Oration, Australian National University, Canberra, April 27, 2004.
Economic Developments in India, Vol. 77.

2

Towards a New Development Paradigm

ARVIND VIRMANI

Introduction

The old paradigm of development was based on the assumption that the active involvement of the State is essential for economic development and poverty removal. Over the decades, this was used to justify intervention in an entry of the state into every sphere of economic activity. Under the guise of noble purpose, the government gradually usurped the space occupied by the private sector, cooperatives, individuals and social groups. This spread of Leviathan was accompanied by a gradual but pervasive deterioration of governance.[1] Though this deterioration started with specific areas of government operations and specific regions of the country, by now it encompasses the entire country, every state and every field of activity in which government is involved. In some states and in regions of other states, government failure has now reached a point at which government has become non-functional; it cannot even fulfil the basic role, the provision of 'public goods', that it has played for centuries, leave alone the grandiose development role envisaged for it in the (old) development paradigm of the second half of the 20th century.

There is therefore the need for a new paradigm at the beginning of the 21st century, that recognises that 'government failure' is a much more important problem than 'market failure'. 'Privatisation' of government services by its employees and government's monopoly of power are the real problems today. The new paradigm must be based on a clear and non-ideological recognition of the strengths and the weakness of the state and the people. A democratic society has enormous potential for entrepreneurship, innovation and creative development. The people, their diverse forms of activity and association such as companies, cooperatives, societies, trusts and other NGOs must be allowed

---

1. It has also distorted the attitudes and operations of business, workers and farmers.

and encouraged to play their due role. The state must focus on what only it can do best and shed all activities that the people can do as well or better. The heavy hand of government in the form of incentive distorting laws, rules, regulations, procedures and red tape, have also corrupted industry and business and other organised interest groups. These must be removed so as to release the energy of the people. The state should confine itself to managing the economy so as to accelerate employment and income growth in a self-sustaining manner, ensure that all citizens receive their basic entitlements of basic public goods and services and empower the poor so that they have equal rights (and responsibilities) as the better-off citizens.

Paradigm Shift

The old paradigm of a moral, benevolent, omniscient and all powerful state has failed. Though this paradigm had some validity in the mid-20th century, postwar and newly independent India, it gradually lost its validity, to reach a point at which it became counter-productive. The deterioration in governance is broad-based and universal. Civic amenities, publicly provided utilities, public education and health, law and order and justice have deteriorated, in some places beyond belief. Both availability and quality continue to decline.

The old paradigm was characterised by approaches and policies that had two underlying problems. These are distorted incentives and the corruption of power. Existing systems have distorted the incentives for working efficiently and productively and for investment and entrepreneurship. In the case of public servants (bureaucrats and politicians) the disincentive is compounded by the imbalance of power between the state and the public. Power corrupts and absolute power corrupts absolutely.[2] As the systems of governance deteriorate under rent-seeking, rent-creation and corruption, the power to do good falls relative to the power to harm. The result is that today the latter is much greater than the former, so that the rare employee wanting to do good has the dice loaded against him/her.

The insights of modern economics, that incentive structures are important for how economic agents behave, were largely ignored in setting up institutions and in devising economic and other policies. The role of moral and social conventions in ensuring respect for and implementation of law was given undue weight. Though post-independence leaders in India were imbued with ideals that defied economic incentives, this has long since ceased to be

---

2. These are a modification of the famous remark by Lord Acton that "power tends to corrupt".

true. Countries that built institutions and systems with some recognition of economic incentives have sustained good governance much longer.[3] Unfortunately, this was not so in India, so that we are now faced with comprehensive failure of governance.

Towards a New Paradigm

Economic theory tells us that under certain conditions market competition produces results that are the most efficient. As the obverse of monopoly, it is a useful goal even when the ideal is not attainable. It has therefore come to be widely accepted over the last two decades that market incentives are the most sustainable incentives for business, workers and farmers and that market competition is the best handmaiden of the social purpose. The best antidote to exploitation by corrupt businessmen and bureaucrats, lazy organised sector workers and shoddy products and services is competition.

Competition is also the best means of dispersing economic power. In an ideal system, competition would ensure that wealth could only be garnered through innovation and acquisition of special skills, hard work and thrift. Such wealth generation is, therefore, in the interests of the entire society. Monopoly (or oligopoly) is the anti-thesis of such competition as it allows generation of profits without any such meritorious activity. Government created monopolies, whether deliberately created or the indirect result of distorting policies, are the worst culprits in this regard. 'Natural' monopolies have to be regulated to ensure that 'monopoly profits' are minimised.

Ideal competition is just that and market incentives are not perfect. There will be market failure and non-existence of markets. Market economics itself helps identify, analyse and suggest the best way of dealing with such problems, appropriate policies, developmental actions and regulatory institutions.

The second underlying problem can only be addressed by the dispersal of the government's enormous power. This requires right-sizing of government, shedding of activities that can be performed by others, decentralisation of governmental functions to lower levels based on the principle of subsidiarity, the creation of countervailing power, transfer of regulatory functions to independent professional regulators, empowerment of citizens and civic groups, giving voice to the under-employed and creation of checks and balances.

---

3. Singapore is the widely cited outlier.

Incentives, Efficiency and Productivity

Law and Incentives

Laws, particularly economic laws (including contract law), do not merely define what a citizen/resident can or cannot do. They create a system of incentives and disincentives for economic agents and those charged with implementing the law. Most economic laws have had consequences that the originators had no inkling of. The common result of the myriad such laws is to create incentives for rent-seeking, rent-creation, bribery and corruption.

Competition and Efficiency

The same basic principles of competition apply to infrastructure services and factor markets as to the goods market. Decontrol and delicensing must be completed in the remaining items such as drugs, fertilisers, coal, petroleum, sugar and small industry.[4] SSI reservation is perhaps one of two main reasons why India, unlike China, has not become the 'manufacturing base' for the world supply of labour intensive goods. Lakhs of new jobs have been lost in exportable industries in a futile attempt to preserve the profits of existing small scale industrialists.

State Monopolies

State monopolies, whether they are departmental public enterprises or public sector units, have proved to be as inefficient and antithetical to consumers/public interest as private monopolies. Such monopolies not only invite extraction of monopoly rents and X-inefficiency, but also confer additional power on government departments and their ministers that is easy to misuse. Introduction of competition and dispersal of this power requires free private entry, unbundling of all natural monopoly elements and their regulation by independent regulators, and privatisation of all contestable elements (core and non-core) so as to introduce genuine competition into the latter. Public sector and nationalised banks also constitute a near-monopoly as around 80 per cent of the entire banking system is owned by the government. This is the highest percentage in the world. As we already have one of the better regulatory systems (RBI) and banking has no natural monopoly elements, the banking system will only become competitive if these are privatised.

---

4. Though notionally the petroleum sector has been decontrolled the reality is much more ambiguous.

Role of Government

The role of government must be redefined to abandon the many functions accumulated over decades where the government adds no value (even theoretically under ideal conditions) and focus on the basic functions of governance that only the government can perform, but have been neglected. Right-sizing of government requires both downsizing and refocusing of government attention on essentials.

Downsizing

Downsizing of the government requires privatising of production, shutting down of control department and ministries and eliminating producer and middle class subsidies. All these add to the power of government and thus undermine the power of the public and accountability of the elected representatives to the people. This is particularly so when the power to harm is so much more than the power to do good. Use of such production units and producer and middle class subsidies for personal vote-yielding populist measures is one of the reasons for fiscal bankruptcy.

Privatise Production

The government must get out of the production of (what are technically defined as) 'private' goods and services, i.e., those that can be sold to and consumed by individuals on an exclusive basis. These are not 'public goods' in the sense that consumption by one individual does not diminish the consumption by another (non-rivalry) or are non-excludable. They are 'quasi-public' in that they meet the criteria approximately and have some element of externality.[5] There are several reasons for this. Firstly, they can just as well be produced and sold by non-government (commercial, cooperative or non-profit) organisations, so there is no positive reason for government to produce them.[6] Their production has been usurped by a 'Leviathan' government in its unquenchable thirst for power.

Secondly, the incentive structures in government are not conducive to efficient commercial operation. The layers of government hierarchy (PSU/DPE,

---

5. For instance, even though urban piped water and education are 'private' good/service, I would define 'clean drinking water' as a 'quasi-public' good as consumption of dirty water can lead to public health epidemics. Similarly literacy and primary education have externalities in that the entire society (including the educated) benefits from the expansion of the pool of literates. Further, in rural areas, even piped water and primary education may not be private good/service.

6. That is, government does not have any advantage even at a theoretical level.

concerned ministry, cabinet and parliament) as well as the CVC and CAG system is not conducive to making management decisions in a complex economy or to risk-taking in an inherently uncertain world. Thirdly, the rate of return on the assets employed in these units is less than the interest rate that could be earned on the sale value of these assets and much less than the rate of return of similar units in the private sector.[7]

Privatisation of competitive and contestable goods (including units producing civil and dual use items for defence forces) can be done with all deliberate speed, while that of natural monopoly (such as power distribution) must be accompanied by setting up of appropriate regulatory systems. Regulators already exist for the financial system (RBI and SEBI), so privatisation of banks and other financial institutions (e.g., UTI) can be initiated without delay.[8]

Eliminate Departments

Many areas have been decontrolled and delicenced; yet the staff, divisions, departments and ministries set up to implement such controls and licences continue. These must be eliminated to remove the threat of *ad hoc* interference and red tape and root out the control mentality that has wormed its way deep into the government. Similarly, there is no need for ministries and quasi-public institutions dealing with 'private' goods and services such as steel, sugar, fertiliser.

Phase Out Non-poor Subsidies

Subsidies must be targeted on the poor, which for this purpose should include the less well off half (50 per cent) of the population. Impact studies show that the poor benefit less than or at best proportionately to the middle-upper income groups. Better targeting requires a systematic effort to eliminate both producer and middle class subsidies and search for channels that can be used to focus subsidies on the poor.

The origins of many subsidies have long been forgotten and they continue because large subsidies always build strong vested interests. The fertiliser (urea) subsidy is a good example. Its original justification was to induce small

---

7. Note that the 'resource rent' on natural resources, such as oil, that have scarcity value can and should be mopped up by government through a royalty or other resource rent tax, whether the producer/user is a government or private company. The proper comparison for oil producer/user companies is therefore net of oil resource rents.

8. Those who genuinely believe that government is to blame for recent financial failures, should realise that systemic tinkering or change of government will not change the basic incentive structures. Similar, perhaps worse crises are inevitable in the future if ownership remains in government hands.

and marginal farmers to adopt new HYV technologies, as higher fertiliser usage was an inalienable part of the HYV package. Over the years it became a subsidy for large surplus farmers, particularly those producing foodgrains for the market. More recently it has become a subsidy for fertiliser producers as the gap between farm price and world prices has disappeared. This subsidy can be eliminated by complete decontrol of fertiliser with the subsidy phased out over three years (say). This will allow the fiscal deficit to be reduced and larger funds to become available for irrigation and rural infrastructure that helps all rural poor including small and marginal farmers.

Refocusing Government

Broadly speaking, the government has three broad functions that it must perform for the economy and society.[9] This is the provision of 'public' goods and services, the correction of 'externalities' and 'social welfare'. The former has been most neglected over the past three decades.

Public Goods

'Public good', is an economic concept with a precise technical definition, one element of which is 'non-excludability' and another is 'non-rivalry.' The classic 'public good' (actually service) is 'defence' where exclusion is literally impossible and once provided, everybody shares in it. Other services that meet the definition are general administration, the judicial system, police, roads and prevention/control of communicable/epidemic diseases. Though in principle government could charge individuals for the use of local roads, it is prohibitively expensive to do so (economic non-excludability). Rural roads, once built, satisfy the non-rivalry condition in that the traffic is very light (and they are thus empty) most of the time. Inter-city roads have very strong element of externality (marginal cost-zero relative to average fixed cost), so that they are also considered 'public goods'. Similarly, public health measures such as public (not individual) supply of clean drinking water, sanitation and sewerage, population control and public education about nutrition, cleanliness, etc., correct negative externalities and are accepted as 'public' goods. Similarly, literacy and basic education have positive externalities for other educated people and can be similarly classified even though it does not meet the exclusion criteria in urban area.[10] Because of limits to divisibility and the

---

9. The issue here is expenditure related functions, not macroeconomic, tax and other policies.

10. In general both basic public health and basic education services are more accurately defined as 'quasi-public' goods.

sparseness of population, many basic infrastructure services (drinking water, primary education) in rural areas have very high average fixed costs relative to marginal costs and can be classified as 'public goods'.[11]

Fifty years after independence, the population coverage and the quality of supply of these basic services is pathetic and globally embarrassing. Much more attention, time and funds need to be spent on these basic public goods and services. Government responsibility for supply means that government must provide the required funds but it need not produce all these services.

Correcting Externalities

Externalities are a known form of market failure even in a competitive economy and need to be dealt with through government intervention. Apart from the externalities that we have incorporated in the concept of 'quasi-public good,' the most important externalities relate to knowledge and information and environment/pollution. The significant areas in the former are science and technology, higher education in special fields of national importance, development of strategic technology (e.g., aerospace and nuclear)[12] and research and development and the spreading of knowledge especially in agriculture (information/extension).[13] This is best achieved through a mix of government expenditures and tax/direct subsidies. The optimal mix can be different for different sectors and also changes over time. The private sector can play a much greater role in correcting these externalities at lower cost to the exchequer, but Government will also continue to be an important player in this area. Similarly, solutions apply to environmental externalities, of which control of water pollution is the most important from the expenditure perspective.

Social Welfare

The third important expenditure-related function of government is social welfare. The definition of social welfare has a large element of context specificity, in that it cannot be defined independent of the average income and wealth of the country. Equally there is a basic minimum that even a relatively

---

11. Once a primary school is built and teacher provided, or piping for drinking water established, the marginal cost is almost zero (relative to the fixed cost).

12. Technologies of power where normal commercial considerations do not apply and availability depend on geostrategic considerations.

13. Thus government must provide facility grants to R&D organisations and scholarships to Ph.D. students in S&T.

poor, democratic country must ensure in the 21st century. We cannot allow people to die of starvation or to be chronically hungry. Society must also take ultimate responsibility for the old, infirm and disabled and for abandoned or destitute children. Every citizen has the right to life, physical security, basic human dignity and equality before law and constitution. The government has the duty to eliminate pockets of feudal oppression and bandit government that still prevail in parts of the country.[14] Known criminals, dacoits and murderers cannot be allowed to publicly hold the law to shame because of their muscle power, political power or (sometimes ill gotten) wealth.[15]

Countervailing Power

Decentralisation

The Central and state governments have accumulated too much administrative power and this power must be dispersed to lower levels of government, the *Panchayati Raj* Institutions (PRI) and *Nagar Palikas* (NPs). This requires further changes in the PRI and NP and municipal acts. The principle of subsidiarity must be applied so that all functions that are best carried out at the lowest level are devolved to them, and a similar allocation is done to the next higher level and so on up the ladder. In particular, responsibility for provision of local public goods (drinking water, primary school, PHC, irrigation water distribution, local roads) must be devolved to PRI and NP along with the power over local taxes and any additional funds required. This is, however, only the first step. These PRIs must also be made accountable to the local public so that powerful caste and other sub-groups do not hijack them.

Accountability: People's Power

User Groups

One way to ensure accountability for provision of particular services is to require the setting up of specialised user groups for monitoring the availability

---

14. 'Bandit' or 'predatory' government is a particular form of pre-feudal government defined in the theory of political economy.

15. The T&D mafia can arrange to steal half the power supply of the capital city of Delhi, its inspectors can institute false charges of electricity theft and set the DESU equivalent of the CBI on a doctor whose employee inadvertently charged his relative and a government servant has to approach the union power secretary to ensure installation of functioning (rather than a faulty) meter at his house, while commentators still refer to 'pilferage' and theft of power by industrialists.

and quality of specific services. Thus, for instance a user group that includes parents and grandparents of school-going children along with the teacher would have a much greater incentive to ensure proper functioning of the local primary school. The user groups for Primary Health Centres must have majority representation from senior citizens, potential mothers and mothers of pre-school age children and disabled/infirm/chronically sick or their close relatives. Similarly, an oversight group for a 'food for work programme' must have adequate representation of the landless and marginal farmers and a water distribution user group must have adequate representation of farmers.

Non-governmental Organisations

The government must also actively support and strengthen self-help groups and civic groups doing social work (NGOs). The existence of NGO entrepreneurs siphoning off funds for personal use cannot be used to discredit the entire movement, just as the existence of numerous charlatans who have made religion into a virtual industry does not discredit all religious figures. Vested interests, whether bureaucratic or political, will inevitably make such charges and demands to preserve their own rents.

Cooperatives

The interstate cooperative law as well as the co-operative laws of states must be modernised to exclude *ad hoc* intervention by government and increase their autonomy and accountability.[16] Any oversight by government must be through transparent institutions such as an independent professional regulator, who can ensure professional management of cooperatives and accurate audited accounts.

Independent Regulators

There are three sectors of the market economy that clearly need regulatory systems for overseeing private (or government) provision and supply. These are infrastructure service segment that have natural monopoly, the financial sector because of its fiduciary responsibility and two social sectors—education and health—because of potentially large and irreversible human consequences. The modern approach to regulation is to ensure availability of information, transparency and detection and punishment of fraud, lying in the grey area between outright illegality and bad luck. Honest, professional suppliers of

---

16. A few states such as Andhra Pradesh have already reformed their law.

these services therefore welcome and support such regulation, making them the first line of administration through self-regulatory organisations.[17]

There are several reasons for removing the regulatory functions from government proper and putting them in a separate organisation. First, the generalist government has neither the expertise nor the professionalism needed to do a good job of regulation. A professional organisation staffed with adequate specialised skills and knowledge is essential for efficient regulation and this is best created within a separate autonomous and independent organisation. Second, such an organisation can be better insulated from the day-to-day pulls and pressures of democratic politics as has been demonstrated in the case of the RBI. Third, it allows government to act as a higher court of oversight in that it is available to act in the (hopefully) rare situation in which the regulator is tempted to extract rents.

Civil Service Reform

Even if the government restricts itself to its basic functions, the civil service will still be needed to perform these functions. One view is that the service is too politicised to even perform these functions effectively, unless its autonomy is restored to levels that prevailed during the first few decades of independence. This requires the process of selection, appointment, posting and promotion to be distanced from politics and made relatively autonomous. Another view is that once the government sheds all the lucrative rent generating functions that it has accumulated over the years, it will become less attractive to those who view politics and government as a (privately/personally) profitable business or occupation. The extreme forms of deterioration can then be controlled through the creation of countervailing power and new checks and balances. Though efforts must be made to reform the system as proposed in the first viewpoint, in our judgment these are either unlikely to take place or will be effectively undermined by the system. These efforts must therefore be focused on the most critical area, namely, the police. For the rest of the bureaucratic system it would be more pragmatic to take the latter viewpoint as the working hypothesis.

Checks and Balances

There is an urgent need to strengthen the checks and balances in the political system. Though the framers of our Constitution paid a lot of attention

---

17. This approach contrasts with the control approach that assumes that the policy maker or administrator knows exactly what the producer should or should not do in the interest of some higher purpose.

to the potential for corruption in the bureaucracy, they made the fatal mistake of assuming that all future elected representatives would be incorruptible and selfless like those who fought for independence. They could not imagine that the judiciary could also be corrupted.

Criminal Legislators

There is an urgent need for electoral reform to reduce the currently, overwhelming incentive for corruption. If the *'neta*-criminal' nexus is not broken, a time will come in the not too distant future when it will become virtually impossible to stop the criminalisation of the entire police force. In our view the minimal elements of a solution are: (a) state-funding of elections through a matching funds approach; (b) freedom to companies to donate funds subject to shareholder approval; (c) transparent accounting and mandatory auditing of the accounts of political parties that receive state or company funds; (d) mandatory bar to running for any political office by any one against whom criminal charges have been legally framed; and (e) special courts to try politicians/potential candidates against whom such charges have been framed so that those who are the object of motivated/false charges can be tried and cleared quickly.[18]

Police

The police force has over time become an important instrument of political power. The police are therefore no longer an independent instrument for enforcing and upholding the rule of law and for providing personal security to all its citizens. The misuse of police by the political masters for personal ends as well as the use by the police of state power vested in them, for their own personal ends, is not merely a theoretical possibility but a frightening reality. This enormous power of the police to do harm must be checked before it becomes uncontrollable.

A number of commissions from the Dharam Vira Commission to the Law Commission have suggested the creation of a buffer between the political bosses and the day-to-day operation of the police. One approach is to set up an autonomous police commission in each state along with open and transparent process for appointing the senior officers of the commission. There is also need for an independent public prosecutor whose job is to take cognizance of oversee investigation of and prosecute major crimes (e.g. murder,

---

18. Penalties could also be prescribed against those who wilfully make false charges.

armed robbery/dacoity, kidnapping, rape, police crimes). To ensure accountability to the public, which has become the object of police harassment, each police commission and public prosecutor would be accountable to an oversight committee of representatives from all walks of life (including the administration and judiciary). This would ensure that the police themselves obey the law and the law-breakers among them are given exemplary punishment.

Media

A free media has a vital role to play in checking the abuse of power by the state. One of the less remarked benefits of economic liberalisation during the 1990s has been the flowering and expansion of the media. Even traditional media such as newspapers and magazines have been galvanised by the entry of new private TV and other media. A responsible and responsive media can be an invaluable protector of the rule of law and the civil rights of its citizens. Our media has demonstrated over the past decade that it can do so while taking due care to guard the national interest against hostile foreign nations and the terrorists sponsored by them. This role can be further strengthened by further decontrol and strengthening of self-regulatory media organisations.

The article is drawn from my book *Accelerating Growth and Poverty Reduction: A Policy Framework for India's Development*, Academic Foundation, New Delhi, 2004.

Economic Developments in India, Vol. 89.

3

Growth, Poverty and Reforms

JAGDISH BHAGWATI

At the outset, let me address and counter the frequent assertion that what went wrong in our assault on poverty in the past, and hence, what is wrong with reforms today, is that our planners were interested in growth as the objective of their planned developmental efforts, not in poverty. This assertion, if true, would be pretty serious and could undermine the reformers since they wish to improve the policies that have undermined growth and hence, in their view, the reduction of poverty. In short, while the critics say that growth was an objective desired in itself by planners indifferent to poverty, economists such as myself argue that growth was, and is, desired because it would reduce poverty.

I will argue presently that growth helps to reduce poverty because of three central reasons:

- It creates jobs that 'pull up' the poor into gainful employment by providing more economic opportunity.

- It provides the revenues with which we can build more schools and provide more health facilities for the poor.

- It creates the incentives that enable the poor to access these facilities and also for the advancement of progressive social agendas generally.

But many of the critics of reforms today choose not to engage these substantive arguments (which in fact favour, not destroy, the case for economic reforms), but to pretend that India's problem has been that growth, not poverty reduction, was the target of our efforts and that they are correcting that mistake. I simply urge you to throw that assertion back in the face of the critics, so that we can focus on the substantive, not illusory, issues at hand. Ask them to read, from a vast literature, the writings of Dadabhai Naoroji in 1901, and of our great leaders such as Gandhiji and Pandit Nehru. If they think these had no relevance to our planning, ask them to take down from the library shelves the successive Five Year Plans from the first in 1950 and, prior to that, the documents of the National Planning Committee of Mahatma Gandhi's Indian National Congress and its 1940 resolve, in Pandit Jawaharlal Nehru's words in 1946, to:

> "Insure an adequate standard of living for the masses; in other words, to get rid of the appalling poverty of the people...[To] insure an irreducible minimum standard for everybody, the national income had to be greatly increased... We calculated that a really progressive standard of living would necessitate the increase of wealth by 500 or 600 per cent. That was however too big a jump for us, and we aimed at a 200 to 300 per cent increase within ten years."

I believe that the truth of the matter is that few serious politicians and economists ever thought of growth as anything except as an instrument for reducing poverty. The focus on poverty was always there, at least in India. Indeed, when I joined the Planning Commission, right after finishing my education abroad in 1961, my first task was to help Pitambar Pant, a great planner, devise the strategy for raising the 'minimum incomes' of the poorest third of the population: and I led him to the view that growth was a critical component of that strategy. True, we could redistribute incomes, assuming that was politically possible, but we had to think of sustainable attack on poverty, not a one-shot effect. The difficult task of sustainability is precisely the problem that faces Kerala (and, to some extent, West Bengal and also Sri Lanka), regions of low growth performance, which used to be cited by the critics of reforms as the great 'alternative' example for us to follow. And sustainability inevitably required us to think of growth, a *sine qua non* of an anti-poverty strategy for reasons I set out earlier in this address.

So, as new members of the educated citizenry who must use their education to think, reflect and challenge, you must reject the argument that we have been guilty of neglecting poverty because we did not value its removal. The debate must focus instead on what was wrong in our policies.

And let me say that, once you do that, the conclusion is inescapable: the economic reforms, which today require a forceful accentuation of the policy changes spearheaded by Dr. Manmohan Singh, are the way to go if India is finally to fulfil its ambition to reduce massively its poverty and destitution. Let me explain this since it is easy to fall prey to the notion that markets, globalisation, privatisation and other such 'neoliberal' reforms are for the likes of us, not for the poor.

First, central to our economic strategy of alleviating poverty was the acceleration of growth and the creation of jobs for the poor. This requires, of course, that our policies promote growth, else the expected benefits in alleviating poverty will not materialise. But, as I argued in the 1960s when I was almost alone (except for my co-authors Padma Desai and later T.N. Srinivasan) and as nearly all except a few diehards now agree, the growth strategy itself was undermined because of our policy framework.

The Indian experience has been that our policies produced an annual growth rate of nearly 3.5 per cent for almost a quarter of a century up to the early 1980s. The economist Raj Krishna described this as the Hindu growth rate, implying perhaps that deep cultural factors destined us to such an unfortunate outcome when the star performers in the Far East had delivered growth rates at almost double digit levels over the same period, transforming in astonishing ways their economies and their standards of living. I doubt this characterisation of Raj Krishna's, believing that we can transcend cultural factors: indeed, the irony is that if the Vajpayee government of the BJP succeeds in cementing the growth-friendly reforms, it will be a Hindu party—the BJP is popularly described in the Western press, interestingly without refutation by the government, as the Hindu Nationalist Party even though BJP translates as the Indian People's Party—that will have finally killed the Hindu rate of growth!

These abysmally low growth rates, it is now agreed among all thoughtful observers who are not wedded to ideology and hence cannot learn from experience, were a result of four sets of policies:

- Anti-globalisation policies that meant that India failed to take advantage of the opportunities provided by the growing world economy regarding trade and inward flows of direct foreign investment.

- Off-the-charts reliance on public sector enterprises which, afflicted by inevitable overstaffing and lack of incentives, steadily led to losses that meant serious inefficiencies and also a serious strain on our revenues.

- Defence of capital-intensive choice of techniques that led to a tolerance of the huge white elephants in the public sector that intensified the sorry performance of these enterprises.

- An overwhelming expansion of direct controls to a Kafkaesque level that also made India a template, a model, of what not to do in order to grow your way to sustained development.

I must urge you to learn to be sceptical of claims to the contrary even when they come from eminent economists and politicians, especially as we are what sociologists call an ascriptive society (i.e., one where ascribed status matters most) and therefore there is a tendency to think that if successful politicians and economists tell you something it must be true. The next time you hear any of them talk about poverty, and how we have fallen short, just ask them: where were you on these four issues during the nearly three decades that we lost altogether to bad growth and inevitably to worse outcomes on poverty alleviation? And also ask them: where are you now, as dedicated and informed reformers are trying desperately to purge the system of these unproductive, indeed counterproductive, policies?

But let me also assure you that the proponents of growth as an effective and necessary instrument for attacking poverty have always been aware of necessary nuances. Thus, growth can certainly by-pass some segments of the poor: if you are in a tribal area which has little connection through economic interdependence or labour mobility outwards to the mainland, growth in the latter will not help the poor tribals. So, you need supplemental policies: who denies that?

Again, growth may actually hurt certain groups, including the poor. In 1958, I even produced an analysis of the paradox of Immiserising Growth that fortuitously made me known worldwide: it established the conditions under which growth, say in Bangladesh, of additional jute for export would drive down world prices of jute so much that the decline in what economists call Bangladesh's 'terms of trade' (i.e. in what exports will fetch by way of imports) would entail a loss that more than offset the gains from the added production. But the answer again is not to oppose growth but to use an appropriate policy of diversification that, in tandem with the growth policy, ensures that immiseration does not occur.

Think again of the mega-debate that growth with green revolution would harm the poor by introducing a new divide between the rich and the poor, the former using and the latter unable or unwilling to use the new seeds: many feared, and some hoped, that the green revolution would then usher in the red revolution! This did not transpire: the green revolution increased the demand for labour and worked benignly with regard to workers' wages.

What we need to remember, and this is a point that we knew from the earliest days, is that growth requires complementary policies where necessary to prevent hurtful outcomes or, better still since it is often difficult to foresee where problems may arise, to offset them as and when they materialise. We see the wisdom of the latter way of doing things when we see how we damaged growth by shielding the small-scale sector through a policy that constrained investment and production in the large-scale sector in industries such as textiles and soap. Does anyone seriously think that our planners were not foolish in assuming that the growth of the large-scale sector would necessarily hurt the small scale sector? Is the soap or *khadi* made in the small scale sector a real substitute for the soap and textiles that come out of modern factories? Cannot both coexist and expand simultaneously? And is it not more sensible to let the large scale sector expand without restraints and to have an adjustment programme in place that is activated only if and when problems arise for the small scale sector?

Then again, we might ask: has growth, once achieved, managed to improve poverty levels in India? In the 1980s, we changed to a higher growth rate of roughly 5.5 per cent annually; but most analysts agree that it was based on unsustainable borrowing and spending policies. In fact, these policies, along with continuing lack of real reforms, produced the 1990-91 crisis. After 1991, we have had similar growth rates, even higher ones, and these are more sustainable and do reflect the ongoing reforms (though the current Bangalore-led Information Technology Revolution promises yet higher growth rates, and impact on the poor, in ways that I cannot explain here).

Doubtless, you know from the newspapers that there has been a big statistical debate whether poverty has declined during the period of higher growth rates. It is clear now that it has. The necessary corrections to the data confirm this. Also, regional disaggregation confirms that the more rapidly growing states have had better impact on poverty. As I tell non-economists among my friends: sometimes economics and common sense do go together!

But let me also emphasise to you that it is not only poverty that will fall with sustained growth but also we will improve literacy and health, even other social agendas. Why? Partly, it is because a growing economy will generate resources, at given tax rates, for the government to spend on schools and public health. Without such revenues, you can profess, but not deliver on, your good intentions. Thus, when our distinguished President Narayanan told us on Republic Day that we must build bridges to the poor, my reaction was mixed. Indeed, I said to myself: how true. But then I also recalled that every politician since Independence (and indeed for decades before then, as I reminded you) had said little else. The real problem, which I have been talking to you about today, has been, to use the President's metaphor, to find the resources with which to buy the cement and mortar to build the bridges. And, there, I am afraid that our distinguished President disregards, or underemphasises, the role of the reforms that have engaged the energies of our governments. And, in so doing, he accentuates from his high office the very poverty that he deplores.

Then again, let me just indicate how growth can aid the advancement of social agendas. To get literacy up, we have to build the schools and pay teachers better salaries, which requires both a commitment and the resources which only a growing economy can provide. But we also need incentives for the poor to send the children to school, in face of the compulsion felt to send them to work instead to augment their poor incomes. This is what economists call 'supply response'. Is there any doubt that in a stagnant economy, with few new economic opportunities materialising, impoverished parents are most unlikely to make the choice in favour of sending their children to schools instead of putting them to work? Again, if you have social legislation that says that you cannot beat your wife, that helps as a norm. But unless the wife can walk out on her husband and support herself with a job, something that is greatly aided by a rapidly growing economy, how is the legislation going to be truly effective? The cute phrase 'empowerment' which the World Bank has discovered works best when the minorities have economic alternatives which can come, in the end, only from expanding economic opportunities, (albeit interacting with a political democracy where effective universal suffrage gives all a vote and hence a voice).[1]

In short, sometimes all good things do go together: growth improves incomes, pulls up people out of poverty, improves literacy, helps spend more on public health, and does much more along these lines. And economic reforms, aimed at a reversal of the anti-globalisation, anti-market, pro-public-enterprise attitudes and policies that produced our dismal growth performance, are therefore the most important thing that we need to do.

And, in conclusion, let me urge you, not just to think on a bigger canvas about reforms and their favourable impact on poverty and social agendas, but to think concretely and at a level of personal experience about them and ask: how does each of the reforms work out for the common man? I would venture the thought that the reforms will come out smelling like roses once you do that. Let me just quote to you what I said in reviewing a recent book by two distinguished economists (whom I shall not name because of diplomacy on this solemn occasion but which I urge you to avoid in public debate where no reputation must be a shield against error and cant). These economists had

---

1. See my Rajiv Gandhi Memorial Lecture on "Democracy and Development", 1994, reprinted in my collection of public-policy essays, *A Stream of Windows: Unsettling Reflections on Trade, Immigration and Democracy*, MIT Press, 1998, Indian edition by Oxford University Press, 1999.

made the following astonishing, backward-looking, observation on Indian reforms:

> "Debates on such questions as the details of tax concessions to multinationals, or whether Indians should drink Coca Cola, or whether the private sector should be allowed to operate city buses, tend to 'crowd out' the time that is left to discuss the abysmal situation of basic education and elementary health care, or the persistence of debilitating social inequalities, or other issues that have a crucial bearing on the well-being and freedom of the population."

Mindful of the damage that such attitudes have done to the cause of poverty reduction in India over decades, I was moved to remark in my review:

> "Much is wrong here. No one can seriously argue that there is a crowding out when the articulation of Indians is manifest in multiplying newspapers, magazines and books and the expression of a whole spectrum of views on economics and politics; this reviewer has noticed no particular shyness in discussing social issues, including inequality and poverty in India... But more important, the put-down of attention to multinationals misses the point that India's economic reforms require precisely that India join the Global Age and that India's inward direct investments were ridiculously small in 1991, around $ 100 million, and that this was an important deficiency that had to be fixed. The reference to Coca Cola is no better, serving as a cheap shot against multinational investment; but it also betrays the assumption that Coca Cola is drunk by the elite or the westernised middle class, not by the truly poor. It is more likely, however, that the rich derive their caffeine from espresso coffee as well whereas the rich are the ones who must depend on coke instead!"

Indeed, the contemptuous reference to the privatisation of bus transportation in the cities could come only from elite economists who travel by private car and are unaware that the common people travel by buses where efficiency needs to be improved by privatisation (accompanied by necessary regulation). Again, let these economists reflect on the fact that when state-run electricity generation and distribution has led to long-accumulating problems that result in continual breakdowns of supply, whom does that hurt? Not the elites of Delhi who, perhaps like the ones in Chandigarh, have their own private generators so they continue sleeping in airconditioned comfort; but the common man who sleeps on the coir cot, with an Usha fan that can no longer function when electricity supply has broken down.[2]

---

2. Perhaps I can speak from my own experience as, for nearly 18 months, when I was a young professor at Delhi School of Economics, my life was characterised by the absence of a private generator and the presence of a coir cot and an Usha fan!

In short, these economists are like the politicians who espouse the cause of the poor but are themselves the unwitting cause of the perpetuation of that poverty. This is not just ironic; it is tragic. The true heroes in India, I urge you, then are not those who go around talking about development with a 'human face', or noting with a touch of moral fervour the need to eliminate 'abysmal poverty' in India. Rather, they are those who, like your alumnus Dr. Manmohan Singh, have vigorously worked for the reformed policies which alone can translate these time-worn sentiments into concrete reality.

I urge you then to join forces with these men and women. After all, you are the young generation that must carry this task forward. It is in your own hands to achieve the ideals of our great leaders, Gandhiji and Panditji. Let me assure you, as an economist who began his career in India's Planning Commission some 40 years ago by addressing this very problem and has worked on these issues ever since, that victory is within your grasp if you only turn your backs with contempt on the populist and beguiling rhetoric and reach out for the prize by standing on the shoulders of the reformers of today.

Convocation Address at Panjab University, Chandigarh, December 2000, *Economic and Political Weekly*, March 10-16, 2001.

Economic Developments in India, Vol. 39.

4

Redefining the Approach to Poverty Reduction and Development

N.A. MUJUMDAR

India has been in the business of poverty reduction for more than 50 years since the inception of planning in 1950-51. And yet more than a quarter of the total population continues to live below the poverty line even today. If China could reduce the magnitude of its poverty to a mere 3 per cent of the population in a span of two decades, what went wrong with India? Even assuming that the Indian economy would manage to remain in high growth trajectory of 8 per cent of GDP growth in the coming years, it would take perhaps another two decades to eliminate poverty. We have lived with the wretchedness of absolute shortage of foodgrains supplies in the 1960s, when the average annual imports of wheat hovered around 3 million tonnes. We survived through the munificence of America which supplied wheat to India under its PL 480 programme. In sharp contrast, India today has emerged, as contemporary policy makers would have us believe, as a major exporter of rice and wheat in the world market; India's exports of rice and wheat aggregated to staggering figure more than 10 million tonnes in 2003-04. The coexistence of alarmingly large unsatisfied domestic demand for foodgrains with massive exports of foodgrains is a clear reflection of our muddle-headed food management policy formulated on the basis of market theology: abolish subsidies for domestic consumption of foodgrains but encourage subsidisation of foodgrains exports. It is this mess of food management policy which warrants redefinition of our basic approach to poverty reduction. Eliminate hunger first and poverty later. For this rather unconventional approach, which is appropriate for the present India-specific situation, to succeed three ingredients of development policy mix are essential: decentralised and broad-based growth, good governance and concern for social safety net. The package of programmes to be undertaken under such an approach can be so designed that many programmes become economically viable and the package, taken as a whole, can be rendered fiscally sustainable.

Poverty and Foodgrains Exports

The Tenth Five Year Plan begins the discussion on poverty alleviation in the following words:

"At the beginning of the new millennium, 260 million people in the country did not have incomes to access a consumption basket which defines the poverty line. Of these, 75 per cent were in the rural areas. India is home to 22 per cent of the world's poor. Such a high incidence of poverty is a matter of concern in view of the fact that poverty eradication has been one of the major objectives of the development planning process. Indeed, poverty is a global issue. Its eradication is considered integral to humanity's quest for sustainable development. Reduction of poverty in India, is, therefore vital for the attainment of international goals."[1]

Or, take the Budget speech of the Finance Minister, who while presenting the Interim Budget on February 3, 2004, stated:

"We believe, Sir, that both are necessary: a vision for a resurgent India and, simultaneously an awakening so that the disadvantaged of our land are lifted beyond poverty. We hold that economic development is not about economics alone, it is always, simultaneously, a political statement too, for 'development' devoid of compassion is a misnomer. Of course, growth statistics are very important, they are vital inputs; but they must also be the indices that assist us in designing distributive justice. It is for that reason that 'gross national contentment' is so important, as the catalyst that motivates redoubled national endeavour. It is from seeking national contentment that objectives are born: *Garib ke pet me dana, Garibini ki tukia main anna.*"[2]

Nobel sentiments indeed. But look at the situation at the ground level. India's exports of rice and wheat are estimated to have reached or even exceeded 10 million tonnes in 2003-04. Shri Sharad Yadav, Minister for Consumer Affairs, Food and Public Distribution[3] exults in this achievement. "Today, India has emerged as the World's third largest exporter of rice and the seventh largest exporter of wheat. The country has earned foreign exchange of $ 4 billion through these exports. Though maintaining domestic food security will continue to be top priority, the country's newly acquired position as a major exporter of foodgrains will be protected."[4] In a similar vein, Food

---

1. *Tenth Five Year Plan*, 2002-2007, Planning Commission, New Delhi, Vol. II, pp. 293.
2. Budget Speech of Finance Minister, Shri Jaswant Singh, on February 3, 2004.
3. *Economic Survey*, 2002-03, Government of India, page 172.
4. For excertps from the Interview with the Minister, see *Swagat* Magazine, December 2003.

Corporation of India (FCI) in a recent advertisement proclaims: "Congratulations to our farmers who have created surplus stock of foodgrains, ensuring no death from hunger."[5]

Concern for good governance and for social safety net must form important ingredients of any meaningful development plan. Unfortunately, contemporary policy makers in India seem to be unwilling to look into subtleties of development beyond the IMF/World Bank models built on market theology. In fact such concerns for the poor, as illustrated above, are being used to merely window-dress growth strategies drawn up on the basis of market theology.

Is there, a surplus of foodgrains in today's India? India continues to be the abode of 260 million people who are in a state of chronic semi-starvation, as admitted by the Planning Commission. In addition, UNDP estimates that over one-half of all Indian pre-schoolers suffer from malnutrition. Against this background, how does one justify the export of foodgrains on a massive scale as in 2003-04? Neither the scholarly document of the Tenth Plan nor the Budget Speech even attempt to provide the rationale for such massive exports. Export of small quantities of high value branded foodgrains like the Basmati rice is indeed understandable. Do we need the foreign exchange so badly that we are compelled to export foodgrains at the cost of domestic food security? Not at all. Our foreign exchange reserves have soared to an unprecedented level of more than $ 100 billion and the Reserve Bank of India is trying to reduce this embarrassingly high level by liberalising the out-flow of foreign exchange with reckless abandon. In fact what did we do with $ 4 billion of foreign exchange earned by foodgrains exports? We imported gold: the average annual imports of gold were around $ 5 billion during the last three or four years. It is as if the contemporary policy makers are asking the people: never mind if you cannot afford to buy foodgrains, deck yourself with gold ornaments and be happy!

Market theology has messed up the situation and led to the formation of the muddle-headed food policy. In the first place, market theologists were keen on abolishing domestic food subsidies. This resulted in raising the issue prices of foodgrains distributed through the public distribution system (PDS) successively. The net result was that the off-take of foodgrains from the public distribution system declined substantially over the more recent years thereby swelling the stocks with the Food Corporation of India (FCI). In other words, foodgrains became increasingly inaccessible to the poorer sections of the

---

5. See *The Times of India*, January 28, 2004.

population. These stocks soared to more than 60 million tonnes at one point of time. Embarrassed by such huge stocks coexisting with large unsatisfied domestic demand for foodgrains, the government sought an easy way out: exports of foodgrains. What is worse, our exports of foodgrains are highly subsidised. For instance, during the four years 2000-01 to 2003-04, the price realised on rice exports by FCI has been generally lower than the issue price of rice through the PDS (See Appendix A-4.1). In other words, the issue price of grains for exports was highly subsidised. The same market theologists, who are crying hoarse against domestic food subsidies are encouraging the subsidising of foreign consumers of Indian foodgrains! This is a concrete proof that the refrain of the Tenth Plan that we are pursuing growth with equity, or of the budget speech that we are aiming at development with compassion, are no more than rhetoric.

Redefining the Basic Approach

The need to redefine our basic approach to poverty reduction stems from the following three factors. First, conventional wisdom stipulates that the problem of poverty can be tackled through higher GDP growth, expansion of employment, and generation of supplementary income through subsidiary occupations and so on. But the process is a long haul and may take at least two decades. This is the conclusion one can derive from the analysis of trends in poverty as provided in the Tenth Plan. The mandated reduction in poverty rate of 5 per cent point during the Tenth Plan and another 10 per cent point reduction during Eleventh Plan will still leave more than 11 per cent of the population or about 130 million people below the poverty line in 2012. This is predicated on the assumption that high GDP growth of 8 per cent would be sustained throughout the period. To eliminate poverty totally or nearly totally may take another decade. It is as if the policy makers are throwing up their hands, declaring that the situation is hopeless. Do the contemporary policy makers expect the 'semi-starving India' to remain with us always?

Second, the coexistence of embarrassingly large stock of foodgrains with FCI with alarmingly high level of unsatisfied domestic demand for foodgrains is an anachronism. The so-called 'surplus' foodgrains, on the basis of which contemporary policy makers seem to build their strategy for growth is only an 'effective demand surplus' and not a genuine surplus. If domestic food security is to be ensured, the so-called surplus evaporates. In any other country such massive exports of foodgrains against the background of under-fed and under-nourished population of a sizeable proportion would have exploded in to a revolution. But ours is an ancient civilisation known for its quiescence. The tragedy of Indian planning is that over the years, we have developed the technology and the institutional framework to produce adequate quantities of foodgrains, or cereals at any rate: but we simply do not know how to reach these foodgrains to the needy. The muddle-headedness of food management policy discussed earlier reflects this tragedy. Food security in a meaningful sense, is ensured not by merely producing an adequate quantum of foodgrains but also by reaching of these grains to the needy. In fact the issue is so important that the Tenth Plan should have devoted a whole chapter to find an appropriate solution to the problem of food delivery mechanism which would ensure food security. In any case, we must redefine our basic approach to poverty reduction by stipulating: eliminate hunger first, and poverty later. This redefined approach meets the test of 'immediacy' because we do not have to wait for two decades to achieve the objective. Fortunately, we have the wherewithal to eliminate hunger, here and now.

The third factor relates to the *modus operandi* of reaching food to the needy. FAO defines food security as: "The physical economic access for all people at all times enough food for an active, healthy life, with the non-risk of losing such access and as such is directly connected with livelihood in developing countries." The task of providing access to food is thus inextricably interwoven with the livelihood or employment, because a majority of the poor is not only asset-less but also without any assured or continuous employment. This brings us to the employment situation. The current backlog of unemployment is around 9 per cent or equivalent to 35 million persons and this is far too high. On the basis of the Prime Minister's vision of creating 100 million employment opportunities over the next 10 years, the Tenth Plan has set a target of creation of 50 million jobs during the next five years. If this target is achieved, unemployment is likely to decline to some 5 per cent by the end of the Tenth Plan. To be able to realise this target, the focus will have to be on a wide range of sectors such as agriculture and allied sectors, construction, tourism, transport and small scale industries (SSI), micro-enterprises, retail trade and so on. The organised sector can do precious little to meet the enormous employment demand and thus the focus would have to be on decentralised and broad-based growth.

The redefined approach to poverty reduction could be summed up as follows: even assuming that the Indian economy continues to remain in a high growth trajectory of 8 to 10 per cent GDP growth in the next decade, reduction of poverty to an acceptable level will take a long time. We cannot afford to live with a semi-starving population of an alarming magnitude for long, especially when we have been able to produce adequate or nearly adequate quantity of foodgrains. Elimination of hunger in the immediate run by utilisation of all the quantities of foodgrains we produce—making allowance for buffer stocks—should therefore be accepted as the 'second best' solution in the given configuration of circumstances. Contemporary policy makers must realise that, there are no 'exportable surpluses' of foodgrains; they should also grow out of their received wisdom of market theology and begin to design an appropriate foodgrains delivery mechanism to reach foodgrains to the needy. This mechanism would be consistent with broad-based and decentralised growth and in fact the two could be made mutually reinforcing. The constellation of this mechanism and other supportive policies could be rendered fiscally viable, making some allowance also for an element of social safety net.

Decentralised Growth

Employment expansion is the ideal way by which the poor would be empowered to have access to foodgrains. Food for Work Programme lends itself admirably to serve the purpose. More about this later. In fact there is no reason why the National Highways Development Project which includes the Golden Quadrilateral connecting the four metrocities of Delhi-Mumbai-Chennai and Kolkata, could not have been converted into one of such programmes. At least part of the wages of the labour employed on the project could have been paid in kind, that is, in foodgrains. This needs to be supplemented by other modalities such as linking rural development works like micro watershed development programmes to utilisation of foodgrains, instituting 'Grain Loans Facility' for all institutions involved in rural development programmes like rural cooperatives, RRBs and NGOs. I have spelt out the possibilities elsewhere.[6] There is enormous scope for enlarging the coverage of the mid-day meals scheme, to provide children in government and government assisted primary schools with prepared meals. This scheme confers multiple benefits to the economy. In fact universal and nutritious mid-day meals would be a great leap forward towards the realisation of the right to food. The Centre for Equity Studies (CES), New Delhi, recently reviewed the functioning of the mid-day meals programme in three states: Chhattisgarh, Rajasthan and Karnataka and came to the following conclusion: "As things

---

6. "Rural Development: New Perceptions", *Economic and Political Weekly*, September 28, 2002.

stand, mid-day meals programmes may have many flaws, but the way to go is forward and not backward. With adequate resources and quality safeguard, mid-day meals can play a major role in improving school attendance, eliminate class room hunger, and fostering social equity."[7]

The Tenth Plan document itself provides a number of concrete programmes which would generate sizeable rural employment. The new 'watershed plus' approach to watershed development seeks to ensure convergence of all other programmes that promote economic activities and generate increased employment opportunities. Conscious efforts to promote non-farm employment and increased land access for the landless as well as promotion of self-help groups (SHGs) form part of the new approach. Then again, the utilisation of wastelands. Out of the estimated area of 107 million hectares of degraded land, 64 million hectares are categorised as wastelands. Under this programme, all such lands under the control of government or *Panchayats* would be parcelled out in viable units and allotted to landless scheduled caste and tribe farmers, small and marginal farmers, and educated rural youth, for cultivation. Besides the wastelands, some of the areas under reserved forests are also unutilised or underutilised. It is envisaged that local community access would be provided to grass and fodder from the forest area and the community would be encouraged to produce grasses and fodder and the medicinal and aromatic plants in the underutilised areas under forest cover. Rainwater conservation and harvesting hold the key to sustainable development of rainfed areas. Hence there is a need to move way from the conventional soil conservation approach of safe disposal of run-off water to rainwater harvesting and conservation. Then there is organic farming, with organic seed and compost preparation.

The point is that there are a thousand ways by which rural employment could be generated and the particular programme chosen needs to be area-specific. In the final analysis, productive utilisation of all foodgrains domestically—and not through exports—should be the overriding objective of development policy.

To what extent these and related schemes would be economically viable and fiscally sustainable? Obviously, many of the schemes discussed earlier would create economic and social over-head capital. Use of foodgrains through mid-day meals is tantamount to investment in education. In fact we should not feel shy of devising some schemes like community kitchens for the old and the

---

7. "Future of mid-day meals", Jean Dreze and Aparajit Goyal, *Economic and Political Weekly*, November 2003.

destitute in the villages. India cannot afford, as yet, to institute a comprehensive social security scheme on the lines of those provided in developed countries like the UK or USA. Through the various modalities discussed earlier and with appropriate supportive policies in place, India can at least seek to guarantee the right to food to all its citizens. If necessary, an 'employment cess' can be levied on all those employed to guarantee resources to support the network of programmes outlined above. Taking the package as a whole, it seems feasible to render it fiscally sustainable.

Governance in Rural Administration

Good governance in rural administration as also in the management of rural financial institutions is a crucial determinant of the success of rural development programmes. Three concrete cases can be cited to demonstrate how lack of or bad governance frustrates the successful implementation of rural development programmes. First, take the case of the Food for Work Programme, which was started in 2000-01 as a component of the Employment Assurance Scheme (EAS) in eight notified drought affected States of Chhattisgarh, Gujarat, Himachal Pradesh, Madhya Pradesh, Orissa, Rajasthan, Maharashtra and Uttaranchal. The Programme aims at augmenting food security through wage employment. Foodgrains were supplied to States free of cost. Unfortunately, the record of the lifting of foodgrains allotted for the scheme from the Food Corporation of India (FCI) has been very disappointing. For instance, against an allocation of 35.31 lakh tonnes of foodgrains, only 21.26 lakh tonnes were lifted by the target states up to January 2002. Was the Centre not persuasive enough? Or, do the States need to be sensitised[8] about the misery of poverty, unemployment and the state of semi-starvation? In all the target states, there is enormous scope for launching schemes to utilise foodgrains provided by the Centre at zero cost.

Second, take the case of utilisation of funds, under Rural Infrastructure Development Fund (RIDF). This fund was originally set up with NABARD in 1995-96 with a corpus of Rs. 2,000 crore with the major objective of providing funds to state governments to enable them to complete ongoing infrastructure projects pertaining to irrigation, flood protection, rural roads and bridges. The scope of RIDF has been progressively widened to include lending to *Gram Panchayats*, self-help groups for implementing village level infrastructure projects. Although the total corpus adds up to Rs. 34,000 crore as of 2002-03,

---

8. *Tenth Five Year Plan, 2002-07*, Government of India, Vol. I, p. 297.

the overall utlisation of these funds by the states has been dismal at only 58 per cent. In fact the percentage of[9] utilisation declined to 40 and 18 in 2002 and 2003. Are the reconnaissance efforts of NABARD to identify eligible projects unsatisfactory? Or, are the states indifferent to rural development? One begins to wonder.

The third case relates to the financial institutions. As I have demonstrated elsewhere the financial sector reforms introduced in the 1990s have, in effect, succeeded in alienating the financial system from the business of development.[10] Admitting this conclusion, the Tenth Plan states: "It is being evident however, that the organised financial sector in India is either unable or unwilling to finance a range of activities that are of crucial importance both for growth and development. Agriculture, unorganised manufacturing and services and various types of infrastructure are instances of such sectors. The recent financial sector reforms have naturally focussed primarily in improving viability and stability of financial institutions, without adequately addressing this issue. It is therefore necessary to consider methods of encouraging the financial sector to finance such activities, without impinging on its viability or compromising on prudential concerns."[11] Public sector banks which have historically played a pioneering role in reaching out to farmers in the post-nationalisation period, have failed even today to meet the credit target of 18 per cent of net bank credit to agriculture: the actual level was some 15 per cent in 2002-03. This is not because of their inability, since banks have remained highly liquid during the recent years with credit deposit ratio hovering around 50 per cent. It is high time that public sector banks and financial institutions changed their post-reform attitude to agricultural and rural development.

Overall, the picture that emerges is clear. Agricultural growth or rural development in general is not constrained by lack of resources, both financial and in terms of wage-goods. It is lack of governance which is hampering growth. Fuller utilisation of these resources would go a long way towards facilitating higher growth and eliminating hunger. And good governance is a prerequisite for fuller utilisation.

---

9. *Report on Trend and Progress of Banking in India, 2002-03*, Reserve Bank of India, 2003, p. 103.

10. For detailed discussion see the book: *Financial Sector Reforms in India's Economic Development*, N.A. Mujumdar, 2002.

11. *Tenth Plan*, Vol. I, p. 13, para 1.52.

Concluding Comment

Without waiting for two decades or so to eliminate poverty through the conventional route, it makes sense to redefine our immediate development objective in terms of eliminating hunger here and now, by utilising what contemporary Indian policy makers consider as 'surplus foodgrains'. Let our policy makers disabuse their mind of the idea of 'surplus' and seek to match the so-called surplus with large unsatisfied demand for foodgrains. To be able to achieve this objective in the short-run, decentralised and broad-based growth of the economy needs to be promoted. Although the Tenth Plan attempts to sketch the broad contours of such growth, it does not provide a blueprint of the institutional framework which can translate such growth into reality. Microcredit institutions, micro-enterprises, self-help groups (SHGs) and NGOs and the private sector on the one hand; establishing and strengthening links and cooperation between, government, panchayat raj institutions. NGOs and the private sector on the other hand. Such networking needs to be institutionalised taking into account the state-specific circumstances. Such institutionalisation also can facilitate decentralised and broad-based growth.

Appendix A-4.1

Prices of Rice Sold by Food Corporation of India (FCI)

(Rs. per Quintal)

Year	For Export	Issue Prices for BPL Families	Issue Prices for APL Families
2000-01	420	565	830
2001-02	495	565	830
2002-03	551	565	730
2003-04	581	565	850

Note : These data, published in *The Economic Times* on 2-1-2004, are based on an answer provided by the Minister of State for Consumer Affairs, Food and Public Distribution to a question in Rajya Sabha.

BPL - Below Poverty Line.

APL - Above Poverty Line.

This is an edited version of the Lecture delivered on February 11, 2004 at the National Institute of Rural Development, Hyderabad.

Economic Developments in India, Vol. 79.

5

Poverty and Development Policy

A. VAIDYANATHAN

I

BACKGROUND

The idea that eradication of abject poverty must be a central concern of public policy has gained wide currency in current academic and public discourse on development. Time was when the focus used to be on the rate and pattern of growth, and on inequalities in distribution of income and wealth. Even as these continue to be important concerns, increasing attention is being given to the extent to which people in individual countries and the world at large are deprived of the minimum requirements for a long, healthy and fulfilling life.

The idea is not new. In India it dates well back into pre-independence era—recall Naoroji's book *Poverty and Un-British Rule*—and was prominent in the deliberations of the Congress Party. The National Planning Committee report in fact spelt out in concrete terms the concept and content of minimum living standard. The 15th Indian Labour Conference which deliberated on the basis for fixing fair wages also spelt out the constituents of a living wage. A committee on economic policy (headed by Nehru) appointed by the AICC suggested that assurance of a national minimum standard in respect of 'all the essentials of physical and social well-being to every family within a reasonable period of time' should be the practical goal of all schemes of development. The Constitutional provisions on the Directive Principles of State Policy specifically enjoined the government to ensure adequate livelihood and employment, health and nutrition, education and security to the citizens.

However it took a long time for government to define its developmental objectives and policies with reference to these principles. The first three Five-Year Plan documents saw sustained high rates of growth as the principal means to alleviate malnourishment, unemployment, illiteracy and other manifestations of poverty. There was much talk in political rhetoric and in policy pronouncements about reducing inequalities of income and wealth through land reforms, public ownership and control of key sectors, and progressive taxation. But with actual growth proving to be much slower than expected, and redistributive measures proving to be ineffective, the appalling conditions in which the bulk of the population continued to live and the necessity to address their problems seriously came into sharp relief. The late Ram Manohar Lohia dramatised it by calling attention of parliament to the fact that more than half the population subsisted on less than 6 *annas* per head per day!

In 1962, an unofficial seminar,[1] in which several leading economists, political figures and social activists participated, gave a fresh impetus to the idea that planning should aim at ensuring a minimum standard of living to every one within a reasonable period. They suggested that the national minimum should include a time-bound target of minimum income (Rs. 20 per capita per month in rural areas and about Rs. 25 in urban areas); expenditure on education and health to be provided by the state according to the Constitution[2] transfers and social welfare expenditure to ensure minimum for the poorest 20 per cent of the population who are not likely, for various reasons, to benefit automatically from growth.

Soon thereafter the implications of planning for this minimum living were worked out in a paper[3] prepared by the perspective planning division of the Planning Commission and further elaborated entitled "Notes on Perspectives of Development India's 1960-61 to 1975-76" (GoI, PC, 1964). The latter was considered but not formally approved by the Planning Commission. In the event, for a variety of reasons (including Nehru's death, the aftermath of military engagements with China and Pakistan, and the droughts) it was shelved. The Fourth Five-Year Plan did not even mention minimum living standard or basic needs!

---

1. It merits noting that the late Pitambar Pant, who was then personal assistant to Nehru in his capacity as chairman of the Planning Commission, was the moving spirit behind the seminar on Planning for Minimum Living and, as head of PPD, the preparation of a perspective plan based on its recommendations.

2. Interestingly this was followed by a phrase 'in the light of its other commitments' which in effect diluted the force of this commitment.

3. This paper, titled "Perspective of Development 1961-1976: Implications of Planning for a Minimum Level of Living", is reprinted in Srinivasan and Bardhan (eds.) (1974).

The late 1960s witnessed a spurt of interest among economists in the study of poverty both at the conceptual and empirical levels. At the conceptual level, questions began to be raised about the validity of using per capita GDP or per capita consumption as a satisfactory measure of well-being. A strong case was made for a much broader concept of 'quality of life' which would include nutritional status, life expectancy and literacy. Attention was also focused on the possibility—based on the example of Kerala in India and Sri Lanka—that the quality of life in the broader sense is not necessarily contingent on high level of income. The factors—largely social and political—which made this possible have attracted much attention and discussion (United Nations, 1975; Sen, 1981; Bhalla, 1988; Streeten and Burki, 1978).

The findings of the Mahalanobis Committee (GoI, PC, 1964, 1969) and Hazari's study (1967), as is well known, found no reduction in inequalities in consumption, incomes or in concentration of economic power. A number of researchers took up empirical and theoretical studies focused on absolute poverty and strategies to eradicate it. Dandekar and Rath's (1974) well known monograph 'Poverty in India' argued for defining the poverty line on the basis of the minimum income required for nutritional diet and other essentials, provided estimates of the number of people who fell below this line, and outlined a strategy (based on a massive public works programme) to give them the needed additional incomes to reach the minimum. Around the same time a number of others discussed estimates of inequalities in income distribution, incidence of and trends in poverty, conceptual and measurement problems involved, and strategies for tackling poverty.

This research highlighted significant differences in estimates of mean incomes and consumption, inequality indices and poverty incidence obtained from different sources. There was a major controversy over whether or not poverty incidence had declined during the 1960s. This stimulated serious investigation into theoretical aspects of concepts and measurements, the merits and weaknesses of different sources of relevant data, the interrelation between growth, distribution of assets and income, employment and poverty; and different strategies for rapid reduction of poverty.[4] All these themes continue to figure prominently in the ever growing literature on this subject both nationally and internationally. The discussions have of course become more detailed, technically more refined and wider in scope.

---

4. Much of the work of this period is published in Srinivasan and Bardhan (eds.) (1974).

By the early 1970s, development economists, both within the country and abroad as well as in international agencies, had veered round to the view that overall growth, while necessary, would not by itself be able to take care of the needs of the poor. The pace of growth is unlikely to be uniform across regions; all segments of the economy and sections of the population are not integrated into the wider economy; and large sections are not equipped (for a variety of reasons) to take advantage of the opportunities arising from growth. Therefore programmes for 'direct attack' on poverty came to be accepted as desirable even by agencies like the World Bank.

This perception did not long remain a matter of academic interest. In India, the set back to the economy during the late 1960s, (slow growth, cut back in investment, inflation), heightened apprehensions of increased inequalities, growing unemployment and worsening of poverty. It happened to coincide with the struggle for political power in the (then dominant) Congress Party. 'Radical' measures, (like bank nationalisation and abolition of privy purses) ostensibly meant to contain the rich, were tried but they were limited in scope and did not mean much to the poor. In this conjuncture, Indira Gandhi sought to broaden her political base by adopting the *Garibi Hatao* slogan and launching a number of poverty alleviation schemes.

Apart from a Minimum Needs Programme, a number of other initiatives—notably special schemes for small and marginal farmers (later replaced by Integrated Rural Development, IRDP for short), rural employment schemes, mid-day meals for school children, and subsidised public distribution of food and other essential commodities—were launched. Some were new, others essentially were refurbished versions of older schemes. That they did not remain slogans, but were backed by substantial financial allocations made them politically credible. That it struck a positive chord among the people is evident from the resounding electoral success of Congress Party under Indira Gandhi's leadership.[5]

For the first time, assurance of basic minimum needs found an explicit and prominent place in the Fifth Plan. The concept included not only an assurance of purchasing power sufficient to procure a collection of basic items of consumption deemed to constitute 'basic' or 'minimum' collection, but also elementary education for all children up to 14 years of age; minimum public health facilities integrated with family planning and nutrition for children;

---

5. Notable subsequent collections include Bardhan and Srinivasan (eds.) (1988); Harris *et al.* (eds.) (1992); Dreze and Sen (1995); Krishnaswamy (ed.) (1990); Bhattacharya *et al.* (1990); Rao (ed.).

protected water supply; amenities for landless labour and slum improvement in larger towns; and rural roads and rural electrification.

The idea of direct, targeted poverty alleviation programmes quickly took root and gained widespread acceptance across the entire political spectrum.[6] Governments, at the centre and in the states, have since vied with each other in increasing allocations and devising new schemes (or the same schemes under different names) under this rubric. Along with the number and variety of schemes, financial allocations have also increased progressively. Motivations were of course not as high minded as the slogans made out. They reflect cold political calculations. That the programmes provided opportunities for large-scale, widespread and diffused patronage as well as opportunities for personal gain for political leaders and cadres obviously made them highly attractive to parties in power.

Having reviewed, briefly, the evolution and acceptance of minimum living standard among the objectives of policy in the agenda of political parties as well as governments, we now turn to a consideration of some important issues concerning concepts and measurement of poverty as well as the design and implementation of policies to tackle the problem.

II

CONCEPTUAL ISSUES

In India, there is a broad consensus that the minimum should include (i) a nutritionally satisfactory diet, a reasonable standard of clothing, housing and other 'essentials'; and (ii) access to a minimum level of education, health care, clean water supply and sanitary environment. Norms for specific elements under both categories have been specified. The income necessary for people to afford the elements constituting the first category defines the 'poverty line'. Ensuring the minimum standards for various social services and amenities are deemed to be the responsibility of the state. These concepts as well as the specific content of the minimum standard have gained wide currency in public discourse on development policy. Minimum living standards and poverty are however deceptively simple notions. Complex and contentious issues are involved in deciding the basis on which the minimum bundle is to be determined and valued; whether the status of individuals or households is to

---

6. For a review of the evolution of these programmes and their problems see Vaidyanathan (1994a).

be judged in relation to affordability of the bundle as a whole or on the basis of actual consumption/use relative to the norms for individual items; whether the bundle should be uniform or allowances be made for differences in need and circumstances across space and between classes.

Of the various ingredients entering minimum income consumption, food has received the most attention. The emphasis on food is obviously justified. The fact that nutrition experts have worked out the level of nutrients (calories, proteins, fat, etc.) necessary for healthy, active functioning of human beings would appear to give an objective basis for determining minimum norms. The normal practice has been to work out the per capita norm for a reference population of specified composition (in terms of age, sex, body size and activity) in rural and urban areas. The appropriateness of a uniform per capita calorie norm has been questioned on the grounds that the relevant characteristics of the population (age and sex composition, body mass and activity) vary across and even within regions and there are biological mechanisms which enable individuals to adapt to lower intakes, over a sizeable range, without any adverse effects on health or activity.[7] Nevertheless, there is a strong case for such a uniform norm and it rests basically on three grounds:

(1) The purpose of the norm is to help define a standard of consumption which is socially accepted as the minimum desirable. This standard covers not only food but also other items.

(2) A uniform standard provides a common yardstick for comparisons across regions and of directions and relative rates of its change over time. It is also essential for meaningful discussion of the public policy for poverty alleviation and their effectiveness in different regions. This consideration acquires added force when poverty incidence (or the numbers of poor) is used—as it has come to be used—as an important criterion in deciding the sharing of central tax revenues, central government assistance for state plans and also of allocation for poverty alleviation between and (increasingly) within the states.

(3) A standard basket of food products corresponding to the calorie norm also helps comparability. One could in principle estimate the minimum cost food basket taking into account food habits and prices prevailing in different regions. But the practical problems (in terms of

---

7. For a comprehensive and detailed discussion of the complex issues involved see Srinivasan (1981); Osmani (ed.) (1992); and Sukhatme (ed.) (1992).

information requirement and computational complexity) make it difficult to do so. Reasons of both comparability and convenience therefore argue for using a uniform commodity composition for determining the poverty line. The current practice in India is to use the NSS data on commodity composition of food basket of people whose calorie intake is equal to the nutritional norm. This is done separately for rural and urban area using national level data.[8]

(4) The levels and composition of non-food items included in the minimum standard are taken to be whatever happens to go along with the fulfilment of the calorie norm at the national level. Together they also used to determine the value of per capita consumption expenditure which defines the national poverty line for rural and urban areas. This procedure for determining the non-food components of the minimum is obviously quite arbitrary. Hardly any thought has gone into working out norms for clothing, housing and other elements under this category. The necessity to consider explicitly and systematically the basis for determining levels and components of non-food consumption to be included in the minimum and the need to review and revise the specification of the minimum bundle at periodic intervals hardly needs emphasis.

While there are good reasons for adopting a standard commodity basket comprising the national minimum, there are no good reasons to ignore differences in level and structure of prices between states (and also between rural and urban area) as well as their behaviour over time. On the contrary there is a strong case for taking these into account in as much as the income necessary to afford the minimum consumption bundle is a function of price level and structure. There may also be a case for taking regional difference into account in fixing norms for social amenities. Following the recommendations of the Lakdawala Committee (GoI, PC, 1993), the earlier practice of using a single national level poverty line and deflator (to adjust for price changes) for state level estimates has been given up. Instead state level poverty lines, adjusting for differences in base year price levels and deflated on the basis of state-specific price indices, are used.

Ensuring that households have sufficient incomes to acquire the minimum consumption standard and that norms for publicly provided schools, health care and water supply and connectivity are met, does not automatically ensure

---

8. For a detailed and critical discussion of this procedure see Rudra (1974, 1978); Dandekar (1996).

that people actually obtain and consume the bundle of goods and services or use the amenities as envisaged in the standard. Actual consumption patterns depend on individuals' decisions which are influenced by numerous personal, familial, environmental and cultural factors. If they choose not to acquire the normative minimum bundle the state can do little about it. Furthermore, consumption data, which usually are obtained for the households do not tell us much about what individual members get and whether it meets the minimum standard for them. The extent to which the poor and the under-privileged actually use and benefit from social services and amenities to be provided by the state also depends to a considerable degree on the decision of individual households which in turn is influenced by the economic circumstances and socio cultural attitudes as well as by the quality and cost of services provided by these public facilities. Because of these factors, the actual position of households, including poor households, may differ substantially from the potential for achieving to minimum living standard even where growth and state policies enable them to do so. Such deficiencies cannot be attributed to failure of government policy except in so far as they are the result of deficiencies in design and implementation of government programmes.

At a more fundamental level, minimum incomes and minimum standards of social amenities are not all desired solely or even mainly for their own sakes but for what they do to peoples' well-being.[9] Amartya Sen, who has done so much to clarify the complex issues involved in the assessment of well-being and suggesting ways to deal with them in a practical way, has strong and persuasive arguments to show that well-being of persons cannot be judged only on the basis of their incomes or access to education and other amenities or of the volume and composition of goods (and services) they have. While these are indeed important, goods and services are not sought for their own sake but as means to achieve desired states of what he calls 'being and doing' (such as leading a well nourished, healthy and long life, being well clothed, mobile, able to take informed part in community life, etc.). The particular combination of functionings which individuals choose depends on the resources (income) available to them, the different combinations of goods from which they can choose and the kinds of functioning they make possible. Together they define the domain of choice effectively available to individuals which Sen calls "capabilities".

---

9. The ensuing summary of Sen's arguments is based on Sen (1985).

The choice within this domain reflects the valuation which individuals place on different kinds of functioning which in turn depends on their personal and social characteristics. Choices are constrained not just by resources at their command as well as by social conditioning. The availability and quality of education, healthcare, sanitation, transport/communication networks and other facilities—which are not determined solely by individuals but depend to an important degree, on the efforts of society and community, governments and non-government organisations—have a direct bearing on peoples' well-being, the choices open to them as well as their perception of the choices. One must also bear in mind that people often have a tendency to restrain their aspirations within limits of what they consider realistically feasible.

The assessment of well-being in a society needs to take into account not only individuals' choices but also assess different social states. The problems involved in doing this are at the heart of the continuing debate among economists and social philosophers. This debate has highlighted the limitations of the market as the arbiter of social states and the difficulties in arriving at a generally acceptable consensus on desirable social states based on a consistent and complete evaluation of available alternatives.

A satisfactory general solution to this problem remains elusive. However, this is much less of a problem in the context of poor countries where large sections do not have adequate and nutritious food, are prone to disease and relatively low life expectancy and are not equipped to access the knowledge and skills needed to function in a complex economy, take advantage of economic opportunities and participate in community life. Under these conditions, it is not surprising that assurance of adequate food (in quantity and quality), basic education and healthcare facilities and connectivity with the outside world figure prominently in the concept of 'minimum living standard' in India and other similarly placed countries. Though, as noted earlier, concretising this and relating it to well-being is a difficult task.

Moreover, if our concern is 'well-being', conventional indicators such as the proportion of population below the poverty line, mean calorie intake, mortality rates, literacy and school enrolment are inadequate basis to assess progress towards poverty eradication. Important as these are, one needs to supplement them with assessments of nutritional and health status, duration of education as well as quality aspects, and gender and group disparities. This calls for considerably wider and more detailed information through surveys to ascertain people's perceptions of their state as well as direct, non-market observations of access to basic goods and functionings at the individual level. There is also a good case to broaden the scope of 'well-being' to cover such aspects as freedom, fresh air, absence of crime, child and women abuse, social peace.

Broadening the notion of well-being and the indicators used to evaluate it has gained currency thanks to the United Nations' Human Development Reports put out by the UNDP. Even those, like the World Bank, who have reservations about preoccupations with poverty and minimum standard of living as the main focus of policy, now include them in their list of development indicators. Increasingly researchers outside government are also broadening the scope of their investigations. However devising objective and measurable indicators for this purpose is daunting and fraught with great difficulties.[10]

III

MEASUREMENT ISSUES

Conceptual problems are compounded by problems of empirical measurement. The Indian statistical system generates an extraordinarily vast and rich amount of data on different aspects of economy and society. The most important and richest source for assessment of poverty and levels of living is the National Sample Survey (NSS). The NSS, which has been in existence for nearly 50 years, has conducted large-scale sample surveys on a variety of subjects relevant for this purpose (ownership of land and other productive assets, household consumption, employment, educational levels, school enrolment, morbidity, health care, access to and the benefit from various programmes meant for the poor and the underprivileged, disability, housing, water supply sources and sanitation). Several of these surveys, particularly those relating to employment and consumption, have been repeated periodically. Published reports provide estimates of mean value of key characteristics and their distributions, as well as their composition for rural and urban areas of the country as a whole and in most cases at the state level. Until recently these were the principal basis for estimation and analysis outside the government. The recent policy decision to make primary household level data available for researchers makes possible vastly more intensive and detailed analyses.

---

10. The theoretical and measurement problems involved are discussed in the Development Reports and their background papers published by the UNDP.

Large-scale sample surveys of household incomes and consumption, education and health have also been done by the National Council of Applied Economics Research (NCAER),[11] though at a lower frequency. The National Nutrition Monitoring Board (NNMB) has been conducting for over 20 years detailed surveys of actual food intake and nutritional status of individuals on a small sample basis in several states.[12] The National Family Health Survey (NFHS) provides detailed information especially on children and women.[13] The ICRISAT survey of 26 villages in semi-arid tropical regions of the country, and a common set of households for a period of 12 years provides a rare and rich body of panel data on practically every aspect of rural economy.[14] In addition, there are a large number of micro studies assessing the impact of government's poverty alleviation programmes and exploring particular aspects of nutrition, health education and social amenities.

Published reports on NCAER surveys are generally less detailed and give less information on design, concepts and comparability compared to NSS. Far more detailed information and analyses based on them is available for the ICRISAT survey and the NFHS. The primary data from both of them are also freely accessible to researchers. The ICRISAT survey data in particular have been extensively used for exploring—in a degree of detail and depth not feasible with published NSS (and more so NCAER) reports—the characteristics of the poor, adaptations to fluctuations and shocks, transient and permanent poverty, participation and impact in employment schemes and other related issues. Of late, the NSS has greatly liberalised access to its primary data which can now be purchased at nominal cost on CD-ROMs and diskettes. NCAER is also giving researchers access to its primary data.

On the whole, the use of these data have, until recently, tended to focus heavily, if not exclusively, on definition of the poverty line and estimating poverty incidence and its trends. Factors underlying regional and temporal variations in these respects and policy interventions have also been explored

---

11. Noteworthy among these being the All India Household Surveys of income, savings and consumption conducted in 1967-68 and 1975-76; panel surveys of sample rural households in 1970-71 and 1981-82; Market Information Surveys of Households (done more or less regularly since 1985); a survey of social indicators (1998); and a household survey to assess macro impact of macro adjustment policies.

12. Reports of NNMB's annual nutrition surveys, which are being conducted more or less regularly since the mid-1970s, are published by the National Institute of Nutrition, Hyderabad. Unfortunately these reports, not to speak of the primary data, are not easily accessible.

13. International Institute of Population Studies (1995).

14. A description of the scope, aims and methodology of the surveys is available in Walker and Ryan (1990).

but not to the extent one would expect. Other aspects such as gender discrimination, educational participation and attainment, health and nutrition are beginning to get greater attention among scholars but do not figure at all in official assessments of the poverty situation.

The methodology of poverty estimates has long been the subject of debate. The first time this came into prominence was in the context of sharply divergent estimates of trends in poverty incidence during the 1960s: one estimate pointing to a significant rising trend in the headcount ratio and another to a falling trend. It was apparent that much of this difference was traceable to the different estimates of mean consumption used by them: one relying on the NSS and the other National Accounts estimate. Systematic differences between the two sources in the estimated consumption expenditure, both overall and for major commodity groups, as well as their time profiles was brought out in the course of that debate.

This led to a critical scrutiny of the assumptions and procedures underlying NSS and official estimates of consumption per head (Kansal, 1965; Srinivasan *et. al.*, 1974; Vaidyanathan, 1986; Minhas *et al.*, 1988). Significant differences in scope, coverage, data sources and basis of evaluation were identified. Minhas and Kansal (1989) attempted a systematic assessment of the effect of these differences and more importantly the relative merits of estimates for various specific items from these two sources verifying them in some cases with other independent data sources. They also offered several important suggestions to reconcile the differences and for ensuring greater comparability in future. Useful as these are, problems remain.

For one thing, the differences in scope of methodology and basic data sources are too large to permit reconciliation or even reasonable degree of comparability. To the extent this is possible, it can be done at best for aggregate private consumption for the country as a whole; nothing can be done about rural-urban or state level estimates.[15] Assessing the relative merits of the two-time series in capturing changes over time is problematic; the scope, concept and assumptions underlying NAS and NSS have both changed over

---

15. One could compare SDP per capita estimates and per capita weighted mean consumption from NSS at the state level. But output originating is not a good proxy for incomes accruing to the population in a state, which is more relevant for determining consumption. In the case of rural areas SDP in agriculture may not be a good indicator of even total output originating (let alone income accruing) in rural areas. At the all India level, there seems to be a significant positive correlation between official estimates of agricultural GDP per head of rural population and NSS estimates of per capita real consumption (both at constant prices) in the post 1973 period. But at the state level in many cases agricultural GDP per rural population is not strongly correlated with per capita real consumption.

time; and both are prone to errors of observation and estimation of unknown magnitudes.

There have been significant changes in the scope, design and procedure of NSS consumption surveys. The 1950s were a period of experimentation about sampling, questionnaire design, reference periods and the relative merits of single *versus* multipurpose surveys, which continued into the 1960s when consumption data were for a while compiled through integrated household surveys. There is much greater comparability after the early 1970s when NSS switched to quinquennial consumption-cum-employment surveys. But as we shall see presently, some changes in sampling design and reference periods have raised doubts about comparability of more recent data.

Changes have also been made in the NAS estimates. The changes were no doubt implemented after discussion with experts with a view to ensure firmer empirical base and minimising arbitrary assumptions. While the general consensus is that these have led to significant improvements, serious gaps and weaknesses in basic data remain: the system for obtaining output data for agriculture and even organised industry has visibly deteriorated. State-level estimates suffer from even more serious deficiencies in basic data. The basis for back-casting the series for earlier periods at every revision, though transparent, can hardly be called robust. The arbitrary manner in which estimates for agriculture have been revised recently hardly helps to increase confidence. In view of the above, the revised NAS series cannot be accepted without question and there is certainly no basis to assume that they are better than the NSS.

During the 1970s the Planning Commission—which puts out the official estimate of poverty—reviewed and revised the poverty line essentially by refixing the calorie norms, but did not address the problem of discrepancy between NAS and NSS estimates.[16] Instead it used NAS estimates of consumption expenditure, and NSS estimate of the distribution of population by level of consumption to estimate poverty incidence. That the NAS does not provide separate estimates of consumption for rural and urban areas at the national level or estimate of even total consumption expenditure of the state level, did not deter them from providing disaggregated estimate of poverty. The highly arbitrary and questionable assumptions underlying this procedure were highlighted by the Lakdawala Committee (GoI, PC, 1993).

---

16. For details of these revisions see GoI, PC (1993) Ch. 3.

This committee examined the possibilities of cross validation of NAS and NSS estimates. They noted that even if one could find a satisfactory procedure for reconciling the differences in estimates of aggregate consumption and making appropriate adjustments to in the estimate of size distribution, problems arising from "...differences in coverage, time period classification schemes and implicit prices..." will remain. Adjusting NAS to get state-level estimates and estimates for rural and urban areas would involve far too many arbitrary assumptions. They noted that the NSS gives statewise estimates of size distribution and commodity composition of consumption for rural and urban areas separately derived from surveys which are carefully organised, use uniform concepts and procedures across the country and sampling is rigorous. While NSS data are not free from errors and sustained efforts to improve their quality is essential, it remains the best available source for assessing poverty incidence and characteristics of the poor across space and time. They therefore suggested that 'if estimates of incidence are to be made with minimum recourse to adjustments based on arbitrary assumptions, the best course would be to base them entirely on the NSS.' The Planning Commission has since accepted these recommendations and official estimates of poverty are based entirely on the NSS.

During the 1970s and 1980s the NAS and NSS showed similar, though not identical, time profiles of change in mean consumption at the national level. Using NSS estimates of inequality, both showed a declining trend in the headcount ratio. However, the NSS, whose estimate of mean consumption was lower and its rise considerably slower than the NAS, showed poverty incidence to be higher and declining much more slowly than the official estimate.[17] But since both showed a decline, the relative reliability of the two sources did not figure prominently in the debate.

But after 1987-88 the NSS began providing annual estimates of mean consumption as well. This shows no significant trend in either inequality or mean per capita consumption in rural areas, and therefore in the incidence of poverty. In urban areas, according to NSS, poverty has declined largely because of an increase in per capita real consumption. Overall poverty incidence in the country has not changed significantly. That this happened during the decade of major changes in economic policy and despite the relatively high rate of

---

17. According to official estimates poverty incidence fell progressively from 51.5 per cent in 1972-73 to 29.9 per cent in 1993-94; while the NSS based estimate showed a decline for 54.9 per cent in 1972-73 to 39.3 per cent in 1993-94 (GoI, PC, 1993).

overall growth indicated by NAS is cited by critics of the reforms as evidence of its anti-poor character. The reliability of NSS data in capturing changes in consumption levels and distribution has, therefore, again become an issue.

While the NAS estimate of consumption no longer enters poverty estimation, the striking difference between the time profile of consumption growth during the 1990s obtained from it and that of the NAS deserves notice. This comparison, which is possible only at the national level, shows that while according to NAS, per capita real consumption expenditure increased progressively at an average annual rate of over two per cent during the 1990s, the NSS showed an erratic trend and a much smaller rise.[18] However, using the same deflation procedures, the movement of the two series based on the quinquennial data from 1973-74 to 1993-94 turn out to be more or less similar. Therefore the divergence between two in the 1990s seems unlikely to be due to deflation procedure. We have to look for other explanations, in terms of changing designs, procedures and biases in the NSS itself.

One aspect of the post 1988 NSS series which has attracted notice is that, except for 1993-94, they are based on so-called thin samples. In the quinquennial surveys, whose primary focus is consumption and employment, the sample size is large enough to provide state level estimates at an acceptable margin of sampling error. In other years consumption and employment data are canvassed on a much smaller sample, and subsidiary to the main theme which varies each year. Sampling and survey design being the same, the smaller size of the sample in the annual surveys by itself should not make any difference to the reliability or comparability of their national estimates, with those of large samples. The fact that the primary focus of annual surveys is on other subjects could however affect the quality of consumption data obtained through them: being secondary themes the investigators and their supervisors may not give as close an attention to this part of the survey as for the primary theme.

While this may increase the scope for non-sampling errors, there is no basis to suppose that they would affect the nature or extent of such bias NSS data may be generally prone to. There is a widespread belief that richer households tend to be less cooperative and tend to underestimate their consumption more than the poor. But we do not have information to test the

---

18. A point-to-point comparison shows that the mean per capita consumption (in real terms) during the triennium ending 1997 was about 14 per cent higher than during 1989-91 according to NAS and only 3 per cent higher according to NSS.

validity of this supposition and how large its magnitude is. Unfortunately, despite repeated suggestions NSS does not provide information on the relative incidence of non-response or the characteristics of non-responding households, nor the investigator's impressions about the cooperativeness of the respondents and their willingness to provide information. Unless the under reporting bias of richer households in the thin sample rounds is higher for either of these reasons, and has increased over time, there is no reason to question comparability of the series on this ground.

It is also arguable that the underestimates of consumption by the rich does not affect the poverty estimates so long as the not-so-well-to-do people report their consumption correctly. The rich may have an incentive to understate much more than the poor. While this is true, it needs noting that if NAS estimate is correct, and the poor accurately (or at least far more accurately than the better-off) report their consumption to NSS, the degree of under-estimation by the rich, and therefore inequalities, must have increased. But this is pure conjecture.[19]

Changes in sampling, reference periods, questionnaire design, and interview procedures can however make a difference. A significant change in sampling design allowing for stratification of households according to broad income class, and a higher sampling fraction of richer households, did take place in the 1980s. But this should not affect the comparability of the series from the late 1980s through 1998 unless—let me repeat—the degree of non-response or non-cooperation of the better-off can be shown to have increased.

Another source of non-comparability is changes in reference period. That the length of the reference period affects the respondents' estimate is well known. After some initial experimentation, the NSS decided on a uniform 30-day reference period for all items of consumption and kept to this practice for nearly 30 years. In the 1980s this aspect was again reviewed. The effect of changing reference period from 30 days to one year on the responses of reconsumption of clothing and durables was tested by canvassing two independent sets of sample households. The differences were expectedly substantial. Subsequently, from 1991, this experiment was extended to all commodities getting information from two independent subsamples one on the basis of a 30-day reference period for all commodities and another using different reference periods for different commodity groups. This was expected

---

19. If the conjecture is valid, the criterion that the reforms have accentuated inequalities would stand vindicated.

to assess the direction and magnitude of difference in reported consumption with different reference periods. Reference periods did indeed make a difference, more in some commodity groups and less in others. The difference in reported consumption of food, drink and tobacco based on a 30-day reference and seven-day reference period turned out to be quite large, the latter being much higher. In the case of clothing and durables, the figure reported with 30-day reference period was lower, and substantially lower in the case of durables, than for the 365-day reference period. Such exercises are essential to provide a basis, after systematic analysis and, if need be, further experimentation with different sets of reference periods, to improve the survey design. So long as this is done on independent subsamples we get a comparable series using the prevailing practice and the difference changes make to the magnitude. When the prevailing practice is changed we also have a clear basis to link the earlier and the new series without losing comparability.

While these precautions were taken care of up to 1998,[20] the large sample survey of 1999-2000 made a significant departure by canvassing information on consumption using two different reference periods, on all sample households. This, it has been rightly pointed out, vitiates the estimates obtained from the latest survey and makes it difficult to compare them with those of earlier surveys including the 1993-94 surveys. Those, like me, who believed that a comparison of the 1999-2000 results with those of 1993-94 ratio provide a better basis to assess the impact of reforms on consumption levels, inequality and poverty at the national and state levels are understandably dismayed!

As already mentioned large-scale surveys of household income, consumption and several other aspects have also been done by NCAER. Estimates of mean consumption, inequalities and poverty incidence reported on the basis of these surveys differ significantly from the ones widely in use: For instance 1968-69 survey (Bhatty, 1974) found per capita consumption close to the official estimates, but there were large differences compared to NSS rankings of states by levels of consumption expenditure and inequalities. Based on panel survey of rural households at two different time points (1970-71 and 1980-82), NCAER concluded that incomes have grown considerably

---

20. These points are discussed at length by Abijit Sen (2000) and Visaria *et al.* (2000) and in an as yet unpublished note by Deaton.

across all classes; (and more so at the lower end) and that poverty had declined substantially more than shown by NSS (NCAER, 1987). There are obvious and large differences in scope, aims design and methods between NSS and NCAER surveys (Bhatty, 1974) and between NCAER surveys at different points of time (Bhalla, 1988; Pradhan *et. al.*, 2000).[21] These differences have not attracted the degree of critical scrutiny which one would have expected.

That different sources, using different methods, give quite different estimate is confusing. Much greater attention must be given to assessing the purposes, concepts and methods underlying different data sets, their reliability and suitability for generating reasonably and comparable estimates of mean consumption and inequality. The scope for confusion could be reduced if these details were available for critical scrutiny by scholars and informed analysis of the reasons for differences in the estimates. Better still if different survey organisations get together and agreed on minimum degree of comparability in scope and concepts in the conduct of such surveys.

With the best of efforts, however, these issues cannot be fully resolved. The fact is that here is nothing like perfectly accurate and reliable data. The challenge is to make ingenious use of imperfect, incomplete information subject to sizeable, and often unknown, margins of error, and to squeeze such insights as we can legitimately extract from them. Plurality of data sets is useful as cross checks. If independent sources reveal the same or similar patterns we can be more confident of the patterns they indicate. But it is necessary to recognise and allow for defects and non-comparability and to maintain pressures to ensure the integrity and transparency of the statistical system.

An equally important lesson to be drawn is not to be preoccupied exclusively, or even primarily, on poverty incidence as the sole index of well-being. It is necessary to broaden our inquiries to cover other aspects which affect and reflect well-being; and to pay much more attention to the characteristics of those at the bottom of the socioeconomic pyramid, how their conditions are changing and how effective public interventions are in improving their conditions and opportunities.

---

21. The aims, scope and design of these surveys vary. Some were focused primarily on household incomes, others on market for branded manufactures and yet others on social indicators. This and the fact that, in some cases, two different surveys give very different estimates raises serious questions as to their comparability and reliability especially for assessing changes in inequality and poverty incidence. Even in the case of the panel survey of 1970-71 and 1981-82, more than one-fourth of the 1970-71 sample could not be traced in 1971-72; and not all the panel responded. The characteristics of the missing households is not indicated.

It is for these reasons that the Lakdawala Committee recommended that, apart from estimates of the proportion and number of poor, a fuller picture of the living conditions and well-being of the poor must cover the following aspects:

(i) The composition of the poor population in terms of dominant characteristics, i.e., their distribution by region, social group, family characteristics (e.g., size, education, age, sex of household head, dependency ratio) and the way this is changing over time. Much of this can be done by appropriate tabulation of NSS employment and consumption survey data.

(ii) Nutritional status of the population: levels of intake of principal nutrients, incidence of malnourishment, anthropometric measurements and activity patterns by age, sex and socioeconomic categories. This can be done by the National Institute of Nutrition.

(iii) Health status: mortality (overall, infant and child, maternal), morbidity, access to and use of health services (public and private) and costs. The quinquennial surveys of public consumption as well as mortality indicators based on the Sample Registration System and the morbidity surveys of NSS need to be put on a systematic and continuing basis.

(iv) Educational status: school enrolment by region, sex and age group and by economic social class, reach and quality of public education services and costs. Here again information from the NSS social consumption enquiries and the all-India Education Surveys suitably restructured would provide the basic data.

(v) Living environment: distribution by density of settlement: living space per head, type of houses, access to safe drinking water and sanitation, access to amenities (post office, telephones, railway, *pucca* road, markets, etc.).

The committee further suggested the preparation of a 'State of Poverty' report every five years covering the above aspects and highlighting the condition of the poorest 30 per cent of the country's population. Unfortunately, there appears as yet no signs of these suggestions being implemented by the Planning Commission.

IV

CORRELATES AND DETERMINANTS

Having discussed the problem of data and measurement at length and cautioned about assessments of changes in overall poverty incidence, I would like now to turn to what we have learnt from the available data, and from studies based on them, about incidence of poverty, its characteristics and determinants.

It is indisputably clear that a large proportion of the country's population cannot afford the bundle of goods and services including food, education, health which constitute the currently accepted norms of minimum living standard. The deficiencies, both in absolute and relative terms, are considerably larger in rural India than in urban areas. It is also evident that in rural India asset-poor households, those dependent mainly on wage labour, and those with relatively large families and a high proportion of children relative to adults figure far more prominently among the poor than those with land (especially those with relatively large holdings), self employed in non-agricultural activities and those with better education. Scheduled castes/tribes households, being disadvantaged on all these counts, have a considerably higher incidence of poverty then other groups (Visaria, 1978, 1979; Lipton, 1981).

Poverty incidence shows large variations across states. In 1993-94, rural poverty incidence varied from about 2 per cent in the Punjab to 58 per cent in Bihar. Broadly speaking, the proportion of rural population living below the poverty line is higher than the national average in east and central India and well below the average in the southern states. About two-fifths of the country's rural poor are concentrated in Bihar, Orissa, MP and West Bengal. The NSS data also show the rate of poverty reduction in these states to be much slower than in others. This implies an increase in the geographical concentration of poverty.

Overall poverty incidence in rural areas seem to be largely a reflection of differences in mean per capita incomes across states and less to inequalities within states (Bhattacharya *et al.*, 1988). More detailed analysis using household level data from an NCAER survey (Gaiha, 1988) suggests that the likelihood of a household, being poor is influenced by the social and economic infrastructure of the village they live in, some characteristics of agricultural technology and the demographic and other feature of the household. The effect of agricultural technology being the largest followed by household characteristics. Both are seen to have a more marked influence on poverty incidence among cultivator households than other categories. The relative importance of factors varies between different groups.

Sundaram and Tendulkar (1988) constructed and estimated a model to assess the impact of demographic pressure on land (the principal productive resource of rural areas), the value of productive assets per head, and the inequality in their distribution, the productivity of land, wage labour incidence, employment and the interactions among them in accounting for variations in rural poverty. Estimates of the reduced form of the model showed that poverty incidence tends to be lower (to a statistically significant extent) in regions with relatively low demographic pressure (low land-man ratio), higher productive assets per head and more equal distribution of these assets. Other things being the same, the higher productivity per unit of land goes with lower poverty incidence. This line of approach to understanding determinant of rural poverty, with refinements to take into account price differentials, the determinants of land productivity, diversification of employment and such other elements seems promising. But not much further work on these lines has been done since.

Attempts to explain trends in rural poverty incidence in terms of trends in agricultural production and prices have given some useful insights. The factors underlying them have also been extensively examined but for reasons already cited the conclusions are much less robust. An early attempt along these lines (Ahluwalia, 1978) found that at the all-India level there was a significant negative relation between the value added by agriculture per head of rural population and rural poverty ratio; and that there was also a significant element of secular decline over time on account of other (unspecified) factors. Subsequently Ahluwalia (1986) showed that the price index for the poor relative to the average for the population also has a significant bearing on rural poverty trend: the higher this index, the higher the poverty. But in this case there is no time trend independent of production and prices. At the state level the inverse relation between agricultural production and poverty was found to hold in several but not all states.[22]

---

22. Significantly during the period covered by his study, the rate of decline in poverty is not significantly correlated with the rate of agricultural growth. Punjab and Haryana, which recorded among the highest growth rates in this period, showed no significant fall in poverty.

The rationale for inclusion of price and its specification has evoked a lively debate [Mellor and Desai (eds.) 1988]. The argument for taking the overall inflation rate as an explanatory variable is not clear. Presumably it would impact on poor *via* the wage rate. But this depends on the extent and rapidity with which rural wage rates adjust to changes in the general price level. Very little is however known about this. Moreover, as many have pointed out, changes in consumer price index for the poor relative to that of the better-off may be more relevant than the general rate of inflation. A better specification (and one used in several recent studies)[23] would be the relative price of food to non-food items in as much as food dominates the poor's consumption and accounts for a much higher proportion of expenditure than the better-off.

Till recently the debate on rural poverty focused mainly on agriculture and has been marked by an underlying concern that emerging patterns of technology and production tend to increase inequalities and that, therefore, agricultural growth may not automatically reduce poverty. The HYV fertiliser-irrigation centred strategy was, and to some degree still is, widely believed to be biased against small and marginal farmers and the growing class of wage labourers. Relatively small farms cannot afford the resources needed to make effective use of the new technology. Also the new technology does not generate fast enough increase in employment opportunities to absorb the growth of labour force particularly for the burgeoning class of wage labourers. This led to predictions of increased unemployment, reduced real wages and worsening inequalities in rural areas. And in the context of relatively slow growth in the rest of the economy, this tendency was expected to spill over into the non-agricultural sector and urban areas as well. The evidence from actual experience is mixed.[24] Access to irrigation has traditionally been relatively higher among small holdings compared to large ones. But during the last three decades irrigated area has increased much faster than average among larger farms. This would tend to accentuate inequalities. There is also evidence of increased inequality in the distribution of operational holdings in some areas due to dispossession of tenants and the spread of 'reverse' leasing. On the other hand the adoption ratio of HYV and fertilisers, which used to be relatively low on small farms compared to large farms in the early stages of their spread, is no longer so. This narrowing difference in adoption of bio-chemical technology offsets the impact of large farmer bias in irrigation, though to what extent remains an open question.

---

23. Two recent examples being Ravillion and Datt (1995) and Abijit Sen (1996).

24. The relevant data are summarised in Vaidyanathan (1994, 1996).

Agricultural employment has increased much slower than agricultural output partly because of the spread of mechanisation. Over time this tendency seem to have intensified. While the share of wage labour in total rural labour force has increased rapidly, agricultural employment has remained virtually stagnant. However, the expected worsening in rural unemployment and in real wage rates has not materialised. On the contrary, non-farm employment has risen at a surprisingly rapid rate during 1970s and 1980s and real wage rates have everywhere risen.

This has led to broadening the scope of the explanatory hypotheses regarding determinants of rural poverty to include the extent of non-agricultural employment (which captures differences in the degree of diversification in the rural economy), commercialisation, real wage rates and public development expenditure. But specifications vary in terms of the variables included without a convincing a priori basis to choose between them. Most of them do well in terms of the proportion of variance explained (R squares exceeding 85-90 per cent) in both national time series and pooled state cross section and time series. The coefficients for individual variables have the expected signs and are statistically significant (Ravillion and Datt *op. cit.* and Abhijit Sen *op.cit.*).

It is noteworthy, however, that inequality in distribution of productive resources or determinants of labour supply and demand do not figure in these exercises in the manner attempted by Tendulkar and Sundaram. There are also data problems arising from the marked deterioration in the system for compiling official agricultural statistics. The levels and, more importantly, time profiles of change in agricultural output per rural person and NSS estimates of real consumption per capita are often dissimilar. Also as noted earlier, changes in scope, methods and basis of estimation, which affect both NSS and official estimates, vitiate comparability across different periods and raise questions about the validity of time series analysis especially for long periods as done in some world bank studies.

Poverty studies deal mostly with rural areas. Urban poverty has received comparatively less attention even at a descriptive level.[25] Available surveys show urban areas to have a higher level of mean per capita consumption as well as higher inequality. Mean per capita consumption in urban areas is higher and more unequally distributed than in rural India. Regional variations

---

25. For a recent overview see Rakesh Mohan and Pushpa Thottan (1988) and Minhas *et al.* (1988). Also GoI, PC (1993).

in both respects are marked: poverty incidence being higher than average in Bihar, MP and Orissa and less than average in Assam, Punjab, Haryana and West Bengal.

There seems to be no significant association, across states, between poverty incidence and mean consumption. However, states where urban poverty incidence is persistently higher than the national average, price levels as well as inequalities are higher than average; the contrary being the case in those where urban poverty rate is persistently below national average. In both cases differences in inequality are more important than price differentials (Minhas *et. al.,* 1988).

NSS data points to a progressive decline in urban poverty since the early 1970s reflecting a modest rising trend in mean per capita consumption without any significant change in the inequality index (Datt, 1999). The trend towards urban poverty reduction is noticed in all states but in varying degrees. The differences largely reflect differences in the pace of increase in mean per capita consumption; there seems to be no significant urban trend in inequality in most states.

Factors underlying regional and temporal variations in urban poverty have not been explored even to the limited extent attempted in the case of rural areas.[26] Very little is known about the characteristics of the urban poor. There are isolated location specific studies of the informal sector, slum and pavement dwellers. But these need to be considerably expanded in scope and integrated into a wider framework to better understand urban poverty. Here perhaps the focus of comparative studies could be on towns of different sizes and different degrees of economic dynamism. Understanding urban poverty naturally would also require greater attention to the migration patterns and more generally to the nature of rural-urban linkages in terms of commodity, income and labour flows.

Refinement in mapping and analysis of income poverty is necessary but not sufficient. Their scope needs to be widened to include different aspects of the poor's well-being in its broader sense. Also deeper investigations are necessary to understand how the poor and the underprivileged cope with vicissitudes, how they adapt to reduction in employment and incomes, how far they are

---

26. Abhijit Sen's (1996) attempt to explain trends in urban poverty incidence at the all India level in terms of changes in agricultural incomes per head of rural population, per capita non-agricultural incomes, commercialisation, etc., are not as convincing as in the case of rural areas both in terms of the underlying logic and the consistency, significance and stability of the estimated coefficients.

able to take advantage of opportunities opened by the growth of the economy and various poverty alleviation and affirmative action policies of the government.

Some aspects—notably food intake and nutrition, transient and chronic poverty, gender disparities, literacy and educational levels, and access to health care—have been the subject of study based both on macro data and in depth micro-level studies. But there is much room for extending and refining such work and making them an integral part of the effort to better understand the nature and role of socioeconomic deprivation. Trends in level and composition of food intake, both overall and for different fractile groups, intra-family allocation of food (especially between males and females), the effectiveness of special nutrition programmes and subsidised food supply and the relation between food intake and nutritional status have attracted much attention.[27] Despite their limitations, the mean level of calorie intake and the proportion of population with intakes below the calorie norm continue to be widely used as an indicator of nutritional status of the population. The NSS data show a trend of decline in calorie intake of the better-off and the very low elasticity of calorie consumption even among the poorer groups, whose calorie intake remains well below the norms. There have also been significant shifts in the pattern of consumption, including especially among the poor, from food to non-food items, from cereals to more costly non-cereal foods and, within cereals, from cheaper to more expensive grains.[28] But there has been hardly any serious investigation of the factors underlying these changes or their impact on health and nutritional status.

If the data on food consumption trends of the poorer segments is correct, one must explain why, despite near stagnation of calorie intake, there are no signs of deterioration in height, weight, health or activity indicators even in states, which, by all indicators are very poor.[29] Surprisingly this apparent puzzle has not attracted much attention.

---

27. On the nature and extent of these shifts use Radhakrishna and Ravi (1992); Suryanarayana (2000) and Meenakshi (2000).

28. State level time series for education and mortality indicators compiled from official sources are collated in Nayyar 1992. Information on morbidity and access to medical care is available from the social consumption surveys conducted by the NSS in 1986-87 and in 1996-97. NNMB surveys give data, for small but representative sample of households in major states, of measured food intake, anthropometric measurements and assessment of clinical signs of nutrition deficiencies. There has been little analysis of the NNMB data. For analysis of nutrition data from the ICRISAT village surveys see Walker and Ryan (1990).

29. See Visaria and Gumber (1996) for a comprehensive and comparative analysis of NSS data on morbidity and health care utilisation and expenditure pattern in different states in 1986-87.

Nutritional status obviously cannot be judged by food intake levels alone. Education, safe drinking water, hygiene, incidence and control of infections— all of which have a bearing on how efficiently food is utilised—must be taken into account. While the standards in all these respects are no doubt far below desired levels, improvements have taken place partly because of as a result of public policy and partly because of the spread in availability and use of antibiotics. Both may have contributed to an overall improvement which indicates nutritional status despite stagnation in calorie intake at low levels. This is only a conjecture whose validity (especially for the poorer socioeconomic groups) needs much closer investigation.

On other aspects of living standards—e.g. clothing, housing, education, water supply/sanitation, and health facilities—considerable amount of information is available in numerous surveys and studies based on them. Literacy rates, enrolment and admission of children in school, mean years of schooling, costs, inter-group disparities and other aspects of education are well documented [PROBE Team, 1998; Vaidyanathan and Nair (eds.), 2001]. So are mortality rates, morbidity, availability and use of public and private health care facilities in different regions and socioeconomic groups. We know that, while considerable improvement has taken place in most of these respects, they are generally inadequate and highly uneven with rural areas and poorer sections of the population invariably reporting lower access and use the facilities and at a higher cost relative to their incomes, than the rich.[30] These data sources, and analytical studies to interpret factors underlying spatial and temporal variations, need to be given a much more prominent place in the study of poverty and well-being. Another example relates to the attempt at differentiating between different types of poverty (seasonal and annual; transient and persistent; poor and ultra poor).[31] Macro surveys can tell us little, if at all, on these matters or of the process underlying them. Only detailed micro-level inquiries and panel type surveys can provide the needed information. We do have some micro studies which give an idea of diverse strategies that poor people adopt to tide over bad years and lean seasons. They include maintaining emergency reserves, borrowing, sale of assets, migration, changing nature, and intensity of activity and altering intra-fairly food allocation. Panel surveys have been used to focus on households who are persistently below the poverty line (Gaiha, 1988).

---

30. See for example Lipton (1983); Chambers (1988) and Sahn (eds.) (1989).

31. Notable and pioneering works on this subject include Guhan (1988); Chen (ed.) (1998); Dreze and Sen (1989).

The role of formal and informal social security mechanisms to take care of the aged, disabled and widows among the poor is attracting increasing attention in research and policy discourses. The coverage, organisation and scale of arrangements for the organised sector are best documented. Descriptive accounts of informal and traditional social mechanisms (family, kin networks, charitable institutions) as well as of various government sponsored pension and insurance schemes for the poor are available.[32] But critical studies of their working and impact have not received as much attention.

The nature, extent and manifestations of persistent gender disparities in access to family resources for food, education and health care have been extensively documented and commented on.[33] The deprivations and disadvantages suffered by underprivileged social groups (especially scheduled castes and tribes, artisans) are also well documented. That they figure prominently among the poor and are prone to various forms of 'exclusion' which handicaps them in taking advantage of opportunities generated by growth and that they are specially vulnerable to the introduction of new products and processes is well known.

There is compelling evidence that the position of these groups in terms of practically every indicator of well being remains much below the average. However, the evidence also shows that there have been substantial improvements and in some respects at least a substantial narrowing of the gap between them and the rest of the population.[34] The extent of this phenomenon however varies considerably between and within regions. The reasons for these variations in the extent and manner in which some segments of this excluded groups are able to improve their condition while others continue in chronic deprivation; the way affirmative action and other government interventions meant to mitigate their disadvantages actually work; and the reasons why, even when basic amenities are in place, some groups do not make effective use of them deserve far more attention than they have received so far.

---

32. See for example Lipton (1983); Sen *et al.* (1988); Bardhan (1988); Walker and Ryan (1992); Kumar and Stewart (1992); Agarwal (1994); Vaidyanathan (1986, 1994).

33. The censuses and the NSS collect and publish data separately for scheduled castes and tribes in respect of demographic features, education, vital rates, employment and land ownership. They show that while their position in all these respects remain well below the average, there have been substantial improvements both in absolute and relative terms. The large variations in these respects between and within regions and in particular the underlying factors (including the effect of affirmative action policies) have received surprisingly little attention.

34. The literature on effectiveness of policy interventions is vast. For useful summaries of current debates and bibliographies on IRDP see Copestake (1988); on employment, Mahendra Dev (1993) and Gaiha (1997), on nutrition, Subba Rao (1988), Osmani (ed.) (1992).

V

POLICY

Some people—especially among those who see rapid overall economic growth as both a necessary and sufficient condition for eradicating poverty and who see excessive state intervention as the major impediment to growth—consider this obsession with poverty, and counting the number of poor, as distracting attention and resources from growth promoting policies. The government according to them should confine itself to ensuring law and order, enabling markets to function freely, facilitating free trade and capital movements and providing universal elementary education, health care, water supply, sanitation and essential infrastructure. On the other hand, they question the efficacy of various poverty alleviation programmes and, by implication, the justification for spending huge amounts on social programmes. These arguments are fundamentally flawed.

Growth—necessary as it is—does not 'benefit' automatically and in equal proportion to all regions and sections of the population. For a variety of reasons—historical factors, resource endowments, social and political conjunctures and, of course, government policy—growth happens to be very uneven across regions. This fact is beyond dispute. It also happens that regions which are poorly developed to begin with have also grown at a slower rate than average. This tendency cannot be dismissed as an inevitable but transitional phase which will get corrected over time. Nor can one accept the proposition that so long as there is no decline in level of development in any region and all record some improvement, there is no need for intervention. Such a proposition, apart from being questionable on merits, is politically unacceptable in a democracy. Concern for equity and political necessity are compelling arguments for government intervention to correct the imbalance.

This argument acquires even greater force in relation to people: both as a proportion of the population and in absolute terms, those who do not have and cannot afford even the quite modest minimum living standard currently accepted as the norm in the Indian context are very large. And they happen to be concentrated in the poor regions, among sections of the population who suffer the cumulative consequences of systematic exclusion and the attendant social and economic disadvantages. That basic needs and minimum living standards figure so prominently not only in rhetoric of all political parties, but also in the sizeable public resources committed for this purpose is a reflection of both moral and political compulsions.

The evolution of policies and programmes meant to tackle this problem may be haphazard and in some respects even incoherent. Nevertheless, one can see a clear pattern in the way they seek to recognise and address differing needs of backward areas with special problems, and of different segments of the poor and underprivileged. Broadly they can be divided into the following groups:

(1) Affirmative action by way of reservations for scheduled castes and tribes in elected bodies, public sector jobs and educational institutions supplemented by special programmes, with earmarked allocations, for their development and welfare.

(2) Programmes (notably IRDP, TRYSEM, DWACRA) designed to help poor segments to acquire or add to their productive assets and enable them to make more productive use of such assets.

(3) Various special programmes to provide additional employment to the poor.

(4) Schemes to ensure that all villages have access to a minimum standard of educational and health facilities, safe drinking water and roads.

(5) Various forms of direct transfers by pension and insurance schemes for aged, disabled and widows, school feeding and child nutrition programmes and subsidised distribution of foodgrains and other essential commodities to the poor.

(6) Special programmes for the development of production potential for hill tracts, deserts and drought prone areas.

For the most part these programmes are conceived and funded by the central government which determines the criteria for allocation between states (and in some cases within states). Actual implementation is left to the state government agencies subject to guidelines (sometimes quite detailed) regarding the scope and content of schemes, and their targeting and implementation procedures. Only a few (notable being the Maharashtra Employment Guarantee Scheme and Tamil Nadu's Mid-day Meals Programme for school children) have been taken up entirely at the initiative of states.

Over the years the functioning of these programmes and their impact on the poor has attracted a great deal of attention. Numerous studies—several under the auspices of the government, and many more based on independent surveys, micro studies and analyses of available macro data—have highlighted their achievements as well as weaknesses.[35] A healthy and wholesome feature

---

35. For a recent and thorough discussion of issues See Krishnan and Krishnaji (eds.) (2000) and Swaminathan (2000).

is the extraordinarily free and open discussion of deficiencies of particular schemes, the relative merits of different interventions and suggestions for restructuring and reorientation.

Official claims of the number of beneficiaries, works carried out, additions to productive assets and employment generated are unreliable and exaggerated. Poor targeting is reflected in the high proportion of non-poor and other non-eligible persons among the beneficiaries. Leakages due to inappropriate works, inefficient implementation and corruption are high. Quality of assets provided/created under these programmes is poor and their impact on income level of beneficiaries dubious. Assets and schemes are frequently not appropriate to the needs and potentials of particular regions or groups. There is little consultation with, not to speak of involvement of local communities generally and target groups in particular, in deciding and implementing schemes. Lack of accountability remains a major problem. The structure, content and funding of these programmes remain mostly in the hands of the central government. There is considerable overlap among these schemes as well as between them and development schemes included under the normal state plans. Typically each programme is administered by a separate agency each with its own line hierarchy and operating independently. These features, taken together with the rigidity of central guidelines, make for fragmentation and duplication of schemes. Coordination is difficult; so is monitoring of accomplishments in terms of efficacy of targeting, quality of works actually completed and impact on the beneficiaries.

The programmes tend to emphasise loans and subsidies and provision of current wage employment rather than ensuring that they are used to augment productive capacity for achieving a higher level of employment and income on a sustained basis. The selection of beneficiaries, the distribution of loans and subsidies, and the recovery of loans offer much scope for patronage and corruption at the political and bureaucratic levels.

The public distribution system (PDS) does not accomplish its ostensible aim of ensuring essential consumer goods to the poor at reasonable prices. Large parts of the country (especially states which have the largest concentration of poor) simply do not have a distribution network to reach the supplies where they are most needed. In states (Kerala, West Bengal, Tamil Nadu) which have such networks, the coverage is not limited to the poor. And attempts to ensure better targeting have been thwarted by administrative difficulties and political opposition. The efficiency of PDS as a poverty alleviation measure and the desirability of continuing it in the present form is being questioned. Supporters of PDS, who see it as a major instrument for ensuring food security for the poor, strongly oppose this prescription even as they recognise the need for restructuring the programme.[36]

These widely known and documented deficiencies have given poverty alleviation programmes a bad name. Critics argue—some explicitly and more by implication—that the effective contribution of these schemes to sustain poverty reduction is not commensurate with the resources spent on them. That given the high level of fiscal deficits and the severe shortage of resources for infrastructural investments needed for overall growth, the country can ill afford this luxury.

It is certainly true that outlays on targeted poverty alleviation programmes have increased rapidly both in absolute terms and relative to total public sector plan outlay. Prior to 1970, these were limited to special schemes for nutrition, scheduled castes and tribes, social welfare, backward areas, and a minuscule rural works programme during the Fourth Plan (1969-74). Total outlay for these was Rs. 6 billion, or less than 4 per cent of public sector plan. During the Eighth Plan (1992-1997), the outlay on a vastly larger and more varied poverty alleviation programme amounted to Rs. 460 billion (about 11 per cent of the total public sector plan).[37] Also, outlays on PA programmes have grown considerably faster than total plan outlay in a period marked by severe infrastructure shortage and bottlenecks. However large these figures might seem, the fact remains that they account for barely one per cent of the GDP, and barely a sixth of the gross fiscal deficit of the centre and the states put together. The public sector resource crisis cannot be laid at the door of PA programmes. The more important and deeper causes lie in the falling tax to GDP ratio, the inability to contain runaway increase in revenue expenditures and the huge and burgeoning deficits incurred in providing public services.[38] All of these are due to policies—be it taxation, salaries and allowances of public sector employees, subsidised supply of water and power—which largely benefit the better-off segments in fact the top quintile of the population. A

---

36. The estimate for the Fourth Plan includes outlays on area development, village industries, backward areas, slum improvement, social welfare and special area programme. That for the Eighth Plan includes rural development, scheduled caste and tribes, social welfare, nutrition and village industry. Including outlays on minimum needs programme, for which separate for as figures are available the total is substantially higher bringing the total outlay on targeted PA programmes to 17 per cent of the public sector plan outlay.

37. In 1994-95 unrecovered costs of publicly provided goods and services are estimated at Rs. 1,370 billion which exceeds the public sector plan outlay by 30 per cent and overall fiscal deficit by 40 per cent.

38. The subsequent arguments draw heavily than earlier paper of the author, Vaidyanathan (1998).

disproportionate share of the food and fertiliser subsidies also accrue to the better-off. Under these conditions cutting back the allocation for poverty alleviation is no solution to the fiscal problem, and it is certainly not justified morally or politically.

This is not to deny the need and immense scope for improving the efficacy of poverty alleviation programmes by better targeting, reducing waste and corruption, making the programmes more meaningful in terms of relevance to local needs and priorities, and creating institutional conditions for greater accountability. The focus should be on rationalising the approach, organisation and priorities of the PA programmes rather than on cutting back the outlays. The number of PA programmes can, and should, be drastically reduced and streamlined to minimise duplication and fragmentation. We need distinguish only between 3 and 4 basic PA programme categories: (1) Those which are meant to ensure that all communities in the country have a minimum standard of school, primary health care, water supply, sanitation and connectivity. (2) Those which are meant to enable resource poor segments of the population to acquire productive assets and to use them effectively. (3) Programmes to provide additional employment opportunities to those poor who do not have productive assets and depend on wage employment. (4) Programmes to enable scheduled castes and tribes to take advantage of educational and health facilities so that they are better equipped to take advantage of growing opportunities.

There are already accepted norms of minimum standards mainly in terms of distance of each community from each facility as well as physical facilities and personnel at delivery points. The norms may in some cases need review and redefinition. Once this is done, a comparison between existing ground situation and the norms would provide an objective basis for identifying, fairly precisely, the areas and locations which are deficient, as well as quantify the extent and nature of the deficiencies. Investment in physical facilities to make up these deficiencies should of course be part of a national Minimum Needs Programme. But creating physical facilities will not suffice. The tasks of ensuring that the prescribed staff are in position, that they function regularly and well, that the underprivileged segments can readily access them and get proper attention are equally important. These will need action in the sphere of administrative reform and social mobilisation.

Category 2 covers the present IRDP and also special area programmes: the former, which provide loans and subsidies for purchase of non-land assets by the poor, has proved to be wasteful and far less effective than expected. The latter are meant to develop productive resources in drought prone, desert and hill areas to facilitate more effective use of resources and open up opportunities for increased production in a variety of activities. These two have not been effective partly because they overlap with schemes which are part of the sectoral programmes and also because of poor design and implementation. All these schemes are in need of drastic change.

IRDP in its present form deserves to be scrapped. Identification of poor, the kinds of assets to be provided, ensuring the back up needed for their programme cannot, as experience has shown, be managed efficiently by government. The difficulties are compounded when they involve heavy subsidies and are implemented by a bureaucracy to political interference. Instead, public investment ought to concentrate on providing infrastructure to facilitate overall development and in each region according to its resource potential thereby opening up greater and more diverse opportunities for employment and entrepreneurial activity.

The poor of course need special help by way of information, technical advice and training to take advantage of growing investment opportunities. The government has a key role in providing this help. But it is neither necessary nor desirable for the government to decide what assets are to be provided, to whom and on what terms. These tasks are better left to individual's choices. Those who want to invest in any enterprise can seek credit from financial institutions who must be left free to judge the viability of the loan and the borrowers. The government's role here would be essentially to lay down guidelines (such as priority sector lending) and providing interest subsidies or insurance of loans given to the poor.

There is also a strong case for including land among the assets eligible for institutional credit for the rural landless and land poor. Redistribution of land through conventional approach to land reforms has not worked and seems unlikely to make much headway. However, the spread of education among the bigger farmers is leading to increasing migration to urban areas; they are also seen to be investing their surplus in non-agricultural activities. The resulting weakening of their economic stake as well as their power in the village communities is creating a situation where they are willing to sell their land. This process has already occurred on a significant scale in several parts of the country and seems to be spreading. In such a situation, asset poor households wanting to acquire land—the most important productive resource in rural areas—deserves as much emphasis in poor-oriented credit programmes as for the acquisition of other assets or setting up other enterprises.

The rationale for special area programmes as a separate category is also questionable. Practically all the components of these programmes figure in the sectoral programmes. Scrapping the special area programmes and merging them into sectoral and area development programmes will make for more effective use of public funds by eliminating dysfunctional and wasteful fragmentation of resources and effort. From the viewpoint of poverty alleviation, agriculture and related activities are the most important. The scale and content of these programmes should however be tailored to the diverse resource potentials in different regions and constraints impeding their realisation. This is the rationale for watershed development and planning on the basis of agro-climatic regions. But these are at present no more than in name. If these are pursued seriously and the organisational arrangements for planning are recast on that basis, there is really no need for special area (or for that matter special crop specific) schemes.

In implementing integrated regional resource planning, it would be perfectly legitimate to earmark allocations, and even provide special extra funds, for use in regions which rank low in terms of per capita income and employment. The distribution of funds between regions must however be based not only on needs, but also on potential for development of land, water and livestock resources as part of integrated area development plans.

Employment schemes can all be merged into one and allocations between and within states determined on the basis of the magnitude of poverty incidence, magnitude of unemployment and development potential. There is considerable room for refinement to get disaggregated estimates of poverty and unemployment (which is feasible with available NSS data by pooling central and state samples and in some cases pooling across years). Information available in the population, agricultural and livestock censuses together with studies of the kind which the agro-climatic regional plans can provide indications of potential for development and interventions needed to exploit them. This would, however, call for a shift from the current preoccupation with generating additional employment in the present as the over-riding objective to giving much greater emphasis to creating assets which by augmenting production and improving socioeconomic infrastructure can lead to a sustained higher level of employment and incomes.

Within the framework of the above broad approach, it is possible to provide earmarked allocations for schemes to ensure minimum standard of amenities and acquisition of assets for scheduled castes and tribes; and for assistance (by way of subsidies or loans) to enable them to finance higher education and skill acquisition. These would make better sense and be more effective when they are part of an overall regional plan.

Targeting

The other, and in many ways more important, issue is targeting. The search for ways to reduce chances of mistargeting has largely focused on more effective monitoring of beneficiary selection; creating credible checks against mistargeting; and creating incentives for 'self selection'. Incomes are notoriously difficult to ascertain. And once it is known to determine eligibility for benefits, there is a strong general incentive to understate incomes. It is better to rely on more easily verifiable attributes (family size, landholding, caste, etc.) associated with poverty. Though this does not eliminate scope for falsification, it certainly reduces the scope for it compared to the income criterion.

Clearly, targeting errors can be reduced if conditions of eligibility and/or the scale of benefits are so defined as to reduce the incentives for those above the poverty line to get into the programme. Insisting on a certain portion of beneficiaries being drawn from poor/vulnerable groups (SC, ST, women) and providing wage employment in employment schemes at wages somewhat below the market/minimum wage rate and at locations away from the residence would be a more effective way of reaching target population than relying on discretionary authority. The reservation idea is now incorporated in the guidelines for all ministry of rural development projects. But the idea of lowering wage rates on work programmes below the legal minimum is not favoured: the government cannot violate its own laws!

Targeting has not only a class/individual dimension, but also a spatial aspect. The poor being unevenly distributed between regions, spatial targeting is an important, but relatively neglected aspect. Except in Jawahar Rojgar Yojana, allocations of PA programme outlays between and within states are not systematically related to poverty, unemployment or deficiency in basic amenities. Richer states generally tend to have larger resources and plan outlays per capita. One would expect the PA programme allocations to correct this imbalance at least to some degree. Data for the early 1980s (Rao, 1992) suggest that, if anything, states with low incidence of poverty had higher outlay on PA programmes both in absolute per capita terms and as a proportion of total state plan outlays.

There is thus a strong case for rationalising the criteria for spatial allocation along the following lines. Allocations for all employment and production oriented PA schemes should be pooled and distributed between states, and within states, in proportion to the absolute number of poor or preferably, income deficit and the number of unemployed. Funds for programmes to ensure a minimum standard of basic amenities (elementary education, health care, water supply and access to roads) can be similarly pooled and distributed in proportion to the magnitude of deficiency in relation to the accepted minimum levels of facility. This would greatly add to the transparency of the programme and its effectiveness.

Accountability

Public accountability for ensuring proper choice of beneficiaries and proper use of funds remains a serious problem. Efforts to publicise the scale and nature of PA programmes in a particular block or district, the criteria by which beneficiaries are selected, the specific benefits to which they are entitled under each programme, and the procedures for availing them have not been effective. Even when the information is available, there are no institutional mechanisms for making complaints or seeking redressal of grievances. Involvement of MLAs, MPs and other local leaders—whether formally as members of advisory committees or because of their ability to exert informal pressure—has not helped. On the contrary, irrespective of their party affiliation, politicians tend to use the opportunity to influence choice of schemes, locations and beneficiaries under these programmes as a source of power, and as instruments for consolidating their political base and often for personal gain. Surprisingly, neither elected representatives nor local cadres of political parties (even when they belong to the opposition) have shown much interest in taking up these issues.

Non-governmental organisations do take up such issues, but they are far too few to make more than a localised impact. Though numerous, they differ greatly in terms of focus, motivation, effectiveness. Some are concentrated on particular activities like education, social welfare and watershed development. Some are concerned with development activities covering several sectors. Funding sources differ. Most use their contacts with sympathetic government officials to secure support and resources for activities in their area. Some get funding from institutional agencies and foreign foundations. Several have innovative programmes to mobilise beneficiaries and building local institutions to make more effective use of government programmes.

NGOs also play a role in making people aware of the various PA programmes and benefits available under them; and interceding with concerned government agencies to secure benefits for eligible people. Some have taken the role of mobilising public opinion to assert people's entitlements under various PA programmes or to press the government to allocate more resources and permit greater flexibility in programming to adapt scheme to local conditions. NGOs have played an active role in lobbying for freedom of information concerning details of public development schemes, entitlements to their benefits and the beneficiaries.

All this has contributed to raising people's consciousness of entitlements under government programme, including PA programmes. There is also a growing awareness, especially among the poor, of their importance in influencing the outcome of electoral politics. There is greater assertiveness on their part in articulating general demands in the political arena. But there is as yet no organised attempt to see that the choice of beneficiaries and implementation of local programmes in particular communities is improved. This does not seem likely unless both the power and the resources for local development are fully devolved to elected representatives of local governments.

The necessity and the wisdom of democratic decentralisation has been a recurrent theme of debates on the structure of government in India. The Constitution did not recognise or provide for representative local government institutions. By the late 1950s a review of the experience of the community development programme emphasised the need for democratically elected local governments for vigorous and equitable development in rural areas. Legislation to create *panchayati raj* bodies were passed by most states soon thereafter. However, few are keen to devolve powers and resources, and there was no legal or political compulsion to do so. Many did not even hold regular elections.

But some states (notably Karnataka and West Bengal) have tried to make it work. After a promising start the Karnataka experiment has stuttered. West Bengal's record in holding regular elections is the longest and most sustained though the devolution process has not gone as far as expected. Nevertheless both experiences have demonstrated the benefits of consultation and participation of local communities in making schemes more relevant to local felt needs, reducing duplication, ensuring that schemes are completed on schedule (often below estimated costs) and also in terms of the functioning of schools and PHCs.

The passage of the 73rd and 74th Constitutional Amendments which provides for a three tier system of local government, mandatory elections every five years and devolution development functions with authority and resources from the state to these bodies, has created a space and opportunity for decentralised participatory local development effort with in-built pressures for accountability. Implementation of these provisions is far from complete. Several states have not held local body elections as required by the Constitution. Even those which have, shown a strong unwillingness to hand over to the elected bodies the authority and the resources to decide and implement local development. They have no power over the staff assigned to them nor the flexibility to hire any personnel on their own; schemes continue to be decided and implemented by the government and its bureaucracy; practically everywhere opposition state- and central-level politicians and the bureaucracy are resisting the process vigorously and in most places successfully.

This is evident even in Kerala which has made by far the most serious and determined effort to implement the spirit of the 73rd and 74th Amendments in all its essential respects. Legislating a statutory transfer of 40 per cent of state plan resources to local bodies—Kerala is the only state to have done so —is a revolutionary step. Efforts to prepare elected members of local bodies for their new role through mass mobilisation and public education training programmes and innovative ways to promote active and meaningful people's participation have been as impressive as they are unprecedented. The process, however, is being impeded at every step by strong rearguard opposition from those with a vested interest in the current dispensation.[39] That this is being increasingly contested by local leaders cutting across party lines and insisting on effective devolution of resources and power to them gives basis for optimism that this opposition will be overcome in due course.

A number of reasons are advanced to justify the opposition. One is the argument that given the highly stratified and unequal socio-economic structure of Indian villages, the dominant landowning caste elites would effectively control power and that they are unlikely to be concerned about the welfare of the poor and the women. Reservation of a specified, substantial proportion of elected positions for SC/STs and for women is meant to give a secure space for the disadvantaged to articulate their needs in the decision-making bodies. Sceptics doubt whether this space can and will in fact be used effectively in all cases and soon. However pessimism on this account seems unwarranted, at any rate exaggerated, for several reasons.

---

39. For a detailed, illuminating and self-critical assessment of the Kerala experience see Isaac (2000).

The growing political consciousness of the so-called lower castes as well as the scheduled castes and tribes is bound to express itself in local government as well. Secondly, villages/blocks differ greatly in caste/class composition: some villages are no doubt dominated by better-off upper castes, but this is by no means the case everywhere. One must expert the outcome of decentralisation will be far from uniform. Even if initially only a fraction of elected local bodies do well, their superior performance will over a period of time act as spur to improvement in others.

The growing economic differentiation of rural society, the rapid diversification of activity and its commercialisation have loosened traditional social structures. The process will, if anything, intensify and lead to a significant realignment of the power structure in substantial parts of rural India favouring the disadvantaged groups. Such realignments will not, of course, occur in all cases spontaneously and in a manner which gives effective voice to the poor and promote their interests. The process initiated by PR and the potential for change created by it are much more important than the immediate outcomes. Interventions in the process must therefore focus on creating conditions which will facilitate and encourage, the realisation of its potential. In this context three aspects deserve special attention.

First, a great deal of knowledge and expertise is needed to assess local resources and their potential, different ways of exploiting the potential, the costs involved and raising resources. This knowledge, much of it technical in nature, is often not available locally. Strong support from state agencies and/ or non-government organisations (including educational institutions) is necessary to make it accessible to the communities and their leaders. A major change in the role of government agencies is also necessary. Instead of planning, deciding and implementing schemes on their own, as they now do, the agencies will have to play a supportive role by providing expertise, helping elected bodies to take informed decision and facilitating coordination between related schemes of different communities and in the larger regional context.

Second, the creation of democratic institutions of local government and assured representation for disadvantaged groups are necessary, but not sufficient conditions to ensure that the latters' interests are safeguarded. The determination of priorities, in the context of limited resources, inevitably involves a process of bargaining between different groups. In order for this to work in favour of the poor/vulnerable, the latter have to articulate their needs and actively persuade and/or pressure the relevant forums to take necessary action to meet their needs. None of these occur easily or automatically.

Conscious measures to encourage and strengthen institutions of civil society are essential.

Non-governmental and voluntary organisations have a particularly key role in obtaining and disseminating information on the working of government (including local government), making people aware of their entitlements and obligations, and enabling them to vent their grievances and seek redress. Besides interceding with the concerned authorities to secure benefits for the eligible and minimise leakages, they have a role in motivating and organising local communities to take active interest in the working of specific programmes and persuading bureaucracy to work with the community for improving the effectiveness of programmes. Over time they can help promote a process of more broad-based changes in institutional mechanisms for funding/managing local development activities to meet the specific local conditions. Active encouragement of NGOs and giving them ample public space is therefore highly desirable for healthy evolution of local government.

Third, rising expectations and assertiveness of the people *vis-à-vis* government and bureaucracy increases pressures on the latter to perform. But better performance often requires a significant change in the relative roles of the three elements involving, among other things, reduced power and increased accountability of bureaucracy. It also involves shifts in the relative power of those who hold political office at different levels and of different segments of the bureaucracy. Reform therefore invariably encounters resistance. Moreover if the elected *panchayat raj* institutions merely generate demands for larger devolution of resources from the state and central governments there is little stake or incentive for them to address the task of efficient use of resources. It is, therefore, imperative that local bodies should be required to mobilise their own resources to meet a significant part of the costs of their programmes and given greater control over their staff engaged in various activities.

All this implies a basic change in the relations between the state and local governments, the role of the bureaucracy and the attitudes of local governments. There are no standard blue prints for accomplishing the change. A great deal of experiment and learning from experience is inevitable. The upsetting of existing power balances between the various groups involved creates an opportunity for engineering desirable changes through a combination of sustained pressures on the system as a whole *via* the general political process along with grass roots efforts to initiate and sustain a discussion of the problem of restructuring among the concerned groups (namely the local and state level politicians, the bureaucracy and its trade unions and non-government organisations).

References

Agarwal, Bina (1994). *Field of One's Own: Gender and Land Rights in South Asia*, Sage, New Delhi.

Ahluwalia, M.S. (1978). "Rural Poverty and Agricultural Performance in India", *Journal of Development Studies*.

———. (1986). "Rural Poverty, Agricultural Production and Prices: A Re-examination" in Mellur and Desai (eds.).

Bardhan, Pranab K. (1988). "Sex Disparity in Child Survival in Rural India" in Srinivasan and Bardhan (eds.).

Bhalla, Surjit (1988). "Is Sri Lanka An Exception? A Comparative Study of Living Standards" in Srinivasan and Bardhan (eds.).

Bhalla, Surjit and Prem Vasishta (1988). "Income Distribution in India: A Re-examination" in Srinivasan and Bardhan (eds.).

Bhattacharya, N.D. Coondoo; P. Maiti and R. Mukherjee (1991). *Poverty Inequality and Prices in Rural India*, Sage, New Delhi.

Bhatty, I.Z. (1974). "Inequality and Poverty in Rural India" in Srinivasan and Bardhan (eds.).

Chen, Martha Alter (ed.) (1998). *Widows in India*, Sage, New Delhi.

Copestake, James (1992). "The Integrated Rural Development Programme" in Harris *et al.* (eds.).

Chambers, Robert (1992). "Poverty In India: Concepts, Research and Reality" in Harris *et al.* (eds.).

Dandekar, V.M. (1996). "The Indian Economy 1947-1992", Vol 2: *Population, Poverty and Employment*, Chapter 6, Sage, New Delhi.

Dreze, Jean and Amartya Sen (1989). "Public Action for Social Security: Foundations and Strategy", *STICERD*, No. 20, London School of Economics.

Gaiha, Raghav (1988). "On Measuring the Risk of Rural Poverty in India" in Srinivasan and Bardhan (eds.).

———. (2000). "Rural Public Works and the Poor: A Review of the Employment Generation Scheme in Maharashtra", *mimeo*.

GoI, Planning Commission (1962). *Report of the Committee on Distribution of Income and Levels of Living*, 2 Volumes, New Delhi.

———. (1964). *Notes of Perspectives of Development, India: 1960-61 to 1965-66*, New Delhi.

———. (1993). *Report of Expert Group on Estimates of Poverty and Number of Poor*, New Delhi.

Guhan, S. (1988). "Social Security in India: Looking One Step Ahead" in Harris *et al.* (eds.).

Harris, Barbara, S. Guhan and Robert Cassen (eds.) (1992). *Poverty in India: Research and Policy*, Oxford University Press, New Delhi.

Hazari, R.K. (1967). *The Structure of the Corporate Prive Sector—A Study of Concentration, Ownership and Control*, Asia Publishing Home, Bombay.

International Institute of Population Studies (1995). *National Family Health Survey, 1992-93*, Mumbai.

Issac, Thomas and Richard W. Franke (2000). *Local Democracy and Development: Peoples Campaign for Decentralised Planning in Kerala*, Leftword, New Delhi.

Kansal, S.M. (1965). "Preliminary Estimate of Total Consumption Expenditure in India 1950-51 to 1963-64", Indian Statistical Institute Planning Unit, *Discussion Paper 5*, Delhi.

Krishnaji N. and T.N. Krishnan (eds.) (2000). *Public Support for Food Security: The Public Distribution System in India*, Sage, New Delhi.

Kumar, Gopala Krishna and Frances Stewart (1988). "Tackling Malnutrition: What Can Targeted Nutritional Interventions Achieve?" in Harris *et al.* (eds.).

Lipton, Michael (1983). "Poverty, Undernutrition and Hunger", World Bank, *Staff Working Paper*, p. 23, Washington, DC.

————. (1983). *The Poor and the Ultra Poor: Characteristics, Explanation and Politics*, Development Research Department, CDS, Survey.

————. (1985). "Poor and the Poorest", World Bank, *Discussion Paper* 25, Washington, DC.

Mahendra Dev, S. (1995). "India's Maharashtra Employment Guarantee Scheme: Lessons and Experience" in Frederick Von Braun (ed.), *Employment for Poverty Reduction and Food Security*, International Food Policy Research Institute, Washington, DC.

Mellor, John and Gunvant Desai (ed.) (1986). *Agricultural Change and Rural Poverty*, Oxford University Press, Delhi.

Meenakshi, J.V. (2000). "Food Consumption Trends in India: A Regional Analysis" in Krishnajis and Krishnan (eds.).

Minhas, B.S. (1985). *Validation of Large-Scale Sample Survey Data in Case of NSS Estimates of Household Consumption Expenditure*, Sankhya: A series B Vol. 50 - Part I.

Minhas, B.S. and S.M. Kansal (1989). "Comparison of NSS and CSO Estimates of Private Consumption: Some Observation Based on 1983 Data", *The Journal of Income and Wealth*, Vol. III, November 1.

Minhas, B.S.; S.M. Kansal and L.R. Jain (1988). "The Incidence of Urban Poverty in States 1970-71 to 1983 in Harris", Guhan and Casen (eds.).

National Institute of Nutrition—Annual Reports on the NNMB Nutrition Surveys.

Nayyar, Rohini (1991). *Rural Poverty in India: An Analysis of Inter State Differences*, Oxford University Press, Mumbai.

NCAER (1987). *Changes in the Structure of Household Income and Distribution of Gains in the Rural Household Sector: An All-India Inter Temporal Analysis 1970-71, 1981-82.*

Osmani, S. (ed.) (1992). *Nutrition and Poverty*, Clarendeon, Oxford.

Parikh, K.S. and T.N. Srinivasan (1990). "Poverty Alleviation Policies in India: Food Consumption Subsidies, Food Production Subsidies and Employment Generation", *mimeo*, Indira Gandhi Institute for Development Research, Mumbai.

Pradhan, Basant K. *et al.* (2000). "Rural Urban Disparities, Income Distribution, Expenditure Pattern and Social Sector", *Economic and Political Weekly*.

Probe Team (1999). *Public Report on Basic Education*, Oxford University Press, New Delhi.

Rakesh Mohan and P. Thottan (1992). "The Regional Spread of Urbanisation, Industrialisation and Urban Poverty" in Harris *et al.* (ed.).

Rao, C.H.H. and H. Linneman (eds.) (1996). *Economic Reforms and Poverty Alleviation in India*, Sage, New Delhi.

Rao, Subba (1992). "Interventions to Fill Nutrition Gaps at the Household Level" in Harris *et. al.* (eds.).

Radhakrishna R. and C. Ravi (1992). "Effects of Growth, Relative Prices and Preferences on Food and Nutrition", *Indian Economic Review*.

Ravillion, Martin and Gaurav Datt (1995). "Poverty in India", Background paper to the 1995 World Development Report, *Working Paper Series* 1405, World Bank, Washington, DC.

Rudra, Ashok (1974). "Minimum Level of Living: A Statistical Examination" in Srinivasan and Bardhan (ed.).

————. (1978). *The Basic Needs Concept and Its Implementation in Indian Development Planning*, ILO, ARTEP, Bangkok.

Sahn, David E. (ed.) (1989). *Seasonal Variability in Third World Agriculture: The Consequences for Food Security* John Hopkins University Press, Baltimore.

Sen, Abijit (1996). "Economic Reforms, Employment and Poverty: Trends and Options", *Economic and Political Weekly*.

————. (2000). "Consumer Spending and its Distribution...", *Economic and Political Weekly*, December.

Sen, Amartya (1985). *Commodities, and Capabilities*, North Holland, Amsterdam.

Sen, Amartya K. and S. Sengputa (1988). "Family and Food: Sex Bias in Poverty" in Srinivasan and Bardhan (eds.).

Srinivasan, T.N. (1981). "Malnutrition: Some Measurement and Policy Issues", *Journal of Developing Economics*.

Srinivasan, T.N. and P.K. Bardhan (eds.) (1988). *Rural Poverty in South Asia*, OUP, Delhi. Srinivasan, T.N., P.N. Radhakrishnan and A. Vaidyanathan (1974).

Streeten, Paul and S.J. Burki (1978). "Basic Needs: Some Issues", *World Development*.

Sundaram, K. and S.D. Tendulkar (1988). "Towards an Explanation of Inter Regional Variations in Poverty and Unemployment in India" in Srinivasan and Bardhan (eds.).

Sukhatme, P.V. (ed.) (1992). *Newer Concepts in Nutrition and Their Implications for Policy*, Maharashtra Association for Cultivation of Science, Pune.

Suryanarayana, M.H. (2000). "How Real is the Secular Decline in Rural Poverty", *Economic and Political Weekly*.

Suryanarayana, M.H. and N.S. Iyengar (1986). "On Reliability of NSS Data", *Economic and Political Weekly*.

Swaminathan, Madhura (2000). *Weakening Welfare: The Public Distribution of Food in India*, Leftword, New Delhi.

UNDP (2000). *Human Development Report*.

————. (various years). *Human Development Papers*. United Nations, Department of Economic and Social Affairs, 1975.

Vaidyanathan, A. (1986a). "On the Validity of NSS Consumption Data", *Economic and Political Weekly*.

————. (1986b). "Food Consumption and the Size of the People: Some Indian Evidence", *Economic and Political Weekly*.

————. (1992). "On Measurement of Nutrition and Health Status".

————. (1994a). "Political Economy of the Evolution of Anti-Poverty Programmes" in T.S. Sathyamurthy (ed.).

————. (1994b). "Second India Series Revisited, Food and Agriculture", *mimeo*, MIDS, Chennai.

————. (1996). "Employment Situation: Some Emerging Perspectives", *Economic and Political Weekly*.

Vaidyanathan, A. and P.R.G. Nair (eds.) (2000). *Elementary Education in Rural India: A Grass Roots View*, Sage, New Delhi.

Visaria, Pravin (1978). "Size of Holdings, Living Standard and Employment in Western India, 1972-73", World Bank, *Staff Working Paper*.

————. (1979). "Poverty and Development in India: An Analysis of Rural Evidence", World Bank, *Staff Working Paper*.

Visaria, Pravin and Anil Gumber (1996). *Utilisation of and Expenditure on Health Care in India 1986-87*, Gujarat Institute of Development Studies, Ahmedabad.

————. (2000). "Alternative Estimate of Poverty in India", *The Economic Times*, June 29.

Walker, Thomas S. and James Rayan (1990). *Village and Household Economics in India's Semi Arid Tropics*, Johns Hopkins University Press, Baltimore.

Kale Memorial Lecture delivered at Gokhale Institute of Economics and Politics, Pune, December 10, 2000.

Economic and Political Weekly, May 26-June 1, 2001.

Economic Developments in India, Vol. 45.

6

Fifty Years of India: A Journey in Time

ASHOK V. DESAI

We do not think of our own times as history. But if we did, we would find them far more interesting and educative. It will never be discovered whether there was a temple of Rama at the precise spot of Babri *masjid* in Faizabad, also known as Ayodhya; if it is discovered, the knowledge will still be irrelevant. But it is possible to find out why suddenly, after 15 years of inflation and shortages, prices began to fall in 1952, the year in which I joined college. And study of that singular event might tell us something about what to do in our own times, when competition is increasing and inflation is coming down.

Pre-independence Period

My first memories are of the war. We moved to Poona just after it began; I remember tanks driving down Ferguson Road. At the foot of the hills in Deccan Gymkhana, where you today find a string of academic institutions, including Brihanmaharashtra College of Commerce and the Film Institute, the area was a wasteland full of ravines; that is where the British army bivouacked. The agricultural college grew potatoes and heaped them along its main road, and covered them up with earth to preserve them. Unfortunately they rotted; after a few months, that road stank to the high heavens. In the meanwhile, in Bengal across the country, skeletons were walking the streets of Calcutta; one by one, they lay down on the street side and died. The scavengers were paid extra for carrying off the corpses, which were cremated *en masse*. Three million people died in the Bengal famine of 1943—a number exceeded only by the casualties of the mass riots of 1947 and 1948.

My foremost memory of my childhood is of shortages and inflation. Rationing of foodgrains was introduced in 1939; it was very different from rationing in recent times. For it was illegal to sell grains except through ration shops; and the ban on private trade was quite effective. So the weekly visit to the ration shop and the time spent in queues were necessary if one was not to starve. That was one reason why there was such mass starvation in Bengal:

there was no open market in which foodgrains could be bought. The other was that trains were requisitioned for the movement of troops and war material. Everything that the railways transported required some official approval. And transport by trucks was virtually non-existent. The trucks in use then were imported 2 or 4 tonnes Bedford trucks; transport by them was expensive, and was largely confined to cities. A good deal of the goods still moved by bullock carts everywhere, and in cities by handcarts.

As Friedrich List pointed out in 1836, transport costs determine the location of economic activity. Cities are concentrations of people; they are nodes of purchasing power, and attract goods from the countryside as a magnet attracts iron fillings. The costlier a commodity is to transport, the closer it is produced to the city. Thus a city is surrounded by concentric circles growing vegetables, foodgrains, meat and so on. And as the city grows, these circles expand, costs of transporting their produce go up, and the cost of living in the city rises. The high transport costs kept down the size of cities; and amongst them, those that had suburban train systems grew bigger. Because of their suburban trains, Bombay and Calcutta were the biggest cities of that time; their population was 4-5 million. The rest were tiny by comparison: Delhi and Madras had half a million, Poona and Bangalore 1,00,000-2,00,000, and most of the rest hardly approached 1,00,000. The growth of cities in postwar India owes much to the fall in transport costs relatively to people's incomes—to larger and more fuel-efficient trucks, lower real costs of petrol and diesel, and rising purchasing power.

The shortages of the 1940s were partly due to lack of transport; but above all they were due to purchasing power that was far in excess of the goods available. Few industrial goods were being produced in the country at that time; and imports were restricted because the government had requisitioned all shipping and was using most of the shipping space for military transport.

The obverse of the shortage of goods was the excess of purchasing power, that arose out of the new theory of war finance that the British government was trying out. John Maynard Keynes, the Cambridge economist, worked in the British treasury during first world war, which was largely financed by borrowing. From its experience he drew the lesson that the interest rate was the price of money; the government could make it what it liked by regulating the supply of money. Money itself is an interest-free loan from the public to the government; and the more money people have, the more government bonds they will buy, the higher will be the price of those bonds, and the lower the interest rate the government has to pay. Keynes was the economic brain behind the British conduct of Second World War; following his theory, the British government issued far more money in that war than in the previous one, and thereby kept the interest costs of the war low. The British government in India followed the home government's lead and followed a cheap money policy.

However, if people have more money in their hands, they will buy more of everything, not just government bonds. Hence unless supply of goods and services responds to demand, cheap money can mean expensive goods—a policy of releasing more money can lead to inflation. In Britain the wartime government kept inflation in check by very strict rationing; for instance, milk was rationed, and people got only so many eggs a week. In India, however, the rationing was less comprehensive and effective, so inflation was rampant in unrationed goods, and shortages were chronic.

It was realised even at that time that a market becomes a black market only because the government declares it so, and that if there were no rationing there would be no black market. The view was often expressed that if only the government abolished rationing, prices would rise and ration out the goods, and shortages would disappear. When he became food minister in 1948, Rafi Ahmed Kidwai tried out this theory; inflation shot up, however, and he succumbed to the outcry and reintroduced rationing after a few months.

But all this suddenly changed in 1952, the year in which we joined college. Foodgrain shortages disappeared, prices started falling, and the feeling of siege that had lasted for 15 years began to dissipate. What changed? Everyone at that time thought that the end of the Korean War eased inflation all over the world. This was no doubt partly true; prices of importables certainly stabilised—and many more things were imported then than now. But foodgrains had never been imported, and yet inflation in food prices eased. What changed in the domestic economy? If the question had been answered then, the answer would have been relevant in the late 1990s, which saw a similar easing of inflation.

The Period of 50s and 60s: Nehruvian Socialism

Although the end of inflation was little understood or analysed, it had enormous political effects. Right till 1952, the new political rulers had felt embattled. They were so taken up by short-term economic problems that they had no time to think ahead or do anything ambitious. But in 1950, Sardar Vallabhbhai Patel died, leaving the field open for Nehru. Between 1952 and

1956 he, with the help of P.C. Mahalanobis, worked out a strategy of state-led, import-substituting industrialisation. There followed nine years of rapid industry-led growth from 1956 till 1965. This was the period when my generation graduated and went to work.

The interesting thing about this period is the contrast between what people thought of it at that time, and what they think about it now. I can think of hardly any contemporary voice against it. Amongst politicians, Rajagopalachari opposed Nehru's policies, and set up the Swatantra party in opposition to the Congress; but he attracted little support, and never came close to power even in his native Tamil Nadu. Amongst economists, B.R. Shenoy fought a lonely battle; but he too attracted no support. The policies were supposed to be directed against capitalists; but industrialists did not protest either. How is it that policies that are generally regarded today as wrong were so widely accepted then?

Part of the answer lies in the urban prosperity of that time. The economy was growing fast, industry was expanding, and employment was rising. Demand was buoyant, and it was easy to make money. The system made industrialisation easy. All one had to do was to borrow from IDBI or ICICI, sell one's shares to UTI and build factories. So industrialists were happy, and so were those they employed.

Industrialists were also happy because British capital was driven out at that time. There was no blatant nationalisation or expropriation; the instrument used was exchange control. The government policed remittance of profits and generally obstructed it. Without any explicit statement, the message was given: that British enterprise was not welcome. And the signal was taken; British managing agents sold out the tea gardens and jute mills and left. They went to Kenya and set up a rival tea industry which later took away India's market. But their sell-out made many Indian industrialists rich. Hence, their support for the government.

This period was particularly good for white-collar workers; and if the middle class was happy, the press reflected it. During the independence movement, one element from which the Congress drew support was educated young men. Opportunities for white-collar employment were poor under British rule. Industry was concentrated in the three major ports. British firms put British employees in senior jobs; there was a glass ceiling beyond which few Indians rose. The nationalist agitation made British employers wary of taking unfamiliar people; so personal recommendations and guarantees carried much weight. Indian industrialists also tended to favour employees of their own caste and language. When I started work, most applications for jobs started with an assurance that the employee came from a respectable family. But during the rapid growth of the 1950s and 1960s, the discrimination in employment began to break down. Hence the rising middle class was quite satisfied with the regime of that kind.

Not everyone was. The early 1950s were the time of the Samyukta Maharashtra agitation. I remember Nehru coming to speak at Chowpatty; we tried to go, but were beaten-off by the police, which had cordoned off the Chowpatty against Samyukta Maharashtra agitators. They also invaded Sydenham College and tried to make us join the strike. Further east, there was an agitation for the break-up of Hyderabad state and unification of Telugu-speaking areas. That was also the time when DMK emerged as a Tamil separatist party. Shiv Sena came later. All this subnationalism was about employment for sons of the soil; the great cities and the provincial governments were too cosmopolitan for local tastes. Nehru opposed the subnationalisms and was defeated by them. But between them and the original Congress nationalism, the middle class obviously preferred the latter.

The trouble with Nehruvian socialism was that it was unsustainable. Its fragility became evident when rains failed in 1965. Foodgrain production at that time was 83 million tonnes; the US gave us 11 million tonnes free that year, and staved off large-scale starvation. I was then a bachelor; I was teaching in Bombay University, and used to forage around in restaurants of Flora Fountain and Colaba. Prime Minister Lal Bahadur Shastri forced restaurants to close on Mondays to save food, and I starved.

That socialist experiment had consequences, some of which were immediate, whilst some are continuing even now. Immediately, once US aid was scaled down in 1966, the payments deficit became unsustainable, and the rupee was devalued. Then, in the absence of aid, government investment had to come down; a three-year plan holiday was declared, and construction of new public sector plants came to a halt. Industries built up in a booming economy behind impregnable import barriers proved unviable; in the early 1970s, thousands of engineering plants and textile mills closed down. West Bengal, which had a large engineering industry, was especially hard hit; its woes led to the eclipse of the Congress, and the rise of CPI (M), which continues to rule West Bengal to this day. Nationally too, economic adversity raised doubts about policies and split the Congress. And the public enterprises, a legacy of that time, still languish, after 11 years of disinvestment and privatisation. Thus

1966 turned out to be a turning point in the nation's history. It was in my history too. That is when my honeymoon with socialism ended. I left my reader's post in Bombay University and went to Delhi to join Delhi Cloth Mills as chief economist.

Seventies: The Turning Point

We did not have to wait long for the next turning point. It came with the oil crisis: in October 1973, the Arab countries took control of their own oil production and raised the oil price fourfold. The blow was both external and internal. Externally, the balance of payments again became unsustainable, and the government had to scramble to borrow money from abroad. Internally, price rise suddenly accelerated, and led to strident demands for wage increases. The government itself was in desperate trouble, and could not meet the wage demands. Hence came the railway strike in 1975, which Indira Gandhi brutally depressed. Soon resistance spread; to suppress it, Indira Gandhi declared emergency.

The emergency is remembered for its excesses—the large-scale imprisonment of political opponents, the mass sterilisation campaign, Sanjay Gandhi's mob rule. Some would also remember it because government servants started going to work on time. But the most important event was the rapid turnaround of the balance of payments—by 1976, the crisis was over for India, and payments became perfectly manageable. Even the mini-oil crisis of 1978-79 could be tackled with great ease. And importantly, many developing countries borrowed heavily in those years, but India did not. All of them had defaulted on their international debts; India had not taken recourse to private loans, and so escaped catastrophe. Then in the early 1980s, oil began to flow from Bombay High, and India's balance of payments looked extremely solid.

By the early 1980s so many developing countries had gone bankrupt, and international bankers were short of borrowers; India, with its solid balance of payments, looked very attractive. Bankers, especially Japanese ones, poured money into India in the 1980s; that was the root of the next payments crisis in 1991.

That crisis has given the 1980s a bad name. The general impression is that Rajiv messed it up. Elected to power in 1985 with the highest proportion of votes ever won by the Congress, he ruined the economy by borrowing too much from abroad, and the polity by overturning the Shah Bano judgment of the Supreme Court.

But the way I see it, the reality was more complex and interesting. India is a peculiar democracy; it is the only functional democracy in which political parties have no stable, legitimate, established sources of income. Most democratic countries have a leftist party supported by trade unions, and a rightist party supported by businessmen; some nowadays have a green party supported by an environmental offshoot of the left. All these parties have loyal supporters, who vote for them, support them and when necessary, fund them. In effect, therefore, they are voluntary organisations funded by members. Out of the contributions they maintain offices and support leaders.

In India, however, it is just the other way round: it is not supporters who fund parties, it is parties that reward members. Thus, trade unions are virtually penniless. When they win wage increases, their members may pay them something out of generosity. Some unions run employment rackets. But trade unions have no regular sources of sustenance. This is equally true of parties. Hence, it is important for parties to get into government, and to siphon off government funds.

This pattern essentially emerged in the period between the oil crisis of 1973 and the payments crisis of 1991. Indira Gandhi had started a business selling government favours to businessmen for money in the early 1970s. Lalit Narayan Mishra was her chief collector. When he was killed, other collectors emerged; some of them are still active in the Congress. But the real need for party funding arose with the emergence of political competition—that is, after Janta Party won power in 1977. Over the 1980s, access to money came to be the primary aim of getting into power.

Politics based on the capture and sale of state power is expensive and unstable. It is expensive because there are too many political forums and hence too many politicians in our country; the fact that politics is an occupation which requires no training makes the supply of politicians highly elastic. And politics is unstable because the chances to collect money are concentrated in the hands of ministers. They are a minute proportion of the vast corps of politicians. Unless they keep collecting enough and feeding the hungry army of supporters, the latter will break away. This is the root cause of dissidence, and of a multiplicity of small parties in this country.

If parties were divided on ideology and could attract loyal supporters, they would need to milk the state for money less. Every once in a while, politicians have tried to build up such parties. Jayaprakash Narayan started a mass movement in 1973 directed against Indira Gandhi's corruption; but he was too old and sick to carry it far. V.P. Singh attacked the nexus between industrialists and Congress politicians in 1985 when he was finance minister; no wonder he was thrown out of the Congress. Then he tried to set up a party of the oppressed, starting with the *dalits*. But Rajiv saw the threat he posed to the Congress, and outmanoeuvred him. The BJP has similarly tried to find a broad Hindu constituency by stirring up Ayodhya. The ploy worked brilliantly—but not so well as to give it an absolute majority anywhere. Repeatedly, the Indian people have rejected ideological appeals; and so they have got fragile governments based on alliances of kleptocratic, opportunistic politicians.

Economically speaking, the 1980s were a golden period. The Hindu rate of growth of 3.5 per cent prevalent from the 1950s till the 1980s was breached; growth went up to 5.5 per cent, well distributed between agriculture and industry. Just as in 1952, as economic constraints were relaxed, the politicians also felt more inclined to experiment. Thus the first experiments in relaxation of both industrial licensing and import licensing were made in the 1980s. And each time they worked. Following relaxation of import licensing in the late 1970s, exports zoomed. That led to progressive relaxation over the 1980s, albeit within the old policy framework. Similarly, V.P. Singh's relaxation of industrial licensing in 1985 led to a great industrial boom. Thus although the 1980s created the conditions for the payments crisis that followed, they also saw experiments that gave politicians greater confidence to experiment with liberalisation in the 1990s.

The Crisis of 1991

Still, they would not have experimented with it if there had been no crisis in 1991. I handled the post of Chief Economic Advisor in the finance ministry from 1991 to 1993, and had a small role in the reforms that were then carried out. What I remember most was the volume of resistance and obstruction. Politicians, without any distinction of party or ideology, did their best to sabotage the reforms. The strongest opposition was within the Congress. For instance, we tried to reduce the subsidy on fertiliser. There was a massive revolt in parliament. It appointed a Joint Parliamentary Committee (JPC) headed by Balasaheb Vikhe Patil, who has the knack of landing on his feet: he was in the Congress then, and now he is a minister in the BJP government at the centre. The JPC he headed sat on the issue as long as it could. Then it made a report that it was sure would be rejected by the government, thereby keeping subsidies intact. It recommended that the subsidies on nitrogenous fertilisers should continue, and those on phosphatic and potassic fertilisers should be abolished. Nitrogenous fertiliser subsidies were the major ones; if they could not be reduced, the government would give up in disappointment. Narasimha Rao accepted the report and abolished the subsidies on nitrogenous and phosphatic fertilisers. But they came back in another guise before long. Vikhe Patil and his politician brothers certainly knew which side of bread was buttered. Similarly, I drafted a proposal for abolishing the sugar subsidy in phases. But suddenly it went off the agenda; I heard that Sharad Pawar, who was then defence minister but always a friend of Maharashtra sugar producers, had stopped it.

The Reforms

In spite of the obstruction, the little reforms we managed to implement worked beautifully. They engendered a magnificent industrial boom. It ended in 1996. But the investment and technology it brought in fuelled fierce competition in industry. For seven years, industrial prices rose less than agricultural prices. So villagers' purchasing power went up; today, a whole range of consumer goods from soap to motor cycles have found big markets in the villages. The millennia-old curse of rural poverty is lifting. With the lifting of industrial licensing, anybody could produce anything. As a result, people have diversified their consumption habits. That is one reason why, despite years of bad harvests, we have a surplus of foodgrains: people have more things to consume, and are eating less rice and wheat.

As industry has become more competitive, the balance of payments has improved year after year; the current account last year recorded a surplus for the first time in 15 years. The last surplus, in 1978-79, was due to massive foreign aid following the oil crisis; if we exclude foreign aid, the last previous surplus was in 1954-55. This year India has virtually stopped taking foreign aid; instead it has lent money to the International Monetary Fund. When I entered Sydenham, India was paying its way; today, as I approach the end of my career, India is solvent again. That is the achievement of our reforms of the early 1990s.

The biggest changes are psychological. Without the financial independence that the reforms brought to India, the BJP government would never have dared test nuclear weapons. Without the liberalisation of exchange control, there would have been no software boom. Our success in software changed the world's image of India. When I went to Germany in the 1960s, I used to think the Germans were the most intelligent people in the world, because even their children could speak German. So I was taken aback when, last year, a German said to me, "You Indians are very intelligent, aren't you?" He was referring to our software engineers.

Within the country, the reforms changed the image of businessmen. In the days of controls, every businessman was looked upon as a criminal. Today all that opprobrium is gone. Today politicians court businessmen; the balance of power has been reversed.

This is where the greatest promise lies, as well as the greatest peril. Although the status of the businessman has changed, his mentality has not; he is still the petty deal-cutter. It is still the norm for individual businessmen to approach the government for favours, and for politicians to use state power to exploit businessmen. Ours is about the most protectionist country in the world; and if you want to know why, just ask who asked for the numerous anti-dumping duties: behind each duty is an industrialist, and in many industries he has a monopoly. Ours is also one of the world's most corrupt countries. Most corruption is related to business, and for every bribe-taker there is a bribe-giver. Corruption is inevitable when a powerless businessman confronts an official backed by the power of the state.

This will change only when businessmen combine in their dealings with the government. Every import duty that benefits a businessman hurts another; if they act together, there will be no import duties. Every bribe helps a businessman against his competitors; if businessmen deal collectively with the government, they will ask for and get an honest administration.

And it is not only a good administration we need. We also need a social conscience. Today the number of the poor is no less than a decade ago; no fewer brides are being burnt, no fewer children are dropping out of school. Our society needs compassion, humanity, sensitivity. Now that businessmen are emerging as the country's leaders, these needs have become their responsibility. We need philanthropy; but that philanthropy must come with a business sense, with a calculation of how we can make people better-off. Does our system of private and public health care make our people healthy? Are there no cheaper ways of improving people's health? P.V. Sukhatme used to say that waterborne diseases of the stomach are the biggest source of both sickness and malnutrition and that protected water supply would make people both better fed and healthier. Our schools are a prison for children; just to make children literate and numerate, they do not have to spend seven years in school. With today's computer technology, with VSAT and television, it is possible to teach children much more, much faster.

Thus, the quest for efficiency, speed and cost-effectiveness, which is the heart of business and industry, affect every aspect of our life, including government and social services. Now that business has been freed from shackles, our CEOs and managers should no longer confine themselves to their own businesses. They must make the business of the nation their own.

Lecture delivered at Sydenham College, Mumbai, July, 2003.
Economic Developments in India, Vol. 70.

7

Public Governance

N.R. NARAYANA MURTHY

Globalisation

Globalisation has led to liberalised trade. It has increased foreign direct investment (FDI) in this country and other forms of capital flows like FII, portfolio investment, etc. In today's global world every country must continually strive to create a hospitable environment to attract capital and technology. There is no doubt at all in our minds that if we want to solve the problem of poverty and to redeem the pledge of the founding fathers of this nation, that all of us made to Mahatma Gandhi that we will strive hard to wipe the tears from the eyes of the poor and the weak. The only way we can do is to make sure that we create more and more jobs, to make sure that everybody has good shelter, good food, good healthcare and good education. And to do this it is very clear that capital and technology are needed, some of it may be available in India, some of it may need to come from outside.

Now, let me talk a little bit about India today. Our nation of a billion people is still far off from achieving many of the goals that our founding fathers set for this nation.

- Our per capita GDP is only about $ 520 or if you want to look at the purchasing power parity, it is about $ 2250 with 35 per cent of the population living below the official poverty line.

- Our adult literacy rate is about 65 per cent.

- Life expectancy is only 62.9 years.

- We are 124th on the human development index out of 174 nations.

- Sixty-five per cent of our population do not have access to essential drugs.

- Sixty-nine per cent of the population do not have access to sanitation.

- Half of the children in this country are underweight and undernourished.

- Only one half of the primary schools in this country have one class teacher for every two classes.

This is really what India is today. So, all of us who are the concerned citizens of this country have to look at this data dispassionately and see what is it that we can do to solve the problem of this country, how do we make sure that we have a more efficient public governance in the country. Also, we have all seen that the disparity between the urban and the rural is gradually increasing in this country. While some of the urban people have access to the latest consumer goods, while some of the urban people's life has been improved, thanks to the liberalisation, but it has not had the kind of impact that all of us wanted when we set out on this path of progress. So, I think that is something that all of us should think about that how do we make sure that we can wipe the tears of the eyes of the poor.

I do believe, in this task, the public or the government sector has a unique place in our economy. Hence, it has to be very responsible as it has an important task of facilitating creation of a fair society.

Democracy

We have always talked a lot about democracy. I have listened to several of our political leaders, several of our corporate leaders and bureaucrats. When we go to outside India and the first thing they say is that one of the greatest achievements of India is that it has had democracy for 55 years. It is true, I am indeed proud of democracy for 55 years, but let's remember democracy does not end with elections which takes place once in 5 years. In fact, democracy just starts there. To me, the aim of democracy is to realise the aspirations of people in a transparent and fair manner with full accountability to the people. This requires an effective governing system and I do believe this is where we have indeed failed. What is an effective governing system. Following are the pillars of an effective governing system. You need:

- A vision and theme.
- Effective leadership.
- Focus on the citizens of the country i.e. focus on the customers.
- Fairness and transparency in every action of the government.
- Accountability of the government and the public governance system.
- Measurable objectives so that we can grow and become better and better.

Vision and Theme

Let me first take up vision and theme. I believe that positive change can be brought about only with a vision. For instance, Mahatma Gandhi created a great vision for our independence and raised the aspirations of our people. Millions of people sacrificed all their comforts and perhaps several thousand sacrificed their lives to make sure that we become a free republic. That was a grand vision. There was a great theme in that. Similarly, Jawaharlal Nehru created a vision for modern India. He realised his vision by building temples of modern India such as institutions of higher learning, the IITs, IIMs, AIIMS, etc. and steel plants, dams, etc.

Effective Leadership

The second thing that we need for effective governance is effective leadership. Effective public governance has to be championed by inspirational leaders who will act as change agents in achieving progress. Leaders have to achieve change by raising the aspirations of people. In fact, as all of you know, it is aspirations that build civilisations. Now these effective leaders have to walk the talk. There is no doubt at all that the leaders who want to be successful will have to demonstrate their belief in sacrifice, in commitment and hard work. Unless we walk the talk, unless the people do not see any dissonance between our walk and our talk, it is unlikely that we will have great leaders. Let me give a great example of this, I will take from J.R.D's life itself.

For instance, he personally inspected each of the toilets in the Boeing 707 in which he was travelling when he was the Chairman of Air India. It was this kind of attention to details, it was this kind of concern for the people at the back of the plane, people in the economy that made Air India under J.R.D's stewardship one of the premier commercial airlines in the world at that point of time.

The other aspect of the effective leadership is this. Mr. K.K. Nohria has referred to it; it is the ability of a leader to put up public good ahead of private good. He or she will have to realise that if you put public good ahead of private good then private good will automatically follow. That I believe is the fundamental principle on which developed societies have been built and we in India need to absorb that message and use that principle. In my own case, I have realised that by putting the interest of the corporation ahead of my own interest, I have every time benefitted in the long term.

Focus on the Citizen

Then the next issue that I would like to talk about is focus on the citizen. I believe that just as the survival of the corporation depends on satisfying and exceeding customers' expectation, I do believe that even in public governance we need to have the client first mindset, we need to have citizen first mindset. Unless, we make sure that we have bureaucrats and political leaders who understand this principle, I am not sure whether we will redeem the pledge that we have made to the founding fathers of this country.

Fairness and Transparency

The next important thing is fairness and transparency. We have to ensure fairness to all the stakeholders of the public governance systems. Who are these people?

- The Civil Society.
- Other people in the government.
- The Private Sector which is a partner on this path to progress and, finally
- Financial Investors.

Whether we like it or not, unless the financial investors in the private sector within India and outside India have great confidence in our ability to use the finances efficiently, to use our resources efficiently, I don't think we will have access to much resource. Whether it is the multilateral agencies which fund us, whether it is FDI, whether it is a portfolio investment, whether it is the investment from our own institutions, it is obviously necessary for these institutions to have full trust and confidence in the public governance system, that system will indeed deliver to the citizens what they have talked about.

The Value System

I believe that the value system will provide a competitive edge in today's nation building. Every nation is in global competition to attract strategic resources. These strategic resources could be human resources in the case of a country like the United States or perhaps some of the developed nations. It could be capital in the case of countries like India. I believe that a value system, which obviously translates to transparency, and fairness with justice is absolutely important for us to make sure that India comes ahead of other nations in the eyes of the investors, in the eyes of other nations who want to do business with us.

Accountability

Next is accountability. Accountability is probably the most important thing that is lacking in the public governance system today. The private sector, fortunately, has a self-correcting market mechanism. For example, if a corporation wastes its resources, then the corporation is likely to make less profit and then people will understand that their earnings per share will be affected and nobody will invest in that corporation, nobody will buy the shares, and people will run away from it. On the other hand, most often in the government there is no system of accountability at all. Let me give you a few examples of lack of accountability. First, after 50 years we are still ranked 124th among 174 countries and we are 55th among 88 developing countries. Forget about the developed countries. One way is to say, look we don't believe in that system of HDI. Another way to say, is there a lesson in what those guys are saying? Can we learn something from it? What is it that other countries are doing? Can we move up in that? Will it help our people? I think, that probably is a mindset that may help us in the long-term rather than saying we don't believe in this kind of index.

Second, is our inability to prevent starvation deaths in the midst of plenty? All of us know last year how several hundreds of people, probably thousands, and died while there was plenty. We had 180 million tonnes of foodgrains in the country but we couldn't somehow deliver those foodgrains to those children who were dying of hunger. I think that is an absolute indictment of the public governance system.

Thirdly, I just can't imagine as to how after 55 years of independence we still don't have power even in major cities. Also we have not built a single world-class airport or a single world-class power plant. It is something unimaginable that at the Delhi airport we had to sacrifice the life of a child in an escalator and even today the system has not been corrected. In fact, it was lying idle for 6 to 8 months. Finally, what happened is that one person is manning that escalator. I don't think that is a kind of efficiency that we need in the public governance system today.

Let me talk about how accountability has been introduced in China. Once upon a time in eighties when I spoke to my friends in the civil service, the batch of 1967-68, some of them were my classmates, they would always tell me, "Murthy, you don't understand, we are a large country and you are talking of South Korea and other smaller countries" but today China is a country, which is three and a half times larger than India in terms of area. It is about 1.2 to 1.3 times larger than India in population. Let us see, how China is managing that. In China, officials are held to targets of 7 per cent economic growth per annum, they are also required to continuously improve environmental quality, build better infrastructure and also lower crime levels. Those people who do not perform have got expelled, and I do believe that they will get expelled if they failed to meet the targets.

Now what is the reason? The reason is simply that we have not provided focus on development. Our civil services has still remained one of administration. I don't think the need of the country today is administration, but the need of the country today is to enhance the pace of development. We have to build bridges, power plants, roads and airports. We have to put in place new laws etc. In some cases the Government may not actually do this for example, airports and bridges, power plants, etc. but they have to make sure that they become partners in enhancing the pace of the implementation of these projects.

Thus, it is very clear to me that today we do not need administrators barring a few select areas like home lands security but even there let me tell you, are we using the limited resources that we have in our country and making sure that we are getting the best returns.

Let me give you another example. A few years ago, I was with a senior official of the Karnataka Government and they said, there is no security check for you guys and you go in. I said no, I am from the private sector; I don't have integrity so you have to check me, so he checked. Then there were three people, one guy was frisking me and I was very happy, the second guy was putting a *chhapa* (stamp). I asked him in Kannada, what man, from morning to evening eight hours a day you really want to put these *chappas*. He got upset; obviously he was not very upset because I was going with senior officials of Karnataka Government. He said what do you mean by that Sir, I have been promoted. It made some sense because here this guy was promoted but then there was one guy who was sitting. I asked him, friend what are you doing. He said I am supervising these two. The point I am saying is simply this that even in administration we have to see that are we using the resources efficiently and that is management or administration, whatever you want to call.

The need of the day in a country like India where resources are extremely limited is to make sure that we use those resources extremely efficiently. Let me say what is it that we can do. I thought a lot about, I read lot of books when I wanted to speak here. I realised that most of the books that I read referred to developed nations. I said, is there something that we can do for India and I looked at Singapore, The United States, The UK, France and South Korea, etc. and I found that a lot of them may not apply to India given our current status and mindset. I said is there something that I can suggest in my lecture today, which will disturb very little the current system, but, however, will bring some improvement.

There is such a system, let me tell you what I think can be done very easily. This does not require any legislation, this does not require any major change. What I am suggesting is when a new government takes over, let them put together a team of Ministers, a few Secretaries and their associates, whatever, their Additional Secretary, Joint Secretary, etc. Let them make sure that these people will work together. They may take 3,4,5 days to announce the ministry, they may have discussions and say, this is the Minister for Power and this is the Secretary and this is the Joint Secretary, etc. Then they must promise, they must make a statement in parliament that during the entire tenure of that government, who knows they may be voted out but that is not within their control, but as long as that government is in power these people will not be shifted except for lack of performance. This doesn't require any legislation, but rather this requires a certain desire to bring out a change, a certain desire to make a difference. The government can say we don't want to do this in all areas. I can understand this is not easy, after all to bring about a major change, though this is not that major in my opinion. They may not be able to do in every area, let them take just one area, be it Civil Aviation, be it power, be it homeland security, or be it anything. It doesn't matter whatever they want to take. Let them take just one ministry and then say we will implement this in that ministry because later on then they can always roll out in other areas.

The second thing that they need to do is they have to create incentives for civil servants to perform. What they can say for this group is that, look if you guys don't perform, you will obviously not be involved in this experiment but those of you who are involved in this experiment and if you complete it well, we will give you great awards. Whatever award the Government wants to give like putting up their names in golden letters and if need be a certain percentage of money that they have saved in the project *vis-à-vis* a project which is in similar stage could be offered as incentive. We don't have to compare with Singapore, we don't have to compare with South Korea, probably we can compare with China. In other words, these people have incentives to perform.

Also these people will have to be chosen on the basis of merit. Let me suggest right now that I am not at all talking about changing the reservation system not at all. All that I am saying is among the people that we have in the civil service, in the political leadership, let us choose people who are best suited to do that job. For e.g. somebody who is extremely good in communicating with the external world will obviously go to the foreign affairs. Somebody who is extremely good in management of projects may go to Power or Civil Aviation or something like that. There is no point in putting the right people in wrong jobs. That's all what I am suggesting. No need for changing, bringing any outsiders, no need for any extraordinary changes in legislation.

We also need to decouple political risk from governance issues i.e. our leaders will have to say, look as long as you guys go ahead and implement this project in a manner i.e. transparency, fairness, etc., don't worry, we will stand up and fight for you in parliament, nobody is going to pull you down. That is, political risk should not become a part of the governance issue because otherwise what's going to happen is that there will be a tremendous overhead premium for uncertainties in the political arena that we will have to pay for in all our economic matters as has happened many times in this country.

Concept of Regulatory Council

Next, we have to provide a quick, predictable and stable legal environment. Obviously we have to cut red tape and reduce cost of compliance with laws. Who will monitor the functions of these ministers and bureaucrats? That is a good question. I suggest that we need to have what I would call a Regulatory Council. Just as it has now become mandatory for all corporations to have outside Directors in all publicly traded companies i.e. to put in people of eminence, we need in the government outside observers, we need people of eminence, we need people from all walks of life including business, who will form this public governance Regulatory Council.

Now, this Council must monitor the progress of all governance initiatives and all those projects and also function as a watchdog plus function as a team, to evaluate the performance of each of the senior functionaries. I am also convinced that if we do it at the level of Ministers, at the level of secretaries, the additional secretaries and joint secretaries, the rest of the people will automatically start performing. Let me also say this that I am not for a second suggesting that civil servants are not interested in performing. As I said I have so many friends in the government and most of them are much smarter than I am and they are all decent as I am, they are all as honest as I am. I do not for a second have any doubt about it but the problem is they are all victims in some sense of a system that we have created, a system that we have not dared to change since our independence.

So, I think it is time for us to dare to change, it is time for us to salute all these public servants, all these civil servants as well as ministers and say look, we have tremendous faith in you and together we will change the system and we will give you opportunity to prove that you are smarter than all those guys in the other sectors. That is the point I am making. All the promotions in the civil service will have to be based on the report of this Regulatory Council and unless the Council has the power to review, power to suggest things and also executive powers, it would have no value.

I have been on so many committees of Government of India and even today I don't see any improvement and I don't see any action. For example, I was a part of the IT Task Force. We had made 108 recommendations. Let me tell you that I don't think more than 10 per cent of them have been implemented; somebody may come and say 20 per cent, it is okay but the fact of the matter is that majority of them have not been implemented. As a member of the Council of the Trade and Industry, I have submitted several suggestions and I have not seen any reply to my suggestions and we have not started any meeting saying that these were the items for which actions was required and this is what has happened and this is why something has not happened, this is when it will happen or it will not happen.

Unfortunately we are an amorphous society. We are people who mistake articulation for accomplishment. I think that mindset has to change. So, let us not go to a big thing, let us start a pilot exercise, perhaps in one ministry, all that we are saying is there will be this identified minister, there will be these identified civil servants. They will be given some incentives in terms of respectability, honour, financial incentives and then they will also be supervised by a Regulatory Council consisting of eminent people from society. I do believe that it is necessary to put in a few bright, energetic and enthusiastic youngsters. There are so many of them in the government and I don't think we are short of them. Having done that, perhaps we can roll it out to other ministries of the Central Government and also the state governments. The other thing is this that these people must clearly define projects when they take over charge of whatever ministry, projects, which don't go beyond two years. They may be huge projects but they may say that this is part one of the project and it will be completed in two years because beyond two years, I find that even in my own company it is very difficult to monitor because you can always postpone, you can always delay and nothing happens.

They should also define some measurable performance and indicators. I am a firm believer in quantifiable parameters, I do believe that if you can't measure you can't improve. It is possible in every area and I have no doubt at all that we can define such performance indicators in every area of public governance. Once we do that then I believe that people will have a clear direction to proceed, people will also be enthusiastic, people will be energetic because they will see progress.

Then there must be one more mechanism that I alluded to earlier i.e. we must set up a Special Fast Track Court, just one, in Delhi or wherever we want with adequate number of judges. Today the number of judges per million people in India is one of the lowest in the world. When you compare it with US, it is much much lower. What we should do is set up such a court only for handling complaints about this Ministry. There may be two, three, or five judges, it doesn't matter. What these judges will do is dispose of all complaints against the Minister and the bureaucrats, ideally within a week.

At the same time, we also should send a very clear message saying that anybody who makes a frivolous complaint will be punished with rigorous imprisonment. This will ensure that, only genuine complaints come and the bureaucrats and the Ministers can get on with their job without being scared of the judiciary.

I think Parliament has to very clearly understand that in this Ministry for this experiment we will set apart extra time, may be part of the time in their proceedings to discuss, debate, and quickly come to a conclusion.

Media Support in Public Governance

In every public governance system you have the executives, Parliament, the legislature, the judiciary, and of course most importantly the media. What I am suggesting is this that every newspaper should carry a separate page every Monday. While in the beginning we may just start with first Monday of every month or so, where they will clearly give details of the progress the money spent, the amount of work completed and the remaining work to be completed and any budget overruns for every one of these 50 projects. This will also carry the name of the Minister, the Secretary, the Additional Secretary, the Joint Secretary, etc. It should be made mandatory that every newspaper and every TV channel will carry it once in a month. It's not too much and I am sure our media will be very happy to cooperate in this area.

The other thing that I find is that today our political leadership is elected, unfortunately, purely on emotions and considerations other than merit and performance. I do believe that the Election Commission should make it compulsory for every party to clearly bring out in quantifiable terms, their performance during their term in office and the credentials of their candidates. For example, we can start with saying that if BJP is in government it will say, this Ministry we took up as a pilot project and it has commenced. Each party will be given an opportunity to talk about its performance and in the beginning they will talk only about the pilot project. Later, of course, it will roll out to the entire government.

Once you do that then I do think that the people will vote on the right parameters. Today people are voting on the wrong parameters, people are voting on considerations that you and I or the poorest of the poor don't want. I think we can also say that the Election Commission will ensure that any party that submits false data will be debarred from taking part in elections.

We must make sure that there is a Regulatory Council that will evaluate the performance of the Minister and other people. Make sure that there is an incentive for the political leadership as well as for the bureaucracy and also make sure that the projects are manageable, no project is more than two years duration. Also ensure that there is wide publicity given in the media because you need transparency. Finally, you need fairness. We must ensure that there is fairness to all, fairness to officers, fairness to the ministers and of course, fairness to the citizens. There must be a judiciary that will look at all complaints quickly and dispose them off in such a way, which is fair.

All that I am saying is that we need to conduct this experiment of accountability, fairness, and transparency. I think if we can bring this on a pilot basis and just make it work in one government department at the Centre or the states, we will achieve a good beginning. Ideally, I would like that it is in each place where different parties are in power, BJP in the Centre, may be Congress in some state, Communist Party in some other state and then the Election Commission should make sure that they fight on the basis of what they have contributed to the people rather than the issues of caste, or saying that all these urban dwellers are bad, these educated English speaking fellows are bad, etc. Let us make sure that development becomes the main focus of the electorate rather than issues that are not really important. I would say that if we can conduct this small experiment, I have no doubt at all that this country will go a long way in redeeming the pledge that our founding fathers made, redeeming the pledge that all of us made to the Father of the nation and that's the only way in which we can wipe the tears of the eyes of the poorest and the weakest.

Fifth J.R.D. Tata Memorial Lecture organised by the Associated Chambers of Commerce and Industry of India (ASSOCHAM), August 1, 2002.

Economic Developments in India, Vol. 56.

Section II

Globalisation

8

India in a Globalising World

MONTEK S. AHLUWALIA

The problems posed by globalisation have been much discussed in recent years and it is interesting to recall briefly how perceptions about globalisation have changed in this period. The early 1990s were characterised by a highly positive assessment of globalisation especially in the West. The collapse of Communism in Russia and Eastern Europe, and the enthusiastic conversion of these countries to market economics, created an environment of triumphalist optimism which was reflected in Francis Fukoyama's premature pronouncement of "the end of history". Many in the industrialised world advocated a drastic reduction in the role of the state and freeing of markets —domestic and external, including liberalisation of capital markets—as a simple and tested formula for accelerated development. It was felt that countries only had themselves to blame if they failed to follow this recipe.

Experience did not validate this simplistic view. In some of the emerging market countries, especially in Africa and Latin America, it became evident that adoption of the conventional package of reforms did not always lead to rapid growth. The liberalisation of capital markets also proved to be a source of problems in certain circumstances, as several emerging market countries experienced severe financial crises from which recovery proved to be a prolonged process, and where the poor were often the worst hit. The industrialised economies also saw growing opposition to globalisation arising from high unemployment rates and fears of lost job opportunities. Careful research repeatedly established that these losses had more to do with technological changes than competition from cheap imports, but public perception remained otherwise, and protectionist fears fanned anti-globalisation sentiments.

This is the background in which India, the world's largest democracy, has been charting her course in a globalising world. Democracies encourage debate and there is a great deal of it in India on issues connected with globalisation.

Politicians of all political parties in India know that globalisation is a reality. Many of them also know that all countries that have grown rapidly have done so by exploiting opportunities in world markets and this can only be done if the economy is globally competitive. But there are also the fears about the impact of globalisation which need to be addressed. These fears relate to two types of negative fallouts. First, there is apprehension that globalisation, and the policies of openness associated with exploiting the opportunities it offers, may lead to negative effects on GDP growth. Second, there are concerns that even if aggregate growth is not adversely affected, indeed even if it increases, globalisation may have severely disruptive distributional effects hurting the economic interests of particular groups, sectors or regions causing a loss of income and an increase in poverty.

Let me first focus on India's growth prospects in a globalising world. India's experience certainly suggests that there is no reason to fear that globalisation will hurt India's growth prospects. On the contrary, India has experienced a distinct improvement in growth in the period when its policies reflected the compulsions of globalisation, compared with the 1960s and 1970s, when the Indian economy grew relatively slowly at an average of around 3.5 per cent per year. Growth accelerated to an average of around 5.8 per cent per year in the 1980s and 1990s and the economy is currently growing at about 6.5 per cent. The present government has targeted a growth rate of between 7 and 8 per cent for the near future. Since population growth has slowed down from 2.2 per cent prior to 1990 to around 1.8 per cent at present, these figures imply that the projected acceleration in the growth of per capita income is greater than in the growth of GDP.

International agencies and independent scholars agree that the economy can achieve growth rates of 8 per cent or so provided supportive steps are taken. A much quoted recent study by Goldman Sachs identified Brazil, Russia, India and China as the set of large emerging market countries projected to grow rapidly over the next thirty years. Within the group, India's potential growth rate was projected to be the fastest—around 8 per cent per year—faster even than China which is currently, and has been for many years, the fastest growing economy but is expected to slow down in future. According to this study, by 2040 India will become the third largest economy after the USA and China. This projection has been adopted by the US National Intelligence Council's 2020 report "Mapping the Global Future".

Are these projections credible? There are good reasons to believe that they are.

Economics tells us that, per capita income in an economy depends upon several key determinants and growth of per capita income depends upon changes in these determinants over time. The first is resource availability, i.e. capital per unit of labour and the quality of human capital. The level of technology available to a country is obviously, an important determinant, and so is the set of policies and economic institutions which together determine the efficiency with which resources are used, given available technology. In an open economy, it is particularly important for the policies to be such that the country can take full advantage of the opportunities provided by interaction with the rest of the world and this aspect has become especially important in a globalising world, where technology has created new opportunities for trade and other interaction which simply did not exist earlier.

Based on these considerations, I have no doubt that India is well positioned to accelerate from its present 6.5 per cent growth rate of GDP to around 8 per cent in the near future. As far as the availability of capital is concerned, this depends upon the rate of investment, which, in turn, is constrained by the rate of domestic savings and the sustainable level of foreign inflow. India's domestic savings rates have risen to a very respectable level of 27 per cent of GDP, and could rise further reflecting the age composition of the population, which is at the stage where the dependency ratio is expected to keep falling. The weak spot in the savings picture is public savings, which is negative, though the latest figures show welcome improvement in this dimension.

In a globalising world, domestic savings can be supplemented by investment flows from abroad and India has reoriented policies towards foreign investment to welcome such flows. India at present attracts only about $ 5 billion of FDI compared with $ 60 billion for China. The government has set the target of raising foreign investment to three times its present level and is taking steps to remove policy impediments to such flows in several areas. With continuing improvement in domestic savings, and an increase in FDI from under 1 per cent of GDP to say 2.5 per cent, India can achieve rates of investment of close to 30 per cent which should suffice to sustain 8 per cent growth. Investment rates in China are much higher—around 40 per cent of GDP—but there is reason to believe that China's very high investment rates reflect some degree of inefficiency in the use of capital.

Human capital is another resource that determines growth and there are two somewhat different dimensions that are relevant. One is the availability of skilled manpower and the other relates to entrepreneurial ability. India has a large pool of technical and higher skilled manpower, reflecting long established socio-cultural biases in favour of education and also the emphasis placed on higher education almost immediately after independence. The country produces about 170,000 graduates in engineering and technology annually; not a large number in relation to the population but very substantial as an absolute flow. While quality varies, the best institutions such as the Indian Institutes of Technology and the Indian Institutes of Management, all part of the Nehruvian legacy, are truly world class. Familiarity with English has proved to be an important advantage, especially in some of the new growth areas created by globalisation such as IT enabled services. These endowments make India a potentially attractive production base, offering high level skills at a fraction of the cost in the industrialised world. The picture is less encouraging when it comes to basic education of the labour force.

The other dimension of human capital relates to private entrepreneurship and this is one of India's major strength. India has a long tradition of private enterprise which flourished even in the period when economic policy strongly favoured the public sector. In those years, businessmen operated in a domestic market, where government control limited domestic competition and high protective barriers limited foreign competition, clearly not an environment that encouraged genuine entrepreneurship. Industry profited more from its ability to 'manage' the bureaucracy and obtain benefits, of one kind or the other, from a system of control that was highly discretionary and non-transparent. There has been a major change in the business environment in the past two decades thanks to economic reforms and this has had a powerful impact on the private sector. Indian firms have re-oriented themselves to deal with both domestic and foreign competition and many have begun to establish or acquire subsidiaries abroad to compete more effectively in a globalised world. Earlier fears that lowering of tariff barriers would lead to a flood of imports that would swamp Indian industry, have been dissipated and Indian industry today is confident about its ability to compete in a globalising world. Some of the best Indian firms have even listed on foreign stock exchanges and now have substantial foreign institutional stakeholders, who are an important force, pushing for greater transparency and better corporate governance. These changes are not easily quantified, but they are real nonetheless and they are an important reason for being optimistic about faster growth in the years ahead.

Economic policies and institutions also play a central role in determining growth prospects. Economists, probably focus too much on the role of policies, and tend to underplay the importance of institutions, because policies can be changed over relatively shorter periods while institutions take much longer to create and to mature. I will touch on institutions also, but for the moment let me emphasise that India has seen major changes in economic policies over the past two decades which will help it to perform more effectively in a globalising world.

The process of economic reforms began in the mid 1980s, following a recognition that India's performance in the 1960s and 1970s was below its potential. Mr. Rajiv Gandhi was the Prime Minister at the time, and he was keenly aware that East Asian countries were outpacing India and a restructuring of economic policies was necessary if India was to realise her growth potential. This was the period when the extensive government controls, which existed earlier, on private investment and technology decisions began to be liberalised. Indian private companies were encouraged to expand in scale and induct contemporary technology. Access to foreign technology was made easier and foreign investment began to be viewed as a mechanism for injecting new technology into the economy. Prime Minister, Rajiv Gandhi was also personally convinced of the importance of telecommunications and paid special attention to the modernisation of this sector. He also encouraged the application of computers and the development of the software industry. These policy initiatives paid rich dividends 10 years later, when India emerged as the most globally competitive emerging market country in software and IT services.

Economic reforms, were intensified in the 1990s following a serious balance of payments crisis in 1991. The present Prime Minister, Dr. Manmohan Singh, was the Finance Minister at the time, and was the architect of those reforms. The internal liberalisation begun in the 1980s was carried further, and was combined with a gradual process of external liberalisation, including lowering of import duties, removal of quantitative restrictions on imports and a major liberalisation of foreign direct investment. The 1990s also saw the start of a process of financial reforms aimed at introducing greater competition and tightening prudential norms in the banking sector, stock exchanges and capital market institutions and the insurance sector.

These reforms were accompanied by efforts to strengthen institutions appropriate for the functioning of a market economy. India is fortunate in this area because it already had commercial and legal institutions necessary for functioning as a market economy in a globalising world. The institutions, I have in mind, are an independent judiciary and the rule of law, the prevalence of acceptable accounting standards, functioning stock exchanges and corporate practices. In a globalising world, these institutional characteristics, sometimes called 'soft infrastructure' to distinguish them from the traditional 'hard infrastructure' of roads, ports, railways, etc. are an important positive factor, especially for attracting foreign investment. India's institutions were broadly patterned on those in the industrialised countries though their functioning certainly needed to be improved. Several steps were taken in this direction, including especially in the area of modernising stock exchange practices and introduction of corporate governance rules. Gaps remain in certain areas such as bankruptcy laws, where procedures take far too long, but the basic structures are in place and they are increasingly being pushed to conform with best practices internationally.

The response of the economy to the reforms that have already taken place gives some grounds for optimism about the future. The reforms of the 1980s produced a distinct improvement in economic performance as the growth rate of GDP, which had earlier averaged only around 3.5 per cent accelerated to an average of 5.8 per cent per year in the 1980s. This was not only much better than in earlier years, it was also better than growth rates in Latin America and Africa in the 1980s which decelerated in the period, later described as 'the lost development decade'. However, India's growth remained well below growth rates achieved in China, which grew at about 8.5 per cent in the 1980s, or even Malaysia and Thailand, which grew at 6 per cent and 7.4 per cent respectively.

The intensification of reforms after 1991, including especially the external liberalisation, was expected to push the economy to a distinctly higher growth path. It appeared to do so initially, as GDP growth averaged 7.5 per cent per year between 1994-95 and 1996-97. India appeared ready to transit to a faster rate of growth and the government even targeted growth at 8 per cent for the Ninth Plan period (1997-2001), but this was not achieved. Growth slowed down in the second half of the 1990s and the average growth rate for the 1990s was not very different from that in the 1980s. More recently, the growth rate has accelerated to around 6.5 per cent but this is well below the growth rate targeted.

The fact that the reforms of the 1990s did not produce significantly faster growth than observed in the 1980s, has led some critics to question whether the reforms of the 1990s, including especially the liberalisation of trade policy and foreign investment, were appropriate or even necessary. The reforms initiated in the 1990s were indeed essential and the reason why growth did not accelerate as much as expected was because the reforms were incomplete in some important respects.

The reforms of the 1990s, were essential because the earlier reforms initiated the process of internal liberalisation, but they did not address the issue of international competitiveness, which required extensive liberalisation of trade policy and liberalisation of foreign investment. In the absence of action in this area, there was not enough improvement in export competitiveness. India's share of world exports had been declining steadily from 2 per cent in 1950 to 0.4 per cent in 1980. This decline began to be reversed in the 1980s but the share increased only marginally to 0.5 per cent in 1990. The balance of payments remained under pressure and the economy resorted to external borrowing, leading inevitably to a deterioration in external debt ratios. Not surprisingly, a loss of confidence in 1990 precipitated a reversal of debt flows and produced a crisis.

The reforms of the 1990s, including the shift to a flexible, largely market determined exchange rate succeeded admirably in correcting this weakness. India's export share in world trade increased from 0.5 per cent in 1990 to 0.8 per cent in 2002. This is still a modest figure, but I should add that it does not include earnings from software exports and from business process outsourcing, which have become very important in recent years and are themselves, indisputably, the outcome of the liberalisation of the 1990s. Higher export earnings in the 1990s have been supplemented by larger flows of foreign direct investment and investments by foreign institutional investors (FIIs) in the stock market. The total inflow from both these sources was around $ 6 billion until 2002-03 and then shot up to $ 16 billion in 2003-04, mainly because of a surge in FII inflows.

The disappearance of the 'foreign exchange constraint' is a major benefit of the economic reforms of the 1990s. It has enabled successive governments to take a number of steps essential for enabling India to compete in a globalising world. Most important of these has been the reduction in import duties, implemented by successive governments albeit at a very gradual pace. There was a brief reversal in this process in the late 1990s, but it was soon resumed, indicating a reasonable consensus on this issue. Indian import duties are still too high—nearly three times higher than in China—but the present government is committed to bringing them down to levels comparable to East Asia and significant reductions were implemented in each of the two budgets presented by the government thus far. Interestingly, Indian industry is no longer alarmed at the prospect and representative industry organisations have publicly recommended a gradual process of duty reduction.

Let me now turn to the question why the reforms of the 1990s did not lead to significantly higher rates of growth of GDP than achieved in the 1980s. I believe there are two reasons for this. First, the reforms in India have been deliberately implemented in a gradualist fashion, a gradualism that reflects the compulsions of India's highly pluralist and participative democracy. It has the obvious disadvantage that the benefits of reforms take time to surface and this may account, to some extent, for the less than expected acceleration in growth. It also tries the patience of investors from around the world who worry about the endless debates and controversies and their impact on the process of economic change. However, it has the distinct advantage that it builds a broad consensus in favour of the reforms being attempted, thereby giving them greater political sustainability. This is evident from the fact that the Congress government, in the first half of the 1990s, which initiated the reforms was succeeded by a short lived left of centre coalition which was followed by a right of centre coalition, and despite these changes the broad direction of economic reforms was continued.

A second reason for the lack of a significant acceleration is that the reforms were incomplete, in some important respects. The most important shortcoming is the inability of the reforms to ensure adequate expansion in infrastructure. Rapid growth in a globalising world requires good infrastructure to attract investment and ensure competitiveness. India's infrastructure is distinctly poorer than in most of the competing countries of East Asia and this has discouraged investment in manufacturing, which in turn has led to inadequate growth in this sector. The Ninth Plan (1997-98 to 2001-02) had targeted a growth rate of 8.2 per cent in the industrial sector against which the actual achievement was only 4.6 per cent. The Tenth Plan (2001-02 to 2006-07) targeted industrial growth at 10 per cent but the achievement in the first 3 years is only 7 per cent per year.

The slow growth of industrial production in the second half of the 1990s is a major cause of concern about the growth process because of its implications for employment. Employment in the organised sector—which is basically the modern sector which generates high quality jobs—has actually fallen in recent years. Indian firms, facing the pressure of domestic and external competition, are downsizing the labour force in their effort to improve productivity and cut costs. This process of improving productivity is unavoidable but it underscores the need to achieve higher growth. Had industrial sector grown not at 6.7 per cent, as it did in the first three years of the Tenth Plan, but at 10 per cent which was the target, the economy would have seen expansion in organised sector jobs notwithstanding the improved productivity. The failure of the economy to generate rapid growth in the industrial sector stands in sharp contrast to the performance in IT enabled services which have grown very rapidly albeit from a low base and where India has been able to penetrate world markets. It is interesting to note that global competitiveness in these services depends not on hard infrastructure as much as upon telecommunications connectivity, where India has done well.

Inevitably, the growth witnessed over the past 15 years is continuously evaluated in terms of its impact on poverty. Critics often argue that the growth produced in the period of reforms has not reduced poverty, but this is not true. Poverty has declined from 40 per cent in 1987 to around 23 per cent in 2003. While the decline is welcome, the performance falls below expectations and targets. India still has a very large number of around 250 million below the poverty line, and the poverty line is very minimal, only $ 1 per day.

Another dimension in which the growth witnessed in the 1990s is less than satisfactory relates to regional balance. Available evidence suggests that even in the first half of the 1990s, when growth accelerated compared with the 1980s, there was an increase in regional disparity in growth, with some of the poorer states actually growing more slowly than in the 1980s. It is not true that the rich got richer and the poor poorer. Two of the richest states, Punjab and Haryana, actually slowed down while some of the poorer states, especially Rajasthan and West Bengal, did better than in the 1980s. None of the poorer states experienced an actual decline in per capita GDP. However, some of the largest low income states, especially Uttar Pradesh, Bihar and Orissa grew more slowly than they did in the 1980s. None of this is surprising. In the pre-liberalised world of industrial licensing, investments were deliberately directed to the more backward states and the resulting inefficiencies in production were sustainable because of protection. With liberalisation of industrial licensing, investment could be expected to flow where productivity was higher and some states would have lost out in this process.

Regional imbalances in growth combined with lower than expected growth and insufficient growth in employment were bound to cause tensions, especially in a functioning democracy where globalisation has raised awareness and expectations. Failure to meet expectations leads to electoral defeat and that is what happened in India in May last year. I do not mean to suggest that election outcomes depend on any single factor and there were other important social issues also involved. But in so far as economics was an issue, the previous government went into the election under the slogan 'India Shining', suggesting that its economic policies had produced results which justified re-election. The electorate clearly thought otherwise.

The election results were described in some quarters as a vote against reforms. This is, in my view, a misreading. The truth is that while the previous government had not reversed the process of reforms initiated by the Congress in 1991, and had even carried it forward in several areas, they had not delivered the high growth rates that were expected and were necessary to create high quality jobs for the new entrants to the labour force. Such growth that occurred was also seen as benefiting only a few. The software and business process outsourcing sectors were clearly 'shining', but performance in critical areas such as agriculture was unforgivably poor. Between 1980 and 1996, agricultural GDP in India grew at about 3.2 per cent per year, but after 1996, it decelerated massively to 1.5 per cent per year. With 60 per cent of the population depending upon agriculture as their primary source of income, the deceleration of agricultural growth to 1.5 per cent clearly showed that the economic reforms had by-passed the rural population.

The critical message of the last election is that the process of economic reforms must generate a wider spread of benefits to be politically sustainable. This calls for a faster pace of growth including in the industrial sector and a better sectoral balance in growth, with much greater attention to the agricultural sector. The present government has read this message clearly. It has indicated that the reforms will be pushed ahead to accelerate growth to 7-8 per cent in the short term. It will also work to make this growth more 'inclusive' and distributionally fairer.

The general strategy of pushing forward with economic reforms involves action on many fronts. It includes continuing with the process of opening up the economy by reducing customs duties, reducing bureaucratic hurdles which make the investment climate less attractive, continuing with the process of reducing the list of items reserved for production by the small scale sector, and continuing with financial sector reforms. A sensitive area which is important for promoting expansion in labour intensive sectors, but where it is necessary to build a consensus, is the need for greater flexibility in labour laws.

Three areas which are crucial for achieving a more inclusive growth and are receiving priority attention are health and education levels especially in rural areas, revival of momentum in agriculture, and improving the quality of infrastructure. Let me comment briefly on each of these.

India's primary education and health indicators lag behind other East Asian countries, not only in comparison with the levels prevailing in these countries today, but even compared to the levels 30 years ago when they began to grow more rapidly. China, in particular, invested heavily in these areas in the early stages of development, with the result that when economic reforms were introduced in the early 1980s, adult literacy was already 85 per cent. In contrast, adult literacy in India in 1991 was only 49 per cent. It can be argued that a base level of literacy of 49 per cent is not enough to generate 8 per cent growth. In a globalising world, which places a high premium on skills and knowledge, improving these indicators should be a matter of the highest priority. As Amartya Sen has pointed out, "This will not only improve human welfare directly, it will also contribute to economic growth over a longer period and furthermore, it will improve the ability of the poor to participate more fully in the growth process."

The government has embarked on a major programme to strengthen primary education, especially in rural areas. The aim is to ensure that 100 per cent of children complete five years of primary schooling by 2007. The programme also includes training teachers to improve the quality of instruction, and the provision of mid-day meals to all primary school children. This will improve the nutrition status of children from poorer families and also encourage school attendance thereby helping to reduce drop out rates, which are too high. The cost of these programmes is being met by imposing a cess of two per cent on all taxes earmarked for this purpose.

A parallel effort is being made in the area of health, concentrating initially on rural areas, where public health facilities are grossly inadequate. A new National Rural Health Mission, has been launched which aims at expanding the availability of public health centres at the village level combined with strengthening of referral health facilities for groups of villages. Improving facilities for assisted childbirth is a critical area where more needs to be done. India's total health expenditure as a percentage of GDP is around five per cent, which is comparable with that in other countries, but public expenditure on health is less than one per cent of GDP, much lower than in other countries. The government proposes to raise this to two per cent of GDP over the next seven years.

I must emphasise that while it is necessary to increase public spending in both health and education, this is only one part of what is needed. Equally important, and probably more difficult, is the need to ensure that the money made available is spent well. This is best done by involving the local communities in supervising and monitoring public agencies which provide these services. This function should be performed by the elected bodies at village, district and intermediate levels which provide the third level of democracy, supplementing elected legislatures at the state and national level.

Constitutional Amendments were introduced in 1994 making it mandatory for states to constitute these elected councils and this was a major step in bringing democracy to the grassroots. What has been achieved is impressive; at any given time there are 3 million elected representatives of whom 30 per cent are women. A great deal remains to be done to strengthen the capacity of these bodies and empower them to supervise local functionaries, but I have no doubt that, in due course, these bodies will take on larger responsibilities and contribute greatly to good governance and increased accountability.

The second area where corrective steps are needed relates to agriculture. We need to more than double the growth rate in agriculture from 1.5 per cent observed in recent years to around 4 per cent, and this requires much more than a business as usual approach. The present government is undertaking a comprehensive review of policies in agriculture and related areas such as irrigation, water management and conservation, agricultural research and extension, rural roads, etc. Large investments are needed in these areas, as also policy changes, including policies on sensitive issues such as the pricing of irrigation water and pricing of electric power to agriculture. The government has already announced a major Food for Work Programme (soon to be converted into an Employment Guarantee Act) aimed at providing at least 100 days of employment at the minimum wage to one member of each poor household in designated rural areas. This is designed as a measure of income support for the rural poor but the programme can also be dovetailed with plans for creation of rural infrastructure by the wage costs of infrastructure development being met though the programme.

Indian agriculture will also have to expand its focus beyond producing foodgrains, towards agricultural diversification, including especially dairying, poultry and horticulture. The scope for development of food processing industries is very large. At present, only about 2 per cent of horticulture production in India is processed compared with 20 per cent or more in many countries. Wastage due to poor handling and spoilage from the farm to the consumer is as high as 25 to 30 per cent and this is reflected in low prices paid to farmers. The development of modern agro-processing would help increase farm incomes but it is currently hampered by outdated laws governing the marketing of agricultural produce which make it difficult for corporations to enter into contract purchase arrangements with groups of farmers. Contract farming would enable farmers to grow the specific varieties needed for agro-processing, with the buyer providing the planting material, extension services, advice on appropriate pesticides and a cold chain from the farm to the processing plant. The laws governing the food processing industry also need to be modernised.

Agricultural modernisation will present new challenges to Indian farmers. India is climatically well suited to the production of high value horticulture, including organically grown crops, which can be marketed in Europe, but this will require compliance with phyto-sanitary standards and European food laws. Biotechnology has the potential of greatly increasing yields of crops tailored to the soil and moisture conditions prevailing in India. However, there are apprehensions and environmental concerns as the development of genetically modified crops faces challenges from NGOs internationally and domestically. India is actively engaged in the WTO negotiations, looking for larger market access for its products and it will have to do its part in the process of opening up. However, opening agriculture creates legitimate fears because of the persistence of heavy subsidisation of agriculture in industrialised countries. Opening up the agricultural sector also exposes farmers to risks when international prices fall. Farmers need to have access to instruments of risk management to deal with such situations such as liquid forward markets and these require institutional development which takes time.

The third area where a complete overhaul of policies is needed relates to infrastructure development. Any visitor to India also familiar with East Asia is immediately struck by the fact that India's infrastructure services, by which I mean the availability and quality of electric power from the utilities, the road network, ports, airports, rail transport, etc., are far behind East Asia. I have already mentioned that inadequate progress in this area is probably the most important reason why the reforms introduced in the 1990s did not accelerate growth as much as was expected. The government is paying special attention to this area. The Prime Minister has established a committee on infrastructure, under his chairmanship, to systematically review policy issues in each of the infrastructure sectors, and to determine an agenda for policy change and monitor implementation.

The investment required to upgrade India's infrastructure is massive and cannot possibly come entirely from the public sector. The strategy being adopted is to increase public resources directed towards infrastructure development and to use them in a manner which most effectively leverages private investment in these areas. In some areas, such as telecommunications, private investment in infrastructure has already taken-off. There are a handful of strong private sector service providers, investing aggressively and competing for market share with the erstwhile public sector telecom companies. The government has recently increased the limit on foreign investment in this sector from 49 per cent to 74 per cent. At the other end of the spectrum are rural roads, where also large investment is necessary, but will have to come entirely from the public sector.

Between these two extremes are a number of sectors where private investment is possible, but there are sector specific problems and policy constraints that need to be overcome. Private investment in ports is relatively easy. Several minor ports are being developed entirely in the private sector, and in the major ports, expansion of new capacity has been successfully privatised. The private sector can also play a major role in airport development. A private sector airport in Kochi has been in operation for some years, and two more have been approved recently for Bangalore and Hyderabad. Bids have also been invited from private investors interested in the development of Mumbai and Delhi airports as joint ventures, with management control in private hands, and the concession is expected to be awarded later in the year.

Roads have been traditionally built only in the public sector but it is proposed to entrust significant portions of future National Highway development to private investors on a BOT basis. The revenue model envisages the investor receiving earnings from tolls, with a capital subsidy to make the project financially remunerative. One such project has recently been completed. Thirty more private sector BOT projects are expected to be awarded in the course of the year.

The most difficult area, of course is electric power. The power utilities in most states are financially unviable, thanks to a combination of large electricity losses in distribution, arising from stealing of power, usually in connivance with the distribution staff, and unrealistically low electricity tariffs for certain categories of consumers. The solution clearly lies in setting rational power tariffs and improving the operational efficiency of the distribution segments. The initiative in this area lies largely with the state governments and some progress is being made. Regulators have been set up in almost all states and have started prescribing electricity tariffs. Two states have privatised electricity distribution, but it is too early to tell whether this shift to private ownership will succeed in reducing losses. Most states have adopted a more limited strategy of separating generation, transmission and distribution into separate companies, and then trying to improve the performance of the distribution company through better management systems. The net result is that despite false starts in the past, some private investment in electric power generation is taking place but not as much as is needed. This can be expected to increase as the distribution companies become financially more viable.

I have listed only some of the major initiatives in the area of infrastructure to give an idea of what is being done. This is a complex area where the reforms needed often require deeper institutional change. Progress will be uneven across states, but I have no doubt that there will be success stories and these will be rapidly replicated, if not in all states, certainly in many. Better infrastructure is central to achieving larger inflows in foreign investment in manufacturing and generating faster growth in this sector which is critical for expanding employment.

Finally, I must emphasise that reforms need to be pursued in a framework of macroeconomic stability. India's macroeconomic parameters are stable, but some of them are not at comfortable levels. There is concern that India's fiscal deficit is too high, and this has been so for quite some time. The government recognises this as a problem and hopes to correct it over time, working within the framework of the Fiscal Responsibility and Budget Management Act, which prescribes a time path for reducing the fiscal deficit of the central government. The states are also being encouraged to adopt similar legislation. As an incentive, they have been offered restructuring of their outstanding debt liabilities to the centre on favourable terms, if they agree to enact fiscal responsibility legislation.

Fiscal balance requires action on both expenditure and revenues. On the expenditure side, the government must contain the growth of public expenditure as much as possible by withdrawing from areas where public spending is not essential or effective, while actually expanding it in other areas where it is necessary and presently inadequate. On the revenue side, there is need for steady pursuit of tax reform, especially reform of tax administration, which should permit larger resources to be raised even at the existing tax rates. An important development in this area is the recent adoption by 19 out of 27 states of a VAT system for sales taxes (which are levied by the states) under which credit will be allowed for sales taxes paid at earlier stages. Experience suggests that this will have a very favourable effect on revenue collection.

I hope the picture that emerges from my lecture is one of an India grappling earnestly with the challenges posed by globalisation, and finding solutions to these challenges within the framework of her democratic polity. As in the past, policy reform in India will continue to be a gradualist process. The present government is a Congress led coalition, with outside support from the Left parties. The partners of the coalition have all subscribed to a consensus document, the National Common Minimum Programme (NCMP).

This document outlines a credible framework to push the reform forward, in a manner which takes care of the deficiencies in past policies and prescribes important corrective steps. The document indicates transparently some important constraints on policy. For example, the government will not privatise profit making public sector companies, though it can sell minority equity in such companies. Similarly, the government is against 'automatic hire and fire' policies, but it will work together with labour to determine desirable changes in the labour laws to give greater flexibility. I recognise that many investors want stronger action in precisely these areas, but democracy is about working within constraints defined by political acceptability. I have no doubt that it is possible to define a reform programme within these constraints, which makes sufficient progress in many important areas to enable India to achieve eight per cent growth per year, and a much more 'inclusive' and socially just growth than in the past.

If we succeed, India could emerge, within 10 years, as an economy well on the way to achieving middle income status, with a much broader middle class whose economic well being is more directly linked to the growth process than is the case today. In Nehru's memorable phrase, "We will have brought about India's second tryst with destiny."

Twenty-seventh Jawaharlal Nehru Memorial Lecture, London, April 20, 2005.
Economic Developments in India, Vol. 91.

9

Indian Economy in the Global Setting

RAKESH MOHAN

In the recent decade, India along with China has emerged as the engine of global growth. This is well reflected in India's share in world GDP increasing significantly from 4.3 per cent in 1991 to 5.8 per cent in 2004. This period has also been one when India initiated structural reforms which encompassed, *inter alia*, a phased opening up of the Indian economy to the external sector. These structural reforms have strengthened India's external sector and have also imparted a degree of dynamism to the Indian economy. The opening up of the Indian economy has not only allowed it to reap benefits of globalisation but India is also contributing to global growth. Against this backdrop, I discuss India's recent economic growth record in order to draw lessons for it to realise its potential in a globalised world.

Recent Economic Growth: Overview and Issues

Economic developments in the recent years indicate a growing resilience of the Indian economy. Illustratively, even as the Indian economy was buffeted by exogenous shocks emanating from a below normal monsoon and record high international oil prices, overall GDP growth was almost 7 per cent during 2004-05. Effective macroeconomic management during the year ensured that India remained one of the fastest growing economies among emerging market economies in an environment of macroeconomic and financial stability. Looking at the post-reform period, real GDP growth has stepped up from 5.8 per cent per annum during the 1980s to 6.2 per cent per annum between 1992-93 and 2004-05. Over the same period, per capita growth has recorded a more impressive increase from 3.4 per cent to 4.3 per cent.

Structural reforms have increased the competitiveness of the Indian industry and this is reflected quite vividly in the robust merchandise export

The assistance of Dr. Narendra Jadhav and Shri Muneesh Kapur in preparation of this address is gratefully acknowledged.

growth since 2002-03—exports have grown (in US$ terms) by more than 20 per cent per annum in each of the last three years. Concomitantly, the services sector contributes more than one-half of GDP, with growing contributions from new impulses of growth such as the information technology, telecommunication and transport sectors and a revival of foreign tourist arrivals.

A noteworthy feature of macroeconomic management is the success with maintaining price and financial stability. Inflation has averaged close to 5 per cent per annum since the second half of the 1990s, significantly lower than that of around 7 to 8 per cent in the previous three and a half decades. This was possible due to effective monetary management, enabled by reforms in the fiscal-monetary interface. This has had a soothing influence on inflation expectations. Thus, despite poor monsoon conditions, record international crude oil prices and sharp increases in a host of non-oil commodity prices, inflation could be contained at around 5 per cent by the end of fiscal 2004-05, reflecting effective calibrated monetary measures supported by timely supply-side and fiscal measures. Inflation in the current year so far has eased to 3.1 per cent, although it needs to be recognised that the pass-through of international oil prices to domestic oil prices remains incomplete. We may also note that unlike previous oil price rise episodes of international inflation has also been contained this time.

Another notable feature of the post-reform period is the improvement in the health of the financial sector. Reforms in the financial sector introduced since the early 1990s have had a major impact on the overall efficiency and stability of the banking system, reflected in improvements in capital adequacy ratios and strengthening of the balance sheets. Furthermore, Indian banks have done a remarkable job in containment of NPLs considering the overhang issues and overall difficult environment. Net NPAs have now fallen to just two per cent of net advances.

The external sector continues to be robust. Despite sharp increase in oil as well as non-oil imports, India's balance of payments has recorded large and persistent surpluses, with foreign exchange reserves at around US $ 144 billion. Increased earnings from exports of services and remittances coupled with enhanced foreign investment inflows have provided strength to the external sector.

In brief, the Indian economy has exhibited a strong performance since the early 1990s in an environment of macroeconomic and financial stability—

higher GDP growth, lower inflation, a resilient external sector and a strong financial sector. All these happened during the 1990s, which was otherwise a turbulent decade in terms of financial instability in many other countries. Nonetheless, it is widely agreed that the growth of the Indian economy remains well-below its potential. Real GDP growth in the first three years (2002-03 to 2004-05) of the Tenth Plan period has averaged 6.5 per cent, lower than the Tenth Five Year Plan (2002-2007) target of 8 per cent per annum. While the economy is doing well in many areas and these gains need to be consolidated, there are also important weaknesses, which, if not corrected could undermine even the potential performance level. In this context, it is interesting to note that the recent years (2001-02 to 2003-04) have seen India recording surpluses in the current account, i.e., we have not been able to find investment avenues to deploy our domestic savings. It is, therefore, important that impediments to investment be removed so that domestic savings can be deployed at home. Of course, to realise the growth potential of 8-9 per cent of the Indian economy, domestic savings will have also to record commensurate increases. Reforms would have to be further intensified in the agricultural sector, in factor markets to promote flexibility, in bankruptcy and exit procedures, in fiscal consolidation and in physical and social infrastructure sectors to accelerate investment.

Although the poverty ratio has declined since the onset of the reforms process, the number of people below the poverty line still remains high, with wide variations across states. Between 1977-78 and 1999-2000, the proportion of people living below the poverty line fell from 51.3 per cent to 26.1 per cent; over the same period, the absolute number of poor people fell from about 330 million to about 260 million, a number that is still sizeable. In 2001-03, for instance, India's per capita income was equivalent to only 9 per cent of the global average and 2 per cent of the per capita income of the high income countries.

With more than half of the people still dependent on agriculture, a key area of concern is that agricultural growth remains low and continues to be monsoon-dependent. Growth in the agricultural and allied sectors has decelerated from 3.2 per cent per annum during 1980-96 to 1.9 per cent subsequently. Per capita agricultural GDP has shown no significant upward trend after 1996-97. The slowdown is wide-spread across crops and reflects a broad based deceleration in productivity growth. The deceleration in output coincided with a downturn in world prices, and this has impacted domestic farm prices more than in earlier decades because of greater openness. The consequence has been that farm incomes became more variable and decelerated more than output in many cases.

A related cause of concern, given that 57 per cent of population is still agricultural dependent, is that the role of agriculture in providing additional employment opportunities was virtually zero during the 1990s. Employment in agriculture remained virtually unchanged at about 190 million people during the 1990s. Concomitantly, annual employment growth for the economy, as a whole, decelerated from two per cent during the 1980s to only 1.1 per cent in the latter half of the 1990s. With employment growth trailing the additions to the labour force, unemployment rate for the economy as a whole is estimated to have increased from 8.87 per cent in 2001-02 to 9.11 per cent in 2004-05, a proportion that is far too high for a country like ours. The generation of productive employment is, therefore, a key issue that needs to be addressed on a continuous basis.

The slowdown in the agricultural sector reflects subdued public investment in agriculture and inadequate crop diversification. A step-up in public investment in rural infrastructural areas such as irrigation, rural electrification and rural roads will become possible through reduction in and better targeting of subsidies that would then enable greater public investment for promoting growth. Efforts are also needed to diversify the cropping pattern to non-traditional activities in line with the changing agricultural demand pattern and making use of recent advances in biotechnology. The process of diversification calls for micro-level planning with emphasis on crop specific inputs, creating proper marketing infrastructure, cold storage, transportation facilities and supportive policies. There is a need for value addition in agricultural products through processing, packaging, and supply chain management so that farm incomes expand, employment is generated and rural poverty is alleviated. Other initiatives to increase agricultural production could cover aspects such as better availability of commodity derivatives to minimise the impact of prices uncertainty; reducing monsoon-dependency through schemes like water harvesting; and, further augmenting the flow of credit to the rural sector. Diversification of agriculture would also provide stable additional avenues of employment generation in the rural sector and enable these sectors to emerge as the main source of growth and employment in rural areas. All these measures will promote competitiveness of the agricultural sector, which is so necessary in the current global context.

As regards social sector indicators, notwithstanding some progress in regard to education and health, India is still far behind its East Asian neighbours. Our social indicators are lower even in comparison with the levels achieved by these countries twenty five years ago, when they first began to grow rapidly. The social indicators also show disturbing gender gaps, large rural-urban differences and wide variation across states. Although the literacy rate has improved encouragingly from 52.2 per cent in 1991 to 64.8 per cent in 2001 and the overall number of illiterates in the country declined from 329 million in 1991 to 306 million in 2001, there are at least seven major States with more than 15 million illiterates each, accounting for nearly two-third of total illiterates in the country. Concomitantly, given India's comparative advantage in services, it is important that the quality of secondary and higher education in the country is improved so that adequate skills are developed to realise the benefits of the knowledge economy. As regards health, the combined government (centre plus states) expenditure on health as a percentage of GDP has stagnated at around one per cent of GDP over the last decade and a half. Total public expenditure on health in India remains even lower than many other developing countries such as Brazil (3.4 per cent), Thailand (2.1 per cent), Sri Lanka (1.8 per cent), China (1.9 per cent) and Malaysia (1.5 per cent). Low public expenditure in India is to some extent compensated by private expenditure which at 4.0 per cent of GDP is comparatively higher than all of these countries except Brazil (4.9 per cent). However, low public expenditure is a cause for concern for the vast majority of the population and primary health care remains of poor quality, unavailable and inaccessible. The infant mortality rate in India is almost double that of China (63 in India versus 37 in China) while the maternal mortality rate at 407 is manifold as compared to China's 56. Hospital beds (per 1000 population) at 0.7 for India are less than one-half of other developing economies such as China (2.4), Thailand (2.0) and Malaysia (2.0). A significant improvement in social indicators is necessary if we want to create the pre-condition for a general improvement in welfare of our population and for genuine equality of opportunity.

Turning to the industrial sector, reforms which encompassed removal of industrial licensing, de-reservation, substantial opening of foreign direct investment and trade liberalisation have imparted a competitive edge to Indian industry. This is reflected in a resurgence of activity in the manufacturing sector in the past two years, and the present phase appears to be sustainable, in contrast to the exuberance—which turned out to be temporary—reflected in high growth in investment and production in industry during 1993-94 to 1996-97. For industrial activity to get entrenched and gather momentum, efficiency in supply of infrastructural inputs will need a large impetus. The subdued performance of the infrastructure sector in the recent months is an issue of concern, given the sector's strong forward and backward linkages in the economy. The increasing demand-supply gap in the availability of power is becoming the most critical issue in the future of India's economic development. In the recent period, shortage of coal and gas has emerged as a serious constraint on power generation with the supply of both fuels falling far short of demand. In this context, given the fact that the Indian economy is among the more inefficient users of energy, highest and urgent priority needs to be given for energy-saving measures, which could include appropriate pricing policies and incentives to invest.

With growing urbanisation, issues related to urban infrastructure have come to the forefront. At present, investment in urban infrastructure is hampered by the fact that local governments are not yet creditworthy and urban infrastructure projects are, therefore, not found to be commercially viable. Strengthened planning and better coordination between various agencies entrusted with maintenance of urban infrastructure would have a positive impact on the overall productivity of economic activity in cities. Given the fact that there is a heavy concentration of economic activity in large cities, weak infrastructural facilities impede the growth of large cities and of overall economic productivity. It is, therefore, of the utmost importance that the quality of urban infrastructure in the large cities is improved significantly so as to maintain and accelerate the momentum of economic growth and productivity enhancement. For urbanising economies like India to replicate the experience of developed countries in the provision of urban infrastructure, it is essential that all aspects of city management, including the fostering of a professional workforce, are strengthened.

The maintenance of vibrant growth in the manufacturing sector will depend crucially on the expansion of small and medium enterprises that then become significant players in the future. For this potential to be realised, there is a need to increase credit availability to this sector at reasonable costs. Banking institutions need to improve their credit assessment capabilities with regard to small-scale enterprises and smallscale must not be equated with high risk. Recent initiatives of the government and the Reserve Bank, such as the new legislation aimed at developing credit information bureaus will help to reduce information and transaction costs that should then lead to lower cost of credit to the SSI sector. Empirical evidence shows that wider availability of credit histories greatly expands the flow of credit as potential borrowers are no longer tied to their local lenders.

The services sector has emerged as the largest contributor to growth in the country. Advances in information technology, liberalisation of the telecommunications sector and availability of skilled labour have permitted India to reap advantages through the globalisation of some services. The initial impetus provided by exports of software and services has now got additional support from the exponential growth of the IT-enabled sector (ITES). According to the National Association of Software and Service Companies (NASSCOM), India's software and service exports recorded a strong growth of 34 per cent in 2004-05. The software sector [including ITES-Business Process Outsourcing (BPO)] now employs more than one million people, having recorded a compounded annual growth of nearly 30 per cent in employment during the period 1999-2005. The software sector also provides indirect employment to 2.5 million people. These data bring forth the growing role of the software sector, but at the same time, they suggest that for this order of growth rates to be maintained in the future, investment in social infrastructure —especially, education—needs to stepped-up. In this context, it is necessary that public expenditure on education should reverse its declining trend: total expenditure by the state governments on education is budgeted to decline from 2.5 per cent of GDP in 2003-04 to 2.3 per cent in 2005-06. Moreover, given the demographic profile, the demand for education is slated to increase further. Accordingly, the improvement in state finances will enable the states to increase their expenditure on education and other social services and thereby improve the quality of overall social infrastructure so that India can realise its potential.

It is now well-recognised that monetary policy can contribute to long-run growth by maintaining low and stable inflation. International experience indicates that a prudent fiscal policy remains the single largest prerequisite for monetary stability. In India, reforms in the monetary-fiscal interface during the 1990s have been a key factor that imparted greater flexibility to monetary policy. These reforms have taken a significant step forward with the enactment of the Fiscal Responsibility and Budget Management (FRBM) Act, 2003 by the Centre. With the Centre's GFD/GDP ratio at 4.1 per cent in 2004-05 (provisional accounts), the FRBM target of 3.0 per cent by 2008-09 appears to be within striking distance. However, with revenue deficit at 2.7 per cent in 2004-05, the elimination of the revenue deficit by 2008-09 will prove to be more difficult. Achieving this target requires continued focused action on containing expenditures, increase in tax revenues and reduction in tax exemptions. Revenue augmentation would critically depend upon improvement in tax/GDP ratio as non-tax revenue is set to decline in the coming years. With the acceleration in overall economic growth that is being observed currently, renewed efforts on tax compliance should yield beneficial results. Achievement of the FRBM target of revenue deficit at zero per cent of GDP will free up resources for public investment which will also crowd-in private investment. Overall, despite the recent improvements in the fiscal position of the central government the effort in achieving fiscal consolidation will have to continue.

International crude oil prices are touching a record high. In previous episodes of such high oil prices, India often faced balance of payments crisis, low growth and high inflation. In the most recent period, the economy has been able to absorb the oil shock relatively comfortably so far. However, in case international oil prices continue to remain at the existing elevated levels, they could have a negative influence on growth prospects internationally. It is important to note that oil intensity—oil consumption per unit of output—in India has increased since early 1970s in contrast to the behaviour of major economies such as the Euro area, the US and Japan. Although oil intensity in India is still lower than that of advanced economies, there is scope for adopting measures to enhance efficiency of oil use in the economy. Energy conservation measures in the backdrop of high and volatile international crude oil prices could help the Indian economy to weather the adverse consequences with relatively lower output losses. In this context, there is a need for policies that permit flexibility in domestic oil prices that respond to the ups and downs in international prices, albeit with some mechanism that cushions the impact on the common man. This will also enable more efficient use of oil in the economy, especially in view of the fact that the rise in international oil prices appears to have a large permanent component.

Given the volatility in the inflation rate during 2004-05, there is a need to consolidate the gains obtained in recent years from reining in inflationary expectations. While sustained efforts over time have helped to build confidence in price stability, inflationary expectations can turn adverse in a relatively short time if noticeable adverse movements in prices take place. Credible commitment of policy to fight inflation is critical to stop translation of higher oil prices into wage-price spirals. In addition, the international prices of non-oil primary commodities may continue to remain firm. On the domestic front, the manoeuvrability on oil prices is getting limited and corporates have a higher probability of gaining their pricing power with a better industrial outlook. The pricing pressure, if it were to occur from the supply side, could get complicated by continuing overhang of excess domestic liquidity. While the economy has the resilience to withstand supply shocks, the upside risks do exist. As such, the inflationary situation, both international and domestic, needs to be watched closely to persevere in maintaining inflation expectations and any complacency on this count could have adverse consequences for both stability and growth.

Global Economic Integration

With the growing external openness of the Indian economy, and given its pace of expansion and size, the debate in the recent period is not only on the contours of the public policy in the context of increasing global economic integration but also to the challenges likely to be faced by the global economy on account of progressively increasing global integration of the Indian economy. The emphasis is of course on successful integration which will no doubt depend on the appropriateness of our public policies and the private sector responses. These issues are addressed next.

Globalisation has several dimensions arising out of enhanced connectivity among people across national borders. In particular, economic integration occurs through three channels, *viz.*, movement of people, of goods and, of finance or capital. In managing the process of economic integration, developing countries face challenges from a world order that is particularly burdensome on them. It is necessary for public policy to manage the process with a view to maximising the benefits to its citizens while minimising the risks; but the path of optimal integration is highly country-specific and contextual. On balance, there appears to be a greater advantage in achieving a well-managed and appropriate integration into the global process, which would imply more effective—but not necessarily intrusive or extensive—interventions by governments. In fact, while there are some infirmities in interventions by government, markets do experience market-failures and cannot exist without some externally imposed rules and prescriptions of the public policy. As the poor, the vulnerable and the underprivileged continue to be the responsibility of the national governments, there is relevance of national public policy— particularly as it relates to global economic integration.

Against this backdrop, external sector policies designed to progressively open up the Indian economy, as observed earlier, formed an integral part of the strategy for structural reforms. In this context, the Report of the High Level Committee on Balance of Payments (Rangarajan Committee, 1993) recommended improvement in exports, both merchandise and invisibles; modulation of import demand on the basis of the availability of current receipts to ensure a level of current account deficit consistent with normal capital flows; enhancement of non-debt creating flows to limit the debt service burden; adoption of market-determined exchange rate; building up the foreign exchange reserves to avoid liquidity crises and elimination of the dependence on short-term debt. It is evident that the external sector policies of the 1990s, based on the Report, paid rich dividends in terms of growth and resilience to a series of external and domestic shocks.

Various reforms in the trade policy regime have unlocked entrepreneurial energies, stepped up productivity gains and improved competitiveness and access to overseas markets. India's merchandise exports have been rising at a rate of over 20 per cent per annum, in US dollar terms, during 2002-05. As a result, the secular decline in India's share in world exports from two per cent in 1950 to 0.5 per cent in the 1980s has been reversed. This share began rising in the 1990s and is currently at 0.8 per cent. These positive developments in the external sector provide the environment of pursuing a further rationalisation of tariffs with a view towards moving to a single, uniform rate on imports, say 10 per cent, and simplify all customs procedures strictly in line with best global practices. This should help to improve competition, exports and domestic consumers. The current external environment including the level of the foreign exchange reserves enables such a move to be made with little or no downside risks.

While the recent trend in imports may continue to persist in the face of high and volatile crude prices and the large increase in domestic demand, an intrinsic link between merchandise imports and exports has emerged and become entrenched. The large expansion in imports is also spurring vigorous export growth. Given the recent experience, especially the fact that workers remittances seem to have acquired a semi-permanent, if not permanent, character, the current level of the trade deficit appears to be manageable at this stage and appears to be consistent with India's growth aspirations.

Given the adverse international experience with unfettered capital account liberalisation, we have been risk averse and have adopted a policy of active management of the capital account. The compositional shifts in the capital account have been consistent with the policy framework, imparting stability to the balance of payments. The sustainability of the current account is increasingly viewed as consistent with the volume of normal capital flows. The substitution of debt by non-debt flows also gives us room for manoeuvre since debt levels, particularly, external commercial borrowings, have been moderate and can be raised in the event of a sustained pick up in the demand for external resources. There is also the cushion available from the foreign exchange reserves.

India has made significant progress in financial liberalisation since the institution of financial sector reforms in 1992 and this has been recognised internationally. India has chosen to proceed cautiously and in a gradual manner, calibrating the pace of capital account liberalisation with underlying macroeconomic developments, the state of readiness of the domestic financial system and the dynamics of international financial markets. Unlike in the case of trade integration, where benefits to all countries are demonstrable, in case of financial integration, a 'threshold' in terms of preparedness and resilience of the economy is important for a country to get full benefits. A judgmental view needs to be taken whether and when a country has reached the 'threshold' and the financial integration should be approached cautiously, preferably within the framework of a plausible roadmap that is drawn up by embodying the country-specific context and institutional features. The experience so far has shown that the Indian approach to financial integration has stood the test of time.

The optimism generated by the recent gains in macroeconomic performance warrants a balanced consideration of further financial liberalisation. At this stage, the optimism generated by impressive macroeconomic performance accompanied with stability has given rise to pressures for significantly accelerating the pace of external financial liberalisation. It is essential to take into account the risks associated with it while resetting an accelerated pace of a gradualist approach. The recent experience in many countries shows that periods of impressive macroeconomic performance generate pressures for speedier financial liberalisation since everyone appears to be a gainer from further liberalisation, but the costs of instability that may be generated in the process are borne by the country, the government and the poorer sections. Avoiding crises is ultimately a national responsibility. The approach to managing the external sector, the choice of instruments and the timing and sequencing of policies are matters of informed judgment, given the imponderables.

As noted earlier, not only do global developments influence India, but the growing size of India has also implications for the global economy which would have also to take in to account the evolving demographic dynamics in countries such as India. Over the next half-century, the population of the world will age faster than during the past half-century as fertility rates decline and life expectancy rises. In Europe, the demographic profile is already tilted towards the higher age group and by 2050, this is projected to accelerate. Projections suggest a turning point between 2010 and 2030 when the European Union, North America and Japan will experience a substantial decline in savings rates relative to investment which may be reflected in large current account deficits. Most of the high performers of East Asia and China are in the second stage of the demographic cycle. Elderly dependency is expected to double in these countries by 2025. Their working age populations will increase modestly first and then shrink. These projections suggest that East Asia could increasingly become an important supplier of global savings up to 2025; however, rapid population ageing thereafter would reinforce rather than mitigate the inexorable decline of global savings. India is entering the second stage of demographic cycle and over the next half-century, a significant increase in both savings rate and share of working age population is expected. The share of the labour force in population in India is expected to overtake the rest of Asia, including China, by 2030. Looking ahead, the rest of the world may increasingly rely on China and India for supplies of both labour and capital and this could significantly influence the evolution of the global economy. It is evident that China and India will have to give high priority to generating employment and both are poised for substantial increases in productivity.

The global economy will have to contend with the implications of these developments on prices, exchange rates, wages and structures of employment in industrialised countries. Over the medium term, it is felt that outsourcing will grow rapidly and may also cover high-end research and development activities. In manufacturing, China has emerged as a leader and India is catching up rapidly. Though agriculture is heavily subsidised in major industrialised countries, such subsidisation would be difficult to sustain from a fiscal point of view, since many of the countries concerned are poised to meet the mounting pension liabilities not to speak of burgeoning health care costs of maintaining the deteriorating demographics. One sector where the industrialised economies continue to show considerable strength and dominance is the financial sector, partly attributable to the confidence factor in financial markets that favours the industrialised economies and traditional international financial centres. It is essential for India to carefully monitor the developments in both real and financial sectors, and to frame the policies in tandem with the global developments so that global integration continues to be a positive sum game for all countries.

While the economic integration of India with the global economy will continue to take place, a successful integration, with due regard to the interests of a vast majority particularly, the poor in our country would be possible only through sound public policies—evolved and redesigned from time to time. Given India's demographic advantages, the quality of labour force (in terms of relevant skills which need to be sustained, reoriented and upgraded in a globally competitive era) and the physical health of the workforce become crucial. Education and health, therefore, provide the link between supply and demand for labour through increases in productivity.

In this context, there is universal recognition of the need to improve both productivity and output in the agriculture and related activities to meet the objectives of growth and employment. There will have to be a massive shift of the workforce from agriculture to non-agricultural avocations and we should be prepared for a large-scale migration of the workforce to the tune of 10 million per year, from rural to semi-urban and urban areas. The quality of urban infrastructure even in the metropolitan cities, as noted earlier, is not conducive to globally competitive economic activity. The inevitable large scale redeployment of the migrating workforce would, therefore, need institutional arrangements, be they in public or private sector, for skill-imparting and skill up-gradation. In these two matters relating to the workforce, some supply-led approaches appear to be in order, rather than waiting for the demand to be generated.

Enhanced investment activity, particularly in the infrastructure area, would necessitate higher domestic savings, especially in the public sector coupled with efficient financial intermediation. In addition, foreign savings need to be attracted and absorbed with a strong preference to foreign direct investment in all sectors though in some sectors like banking, a calibrated approach may be warranted. At the same time, our enterprises should be enabled to attain a strong global presence in all sectors. In brief, our global integration has to be a two way process, encompassing movement of people with some caveats, trade in a free and equitable manner and financial integration on a specially sequenced basis.

Concluding Observations

The structural reforms initiated in the early 1990s coupled with a cautious and calibrated approach to external sector liberalisation has led to a step-up in economic growth and India has emerged as one of the fastest growing economies of the world. Notably, this growth has been achieved in an environment of monetary and financial stability, even as there was a series of exogenous shocks, both domestic and foreign, that hit the Indian economy in the period since the latter half of the 1990s. Looking ahead, the evolving demographic profile in favour of younger population suggests that the growth prospects of the Indian economy remain strong, provided their potential is effectively utilised. At the same time, a lot needs to be done to improve the quality of life. While the proportion of the poor in total population has come down, the absolute number of poor people remains high. India's rank in terms of human development index and gender development index continues to be low compared to many developing countries. There is a need for linking growth with development and fill the gap between macroeconomic performance and social sector development. In this regard, globalisation throws both opportunities and challenges for benefit of societies. Opportunities offered by forces of globalisation offer India scope to improve the quality of life of its people, provided appropriate policies are put in place.

Address at Ninety Ninth Foundation Day Celebration Function of the Indian Merchants' Chamber, Mumbai, September 8, 2005.

Economic Developments in India, Vol. 94.

10

India and Globalisation

BIMAL JALAN

There is a debate not only in India but all over the globe about the pros and cons of 'globalisation'. There is hardly any important global meeting which does not witness vigorous protest marches or picketing by the opponents of the globalisation process.

Equally, on the opposite side, there are those who regard it as panacea for all the world's problems and key to unmixed prosperity and well being for all the countries and all the people. If you take a poll in any assembly, including I am sure this one, you will find some are strongly for and some are strongly against globalisation.

To my mind, neither view—for or against—is correct. The only rational view is to accept it as an emerging and powerful global reality which has a momentum of its own. Our job as an independent nation/state is to ensure that we maximise the advantage for our country and minimise the risks. It has both pluses and minuses like any other major global economic change—say, the industrial revolution of the 18th century. Some countries gained, some lost —partly because of the then prevailing political circumstances. India, for example, lost because of colonialism and fragmented nature of our polity. UK, Europe, US—and later Japan prospered. Same is the case with globalisation. One big difference, however, is that unlike the olden days, today our destiny is in our own hands.

Before we look at our opportunities and challenges from globalisation, it is good to be certain of facts—where exactly India is in terms of globalisation. If we look at some of our own debate, it would seem as if we were already well on the way to globalisation, which was shaking up our economy. A most common measure of globalisation is openness to trade and a country's participation in trade. By this measure, the extent of India's globalisation is insignificant—it is one of the lowest in the world. India's share in world trade is a meagre 0.7 per cent or so. If a map of the world were drawn on the scale of a country's participation in trade, India, with a population of more than 1,000 million, will occupy a smaller area than Singapore with a population of only 3 million. You would need a magnifying glass to locate India on that map!

A second commonly used measure of globalisation is a country's participation in international capital flows, particularly foreign direct investment (FDI). As you know, annual flow of FDI across the globe is more than $ 1 trillion, i.e. $ 1,000 billion. Annual FDI inflows into India is $ 3 – 4 billion only or 0.3–0.4 per cent of the total—that is all. Same is true of foreign institutional investment (FII).

Therefore, the first point that I would like to emphasise is that despite all the talk, we are nowhere even close to being globalised in terms of any commonly used indicator of globalisation. In fact, we are still one of the least globalised among major countries—however we look at it.

An equally important point is that whether the so-called globalisation is considered to be good or bad for a country depends crucially on the sense in which the word is used. The word may be used in a purely descriptive sense to describe a 'shrinkage' of distance among nation states due to technological changes in transport and communication and closer integration of product and financial markets across the world.

Another sense in which the word may be used is the effect of such changes on different countries or groups of countries, such as, developed and developing. In yet another sense, the word may also represent a 'globalisation of ideas or ideology' and may be used as a synonym for triumph of capitalism or dominance of unfettered markets.

In discussing the issue of globalisation in the Indian context, I propose to confine myself largely to the factual and descriptive sense in which the word is used, i.e. the technological changes, and associated policy changes, that have brought the world economies closer and made them more integrated with each other.

In this particular sense, I believe that the changes that have occurred in the patterns of trade and capital flows in recent years are to India's advantage— although, unfortunately, so far we have not made much use of it. Today, in terms of the potential benefits of globalisation, India is in a very different position than would have been the case 50 or even 20 years ago.

This is because the sources of what economists call 'comparative advantage' have changed dramatically in India's favour in the 1990s because of the technological revolution. In the old days, comparative advantage was largely determined by 'factor endowments', i.e. land, labour and capital. Geographical location and early starts in industry also conferred greater advantages.

Thus, at one time, a country's trade pattern, was determined by its natural resources and the productivity of its land. Leaving aside political and institutional factors, a country's level of income was also largely determined by the global demand for its natural resources and its relative efficiency in exploiting them. The importance of land as a source of comparative advantage, however, changed dramatically after the industrial revolution. Today, it is almost insignificant. Thus, except for the United States, countries accounting for a predominant share of the world GDP have a relatively small share of global land area.

After the industrial revolution, the availability of 'capital' or investible resources became the most dominant source of comparative advantage. At this institute, established by the great Prof. P.C. Mahalonobis, I hardly need to elaborate on the importance that was attached to domestic capital accumulation in early development economics. In fact, scarcity of capital and low domestic savings were considered to be, and rightly so, as principal causes of a country's underdevelopment.

Today, availability of capital and productivity are still crucial in determining a country's growth rate. However, there has been a dramatic change in the global mobility of capital, and national boundaries are no longer important determinants of sources and uses of capital. A dramatic illustration of this is the fact that the most developed country in the world, which enjoyed unprecedented growth during the 1990s, is actually a capital-importing country, i.e. the United States. Similarly, the fastest growing developing country, i.e. China, is one of the largest recipients of capital from outside.

Similarly, labour is no longer an important element in cost of production and in determining a country's comparative advantage. In most manufacturing industries in the world, it is no higher than one-eighth of total costs. In India, it may be somewhat higher because of our domestic laws, but the important fact to note is that India no longer needs to specialise only in the production of labour-intensive plantation crops or primary commodities.

A related development which is linked to the above changes, is the 'services revolution'. The focus of attention in conventional economics, was on production of goods—manufactured products and agricultural commodities. It was, of course, recognised that the services sector (which includes transport, communication, trade, banking, construction and public administration, etc.)

was an important source of income and employment in most economies. However, overall, the growth of services was perceived at best as a by-product of developments in the primary and secondary sectors, and at worst as a drag on the prospects for long-term economic growth.

In the last few years, there has been a phenomenal change in the conventional view of services and their role in the economy. This change has been facilitated by unprecedented and unforeseen advances in computer and communication technology. As a result, the development of certain services is now regarded as one of the preconditions of economic growth, and not as one of its consequences.

The boundary between goods and services is also disappearing. Many industrial products are not only manufactured, but they are also researched, designed, marketed, advertised, distributed, leased and serviced.

An important aspect of the 'services revolution' is that geography and levels of industrialisation are no longer the primary determinants of the location of facilities for production of services. As a result, the traditional role of developing countries is also changing—from mere recipients to important providers of long-distance and high value services.

From India's point of view, these developments provide opportunities for substantial growth. For example:

- The fastest growing segment of services is the rapid expansion of knowledge-based services, such as, professional and technical services. India has a tremendous advantage in the supply of such services because of a developed structure of technological and educational institutions, such as this one, and lower labour costs.

- Unlike most other prices, world prices of transport and communication services have fallen dramatically. By 1960, sea transport costs were less than a third of their 1920 level, and they have continued to fall. The cost of a telephone call fell more than 10-fold between 1970 and 2000. Moreover, the cost of communication is also becoming independent of distance. The most dramatic example in this area is, of course, provided by the 'Internet'. India's geographical distance from several important industrial markets (for instance, North America) is no longer an important element in the cost structure of skill-based services.

- It is now feasible to 'unbundle' production of different types of goods and services. India does not necessarily have to be a low-cost producer of certain types of goods (e.g. computers or discs) before it can become an efficient supplier of services embodied in them (e.g. software or music).

At the same time, it must be recognised that the 'death of distance' and the growing integration of global product, services and financial markets in recent years have also presented new challenges for management of the national economy—not only in India but all over the world. The trend towards integration of markets, particularly financial markets, is by no means an unmixed blessing. Unlike the old days, a heavy price may have to be paid by national economies for somnolence, sloth and non-conformity to generally accepted international norms and standards of macroeconomic management, disclosure, transparency and financial accountability.

Another consequence of recent global trends is the greater vulnerability of national economies to developments outside their own borders. A crisis in any one or a group of countries, can be transmitted to other countries—including countries which may not have any strong economic linkages with crisis-affected countries. Thus, the nineties have been marked by a large number of currency crises (for example, in Mexico, Russia, East Asia and Brazil—and currently Argentina and Turkey); substantial swings in exchange rates (including the exchange rate of three leading currencies—the Dollar, the Euro and the Yen); and run ups in asset prices followed by sharp collapse (for example in Japan and East Asia earlier and the United States last year). While the crises initially occur in one or two specific countries, their adverse effects are felt across the world.

While we must be careful, on the whole, in my view—the death of distance, the services revolution, and the mobility of capital—which characterise globalisation—present unprecedented opportunities for India. The primary source of comparative advantages today are: skills and ability to adapt and change. And, India has the advantage—of skills, of entrepreneurship and of managerial competence in taking advantage of these changes.

If what I have said is correct, then, why are we not jumping with joy and optimism? Why are we so 'unglobalised' in terms of our share in trade, investment or communication?

Transition from a closed to a vibrant, open and a more globally dominant economy will certainly take time and will not be painless.

As of now, we also have much greater tolerance for waste, non-work and survival of the inefficient, and the self-seeking than other fast growing countries. Somehow to make this transition—from a less productive and less challenging economy to a more work-oriented and competitive economy—is the real challenge of globalisation.

If we continue in our old ways, I see real social problems and inequalities emerging in our society. We will have islands of prosperity and excellence— IT, beauty parades and media entertainment amidst growing disparity, rising unemployment and immiseration. And as has happened in several countries in the 1990s, including Turkey and Argentina—just now, those who are with us today will be the first to leave.

The principal lesson of recent economic and technological developments, and growing tensions and inequalities within and across countries, is that our fate is in our hands. Our public policies have to respond to our own requirements rather than to any fixed global ideology or a pre-determined and internationally prescribed model of economic progress. In my view, this is the real lesson of the 1990s.

My fervent hope is that as you—the best and the brightest of our country— go out and face a 'globalising' world, you will keep India's interest, its integrity, its indivisibility and its future potential close to your hearts and your minds. I have no doubt that, with your help, India of 2025 will be a very different place, and a much more dominant force in the world economy, than was the case 25 years ago or at the beginning of the new millennium.

Twenty-sixth Convocation Address at the Indian Statistical Institute, Kolkata, January 15, 2002.
Economic Developments in India, Vol. 50.

11

Half-hearted Globalisation

SHANKAR ACHARYA

As with many other topics, we Indians have done a lot more talking on globalisation than action. You wouldn't think so from the fuss that's made of 'WTO diktats' and 'IMF policies'. But the facts are pretty clear. Let's take a look at them and compare to the growing economic superpower to our north, China. Picking China as a comparator is obvious for many reasons. These are the only two countries which will have a billion plus population throughout the 21st century (nobody else will be close). A growing number of analysts have linked the fate of globalisation to its impact on these two populous giants. Most importantly, China has (for the last quarter century) decisively embraced global economic integration as a crucial plank of her dash to superpower status, while we have hummed and hawed. Yes, there was a brief interlude, 1991-1997, when we also seemed to clearly signal a similar desire to engage the world economy. But subsequent events suggest that we soon relapsed to dithering and *chalta hai.*

Three decades ago, in 1970, both China and India were rather closed economies, with the share of exports (goods and services) accounting for less than 4 per cent of GDP, compared to 12 per cent for developing countries as a whole. Interestingly, India's share at 3.5 per cent was almost double that of China's at 1.8 per cent. But that was back then. When China opened up her economy in the late seventies, she did so with remarkable strategic decisiveness and determination. By 1982 her merchandise exports at $ 21 billion were already more than double India's at about $ 9 billion. By 1990 the gap had widened as China's goods exports almost tripled to $ 62 billion, while India's increased sedately to $ 18 billion. But China's truly astonishing export surge has come in the nineties with merchandise exports touching $ 250 billion in 2000, compared to India's $ 43 billion. As players in international trade, the two countries are now in different leagues.

Through her hugely successful domestic and international policies China won growing import shares in the major markets of the world. Professor T.N. Srinivasan of Yale University has compiled data for eight 3-digit SITC product categories, including toys, sporting goods, textiles, garments, footwear, telecom equipment and accessories, plastic articles and certain categories of electrical machinery. By his estimate these eight product categories account for about half of India's manufactured exports and almost 40 per cent of her total merchandise exports. The difference in evolving market shares of China and India in these selected product imports into EEC and North America is striking (Table 11.1). Between 1990 and 2000 India's share in EEC imports actually declined from a meagre 0.8 per cent to 0.7 per cent, at a time when China expanded her share from 3.4 per cent to 9.2 per cent! It was the same story in the North American market: India's share stagnated at a low 1.0 per cent over the decade, while China grew her share from 11.8 to 25.3 per cent. No wonder western shopping malls are full of 'Made in China' products, while you have to search quite hard to find goods of Indian provenance!

I have dwelt on foreign trade indicators for two reasons. First, I do believe that international trade is the single best index of a country's globalisation. Second, trade data are subject to the discipline of partner country data systems (China's exports are other countries' imports) and thus largely immune to the deficiencies of national data systems. Another obvious indicator of globalisation is, of course, foreign investment, especially foreign direct investment (FDI). Here too the contrast between China and India is striking and hugely in China's favour (Table 11.1). As I have noted elsewhere (ET, October 4, 2001) in the five years 1996-2000 China received over $ 200 billion of FDI while India managed a somewhat pitiful $ 13 billion. China's nineties surge in exports and FDI were mutually reinforcing. Much of FDI went into expanding export-driven firms and the huge export success, in turn, attracted increasing flows of FDI. And both these surges were a large part of China's enviable success in sustaining fast growth of national output and employment.

Of late, it has become fashionable in some Indian quarters to argue that India's FDI estimates are underestimated by narrowness of concept, while China's is exaggerated by 'round-tripping' of domestic funds. May be (though if this is so obvious, why doesn't the government's recent Mid-Year Review correct the data for India at least?). But to doubters I can only recommend a quick trip to Shanghai or Guangzhou to see the difference with their eyes (by now lots of our politicians have done this!).

Alright, you say, so what should India do to get greater gains from globalisation? Well, the list of policies has been listed many times by many people, including, most recently, in the Tenth Plan. They include lower government borrowing, much less restrictive labour laws, phasing out of SSI reservations, lowering of our unusually high customs duties, quick reform of the power sector, reduction in 'transaction costs' in taxation, finance and infrastructure provision, decisive privatisations and so on. To even repeat such lists is becoming embarrassing! The problem is not with knowing what's to be done... but to do it. Until we DO sensible economic policies, half-hearted globalisation will continue to yield half-baked results!

Table 11.1

Indicators of Globalisation

	1982	1990	2000
Merchandise Exports ($ Billion)			
India	9.1	18.0	43.0
China	21.1	62.1	249.1
Foreign Direct Investment ($ Billion)			
India	negligible	0.2	2.3
China	negligible	3.5	38.4
Share in EEC Selected Imports* (Per Cent)			
India	-	0.8	0.7
China	-	3.4	9.2
Share in North American Selected Imports* (Per Cent)			
India	-	1.0	1.0
China	-	11.8	25.3

Source : World Development Indicators, 2002 (World Bank) and UN Comtrade Database as compiled by Professor T.N. Srinivasan (Yale University).

Note : * : For SITC Product Categories 764, 778, 842, 843, 847, 851, 893, 894.

The Economic Times, January 2, 2003.

Economic Developments in India, Vol. 61.

Section III

Sectoral Development:
Agriculture, Industry, Financial
and External Sector

12

Reshaping Indian Food and Agricultural Policy to Meet the Challenges and Opportunities of Globalisation

PER PINSTRUP-ANDERSEN

The food and agriculture situation in India today is remarkably different from that of 35 years ago, but too many of India's agricultural policies are still focused on the conditions of 35 years ago. With appropriate changes in policy, Indian agriculture could become an important force for economic growth, poverty alleviation, and competitiveness in the world economy.

As an outsider, it is not my intention to preach to India about the course it should take. On the contrary, I have arrived at conclusions concerning the need for changes in policy based on what I have learned from India's own leading economists and from IFPRI's own research. At the International Food Policy Research Institute (IFPRI), we are fortunate to have Dr. Ashok Gulati as a senior member of our research and management team. Our research on Indian food policy over the years has been carried out in collaboration with leading Indian scholars, among them Professors G.S. Bhalla, V. Rajagopalan, C. Ramasamy, and S. Thorat.

Were we meeting 35 years ago, our concerns would be poles apart from those of today. I think that some of you, like myself, are old enough to remember the middle and late 1960s, when famine was averted in India primarily because of massive external food aid, mainly from the United States. In those days, the conventional wisdom among too many so-called experts was that India would never be able to feed itself, and that the international community should practice 'triage', or lifeboat ethics, abandoning those unable to take care of themselves to their fate.

Because India adopted appropriate policies and was willing to adopt modern agricultural technology, as I will outline later, the country no longer faces food shortages and dependence on external food aid. On the contrary, the central government instead must tackle the problem of what to do with a 60 million metric tonne stock of surplus of wheat and rice.[1]

I would like to proceed to briefly sketch out the current food security situation in India as I understand it, and then focus most of the remainder of my remarks on the current problems facing Indian agriculture, the promise and perils that globalisation poses for a strategy of growth with equity in which agriculture plays a prominent role, and the place of science, technology, and public policies in such a strategy.

Current State of Food Security: Hunger Amidst Plenty

Even though food availability in India might be described today as a state of plenty, India also must grapple with the paradox of persistent hunger. According to the Food and Agriculture Organization of the United Nations (FAO), over 225 million Indians remain chronically undernourished. Alarmingly, this is an increase of 5 per cent from 1991, the year in which the process of economic reform began in earnest, when 215 million Indians were food insecure.[2]

Malnutrition among preschool children is of particular concern. On the positive side, India and its South Asian neighbours have made steady, albeit slow, progress in reducing the incidence of child malnutrition since the mid 1980s, and the absolute number of malnourished pre-schoolers has fallen as well. But over half of all Indian preschoolers still suffer from malnutrition, compared to 33 per cent in Sub-Saharan Africa, where child malnutrition is on the rise.[3] Malnutrition is associated with about half of the 98 deaths per 1,000 live births that occur each year among Indian children under 5 years of age.[4] For those who survive, it usually means irreversible damage to their physical and mental development. Adults whose growth has been stunted by childhood malnutrition are 2-9 per cent less productive than non-stunted adults.[5] Countless Indians will not grow up to be scientists, software engineers, creative artists, political leaders, entrepreneurs or productive farmers and workers because of this scourge.

---

1. Ministry of Finance (2002).
2. FAO (2001).
3. Rosegrant *et al.* (2001).
4. UNDP (2001).
5. Gillespie and Haddad (2000).

A critical factor behind India's high rates of child malnutrition are birth weights of less than 2.5 kilogrammes for the affected children. In South Asia, 21 per cent of the children are born with low birth weights, accounting for 64 per cent of the world's low birth weight newborns. This is usually the result of poor maternal nutrition both before conception and during pregnancy. In effect, malnutrition is directly transmitted from one generation to the next.[6] Cultural practices contribute to this situation: because families of daughters must pay bridegrooms a dowry, girls tend to receive less care and food than boys. Girls, therefore, have higher mortality rates than boys, and those who survive grow up malnourished and likely to have low birth weight babies. The problem is even more compounded for girls born into tribal and scheduled caste families, for such families are far more likely to be poor and food insecure.[7]

Generally speaking, if a person consumes an adequate level of calories, he or she will also take in enough protein. However, this does not guarantee adequate consumption of vitamins and minerals. Insufficient intake of these micronutrients—often called 'hidden hunger'—affects vast numbers of people, with serious public health consequences. In South and Southeast Asia, 76 per cent of pregnant women and 63 per cent of preschool children are anaemic, and around 50 per cent of the world's anaemic women live in South Asia. Deficient iron in the diet is the leading cause of anaemia. The risk of maternal mortality among anaemic women is 23 per cent higher than that of non-anaemic mothers. Their babies are more likely to be premature, have low birth weights and die as newborns. The incidence of anaemia is also high among South Asian infants and children. Anaemia can impair child health and development, limit learning capacity, impair immune systems, and reduce work performance. Iron deficiency anaemia is estimated to reduce productivity by up to 17 per cent for heavy manual labour. Even when iron deficiency does not progress to anaemia, it can reduce work performance. These effects of iron deficiency result in annual economic losses estimated at $ 5 billion for the South Asia region.[8]

Insufficient intake of vitamin A among children in developing countries is the leading cause of preventable severe visual impairment and blindness and contributes to infections and death. Pregnant women who are vitamin A deficient face increased risk of mortality and mother-to-child HIV transmission.

---

6. Allen and Gillespie (2001).

7. Meinzen-Dick *et al.* (1997).

8. ACC/SCN and IFPRI (2000); Haddad and Gillespie (2000).

India has a high incidence of clinical vitamin A deficiency as compared to other Asian countries.

Both the state governments and the central government in India's federal system have established policies, programmes, and institutions aimed at preventing and mitigating famine, improving nutrition, and assuring that poor and vulnerable Indians have access to food. These include the Maharashtra Employment Guarantee Scheme, the Tamil Nadu Integrated Nutrition Programme, the Integrated Child Development Services (ICDS), and the Targeted Public Distribution System (TPDS). The efforts of the state government in Kerala to assure the well being of all the residents of that state, even in conditions of modest growth and widespread poverty, are especially noteworthy. I would also stress, drawing here on the work of India's own Nobel Laureate economist A.K. Sen, that the democratic institutions of this country, including the free press, have played an important role in eradicating famine and reducing chronic undernutrition. A democratic government, coupled with active and independent mass media and engaged organisations of civil society, is more likely to respond to the needs and demands of all its citizens than an authoritarian regime.[9]

Although a number of factors contribute to food insecurity, it is widely recognised that poverty is the primary cause. In a country like India that produces large surpluses of basic food grains, it is clear that large numbers of people remain hungry because they have insufficient resources to purchase all the food they need. Improvements in India's already extensive safety net programmes could help over the short- and medium-term. The long-run solution, however, is investment in human resources (assuring access to health care and education for all), empowerment of poor people to better articulate and pursue their interests, and programmes and policies that assure poor people access to productive resources and employment opportunities. Taking such steps will benefit well-fed and food-insecure Indians alike, given the costs to the economy of hunger and malnutrition that I have noted.

India's efforts to address widespread micro-nutrient malnutrition have had mixed results. The central government has been successful in controlling iodine deficiency disorders (which can lead to severe mental retardation) through an effective program of salt iodisation. Distribution of vitamin A supplements has been a somewhat successful strategy, although this is more of a curative approach than a preventive one. The main approach to iron

---

9. Drèze and Sen (1989).

deficiency, distribution of iron folate supplements, is not regarded as successful.[10]

Unfinished Economic Reform in Agriculture

As this audience knows better than I, for most of the first 40 years after independence, India pursued economic policies characterised by strict regulation of domestic and international trade, with substantial subsidies provided on many goods and services (notably food), and reservation of substantial segments of the economy to national, and especially small businesses. Public sector firms and government agencies played a major role in many areas of the economy, often operating on a monopoly basis. These policies reflected the strong commitment of India's founding fathers and mothers to nationalism, socialism, non-alignment, and self-reliance. Beginning tentatively in the 1980s, with a substantial deepening after 1991, governments led by various political parties have implemented economic policy reforms, including international trade liberalisation, liberalisation of direct foreign investment, a loosening of restrictions on large enterprises, and financial sector liberalisation.

Some of the post-1991 results have been impressive. Despite concerns that greater openness to the global economy would make India vulnerable to external shocks, the Indian economy has grown at an average rate of 5.4 per cent per year since 1997, notwithstanding the Asian economic crisis, increased energy prices, and a slowing international economy. At home, the economy has overcome natural disasters, sluggish agricultural performance, deepening communal tensions, acts of terrorism, and the very real possibility of war with Pakistan. Indeed, no one would think of calling India a 'basket case' these days. Instead, your country is recognised as one of the world's fastest growing and most resilient economies. The urban and urbane middle class is roughly the same size as the whole population of the United States, and seeks sophisticated consumer goods. India is a world-class player in software and information technology.

In the agricultural sector, however, the policy reform process has been tentative at best. Controls and subsidies, created in an era of scarcity, impede the creation of an integrated national food system, and constitute a major barrier to India pursuing comparative advantage in the global economy.

---

10. Allen and Gillespie (2001).

Parastatals continue to play a significant role, particularly in the foodgrain market. Most importantly, these controls and subsidies have not really benefited rural poor people. Instead, at least half of the fertiliser subsidy goes to keep several inefficient domestic fertiliser firms in business, at high cost to the treasury. Irrigation subsidies promote excessive use of agricultural water and actually drain funds from operations and maintenance of water facilities and the creation of new irrigation infrastructure. Power subsidies contribute to corruption and pilfering of supplies that are reported as agricultural uses. It is estimated that subsidies for fertiliser, irrigation water, and power account for over two per cent of gross domestic product (GDP), and nearly nine per cent of agricultural GDP. Agricultural subsidies are a big factor in the central government budget deficit, which is consuming five per cent of GDP in the current fiscal year. The subsidies also contribute to regional inequality, as the states with the largest agricultural sectors reap the biggest harvest in subsidies, but the poorer states, which receive a small share, are the ones that are supposed to benefit.[11]

Whereas input subsidies help to encourage overproduction of foodgrains, and impose heavy storage costs on the government, other agricultural policies impede agricultural growth and diversification. Restrictions on the movement and stocking of grain keep private investments in storage and processing low. Taxes on agricultural processing enterprises are passed on to the farmers, and impede expansion of higher value-added exports.[12] Such policies may have made sense when the government needed to assure cheap food availability in the late 1960s, but they seem wholly illogical at a time when India has more grain than it can use or store.

Two significant biases have characterised Indian agriculture over the past several decades: an emphasis on achieving foodgrain self-sufficiency at the expense of other crops, and a public investment emphasis on irrigated areas and, to a lesser extent, high-potential rainfed areas at the expense of resource-poor rainfed areas. But fruits, vegetables, oilseeds, milk and milk products, cut flowers, and agro-industry offer new opportunities, which could benefit small farmers as well as large, both at home and abroad. About 80 per cent of India's rural poor people live in rainfed areas, with about half living in zones with limited agricultural potential and/or infrastructure and market access.

---

11. Gulati and Hoda (forthcoming); Gulati and Narayan (forthcoming).

12. Gulati and Hoda (forthcoming).

Population densities are increasing in these less favoured areas despite lack of investment, and are likely to continue to do so for the next several decades.[13]

Past and current agricultural policies have also had a negative environmental impact. The increased yields achieved in Green Revolution areas preserved forests, hillsides, and fragile drylands from cultivation. However, poor natural resource management and excessive use of agricultural chemicals in the Green Revolution areas have led to soil salinisation, fertiliser and pesticide contamination of waterways, pesticide poisoning of farmers and labourers, and declining water tables. These problems have implications for agricultural growth, overall economic growth, and food security, because natural resource degradation appears to be worsening, and has apparently led to stagnant and even declining yield growth in some of India's intensive farming areas.[14]

The process of economic policy reform needs to extend much more thoroughly into the food and agricultural sector. Agriculture remains extremely significant in India, and is a potential driver of both overall economic growth and poverty reduction. Value added in agriculture continues to contribute about 25 per cent of gross domestic product (GDP), more than in most East and Southeast Asian countries, though less than in some other South Asian nations. Over 70 per cent of the population lives in rural areas, and 62 per cent of the workforce is engaged in agriculture. The overwhelming majority of Indian farmers have very small farms, averaging less than two hectares in size.[15] The rural poverty rate is about 20 per cent higher than that for urban areas, and agricultural growth offers rural poor people the most likely path to sustainable livelihoods and well-being, whether they work on the farm or in non-farm rural activities that are closely related to agriculture, such as processing, produce marketing, transportation, infrastructure development, farm input and implement production and marketing, and consumer goods demanded by farmers.

I want to emphasise that reforms that make agriculture more market-oriented do not reduce the importance of sound and transparent public administration. Indeed, effective government at both the central and state level is a crucial component of reform. Government action will remain critical to provide safety nets for those who may be adversely affected by economic policy

---

13. *ibid.*; Fan and Hazell (2000).

14. *ibid.*; Hazell (undated).

15. Rosegrant and Hazell (2000); Ministry of Finance (2002); Gulati (2001).

change, to maintain standards such as a system of weights and measures, to enforce contracts, and to make investments in public goods that are essential but that do not offer the private sector the likelihood of a profitable return. A good example of such public goods would be agricultural research and development (R&D) to breed drought tolerant and pest resistant varieties of the crops that poor farmers cultivate in less-favoured rainfed areas. The social return would be high in the form of less poverty, more food security, and higher productivity.

The alternative to the current dysfunctional system of agricultural input subsidies is not simply to cut back on the subsidies and expect farmers to pay higher prices for inputs. Rather, input price reform must go hand in hand with institutional reform. In the case of fertilisers, the subsidies permit domestic industry to remain inefficient and non-competitive. Reform must introduce market forces into the production and marketing of fertilisers, which should lead to lower costs for farmers as protection from import competition is removed. In the case of water and power subsidies, the public supply agencies need to become much more transparent and accountable in their operations. As it stands, these monopolies lack incentives to improve the quality of service and the resources to maintain and enhance infrastructure. Institutional reform may be achieved by engaging agricultural water and power users directly in operations, maintenance, and expansion of water and power systems. Such a participatory approach can make short-term price increases due to removal or reduction of subsidies more palatable, and are likely to facilitate improvements in the quality of service. Increased input prices that reflect true costs offer farmers incentives for better management of inputs and natural resources.[16]

Likewise, substantial reforms are needed on the output side. Trade liberalisation since 1991 has reduced the protection of Indian agriculture from international competition, and controls on the movement of grain have eased. But much remains to be done. Further liberalisation of domestic output markets will have to be coupled with enhanced social safety nets, so that rising input prices do not undermine the livelihoods of poor farmers, and uncontrolled grain prices do not hurt poor consumers (many of whom are themselves farmers). It would be helpful to decouple procurement prices from support prices, which are aimed at assuring that farmers are able to at least meet the paid-out cost of production. While the government should continue to set the latter prices, TPDS should procure its grain from private grain

---

16. Gulati and Narayan (forthcoming).

traders at market-determined prices. The Food Corporation of India should limit its publicly-held grain stock to the minimal level needed to respond to the threat of famine and to stabilise prices in the case of a true emergency situation, e.g. 10 million metric tonnes, plus what is needed to run the TPDS, rather than 60 million tonnes. The controls on the movement and private stocking of some agricultural commodities (foodgrains, edible oils, cotton, and sugar) prevent the development of an integrated national market. Repeal of the Essential Commodities Act, or limiting its use to times of national emergency, would encourage private investment in storage and handling facilities.[17]

Reduction in input subsidies, will free up public funds that can be used instead for investment purposes. Research at IFPRI and elsewhere has suggested a number of priorities for the government to pursue in public investment in agriculture. Since the 1980s, the high cost of subsidies has crowded out such public investment, which grew at an average annual rate of 15 per cent in the 1970s, 5 per cent in the 1980s, and just 1 per cent in the early 1990s. Private investment has not filled in the gap, and is generally not targeted in areas that contribute to poverty alleviation. We have carried out a study of a variety of public investment expenditures in agriculture and rural development: research and development, irrigation, rural roads, education, power, soil and water, rural community development, and health, using state level data from the period 1970-93. We assessed different types of expenditure for their impact on growth and poverty reduction. We found that expenditures on roads and agricultural R&D are the major 'win-win' strategies, with high impacts on both growth and poverty reduction. In addition, education expenditure has a significant impact on poverty reduction, because it leads to increases in rural employment and wages. While irrigation expenditure is important for growth, it has little impact on poverty reduction. All of the other forms of expenditure have lesser impacts on either growth or poverty.[18]

Another IFPRI study lends additional support to the need for investment in agricultural research oriented toward poor farmers and education, with an emphasis on full enrollment of girls as well as boys. We found that the biggest single factor in reductions in child malnutrition globally during the period 1970-95 was female education. Female education and improvements in food availability combined accounted for nearly 70 per cent of the gains in child nutrition.[19]

---

17. Gulati and Hoda (forthcoming).
18. Fan, Hazell, and Thorat (1999); Hazell (undated).
19. Smith and Haddad (2000).

A third study that we have carried out shows that for every type of public investment studied, the highest marginal impact on agricultural production and poverty alleviation occurs in India's rainfed areas rather than in irrigated areas. Investment in high-yielding crop varieties, roads, and private irrigation have the highest production and poverty impact in less-favoured rainfed areas.[20] Hence, the bias against public investment in these areas is not sound agricultural development policy.

Nor is the bias in favour of foodgrains appropriate in the circumstances of serious over-production. Overall economic growth and rising middle-class affluence has increased domestic demand for livestock products, particularly milk and milk production, as well as fruits, vegetables, flowers, and vegetable oils. This means new opportunities for farmers to diversify and specialise. If poor farmers are to have a chance to benefit from these opportunities, then investments are needed in poorer regions in roads, transport, electricity, improved crop varieties, disease control, refrigeration, communications, and food processing and storage.[21] As I have just noted, these investments promise a substantial boost to economic growth at the same time that they contribute to equity and poverty alleviation.

Smallholder farmers, often are more efficient at producing many labour intensive livestock and horticultural products than are larger operations, but they need to have organisations that allow for efficient marketing and access to inputs. India's experience with milk marketing cooperatives shows that they can permit poor people, including landless labourers and women farmers as well as smallholders more generally, to participate in new economic opportunities such as the 'White Revolution.' Co-ops could likewise assure that small farmers and other rural poor people can gain from expanded horticulture and floriculture production for domestic and international markets.[22] At the same time, co-ops and farmer and community associations that are run in a democratic and accountable manner can amplify the political voice of rural poor people.

Eliminating protective policies that keep domestic agro-industry, particularly oilseeds processing, uncompetitive with imports would also open up new opportunities for production of greater value-added products. Indian oilseed farmers are already quite efficient and productive, and much of the

---

20. Fan and Hazell (2000).

21. Hazell (undated).

22. *Ibid.*

output comes from the country's less favoured semi-arid tropics. The domestic processing industry needs to become similarly competitive. Removal or reduction of taxation of agricultural processing firms would help develop this industry. Reservation of groundnut and rapeseed-mustard processing to small scale industries is well-intentioned in attempting to assure that smaller entrepreneurs have opportunities, but it has prevented the industry from capturing economies of scale and cutting costs to become competitive with imports.[23] As larger, higher value-added enterprises develop, it is important that equitable contracting arrangements and other mechanisms allow smallholder farmers to capture a fair share of the benefits from oilseed sector growth. Such enterprises can also create new higher wage rural employment opportunities.

The transition to a more market-oriented agricultural policy will need to be accompanied by reform of safety net programmes. Some of the largest, notably ICDS and TPDS, presently fail to reach large numbers of poor and nutritionally vulnerable people. The programmes would be greatly enhanced by better targeting based on income levels and nutritional need, coupled with community participation in programme design and management so that intended beneficiaries feel a sense of ownership.[24]

The Role of Science and Technology

Science and technology, if applied within a framework of appropriate policies, can do a great deal to advance food security, agricultural growth, equity, and sound natural resource management. Technological change frequently is risky. Thirty-five years ago, India took bold steps to make sure that it could indeed feed itself. Thanks to visionary leadership from policy makers like Agriculture Minister C. Subramaniam and agricultural scientists like M.S. Swaminathan and Norman Borlaug, India launched its Green Revolution, making investments in irrigation and providing farmers in irrigated areas with access to high-yielding rice and wheat seeds, fertiliser, and pesticides. Initially there was scepticism about whether the technology would mostly benefit richer farmers who enjoyed good access to inputs. In fact, the benefits were widely shared. Between 1970 and 1995, while India's population increased by 67 per cent, cereal production grew by 88 per cent. Dietary energy supplies per person rose 15 per cent, so that by 1995, there was

---

23. *ibid.*; Gulati and Hoda (forthcoming).
24. Allen and Gillespie (2001).

enough food available for every Indian to meet her or his minimum calorie needs, if the food were distributed according to need.[25] And indeed, the proportion of Indians who are chronically undernourished fell from 38 per cent in 1980 to 23 per cent today.[26] Rural poverty declined from over 50 per cent in the mid 1960s to 27 per cent in 2000.[27] Small scale farmers as well as larger producers gained from increased yields and lower unit costs of production due to their having adopted the new agricultural technology. Landless rural people found new employment opportunities on and off the farm, and consumers benefited from substantially lower food prices. Agricultural growth stimulated growth throughout the economy, as rural demand for goods and services grew with rural incomes.[28]

India has developed an impressive public agricultural R&D system at both the Central and state levels. Yet the country seriously under-invests in public agricultural R&D: spending only accounted for 0.5 per cent of agricultural GDP in the 1990s, compared to 1.5 per cent for all developing countries and 3 per cent in the United States. Public agricultural research needs to focus more on addressing the problems of poor farmers and regions, as larger farms and better-off regions are likely to attract private research investment.[29]

Public agricultural R&D should focus on development and dissemination of technologies and natural resource management practices that are environmentally sound. Some of these technologies already exist and include precision farming, crop diversification, integrated pest management, pest resistant crop varieties, and improved soil and water management practices. Some of these, if managed appropriately, can increase yields at the same time that they reduce natural resource degradation. More research is needed to create more technology options for poor farmers. Conventional and molecular biology based approaches to research should be used to develop pest and disease-resistant and drought and salt-tolerant crop varieties that do not depend on application of chemicals. In dryland areas, diseases and pests often wipe out the groundnut, pigeon pea, and cotton crops upon which smallholders depend for their livelihoods.[30] Agricultural researchers must work

---

25. Asian Development Bank (2000).

26. FAO (1999, 2001).

27. Fan, Hazell, and Thorat (1999); Planning Commission (2002).

28. Hazell and Haddad (2001).

29. Hazell (undated); Gulati and Hoda (forthcoming).

30. Hazell; Paarlberg (2001).

in close partnership with farmers, and draw on the insights of indigenous knowledge. Farmers in India's semi-arid tropical zones, for example, have on their own devised approaches to soil conservation, and this knowledge could be integrated into research programmes aimed at sustainable intensification of agriculture in these resource-poor areas.[31]

Today, India again must choose whether to adopt new agricultural technology that many critics consider risky. Contentious public debate over the environmental and socio-economic risks of modern agricultural biotechnology have meant long delays in approval of the commercial release of genetically modified crops in India. Last month, the government's Genetic Engineering Approval Committee granted permission to Indian farmers to grow genetically modified cotton commercially, four years after the first field trials.[32] Extensive research on additional applications of modern agricultural biotechnology is underway both through the public Indian Council of Agricultural Research (ICAR) and the domestic and international private sector. Opposition has centered primarily on the involvement of foreign companies, such as Monsanto, in efforts to commercialise genetically modified cotton. While Monsanto was trying to get approval for commercialisation of insect-resistant cotton in India, it was also trying to acquire the US patent on genetic use restriction technology that renders second generation seeds sterile, i.e., the so-called terminator gene. Although Monsanto ultimately agreed not to commercialise the latter technology, concern about sterile seeds was another major factor in opposition to the cotton from Indian non-governmental organisations.[33]

Despite the antagonism towards genetically modified cotton in India, use of similar cotton seeds (containing genes from the soil bacterium *Bacillus thuringiensis*, or Bt, that produce a toxin that kills the cotton bollworm) in China has had significant benefits. It has reduced synthetic pesticide use on cotton farms dramatically, lowered labour costs, increased profits, reduced collateral damage to non-targeted species and water pollution, and, importantly, dramatically reduced pesticide poisoning cases among farmers and agricultural labourers.[34] In South Africa, Bt cotton has led to substantial yield increases where it is commercially available.[35]

---

31. Kerr (2000).

32. Crop Biotech Update (2002).

33. Paarlberg (2001).

34. *ibid.*

35. Njobe-Mbuli (2000).

Since ICAR research is funded by Indian taxpayers, not foreign companies, and focuses on the needs of poor farmers and consumers (e.g. high protein and insect-resistant rice varieties, as well as insect-resistant cotton, oilseed crops, and potatoes), often in collaboration with public international agricultural research centres such as the International Rice Research Institute and the International Crop Research Institute for the semi-arid tropics, there is reason to hope that some of the results of this research will find its way into farmers fields sooner rather than later. As is a necessity before commercial introduction of genetically modified crops can take place, India has already developed an impressive capacity to assess and manage risks to human health and environment, through inter-ministerial bodies including officials charged with responsibility for environmental protection, agriculture, health, and science and technology, along with university scientists. This capacity is adequate to address legitimate biosafety concerns with respect to biotechnology.[36]

Slow progress in enacting intellectual property rights legislation relating to plant varieties has impeded both private sector research and commercialisation of domestic and imported seeds derived from biotechnology. The recent passage of the Protection of Plant Varieties and Farmers' Rights Legislation by the Parliament creates an intellectual property regime that may serve as a model for other developing countries to meet their obligations under the World Trade Organization (WTO) and the new International Treaty on Plant Genetic Resources for Food and Agriculture. It seeks to balance the need to offer incentives for innovation to private plant breeders with provisions on benefit sharing for individual and community holders of traditional knowledge and on the rights of farmers to save and exchange seeds.[37] Such a system should be effective in promoting both agricultural innovation and the equitable and sustainable management and conservation of India's agricultural biodiversity.

R&D should also focus on improving poor rural people's access to India's well-developed information and communications technology. The development of wireless broadband can greatly expand access to telephones and the Internet in poor rural communities. Using a hub-and-spoke approach, one village with full Internet access can disseminate information and receive requests from other villages that have wireless access to the hub, thereby saving on costs. Digitised radio broadcasts *via* satellite can now cheaply reach large numbers

---

36. Paarlberg (2001).

37. Ministry of Finance (2002); Ramanna (2002).

of people. These technologies offer poor rural dwellers vastly improved access to timely market information, awareness of relevant government policies, and access to new agricultural know-how. Information flows at a greater speed, and has far broader reach, than *via* traditional brick-and-mortar agricultural extension. This can contribute to higher incomes for poor farmers and non-farm rural poor people engaged in handicraft production, with positive impacts on household food security and nutritional status. For poor Indian fisherfolk, cell phones already make it possible to compare prices in different markets for their catch. Technologies aimed at collecting geographically referenced data can be enormously useful in food security research and policy making, e.g. improved targeting of safety net programmes and famine early warning.[38]

Making Globalisation Work for Poor People

Many food security and poverty reduction advocates are concerned that agricultural trade liberalisation will hurt poor people, as larger scale producers come to dominate export crop opportunities and cheap imported produce from developed countries (often produced and exported with heavy subsidies) wipes out smallholders.[39] Most analysts agree that globalisation is presently occurring in a highly inequitable context and under rules that have biases against poor people and countries. However, many would argue, in contrast to the above concern, that if governments in developed and developing countries undertake appropriate policy changes, globalisation can be made to work for poor and hungry people.[40]

In the case of Indian agriculture, most domestically produced commodities enjoy comparative advantage on the home market, and many are competitive, or could become so, in global markets. These advantages can, moreover, be enhanced to the benefit of poor rural people with appropriate policies. However, much depends on the willingness of developed countries to open their markets to developing country products, reduce tariff escalation against higher value commodities and processed goods, and reduce trade-distorting subsidies on their domestic agriculture and exports. India is playing a very prominent role as a leader of the developing countries in the current round of global agricultural trade negotiations through the WTO. By putting 'food and livelihood security' on the table as a 'non-trade concern' to be addressed in the

---

38. Chowdhury (2001).

39. See, for example, WTO Watch (2002).

40. See, for example, Diaz-Bonilla and Robinson (2001).

negotiations, India has helped to steer the discussions toward a clearer focus on the potential impact upon poor people.

There are varying patterns of domestic and international competitiveness among India's major agricultural products. Despite the controls and regulations on foodgrains, research has shown that Indian rice and wheat are very competitive with imports, particularly since the productivity gains of the Green Revolution resulted in real price declines. Moreover, since the mid-1990s, India has become a major rice exporter, as domestic prices have been below or equivalent to world prices. Indian rice is likely to remain competitive, especially in Asian markets, given lower freight costs in comparison to the United States. In contrast, India has only made modest exports of wheat in recent years, despite the large surpluses on hand, as domestic prices remain above world prices. Indian cotton is likewise competitive *vis-à-vis* imports, and seems likely to be competitive on export markets as well. Although neither unprocessed Indian oilseeds nor processed edible oils are competitive in domestic or global markets, deregulation of the edible oils processing industry to allow scale economies might change this. The dairy sector is strongly competitive in the growing domestic market *vis-à-vis* imported products, but does not seem likely to fare well in highly distorted global markets. India has long enjoyed a strong position as an exporter of tea, coffee, spices, cashews, jute, and tobacco, although the prices of some of these commodities are too low to make expansion of production worthwhile. In the 1990s, India has increased its exports of both fresh and processed fruits and vegetables, but further expansion will require improvements in infrastructure, storage, transport, processing, and the ability to meet sanitary and technical requirements in developed country markets. The same applies to fish exports, where there is also potential competitive advantage.[41]

The liberalisation of the industrial sector after 1991 improved the terms of trade between agriculture and manufacturing, and spurred private investment in nongrain agriculture, particularly in horticulture products, livestock products, and fisheries. Beginning in 1994, trade liberalisation was extended to agricultural products. However, grain, oilseed, and edible oil imports have remained subject to protection. Agricultural exports of most products are much less restricted than imports.[42]

---

41. Gulati and Hoda (forthcoming).
42. *ibid.*

If India remains hesitant about completing the liberalisation of agricultural trade, it may lose out on opportunities that globalisation offers while facing some very real risks. Now that China has joined the WTO and is deepening its engagement with globalisation, the biggest risk for India may be getting left behind.

The completion of economic reforms in agriculture, that I outlined earlier, would not necessarily focus on exports. India has a very large domestic market, and many domestically produced products are already very competitive on that market. Nevertheless, appropriate investments and institutions could enhance the export competitiveness of Indian agriculture. As in the domestic market, whether or not enhanced export opportunities will benefit smallholders depends on whether they have access to infrastructure (especially all-weather roads and storage facilities), inputs, credit, and markets.

Unless developed countries are willing to open their markets to temperate-zone agricultural exports from developing countries and end tariff escalation against processed and higher value products, however, the benefits that developing countries and the poor people who live in them will derive from globalisation will be limited. In addition, India faces high tariff barriers in some developing country markets for such key exports as mangoes, tea, and cashews.

If developed countries want developing countries to continue to open their markets for agricultural products and other goods and services, they must, in turn, reduce the substantial subsidies provided to developed country farmers. Global agricultural subsidies total US$ 360 billion annually, or nearly a billion dollars a day, of which 80 per cent are in OECD countries. A large number of developing countries are among the 140 members of the WTO, so agricultural trade negotiations can no longer boil down to discussion among the United States, the European Union, and Japan. The Cairns Group of non-subsidising agricultural exporting countries, which includes both developed and developing nations, played an important role in the Uruguay Round agricultural negotiations in the 1980s and 1990s, and may have an even more pivotal role in the current talks. A coalition including the Cairns countries and developing countries with large agricultural sectors, such as India and China, would be particularly well-placed to challenge the current distorted patterns of global agricultural trade. The developed countries cannot expect the developing world to endorse one-sided trade agricultural trade liberalisation *ad infinitum*.

In 2001, India proposed that the concept of 'special and differential treatment of developing countries' in the WTO agreement should recognise the need for developing countries 'to tackle their special concerns such as food and livelihood security while reforming agricultural trade'. The African group has similarly proposed that trade liberalisation take into account 'such non-trade concerns as food security, sustainable development, and poverty alleviation'.[43] Given the importance of agriculture in the economies of the poorest developing countries, particularly in Africa, and its potential to drive poverty reduction, it is clear that some balance between complete trade liberalisation and an ability to promote and protect domestic agriculture without violating WTO rules will be needed for some time to come.

In India's case, however, the country can take the measures needed to achieve food security under the existing WTO rules affecting developing countries. Such measures include input subsidies and product specific price supports up to the level of 10 per cent of the value of production. But reform of input subsidies would serve to advance food security more than maintaining them in their current form. The policy agenda that I have laid out earlier, including programmes to invest in human resources, improve safety nets, and invest in public goods, such as agricultural research that will increase poor farmers productivity and reduce their risks, is likewise permissible under the existing WTO agriculture rules. India's remaining barriers to agricultural imports, particularly high tariff barriers to imported cereals and edible oils, do not advance food security much. Indian cereal production is sufficiently competitive domestically not to require high protection. While further investment and policy reform is needed to expand domestic edible oil production capacity, Indian consumers, and especially poor consumers, would benefit from liberalisation of the import market for edible oils.

Conclusion

Agriculture will remain an important source of livelihood for large numbers of Indians, either directly or indirectly, for a long time to come, as a majority of the workforce remains engaged in farming and related work. Moreover, most poor Indians live in rural areas, so broad-based agricultural growth must be at the centre of strategies to reduce poverty and achieve food security.

In order to achieve this, food and agricultural policy must shift from poorly targeted subsidies to a focus on investment—with an emphasis on human resources, public goods, and meeting the needs of poor people and regions. Key investment targets include less favoured areas, agricultural research,

---

43. WTO (2002).

infrastructure (especially roads and storage), and education, for girls and boys alike. Agricultural research must make use of all relevant tools, including molecular biology, conventional approaches, and better utilisation of farmers' own knowledge, to help meet the needs of poor farmers and regions. Alongside these public investments, agriculture should become more market oriented, with better targeted safety nets to assure that the transition from controls and subsidies does not leave poor people worse-off. Safety net programmes and agricultural and rural development programmes alike need to be designed and implemented with the participation of the intended beneficiaries, rather than in a top-down bureaucratic manner. Agricultural policy also needs to shift from the heavy emphasis of the past on foodgrains to more diversified and higher value added activities. Much greater attention must also be paid to sustainable use of natural resources.

Globalisation can be shaped to benefit poor people. The needed shifts in domestic food and agricultural policy would go a long way to assuring that smallholders and other rural poor people have a stake in export opportunities, namely assuring them access to infrastructure, inputs, credit, markets, and organisations such as cooperatives that can facilitate their participation in markets and enhance their political voice. But these shifts will fall short of achieving what is needed unless the developing countries and their allies can also convince the developed countries to reduce their barriers to developing country exports and other trade-distorting policies.

References

ACC/SCN (United Nations Administrative Committee on Coordination/Subcommittee on Nutrition) and IFPRI (2000). *Fourth Report on the World Nutrition Situation.* Geneva: ACC/ SCN and Washington, DC: IFPRI.

Allen, Lindsay and Stuart Gillespie (2001). *What Works? A Review of the Efficacy and Effectiveness of Nutrition Interventions,* Geneva: ACC/SCN and Manila: Asian Development Bank.

Asian Development Bank (2000). *Rural Asia: Beyond the Green Revolution,* Manila: Asian Development Bank.

Chowdhury, Nuimmudin (2001). "Information and Communications Technologies" in Per Pinstrup-Andersen (ed.), *Appropriate Technology for Sustainable Food Security,* 2020 *Vision Focus 7,* Brief 6 of 9. Washington, DC: IFPRI.

Crop Biotech Update (2002). Posted at *www.isaaa.org/ kc/News/CBTnews/ CBTN_recent.html.*

Diaz-Bonilla, Eugenio and Sherman Robinson (eds.) (2001). *Shaping Globalization for Poverty Alleviation and Food Security, 2020 Vision Focus 8,* Washington, DC: IFPRI.

Drèze, Jean and Amartya Sen (1989). *Hunger and Public Action,* Oxford: Clarendon Press.

Fan, Shenggen, Peter Hazell and Sukhadeo Thorat (1999). "Linkages between Government Spending, Growth, and Poverty in Rural India", *Research Report* No. 10, Washington, DC: IFPRI.

Fan, Shenggen and Peter Hazell (2000). "Returns to Public Investment: Evidence from India and China" in John Pender and Peter Hazell (eds.), *Promoting Sustainable Development in Less Favored Areas, 2020 Vision Focus 9.* Brief 5 of 9, Washington, DC: IFPRI.

FAO (Food and Agriculture Organization of the United Nations) (1999). *The State of Food Insecurity in the World*, Rome: FAO.

————. (2001). *The State of Food Insecurity in the World, 2001*, Rome: FAO.

Gillespie, Stuart and Lawrence Haddad (2000). *Attacking the Double Burden of Malnutrition in Asia*, Washington, DC: IFPRI for the Asian Development Bank.

Government of India (2002). "Honourable Finance Minister's Speech on Budget 2002-2003", February 28.

Gulati, Ashok (2001). "The Future of Agriculture in South Asia: Whither the Small Farm?" Summary Note on Presentation at the IFPRI 2020 Vision Initiative Conference *Sustainable Food Security for All by 2020*, Bonn, Germany, September 4-6.

Gulati, Ashok and Anwarul Hoda (Forthcoming). *Negotiating Beyond Doha*, Delhi: Oxford University Press.

Gulati, Ashok and Sudha Narayan (Forthcoming). *Subsidy Syndrome in Indian Agriculture*, Delhi: Oxford University Press.

Hazell, Peter (Undated). "Priorities for Agricultural Policy Reform in Indian Agriculture", Photocopy.

Hazell, Peter and Lawrence Haddad (2001). "Agricultural Research and Poverty Reduction", *2020 Vision Food, Agriculture, and the Environment, Discussion Paper* No. 34, Washington, DC: IFPRI.

Kerr, John (2000). "Development Strategies for Semiarid South Asia" in John Pender and Peter Hazell, (eds.), *Promoting Sustainable Development in Less Favored Areas, 2020* Vision Focus 9, Brief 6 of 9, Washington, DC: IFPRI.

Meinzen-Dick, Ruth, Lynn Brown, Hillary Feldstein and Agnes Quisumbing (1997). "Gender, Property Rights, and Natural Resources", *World Development* 25:8, pp. 1303-1316.

Ministry of Finance, Government of India (2002). *Economic Survey, 2001-2002*, Posted at *http:// www.indiabudget.nic.in/es 2001-02/ general.htm*.

Njobe-Mbuli, Bongiwe (2000). "Biotechnology for Innovation and Development" in G.J. Persley and M.M. Lantin, (eds.), *Agricultural Biotechnology and The Poor*, Washington, DC: Consultative Group on International Agricultural Research, pp. 115-117.

Planning Commission, Government of India (2002). Data posted at *http://indiabudget.nic.in*.

Paarlberg, Robert L. (2001). *The Politics of Precaution: Genetically Modified Crops in Developing Countries*, Baltimore and London: The Johns Hopkins University Press for IFPRI.

Pinstrup-Andersen, Per, and Ebbe Schioler (2000). *Seeds of Contention: World Hunger and the Global Controversy over GM Crops*, Baltimore and London: The Johns Hopkins University Press.

Pinstrup-Andersen, Per, and Rajul Pandya-Lorch (eds.) (2001). *An Unfinished Agenda: Perspectives on Overcoming Hunger, Poverty, and Environmental Degradation*, Washington, DC: IFPRI.

Ramanna, Anitha (2002). "A Tragedy of the Anticommons? India's IPR Policies in Agriculture", Presentation at IFPRI, March 27.

Rosegrant, Mark W. and Peter B.R. Hazell (2000). *Transforming the Rural Asian Economy: The Unfinished Revolution*, Oxford: Oxford University Press.

Rosegrant, Mark W., Michael S. Paisner, Siet Meijer and Julie Witcover (2001). *Global Food Projections to 2020: Emerging Trends and Alternative Futures*, Washington, DC: IFPRI.

Smith, Lisa C. and Lawrence Haddad (2000). "Explaining Child Malnutrition in Developing Countries: A Cross-Country Analysis", *Research Report* No. 111, Washington, DC: IFPRI.

UNDP (United Nations Development Programme) (2001). *Human Development Report 2001*, New York: Oxford University Press.

WTO (World Trade Organization) (2002). *http:// www.wto.org*. WTO Watch.

Exim Bank Commencement Day Annual Lecture, Mumbai, India, April 22, 2002.
Economic Developments in India, Vol. 56.

13

Food Security in India

Towards Elimination of Hunger and Malnutrition

V.S. VYAS

There is unanimity of opinion in our country, as in most other countries of the world now, that every person in a civilised society deserves to be food secure. A pledge to ensure food security (FS) has been repeatedly made at various policy fora and is incorporated in development plans and policy documents the world over. India is also a signatory to international convents to abolish hunger and malnutrition at the World Food Conference convened by FAO, and the Conference on Millennium Goals convened by the United Nations. It has been endorsed as an important objective in our successive Five Year Plans.

The concept of FS as it is now understood universally goes beyond avoiding starvation. A widely accepted definition of FS suggests, "access to adequate food to all people at all times for an active and healthy life". Food Security, thus, goes beyond merely avoiding starvation. It implies availability of food in adequate quantities (from domestic production or imports) of requisite quality (from a nutritional point of view) and, entitlement to access the food (through production, labour, trade or transfer) by all the households. There are enough indicators to suggest that we are far behind in ensuring to the citizens of this country the kind of FS implied in the definition given above. I shall examine the developments and prospects in ensuring food security, in its wider connotation.

Because of difficulties in measuring FS, it is not possible to be precise on the degree of food insecurity that a household faces. However, food insecurity can be examined at three levels, *viz.*, hunger verging on starvation, calorie deficiency verging on hunger and, malnutrition with or without calorie deficiency. There are obvious overlaps between these categories. Nonetheless, it is useful to accept these categories of food insecurity to distinguish the nature of deprivations faced by the households at these three levels and to arrive at appropriate remedial measures. In the following sections, I shall attempt the same. At the outset, I wish to make it clear that by using household, rather than individual members of the household, as the reference unit, we are not taking into consideration intra-household distribution of food (between men and women, between adults and children), a subject which is of great importance. In fact, it requires separate treatment.

Hunger

It is difficult to define or measure hunger. In India, the main source for finding out the number of hungry people comprises the periodical surveys conducted by National Sample Survey Organisation (NSSO). Their measurement of hunger is subjective, in the sense that what they record is the perception of the respondents regarding their households getting 'two square meals' a day. On this count, there seems to be progressive reduction in the proportion of 'hungry' households among total households, both rural and urban, in every state for which time series data are available.

Even with this laudable progress, the disturbing feature is that in 1999-2000, the latest year for which data is available, there were 1.6 per cent of rural households and 0.4 per cent of households in the urban areas who did not get adequate food, and had to suffer chronic hunger. In terms of percentage of the total number of the rural and urban households, these figures look insignificant, but when translated in to actual numbers, it suggests that over 3 million households, comprising more than 15 million people go to bed hungry every day. For a country, which is aspiring for a growth rate of 8 per cent or more, feeding less than 2 per cent of its people who are chronically hungry should not be an insurmountable task.

Other significant features revealed by the NSS surveys is that some states such as Assam, Bihar, Orissa and West Bengal, continue to record higher proportions of hungry people as compared to the national average. And the proportion of vulnerable groups, on this criterion, is higher among the Scheduled Tribe and the Scheduled Caste households. If we have to fight this scourge, we have to concentrate on the eastern region of the country, especially the socially and economically vulnerable groups therein.

The NS surveys also reveal that hunger is more pronounced in certain months. The period of acute hunger varies from state to state but, normally, it is the post-sowing and pre-harvest months of July, August and September. Naturally, the worst sufferers are those who get only seasonal employment, i.e., the agricultural wage earners and marginal farmers in rural areas of the arid and semi-arid regions. The plight of unskilled casual workers in urban areas is no better. The dry areas of Andhra Pradesh, Gujarat, Madhya Pradesh and Rajasthan show severe incidence of seasonal hunger.

Some relief could be offered by the Employment Guarantee Scheme (EGS) in the fight against seasonal hunger in the rural areas during the most difficult months. If properly targeted, EGS can provide gainful employment of 90 to 100 days to the vulnerable households during the slack period. We do not have any such programme for the urban areas, and this is a big lacuna.

Calorie Deprivation

In India, the poverty line is based on a given quantity of calorie intake together with expenditure on other necessities accompanying the stipulated calorie intake. The base for calorie consumption for this purpose was suggested at 2400 calories per person in the rural areas and 2200 calories per person in the urban areas. Right from the inception, this norm was challenged, basically on two grounds. Some scholars (e.g. P.V. Sukhatme) do not consider a fixed calorie intake relevant indicator at all, as they insist that body's adaptation mechanism determines the calorie requirement. They are not in favour of a fixed calorie norm for poverty estimation. Many more scholars object to the relevance of the prevailing high norms. It has been suggested that, with the changing age structure, male-female composition, living standards, occupational diversification and availability of several facilities to minimise physical labour—all being reflected in the changes in the consumption basket —the norms suggested are too high. This is also borne out by the fact that calorie consumption, even by the richest deciles in some of the major states, is less than the stipulated norms.

There is substantial force in this argument. The threshold calorie intake suggested for defining poverty seems to be on the higher side. However, one can easily agree that there is a minimum level of calorie intake for ensuring 'healthy and productive life' and that consumption below that level signals food insecurity. FAO uses a cut-off norm of 1810 calories for India to represent the lower range of food requirements. Based on NSS rounds, Meenakshi and Vishwanathan in a recent paper *(Economic and Political Weekly, 2003)* have shown that if the measure of, say 1800 calorie per person per day is used, there were in 1999-2000 eight states in the country where more than one-third of the population was consuming 1800 calories or less per person per day. These are Tamil Nadu, Kerala, Karnataka, Gujarat, Maharashtra, Madhya

Pradesh, Andhra Pradesh and West Bengal. It should be recognised that there has been some improvement in the situation as compared to 1983. Only four states—Andhra Pradesh, Karnataka, Madhya Pradesh and Maharashtra—recorded a higher calorie gap ratio as compared to their record in 1983.

Many of these states are not 'poor' states in the Indian context. It has prompted some scholars to challenge these norms as indicators of poverty. Their objection may be valid. However, the over all record in poverty alleviation in a state may hide calorie deficiency in some sections in that state. In any event, poverty and food insecurity are not one and the same thing. That a large number of people in the country are not getting the minimum amount of energy necessary for good health is an incontrovertible fact, unless the NSSO estimations are wrong.

Assuming that the estimates of the number of people suffering from calorie deprivation are correct, such situation can arise possibly due to two main reasons. Poverty is an obvious explanation. Or, the main sources of calories which the poor take recourse to have become too costly, and/or a higher expenditure has to be incurred on other necessities, (e.g. health related expenditure), forcing people to cut on the intake of food at the margin. There can, of course, be willing sacrifice of calories for looks, appearance, etc.! Leaving aside the last motivation for low intake of calories, the other two more serious reasons clearly suggest policy and programmatic interventions. The relative prices of the foods which the poor consume for their sustenance have to be kept low, and the cost of availing of other necessities, particularly health services, has to be restrained. At present, the state is defaulting on both counts.

Nutritional Security

There is some evidence of progress towards eliminating hunger and, to an extent, even correcting calorie deprivation. There are no such hopeful signs as far as nutritional insecurity is concerned. In fact, several indicators of health and nutrition suggest deterioration of the situation. Indicators, such as body mass index, number of stunted and wasted children, maternal morbidity and mortality present a very discouraging picture. Thanks to National Nutritional Monitoring Bureau and National Family Health Survey, we have much better information on nutrition as compared to say, hunger or calorie deprivation. These surveys unambiguously suggest that incidence of malnutrition is extremely serious. In 2000-01 about half of the children and one-third of adults were undernourished. What is more worrisome is the fact that, except for two states, Kerala and Tamil Nadu, there has not been any significant improvement in this regard. In some states such as Madhya Pradesh and Orissa, the situation has worsened.

Paucity of micronutrients, which is aptly described as 'hidden hunger', is equally glaring all across the country. Indepth reports on the plight of the poor in the areas which record alarmingly high child mortality point to the appallingly low nutritional status of children in these areas. (See for example, Report of the Advisers to the Supreme Court Commissioners on the deaths in the Baran District of Rajasthan, 2005). The nutritional status of adults is only slightly better. Chronic Energy Deficiency (CED) was as serious as child malnutrition, again, with the exception of Kerala and Tamil Nadu. Madhya Pradesh, Maharashtra and West Bengal showed the worst performance in this respect. In a large number of states, incidence of malnutrition among females is higher. According to the India Development Report (2004-2005) brought out by the Indira Gandhi Institute of Development Research, medium income states such as Gujarat, Maharashtra and West Bengal do not fare much better than the 'less developed' states such as Bihar, Madhya Pradesh and North eastern states in this regard.

For ensuring nutritional security, special attention should be given to two groups: children in the age group 0-2, and pregnant and lactating mothers. Improvement in the nutritional status of these groups will have a lasting and multiplier effect. Another group, which is becoming important, especially due to demographic transition, is the group of the elderly persons who do not have any family support. Schemes such as old age pension legislated in some of the states have not gone beyond tokenism. The access of the elderly without family support to adequate nutritious food has to be ensured.

In short, the current scenario on the food and nutrition front suggests the following:

- Hunger, in terms of starvation, has largely been eliminated, although there is a disturbingly large extent of seasonal hunger, especially in dry areas.

- There has been progress in reducing calorie deficiency. However, a very large proportion of rural households subsist on below 1800 calories per person per day even in the so-called progressive states.

- There has been no progress in ensuring nutritional security, barring in one or two states. The worst sufferers are young children, pregnant and lactating mothers and elderly persons without any family support. If the present rate of progress in this area continues, India will not be able to reach the millennium goal of halving malnutrition.

In a country which has been aspiring for decades to achieve Food and Nutritional Security these are very disheartening facts.

If we have to redress this situation, review of the economic policies as well as the design and implementation of programmes to ensure FS is necessary. In the next section, we briefly touch upon the relevant economic policies. The following section highlights the efficacy of the different programmes aimed at ensuring FS.

Economic Policies

Economic policies relevant in this context are those addressed to improving availability of food, ensuring stability in the supply of food and entitlement of households to food.

As far as the availability of food is concerned, the last decade marked a reversal of the earlier trend i.e. food production comfortably outpacing the growth in demand for food induced by increases in population and income. In recent years, income-induced growth in demand is slackening and the overall elasticity of demand is estimated to be between 0.2 and 0.3. However, population growth continues to be higher at 1.9 per cent per year. Food production in recent years is creeping at 1.7 per cent per year. It is slower than the growth in population. Per capita foodgrain output is falling since the mid-nineties. The deceleration in the growth of production of foodgrains has been due to the complacency generated by the high level of production in the past. Two prime movers for the growth in productivity, namely investment in infrastructure and generation and propagation of superior technologies, were neglected in the recent years. Complacency was partly induced by the belief that with the opening up of the economy, food surpluses available in the international markets could always be tapped.

So long as a large proportion of the workforce, currently accounting for nearly 57 per cent, depends on agriculture—and to a large extent on foodgrains production, and a sizeable share of consumers budget goes for the purchase of food, it is imprudent to slacken our efforts to raise productivity in agriculture in general and foodgrains production in particular. Once this scenario changes, when non-agricultural sectors account for a bulk of employment and expenditure on food goes down to an insubstantial level, we can relax our policy of food self-sufficiency. Any premature withdrawal from this policy at this stage will jeopardise the food security of a large number of poor producers as well as a substantial section of poor consumers. This is not an occasion to spell out the strategy for imparting buoyancy to the agricultural sector. It is sufficient to indicate that the direction in which we should move is higher investment in land and water along with strengthening the support system of research, extension, credit and marketing. An equitable price policy also plays an important role. However, the present price policy, which has restored the adverse terms of trade for agriculture to a more equitable level, cannot be faulted.

Another important prerequisite at the policy level is ensuring a reasonable level of stability in the flow of food supply and also prices. Agricultural production being seasonal, some fluctuation in food availability and consequently in prices is inevitable and in fact, is even desirable. However, as food is demanded every day and also accessed at frequent intervals, if not daily, by the poorer sections of consumers, excessive fluctuation in prices takes its toll on food consumption. More so as the employment opportunities for a large section of the people are also seasonal. In the situation of comfortable supply at the overall level, a properly functioning market can even out sharp fluctuations quickly and efficiently. The objective of our domestic market reforms is to remove imperfection in the markets and curb tendencies for monopolistic gains.

Procurement of major foodgrains at the minimum support price, coupled with an active buffer stock policy, also helps in assuaging large-scale deficits or surpluses in the availability of foodgrains. The situation can be further buttressed by a complementary trade policy. The government policy in the past was directed to soften the blow of fluctuations in the supply, with timely release or accelerated procurement as the situation warranted. Existence of a vast number of public distribution outlets (fair price shops) and large apparatus for procurement of grains, helped in the implementation of this strategy. In the absence of government interventions, fluctuations in prices would have been much sharper. This is one area where the government cannot abdicate its responsibilities.

The key consideration is the entitlement to food at the household level. For the bulk of the rural poor, who are threatened with food insecurity, entitlement is synonymous with their current income, mainly the wage income or the income from their tiny landholdings. The model of development practiced in our country as well as in many other countries has led to 'jobless growth'. This is also true of agricultural growth, where, with the current production pattern, employment elasticity is coming virtually to zero. The compound annual rate of growth in employment (principal + subsidiary) in agriculture during the period 1983-84 to 1993-94 was 1.39 per cent; it came down to 0.05 per cent during 1993-94 to 1999-2000. In this context, the Employment Guarantee Scheme, if properly implemented, can prove a boon to the rural poor. Also, proper use and development of land and water resources and necessary institutional backing can lead to diversification to more labour intensive crops.

A major factor determining access to food, especially by poor households, is the relative prices of food. A cardinal principle of our food policy in the past few decades was the conviction that the real prices of food are kept low, while the farmers gain in income with enhancement in productivity. In the last few years, public support to enhancing productivity by investment in rural infrastructure and focussed attention to research and extension has been kept on the back-burner, and reliance seems to have been placed solely on the so called 'incentive prices'. The net result is that productivity has stagnated and real prices of foodgrains started creeping up. This policy is counter-productive. Like any other producer, the agricultural producer is concerned with his income, not with the prices *per se*.

A point which has to be made clear at this stage is the nature and justification for self-provisioning. In our anxiety to go for high value agriculture, the traditionally diversified farm economy is being disrupted. Fast disappearance of the crop-livestock nexus at the farm level is an example of blind faith in monoculture, favouring high value crops. So long as the access to inputs and output markets is biased against small farmers and insurance cover is not available to them, it will be a better strategy to encourage self-provisioning of nutritious food such as vegetables and fruits on small farms. I may mention that Thailand, another fast developing country like ours, is encouraging a policy of self-provisioning on small farms with a salutary impact on food and nutritional security.

Programme Interventions

There are three major programmes, which can make an important contribution to FS. These are: (i) the Public Distribution System (PDS) and its variant Antoydaya, (ii) Integrated Child Development Scheme (ICDS), and (iii) Mid-Day Meal Scheme. These are multi-objective programmes, but they can significantly contribute towards food security. A few words on each of these may be useful.

Among these, PDS or its earlier versions, is the oldest programme. A large quantity of foodgrains and a few other necessities are distributed through fair price shops under this programme. In terms of the quantity of foodgrains handled, as well as in terms of the number of outlets, it is one of the largest programmes of its kind in the world. Its effectiveness in reaching the poor has all along been questioned, mainly because of the lacunae in its implementation, and leakages to non-merit consumers. These defects have been progressively corrected, though much remains to be done. In a number of states, its scale and reach among the poor are progressively improving. The Mid-Term Appraisal of the Tenth Plan suggests that correlation between offtake from PDS and total number of the poor in the states is improving.

The real difficulty is due to the persistence of confusion regarding the objectives of PDS. Put simply, policy makers are not clear as to whether the objective is to influence the overall price level for foodgrains through the supplies distributed through PDS, or to provide foodgrains to the targeted clientele at below market prices. Related to it is another question, one regarding the issue prices, i.e. the prices at which foodgrains to be distributed to the poor. If the objective is to provide food to the poor as an indirect measure of income support, the issue prices should be substantially below the market prices. Pursuing this strategy is becoming more and more difficult as the minimum support prices (MSP), which have become synonymous with procurement prices, are progressively rising. The difficulties get compounded once the targeted distribution [i.e., targeted to the below poverty line (BPL) families] of foodgrains is abolished and foodgrains are made available to virtually every one through PDS. The net result is that food subsidy is rising year after year, and that is considered undesirable from the point of view of fiscal management.

The government seems to have taken the easier course. The issue prices are progressively rising, and the scheme has been opened to all types of clientele, —those below the poverty line as well as those above. The paramount consideration is to reduce the subsidy burden. An approach consistent with the original objective of making food available to insecure households at prices below the market prices would suggest that the scheme should be confined to BPL households. This will automatically reduce the subsidy burden. As the number of households below the poverty line will, hopefully, continuously decline, the subsidy burden will come down progressively. The main argument against this approach is the difficulty in targeting. This is not the only programme for which a distinction is made between BPL and APL households.

We have to perfect the norms and procedures for targeting rather than throw away baby with the bath water.

A programme, which can directly contribute to the alleviation of the calorie deficiency, is the Antoydaya programme. Started in December 2000, it was expected to identify one crore 'poorest of the poor' families and make food available to them at highly concessional prices, i.e. Rs. 2 per kg of wheat and Rs. 3 per kg of rice. The number of the poor to be covered has since been raised to 2.5 crore families, and the issue of foodgrains per family from 25 kg per month to 35 kg per month. If the programme is better targeted, it can certainly take care of the calorie deficiency for the worst affected sections.

Two other major programmes to ensure food security are the Integrated Child Development Scheme (ICDS) and the Mid-Day Meal programme. There is also the Annapurna programme to provide foodgrains to indigent senior citizens free of cost. This has yet to make its impact felt. ICDS is aimed at providing supplementary nutrition along with health care to young children and lactating mothers. It is a laudable objective as it addresses the problem of malnutrition of those sections that need urgent attention. By focussing on children and young mothers, the programme ensures lasting benefits to the society. There is nothing wrong with the concept; the difficulties are more at the operational level, and they have to be tackled with foresight and determination. The mid-day meal programme is equally laudable. By providing nutritious food to the school-going children, it encourages school attendance among the children of poor households. Whatever lacunae have been observed exist at the implementation level. An important development that is taking place in this programme in some states is public-private partnership. With the passing of the Right to Information Bill, an important step has been taken to ensure accountability of the programme implementers.

We have, thus, some powerful programme addressing the poor and food insecure. Two vulnerable groups which are yet left out of the safety net are children in the 0-2 years age group and out-of-school youth. There is a need for well-focussed nutritional interventions for these groups.

The ongoing programme, together with the policy reforms mentioned earlier can address the FS issues in an effective way, provided a major handicap, namely poor health and sanitary conditions is addressed simultaneously.

Health and Environment

Over the years, we have gained in terms of life-expectancy. The expectation of life at birth has doubled in the last 50 years. But, this has also given rise to higher incidence of morbidity. Apart from the malnutrition and lessened resistance to diseases, increasing pollution, crumbling sanitation facilities, deteriorating water quality and rampant adulteration of food items have added to the incidence of morbidity.

If the share of expenditure on health services in the total government expenditure, even in GDP, for that matter is taken as an indicator, our record is worse than those of some of the other developing countries, particularly China. For example, we spend 5.3 per cent of the total government expenditure on health as against 11 per cent by China. Further, allocation of the public resources is biased against the rural areas. The private health providers, who have filled the vacuum are far more expensive, though not necessarily more effective. As a result, the share of expenditure on health even among the poorer sections is rising without perceptible improvement in their health status. An inevitable consequence of higher expenditure on private health services by the poor is a decline in the share of expenditure on other necessities. (This, more than Engel's Law, explains the declining share of expenditure on food by the poorer households.) By all accounts, sanitary conditions in the rural as well as the urban areas are appalling. With totally inadequate health care and deteriorating environmental conditions, intake of nutritious food is no better than storing water in a sieve.

The Way Forward

We have made significant progress in eliminating hunger, although seasonal hunger is still rampant, and its incidence on some sections very serious. We have not made much notable progress, in filling in the calorie gap. The nutritional status in large parts of the country is probably deteriorating. If the objective of ensuring a healthy and productive life to all households is to be fulfilled, a time-bound programme to meet four critical requirements for Food Security have to be met i.e. (a) adequate availability, (b) reasonable stability in terms of quantity and price, (c) purchasing power to access food, and (d) desired nutritional intake. Let me summarise some important actions in these areas, based mainly on the previous discussion.

Availability

The first condition for ensuring FS is availability of adequate quantities of foodgrains to meet the requirement of the country's population. In the modern interconnected world, there is always possibility of importing foodgrains to supplement domestic production. This has prompted many analysts to suggest that we need not insist on food self-sufficiency. As I have written elsewhere, food self-sufficiency need not be an article of faith. However, we have to continue with this policy as long as a large proportion of the agricultural producers, most of whom are resource-poor are compelled to depend on food production for their livelihood, and a large part of consumers expenditure— nearly 50 per cent of the total expenditure in the last two deciles—is on food. Once these conditions change, i.e. we have, say, less than a quarter of agricultural producers depending on foodgrains production and a not too large amount of consumers' expenditure, say less than a quarter, being spent on purchase of foodgrains, we can review the policy on food self-sufficiency. These conditions will, hopefully, be met over a period of time. Till then, any heavy dependence on imports will expose the poor producers and poor consumers to risk which they are not in a position to take. Our system is not resilient enough to accommodate all those who are likely to be displaced by heavy imports of foodgrains in other gainful activities, or even to facilitate their switching over to alternative crops on a scale warranted by such a shift in policy.

With concerted efforts we have transformed a heavily import-dependent agricultural economy into one of food self-sufficiency, in fact one with exportable surpluses. It has been largely due to several policy and programmatic interventions, the more important among them being:

- Concerted efforts in research and extension to evolve and popularise high yielding varieties.

- Investment in expansion of irrigation.

- Assurance of a minimum support price and needed arrangements for procurement.

- Orienting the support institutions in credit and marketing to meet the needs of a dynamic agriculture.

All these measures continue to have the same relevance today. A significant change, which has taken place in the agrarian structure since the seventies is a larger proportion of the agricultural land being now farmed in small holdings, of less than two hectares. The supportive institutions, both public and private, have to take account of the small farm character of our agriculture.

Another requisite for ensuring food availability in a large country like ours, with an underdeveloped rural infrastructure, is making sure that the domestic markets function efficiently, especially in the remote areas, and *vis-à-vis* small producers and consumers. The measures, which need to be encouraged in this regard, include:

- Improving connectivity.

- Developing efficient ways for price discovery.

- Expediting the reform process in domestic markets.

- Improving market infrastructure.

- Ensuring an appropriate institutional arrangement to handle small lots in an efficient way.

Stability in Supplies

Food production being seasonal and the demand for food being more or less constant the year round, some degree of fluctuation in availability and in prices is inevitable. Apart from many other costs, the cost of storage over the seasons has to be reckoned with. Consumers also would accept some degree of fluctuation as natural. However, the poorer sections that buy their requirements on a day-to-day basis suffer the most due to the instability in supplies as well as in the prices. In the years of crop failure, the regions where shortfall in production take place, there is always the danger of the hoarding of foodgrains by unscrupulous traders which aggravates the plight of the poor households. An important institution to protect the poor in such circumstances is 'grain banks,' organised by a number of NGOs in different parts of the country. Realising the difficulties faced by the consumers, especially in the 'lean seasons', certain measures seem imperative. These would include:

- A well-formed policy on buffer stocks and their release, i.e. an effective market intervention policy.

- A coordinated price and trade policy.

- Use of PDS outlets to release adequate supplies in the lean seasons.

- Encouragement to organisation of 'grain banks' by the poor, on the lines suggested by the National Commission on Farmers.

Ensuring Access to Food

The most important condition for ensuring food security is entitling the household to avail of adequate nutritious food. For the bulk of the food–insecure people, this means effective demand backed by the necessary purchasing power. For this reason, a high correlation of poverty and food insecurity can be observed. A large number of studies in this country have identified the agricultural labourers and marginal farmers in the rural areas and the casual workers in the urban areas as the most vulnerable groups. As most of the food-insecure households in the rural as well as the urban areas have to rely on wage-paid employment, provision of employment opportunities to these sections is the most important step.

As far as marginal farmers are concerned, gainful non-farm employment is the right answer. However, there is a sub-set of these farmers who are potentially capable of enhancing the productivity of their 'small' or 'marginal' holdings. It is important to remind ourselves that what we categorise as a marginal holding is the average size of holdings in most Southeast Asian countries as well as in China, with a much better record of agricultural productivity. In the past, some attempts were made to address the problems of these sections under Marginal Farmers and Landless Labour Development Agencies. Abolition of this programme has proved a retrogressive step, as it led to neglect of the problems of this vast section of our rural population.

There is a residual section of the population who cannot avail of existing employment opportunities because of their physical handicaps. Old, infirm and physically challenged people cannot be left to their devices to procure food. Societal obligations should give precedence over all other considerations as far as FS to these sections is concerned.

Necessary measures to ensure access to food to the food insecure include:

- Focussing the proposed Employment Guarantee Programme during the lean season in the selected districts.

- Converging all employment related programme in those districts which are not yet covered by EGP.

- Reviving Marginal Farmers and Landless Labour Development Agencies.

- Starting Urban Employment Guarantee Programme with emphasis on skill formation and self-employment.

- Ensuring food security, as a matter of right to those who cannot do physical work.

Nutritional Security

There is no need to emphasise the appalling state of nutrition in our country. Judged by any indicator, Body Mass Index, Child Mortality, Maternal

Mortality or Incidence of Morbidity—India comes near the bottom in list of comparable countries. In fact, on some indicators, we are worse-off than some of the least developed countries. There have been no signs of any remarkable improvement in this respect in recent years. The irony of the situation is that most of the measures to improve the nutritional status do not require huge investments. The more important among the measures advocated by nutrition experts are:

- Giving focussed attention to the children in the 0-2 years age groups and pregnant and lactating mothers.

- Identifying other vulnerable groups and administering food supplements to these people through various government schemes.

- Using PDS outlets for distribution of nutrition-rich food supplements.

- Launching a kitchen garden movement in the rural areas and, wherever possible, in urban areas also, with distribution of seeds, planting material and advice on cultural practices for locally suitable fruits and vegetables.

- Identifying nutrient-rich traditional crops and encouraging research on enhancing the productivity and improving the marketability of these crops.

- Encouraging research on breeding nutrient-rich food crops e.g. high protein maize.

None of these measures will succeed without raising public awareness on the nutrition-related issues. In this task, as for other programme for ensuring FS, civil society institutions will be more effective than the government machinery in mobilising people.

With the growth record of past decade which is likely to continue if not improve availability of necessary institutions, and requisite experience, neither dearth of resources nor lack of expertise can be cited as reasons for further delaying the task of ensuring a food secure India. It can not now be considered an elusive goal or a distant dream.

R.S. Bhatt Memorial Lecture, October 22, 2005.
Economic Developments in India, Vol. 94.

14

Sustainable Use of Water for Irrigation in Indian Agriculture

C. H. HANUMANTHA RAO

Water resources are becoming extremely scarce. According to the projections made by the National Commission for Integrated Water Resource Development Plan, the requirement of water for irrigation in India will grow by more than 50 per cent in the next 50 years. The water requirements for household consumption and for industry would rise even faster. In view of this, even after fully exploiting the usable water resources, the balance between the supply and demand for irrigation water can be achieved only by improving the level of irrigation efficiency in a big way from about 36 per cent efficiency in 1993-94 to 60 per cent in the year 2050 (Government of India, 1999). A 10 per cent improvement in the efficiency of water use would be equivalent to adding some 14 million hectares of gross irrigated area (Saleth, 1996). A model of water supply and demand for 118 countries accounting for 93 per cent of world population, built by the International Water Management Institute (IWMI), shows that around 50 per cent of the increase in demand for water by the year 2025 can be met by increasing the effectiveness of irrigation. Most of this gain in irrigation effectiveness would be in countries with a high percentage of irrigated rice. India and China together would account for as much as one-half of the world's total estimated water savings from increased irrigation effectiveness. Therefore, the capacity of large countries like India and China to efficiently develop and manage water resources is likely to be a key determinant of global food security in the 21st century (Seckler *et al.*, 1998).

Usable water supplies are highly unevenly distributed across the globe and across regions within a large country like India. Therefore, notwithstanding the balance achieved at the national level between the demand for and supply of water, shortage of drinking water would pose a serious problem in the

The author is thankful to Mahendra Dev, V. Ratna Reddy and S. Subrahmanyam for their comments and suggestions.

drought-prone regions of the country, especially because over 90 per cent of rural population depends on groundwater for drinking purposes. The poor who depend upon dug wells, which dry up fast, are the first to suffer. Under such circumstances, the only way to ensure local food security and water security to meet the basic needs for drinking and cooking, is by undertaking rainwater harvesting and groundwater recharge on a large scale through the participation of the community, including especially the women and the landless. This should be possible because, unlike in regions of high rainfall, land area per head is larger in the low rainfall or drought-prone areas where 10 tiny dams with a catchment of 1 ha each can collect more water than one larger dam with a catchment of 10 ha (Agarwal, 2000). Augmentation of groundwater through artificial recharge, including watershed development, by harnessing surplus monsoon run-off can raise the irrigation potential from groundwater sources substantially over and above the existing potential of 64 million ha (Chada, 2000).

Variations in Water Productivity

In the last two decades, we have been faltering in our efforts to augment water resources, even as the use of the available water resources has become increasingly unsustainable. Public investment in major and medium irrigation schemes has been declining, in real terms, throughout the 1980s and the 1990s, even though as much as 40 per cent of the potential still remains to be exploited. We have not taken significant steps so far for improving water-use-efficiency through modernisation/renovation of existing systems which have deteriorated over the years. According to the Mid-Term Appraisal of Ninth Five Year Plan, the progress achieved so far in Participatory Irrigation Management (PIM), designed to improve water-use-efficiency, is rather slow. The irrigated area transferred to Water Users Associations (WUAs) in India is only about 7 per cent as against 45 per cent in Indonesia, 66 per cent in Philippines, and 22 per cent in Thailand (Government of India, Planning Commission, 2000). As regards groundwater, the rate of extraction has been far above the rate of recharge. As a result, the number of over-exploited and dark blocks has increased by nearly 70 per cent over the last 14 years (Government of India, Planning Commission, 2000).

Ultimately, savings in irrigation water can be achieved only by raising the productivity of water, defined broadly as the volume or value of crop output per unit of water used. Definition of water productivity varies in the literature depending on how the denominator in this ratio is specified. When, at one extreme, water released from the system is used as the denominator, water productivity becomes all-inclusive subsuming water-use-efficiency, that is, the ratio of consumptive use of water to the water released. At the other extreme, when the denominator consists of water lost as evapotranspiration by plants in any particular season, then improvement in water productivity can arise basically from the improvement in yields.

Interestingly, water savings in crop production the world over in the last few decades have accrued indirectly basically from rise in crop yields and very little directly from improvement in water-use-efficiency (CGIAR, 2001a). This is particularly so in developing countries like India where the improvement in irrigation efficiency has been very slow. For one thing, a clear focus on water productivity, i.e., productivity per unit of water used is new for the international agricultural research system (CGIAR, 2001b). Nearly 200 years ago, Thomas Malthus focussed on the fixity or scarcity of land in relation to population growth as the cause for recurring famines. This perception prompted the evolution and use of land-saving technologies and practices which substantially raised productivity per unit of land. Until recently, irrigation water has seldom been regarded as a scarce resource in the favourable rainfed areas of Europe, North America and Japan, where water losses on account of evaporation and evapotranspiration are also lower because of cooler climate. In the last century, major breakthroughs in crop yields per unit of land were witnessed in these countries, from where such technologies were transferred to the developing countries. Recently, however, the growing competition for water from industry, urban areas for household consumption and for environmental purposes in these developed countries has been exerting pressure to save water allocated to irrigation. Besides, rising level of water pollution is accentuating the scarcity of fresh water in all the sectors.

The green revolution has substantially raised yields in irrigated areas in India, resulting in a rise in the productivity of irrigation water. Such an increase in water productivity on account of land-saving technological changes can eventually ease pressure on water for irrigation, even when there is no change in water-use-efficiency. Since irrigated area under foodgrains accounts for the bulk of the increase in foodgrains output, growth of foodgrains output in relation to the growth of irrigated area under foodgrains would give a good measure of the changes in the productivity of irrigation water. Despite the green revolution, which was confined largely to wheat in the north-western region in the 1970s, foodgrains output grew at about the same rate as gross irrigated area. Thus, there was no growth in productivity of irrigation water for foodgrains in the country in this decade (Table 14.1). During the 1980s however, green revolution was broad-based covering rice in the central and eastern regions of the country where high rainfall supplements irrigation. Thus, foodgrains output grew at a higher rate than irrigated area resulting in a positive growth in the productivity of irrigation water. However, in the post-reform decade of the 1990s, there was a deceleration in the growth of foodgrains output leading to a significant decline in the productivity growth of irrigation.

The decline in water productivity growth in the foodgrains sector of Indian agriculture in the last decade may be attributed partly to the loss of momentum in the development of yield-increasing technologies and partly to the political economy of irrigation from groundwater sources. For example, there was a sharp decline in agricultural growth in east UP on account of severe cuts in the supply of power for pumping water, which was diverted to west UP to satisfy the powerful farm lobby (Shah, 2001). The known potential from green revolution is yet to be fully realised in the eastern states where productivity of irrigation water can be raised significantly both on account of high precipitation which supplements irrigation water and the controlled nature of irrigation from groundwater sources which are abundant in this region. Whereas eastern India has over one-fourth of India's usable groundwater resources, less than one-fifth of this is developed.

Table 14.1

Productivity of Irrigation for Foodgrains in Indian Agriculture
(Growth Rates)

	1970-71 to 1980-81	1980-81 to 1990-91	1990-91 to 1996-97
Gross Irrigated Area	2.31	1.72	1.70
Output	2.30	2.90	2.00
Productivity of Irrigation	-0.01	1.18	0.30

Sources : (1) Government of India, Ministry of Agriculture, *Indian Agricultural Statistics,* 1992-93, 1997.

     (2) Government of India, Central Statistical Organisation, *Statistical Abstract—India,* 2000-2001.

Sources for Raising Water Productivity

Although research focussed on water productivity is relatively new, the gap between the available knowledge to increase water productivity and its beneficial application appears quite large (CGIAR, 2001a). In the case of India at present, such a gap between knowledge and its application is greater in respect of water productivity than for land productivity. Unlike irrigation water, property rights for land are well-defined and protected which is the single most important factor providing incentives for farmers to successfully participate in the green revolution. Secondly, green revolution has been facilitated by institutional support such as the provision of extension services, credit and marketing. Thirdly, agricultural price policy, whether for output or for inputs, has provided the necessary stimulus for stepping up output per unit of land through input intensification. So far as irrigation is concerned, the failures have been massive on all the three fronts, *viz.*, property rights, institutions and public policy. It would be instructive, therefore, to identify the major problems afflicting irrigation in each of these areas.

But, what are the major sources for raising the productivity of irrigation water? An understanding of these would help to see the problems afflicting irrigation in a proper perspective. We have seen that technological changes which raised crop yields per unit of land have so far been the major source of the rise in productivity per unit of irrigation water. Since genetic improvements for raising the productivity of land further are very much in the realm of possibility, they can, at the same time, significantly raise water productivity, especially if such genetic improvements are targeted towards saving water. These improvements include the development of crop varieties with better tolerance to drought, cool seasons which reduce evaporation and evapotranspiration, and saline conditions. Biotechnology is considered to have a great potential for raising yields and imparting stability in adverse environments (CGIAR, 2001b). In India, technological changes to improve water productivity by raising crop yields seem to hold a better promise in the short and medium-term than the attempts to improve water-use-efficiency, which can be expected to yield significant results only in the long-run, owing to the severe political constraints, and managerial and institutional bottlenecks besetting these efforts.

Secondly, productivity of irrigation water can be raised by skilfully supplementing it with rain water, especially in the high rainfall areas, despite the possible losses on account of evaporation and evapotranspiration. Because of this, agricultural development strategy that accords greater priority to high rainfall areas like the central and eastern regions in the country may result in significant savings on high-cost surface irrigation.

Thirdly, water losses occur from the point of delivery from the system to the farmer's field due to evaporation, flow of usable water to sinks, pollution, salinity and waterlogging. Such losses cannot eventually be recovered at the basin level. These can be minimised with appropriate management practices, provided there are adequate incentives to farmers for adopting water-saving practices. Fourthly, farmers are known to reallocate land and water to high value crops in response to the changing demand. As incomes rise, consumer demand shifts away from some of the water-intensive crops like rice to water-saving horticultural products. However, trade and price policies and policies on input subsidies, including on irrigation water, would determine whether farmers would be induced to switch over to water-conserving enterprises.

Finally, globalisation opens up opportunities for countries faced with water scarcities to specialise in the production and export of water-saving crops and import water-intensive ones. Favourable rainfed areas of Europe, North America and parts of South America may gain comparative advantage in the export of water-intensive crops (Seckler, 1996). A country like India, faced with water scarcity, can safeguard its food security by entering into collaborative arrangements with certain countries which have abundant land and water resources but are short of labour and capital and do not have enough domestic demand, for production and exchange of foodgrains and other water-intensive products like sugar. Such arrangements are already working in the case of fertilisers and petrochemicals (Hashim, 2000).

Government *versus* Market Failure in Water Management

Well-defined and secure or enforceable property rights on irrigation water and volumetric pricing of surface water as well as electricity for pumping water are necessary to induce the farmers to adopt water saving practices. However, under the existing system of public management of irrigation, we have failed to ensure these preconditions for the efficient use of water. The well-known explanation for government failure in respect of irrigation is the lack of accountability of its management to the user farmers and its growing politicisation. The most worrisome manifestation of this politicisation in the recent period is the political rent-seeking by offering free electricity for pumping water which has led to the overexploitation of groundwater resources.

Therefore, a question that arises in this context is whether privatisation of irrigation can provide the necessary correctives. But market failure is as endemic in irrigation and water management as government failure. Market failure is caused, in the first place, by the widespread prevalence of externalities defined as uncompensated costs or benefits accruing to some owing to the activities of some others. Then, there are high transaction costs, for example, costs of infrastructure for setting volumetric pricing and its enforcement. Thirdly, property rights for irrigation water are insecure and ineffective. This is commonly manifested in the farmers at the head reaches of the system appropriating much more water than they are entitled to, at the expense of those at the tail end (Perry *et al.*, 1997). Full-scale privatisation of irrigation under such circumstances, in the absence of necessary institutional mechanisms for correcting the distortions arising from market failure, can lead to serious inequities and inefficiencies in the use of water.

Irrigation Management Transfer (IMT) to the user-farmers is being increasingly advocated and practised the world over to provide correctives to the distortions arising from the failure of the market as well as the state. India has embarked upon Participatory Irrigation Management (PIM), under which the management of some of the systems is being turned over to the Water Users' Associations (WUAs). Conservation of land and groundwater resources through rainwater harvesting is another area where market failure as well as government failure have been glaring. As a solution to this, Participatory Water-shed Development is being evolved and practised in many countries, including India, for the protection and sustainable use of land and water resources.

Performance of Participatory Irrigation Management

The evidence so far on IMT in several countries, and on PIM in India, shows some positive results in terms of an increase in yields, water productivity and farm incomes. Incentives to the farmers to participate and the quality of leadership seems to be the key for the success of these ventures (Guerra *et al.*, 1998). In India, the performance of PIM so far indicates that the unwillingness of the lower levels of bureaucracy to fully transfer powers and functions to the user associations is the major bottleneck in the successful working of these institutions (Brewer *et al.*, 1999). Such a reluctance to delegate powers and functions, by stifling local initiative, prevents the emergence and development of leadership at the grass roots—an essential pre-requisite for the success of these institutions.

Similarly, the experience with watershed development under the new participatory approach in India shows that the immediate results are positive in terms of the rise in watertable, crop yields, employment and incomes of the participants (Rao, 2000). And, where property or use rights on common property resources are well-defined and protected, there has been a significant decline in the distress migration of labour (Chopra and Gulati, 1997, 2001). But there is still considerable uncertainty regarding the long-run sustainability of these institutions, that is, their ability to hold the different social groups together and mobilise resources from the community for maintenance of structures already created and for further development when the assistance under the current officially sponsored programmes ceases (Rao, 2000; Reddy *et al.*, 2001). This holds true even for a relatively promising experiment towards PIM in Andhra Pradesh (Raju, 2000). The performance of Irrigation Management Transfer (IMT) so far in several other countries points to similar uncertainties (Perry *et al.*, 1997).

The present obsession of the bureaucracy in India with the fulfilment of physical and financial targets has to give place, firstly, to greater devolution of powers and functions to the user-associations, including their involvement in the renovation and modernisation of the systems as well as in their management right from the outlet level. Secondly, there needs to be much greater stress on building up social capital through social mobilisation of different groups of user-farmers for sustainable use of land and water through conflict resolution among them and their capacity building by putting in place an autonomous and credible infrastructure for training. The institutions developed in this process need to be integrated with more formal legal or market institutions for sustaining them (Chopra, 2001). Thirdly, independent and professional evaluations of the ongoing programmes can help mid-course corrections that would greatly enhance the fulfilment of programme objectives.

Public Policy

In the area of irrigation and water management, the state should increasingly concern itself with overall public policy to create conducive socio-economic environment for the efficient and productive use of water. The state should divest itself from the tasks of managing the systems, because its failures have been conspicuous in this area which accounts for the major opportunities available for improving water productivity (CGIAR, 2001a).

Governments in the states and at the centre need to accord highest priority to the renovation/modernisation of the existing systems which account for nearly 40 per cent of the irrigated area from the major and medium irrigation projects. The rate of return from such investments would be very high when compared to the projects creating new irrigation potential. Modernisation of the delivery systems and the distribution channels for the existing projects would have a high pay-off, as they would facilitate a clear definition of property rights or entitlements of farmers and their effective enforcement. They would also facilitate the adoption of measures by the water users to improve water-use-efficiency and productivity.

Price and procurement policy of the government has an important bearing on the efficiency and productivity of water use through its impact on cropping pattern. A glaring illustration of this is the price policy for rice and wheat in the recent period which has resulted in the accumulation of over 60 million tonnes of foodgrains—nearly thrice the actual requirement—with the Food Corporation of India (FCI). It has been estimated that for each hectare of paddy raised under irrigated conditions, as much as 16,000 tonnes of irrigation water is applied in the semi-arid north-western Indian states (Dhawan, 2001), from where bulk of the rice is procured by the FCI. One can thus imagine how many billion tonnes of scarce water has been wastefully used over the years in the semi-arid plains of India, which could have been saved or diverted to higher productivity uses if the price and procurement policies were better aligned with the emerging domestic and export demand for foodgrains.

The experimental work backed by the ICAR found that 25-40 percent saving in irrigation water could be achieved through intermittent submergence and transplanting paddy seedlings at about the time of onset of monsoon rains. Similarly, water savings of the order of 50 per cent in the case of drip irrigation and 25 per cent in the case of sprinkler irrigation can be realised (Dhawan, 2001). But, only about 1 per cent of irrigated area in the country is presently covered by drip and sprinkler methods of irrigation. These technologies are not adopted by the farmers because water is available at a very low cost or is even free. The incentives are in fact perverse in as much as the capital cost of drip and sprinkler irrigation is prohibitively high for the Indian farmer due to various taxes and high interest rate (Dhawan, 2001).

The debate on water rates in the country so far has centered round the revenue accruing to the government for covering the Operation and Maintenance charges. The objective of conserving water needs to be brought into the forefront in these discussions. Given that water rates have depreciated very much in real terms, it is not certain that a significant rise in these rates within the feasible range would induce the farmers to save water under the existing system of management. On the other hand, a system of rationing water supplies in water-scarce regions even with moderate charges can induce farmers to increase water productivity, provided the supplies are reliable in terms of quantity and timings as in the case of the Warabandi system in north-western India (Berkoff, 1990; IWMI, 2001). In any case, raising water rates significantly would not be politically feasible unless it is linked with the performance of irrigation services and made explicit that revenues so raised would be reinvested locally to upgrade the services.

Water Users' Associations and panchayats should be fully empowered and induced to charge and collect water and electricity rates from the farmers on the basis of the volume of actual consumption where metering is possible, or, on the basis of the quantities of water received or electricity consumed as estimated by the farmers' associations where metering is uneconomical or otherwise infeasible. The revenues so collected should be allowed to be retained entirely by the Water Users' Associations under the aegis of panchayats for maintenance and development of irrigation services, with possible supplementation from the state governments.

It is clear from the foregoing discussion that given the technology and public policy, institutions concerning water use hold the key to raising water productivity by bridging the vast gap that now exists between knowledge and its application. Water institutions are a relatively new and challenging area of research for social scientists. Also, research in this area is highly interdisciplinary.

References

Agarwal, Ani (2000). "Drought? Try Capturing the Rain", *The Asian Journal*, Vol. 7, No. 3.

Berkoff, D.J.W. (1990). "Irrigation Management on the Indo-Gangetic Plain", *World Bank Technical Paper No. 129*, The World Bank.

Brewer, J., S. Kolavalli *et al.* (1999). *Irrigation Management Transfer in India: Policies, Processes and Performance*, IIM, Ahmedabad and IIMI, Colombo, Oxford and IBH Publishers.

Chada, D.K. (2000). "Ground Water Recharge: Option for Ground Water Management", *The Asian Journal*, Vol. 7, No. 4.

Chopra, Kanchan (2001). "Social Capital and Development Processes: The Role of Formal and Informal Institutions", *mimeo*, Institute of Economic Growth, Delhi.

Chopra, Kanchan and S.C. Gulati (1997). "Population, Poverty and Environmental Degradation: The Role of Property Rights" in Anil Agarwal (ed.), *The Challenge of the Balance-Environmental Economics in India*, Centre for Science and Environment, New Delhi.

———. (2001). *Migration, Common Property Resources and Environmental Degradation—Inter-linkages in India's Arid and Semi-Arid Regions*, Sage Publications, New Delhi.

Consultative Committee for International, Agricultural Research (CGIAR), Technical Advisory Committee (2001a). "Water and the CGIAR", *Discussion Paper*.

———. (2001b). "Water Productivity Research in the Context of CGIAR", *Discussion Paper*.

Dhawan, B.D. (2001). "Technological Change in Indian Irrigated Agriculture: Diffusion of Water Economising Technologies and practices", *mimeo*, Institute of Economic Growth, New Delhi.

Government of India (2001). *Economic Survey, 2000-2001*, New Delhi.

Government of India, Ministry of Water Resources (1999). *Report of the National Commission for Integrated Water Resources Development Plan*, Vol. 1, New Delhi.

Government of India, Planning Commission (2000). *Mid-Term Appraisal of Ninth Five-Year Plan (1997-2002)*, New Delhi.

Guerra, L.C., S.I. Bhuiyan, T.P. Tuong and R. Barker (1998). "Producing More Rice with Less Water from Irrigation Systems", *SWIM Paper 5*, International Water Management Institute (IWMI).

Hashim, S.R. (2000). "From Food Security to Water Security", *The Asian Journal*, Vol. 7, No. 4.

International Water Management Institute (IWMI) (2001). *Basin-Level Use and Productivity of Water: Examples from South Asia, Research Report* 49.

Perry, C.J., Michael Rock and D. Seckler (1997). *Water as an Economic Good: A Solution, or a Problem?, Research Report* 14, IIMI.

Raju, K.V. (2000). "Participatory Irrigation Management in Andhra Pradesh: Promise, Practice and a Way Forward", *Working Paper* 65, Institute for Social and Economic Change.

Rao, C.H.H. (2000). "Watershed Development in India—Recent Experience and Emerging Issues", *Economic and Political Weekly*, Vol. 35, No. 45, November 4.

Reddy, V. Ratna, M. Gopinath Reddy, S. Galab and Oliver Springate-Baginski (2001). "Watershed Development and Livelihood Security: An Assessment of Linkages and Impact in Andhra Pradesh, India", *mimeo*, Centre for Economic and Social Studies, Hyderabad and School of Geography, University of Leeds, UK.

Saleth, R.M. (1996). *Water Institutions in India: Economics, Law, and Policy*, Commonwealth Publishers, New Delhi.

Seckler, David (1996). *The New Era of Water Management: From 'Dry' to 'Wet' Water Savings*, Issues in Agriculture 8, CGIAR, Washington, DC.

Seckler, David, Upali Amarasinghe, David Molden, Radhika De Silva and Randolph Barker (1998). *World Water Demand and Supply, 1990 to 2025: Scenarios and Issues, Research Report* 19, International Water Management Institute (IWMI), Colombo, Sri Lanka.

Shah, Tushar (2001). *Wells and Welfare in the Ganga Basin: Public Policy and Private Initiative in Eastern Uttar Pradesh, India, Research Report* 54, IWMI.

This paper is based on the Presidential Address delivered by the author at the Second Biennial Conference of the Indian Society of Ecological Economics, Indian Institute of Forest Management, Bhopal, December 19-21, 2001.

Economic & Political Weekly, Vol. XXXVII, No. 18, May 4-10, 2002.

Economic Developments in India, Vol. 59.

15

Mission 2007: Every Village a Knowledge Centre

M.S. SWAMINATHAN

At the World Summit on the Information Society (WSIS) held recently in Tunis, a programme titled "Connect the World by 2015" was launched. The aim is to ensure that the benefits of the digital revolution reach every country and every part of each country by the year 2015, which is also a benchmark year for achieving the UN Millennium Development Goals. At a function held in Tunis on November 15, 2005, the International Telecommunication Union recognised India's Mission 2007: Every Village a Knowledge Centre, as the flagship of the 'Connect the World' movement.

Mission 2007 aims to provide knowledge connectivity to every village of India by August 15, 2007, which marks the 60th anniversary of what Jawaharlal Nehru called "India's tryst with destiny". A National Alliance for Mission 2007 was formed in 2003 to provide a platform for multi-stakeholder partnership. Seemingly impossible tasks can be achieved by mobilising the power of partnership, since irrespective of the individual strengths of the alliance partners their collective strength becomes considerable.

The National Alliance currently includes 22 government organisations including the Department of Information Technology, the Ministry of Panchayati Raj, the Telecom Regulatory Authority of India and Bharat Sanchar Nigam Limited; 94 civil society organisations; and 34 private sector information and communication technology (ICT) leaders such as NASSCOM, TCS, HCL and Microsoft. Besides, 18 academic institutions such as the Indian Institutes of Technology and the Indira Gandhi National Open University; and 10 financial institutions such as the National Bank for Agriculture and Rural Development (NABARD) and the State Bank of India are involved.

In addition, an international support group has been formed to provide technical and financial support to Mission 2007. The group is chaired by the Resident Representative of the United Nations Development Programme. It has the active participation of the International Development Research Centre and the Canadian International Development Agency, the Swiss Agency for Development and Cooperation (SDC), the United Kingdom's Department for International Development, the World Bank, the International Crops Research Institute for the Semi-Arid Tropics, the United Nations Educational, Scientific and Cultural Organisations, the World Health Organization, the Food and Agriculture Organization, the World Food Programme, the International Fund for Agricultural Development, the McArthur Foundation, the Jhai Foundation and the Global Knowledge Partnership.

Following the launching of Mission 2007 over two years ago as well as the recommendation of the National Commission on Farmers that village knowledge centres (VKCs) should be established as soon as possible for the knowledge and skill empowerment of rural families, some developments have taken place that give hope that the urban-rural digital divide can be substantially ended by August 15, 2007. These include:

- The decision to establish 100,000 ICT-based community service centres by August 15, 2007, by the Department of Information Technology, Government of India. Leveraging SWAN (State Wide Area Network) infrastructure, community service centres will provide reliable broad-based connectivity to remote villages.

- Setting up village resource centres at the block level by the Indian Space Research Organisation (ISRO) in collaboration with appropriate public and civil society institutions to provide a wide range of services including teleconferencing facilities.

- The decision of the Ministry of Panchayati Raj to establish Internet connected ICT centres in all the 240,000 *panchayats* and local bodies in the country by August 15, 2007. This will help to provide a public space for VKCs, characterised by access for all sections of rural society.

- The rural information society initiative of BSNL which will aim to set up 100,000 VKCs each covering a population of 2,000 or more.

- Support by NABARD through the Rural Infrastructure Development Fund to state governments to organise ICT self-help groups to establish and manage VKCs.

- Promotion of e-governance as a key component of the National Common Minimum Programme and the proposal to include knowledge connectivity as an essential component of the Bharat Nirman Programme.

- Setting up of public tele-information centres (PTICs) through the Universal Service Obligation Fund.

- Inclusion of e-health facilities under the National Rural Health Mission by the Ministry of Health and Family Welfare.

- Enactment of the Right to Information Act (2005).

What is important is to ensure that all such initiatives designed to help rural and tribal families are pro-poor, pro-women, and pro-livelihood in both design and implementation. There are many other initiatives by both the centre (for example, the Department of Science and Technology, and the Council for the Advancement of People's Action and Rural Technology) and the states. In addition, both private industry and academic and civil society organisations are actively involved in bridging the urban-rural digital divide and in assisting rural families to have access to the information they need in relation to health, livelihood, food, water and income security. Well-known initiatives by the private sector include the *e-choupal* of ITC and Microsoft's unlimited potential capacity building programme.

It is obvious that if we can achieve convergence and synergy among the numerous ongoing as well as emerging programmes, the goal of achieving a rural knowledge revolution by August 15, 2007, can become a reality. While the green revolution helped us to improve the productivity and production of rice, wheat and other crops, the knowledge revolution will help to enhance human productivity and entrepreneurship in every sphere of human activity.

The VKC is based on the principle of an integrated and appropriate use of the Internet, cable TV, cell phone, community radio and the vernacular press. To begin with, VKCs will be established in the 240,000 *panchayats* and local bodies. With the help of loud speakers and FM radio, they will be able to cover all the 600,000 villages in the country. Internet-community radio and cell phone-community radio are powerful combinations for reaching the un-reached with timely information. The spot prices of agricultural commodities monitored on a cell phone can be communicated to several villages through a low power FM radio. A group of VKCs will be supported by a block-level village resource centre, which will also provide teleconferencing facilities.

Apart from a sense of ownership by local women and men, the other major requirements for the success of the village knowledge centre movement are in the areas of connectivity, content and capacity building. Fortunately, more than 670,000 km of buried fibre optic cable network nationwide offers the capability to connect an estimated 85 per cent of the villages.

The relevance and timeliness of the content will determine the interest of rural families in VKCs. The content should be demand driven and area culture, and time specific. The National Alliance has suggested that at the level of each district a content consortium may be organised to enable VKC managers to access the information they need in the area of weather, health, entitlements to government projects, e-governance, credit and insurance, agriculture and market. The managers of VKCs will have to maintain active contact with the content consortium. To facilitate the availability of the right information at the right time and place, it is proposed to organise national digital gateways for agriculture, education, health and livelihoods.

In the area of capacity building, it is proposed to train at least one woman and one man from each village in computer literacy, under the auspices of the Jamsetji Tata National Virtual Academy for Rural Prosperity (NV). Those who reveal the capacity to become master trainers will be elected fellows of the NVA. The experience gained under the M.S. Swaminathan Research Foundation's VKC programme during the last eight years shows that rural women in particular are able to master ICT within a fortnight provided the pedagogic methodology is learning by doing. The NVA fellows will be the torchbearers of the rural knowledge revolution.

The Tunis World Summit on the Information Society demonstrated the spectacular progress made in technology development since the 2003 Geneva Summit. The world is thus witnessing two opposite trends. The explosive progress in science and technology is providing uncommon opportunities for health, food, water, work, energy and literacy for all. On the other hand, a considerable proportion of humankind living under conditions of poverty, hunger and deprivation feel a sense of social exclusion and injustice.

Consequently, there is a growing violence in the human heart. While the WSIS was in progress in the midst of a feeling of a brave new world of technological breakthroughs, the main news in the media every day was the loss of innocent lives caused by bomb explosions in different parts of the world. The extensive coexistence of unsustainable lifestyles and unacceptable poverty is not conducive to either harmony with nature or with each other. This is why the success of Mission 2007: Every Village a Knowledge Centre is so important for human security and well-being in our country.

The Hindu, November 25, 2005.

Economic Developments in India, Vol. 96.

16

Unshackling India's Manufacturing—
The Ingredients of a Strategy

BIBEK DEBROY

I. INTRODUCTION

The etymology of the word 'manufacture' isn't certain. But it seems to have a link with the Latin *manu factum*, meaning 'made by hand'. Irrespective of ingredients of technology, capital (plant and machinery), entrepreneurship, and perhaps even land, entering as inputs or factors into production processes, labour remains a core input. And there is no denying that India possesses, or should possess, a comparative advantage in labour. As with every other developing country, that has always been the case, labour is relatively more abundant than capital. In a completely integrated and globalised world, national boundaries should make no difference. But that ideal never happens. Even if cross-border movements of technology and capital are relatively free, there will be restrictions on cross-border movements of labour. Integration of labour markets will only happen in niches, in selected segments. Therefore, India should be in a position to exploit its cost advantage in labour, and in natural resources, to push manufacturing growth. Nor should one forget India's strengths in science and technology and in education. These reinforce the labour cost advantage.

To this traditional labour cost advantage has been added what is called the demographic dividend. Stated simply, this means that populations in developed countries are ageing, whereas in developing countries, the working age population is increasing. Perhaps the most spectacular of extrapolations is the Goldman Sachs, BRIC (Brazil, Russia, India, China) report.[1] This makes the point that in the period leading up to 2050, India alone, among the BRIC

---

1. Wilson, Dominic and Roopa Purushothaman (2003). "Dreaming with BRICs: The Path to 2050", *Global Economics Paper* No. 99, Goldman Sachs, October 1. There have been two subsequent follow-up BRIC reports also.

countries, is unlikely to face a labour constraint. A labour shortage in developed countries means scope for immigration or for outsourcing manufacturing activities. Except for niches and small segments, the former is never likely to be quantitatively significant. After all, even WTO mandated agreements visualise cross-border movements of skilled personnel alone, that too, for temporary periods. In contrast, outsourcing and off-shoring of manufacturing activities is likely to be much more significant. There are estimates that off-shoring of manufacturing activities to low cost countries can be significant and that India can reap part of this dividend.[2] Outsourcing to India has happened and has even figured in election debates in developed countries. But that has been for services. In the 1970s, 1980s and even the 1990s, India missed opportunities in off-shoring of manufacturing. There is no reason why that should happen in the next two decades also.

The Tenth Five Year Plan (2002-07) projects an annual average real GDP growth of 8 per cent. The National Common Minimum Programme (NCMP) of the government targets 7 to 8 per cent growth over the next decade. While an average of 8 per cent during the Tenth Five Year Plan may now be impossible, there is no denying that a trend rate of 8 per cent plus over the next decade and more is feasible. Other countries in the world have exhibited such high rates of growth, even approaching and crossing 9 per cent. Notwithstanding the low base in 2002-03, the GDP growth of 8.5 per cent in 2003-04 is significant and even more significant is the GDP growth of 6.9 per cent in 2004-05, given the high base in 2003-04. In 2005-06, GDP growth should cross 7 per cent. GDP's sectoral composition has primary, secondary and tertiary components. In 2003-04, in constant prices, the primary sector[3] accounted for 24.4 per cent of GDP, the secondary sector[4] accounted for 24.6 per cent and the tertiary sector accounted for 51 per cent. There is often euphoria about tertiary sector growth. However, in the history of economic development, no country has developed riding on service sector growth alone. The transition has been from the primary to the secondary and thereafter to the tertiary. That apart, such sectoral growth rates are not independent of one another. Tertiary sector growth requires secondary sector growth and in India's growth experience, the two have always gone together, the 1990s representing a slight aberration from the trend.

---

2. *Made in India—The Next Big Manufacturing Export Story*, CII-McKinsey, October 2004.

3. With mining and quarrying (2.3 per cent) also included in the primary sector, together with agriculture, forestry, logging and fishing. However, mining and quarrying can also be included under industry.

4. Manufacturing, construction, electricity, gas and water supply.

Sectoral compositions of GDP are not constant. They change over time. However, with the present sectoral compositions, what sectoral growth rates can ensure 9 per cent real GDP growth? Pure agriculture and allied activities (excluding mining and quarrying) accounts for 22.1 per cent of GDP.[5] The historical trend for growth in this sector has never been more than 3 per cent. Even if one assumes that an optimistic rate of 4 per cent is achieved, with a share of 22.1 per cent, this contributes 0.884 per cent to GDP growth. A trend growth of more than 10 per cent for the services sector is unreasonable and with a 51 per cent share, this contributes 5.1 per cent to GDP growth. The 9 per cent target still requires a 3.016 per cent contribution from the secondary sector. With a secondary sector contribution of 26.9 per cent (including mining and quarrying), the secondary sector needs to grow at 11.21 per cent. And this is the entire secondary sector, not just manufacturing. This entire secondary sector or industry includes components of mining and quarrying, manufacturing, electricity, gas and water supply and construction, with manufacturing contributing the bulk of 79.36 per cent.[6] An average growth of 6 per cent in the other three components requires manufacturing to grow at 12.26 per cent. Admittedly, construction may perform better, as it often has in the decade of the 1990s and subsequently. To that extent, the burden on manufacturing, in terms of that growth target of 9 per cent, eases. But on the other hand, the primary sector may not chip in with 4 per cent growth. Therefore, a 12 per cent target for manufacturing ought to be the target growth.

Nor should one forget the employment angle. A quote from the National Common Minimum Programme (NCMP) is pertinent, "The UPA government will set up a National Manufacturing Competitiveness Council to provide a continuing forum for policy dialogue to energise and sustain the growth of manufacturing industry like food processing, textiles and garments, engineering, consumer goods, pharmaceuticals, capital goods, leather, and IT hardware. Household and artisanal manufacturing will be given greater technological, investment and marketing support. In the past few years, the most employment-intensive segment of small scale industry (SSI) has suffered extensively. A major promotional package for the SSI sector will be announced soon. It will be freed from the Inspector *Raj* and be given full credit, technological and marketing support. Infrastructure upgradation in major

---

5. *Economic Survey 2004-05* points to a further decline in agriculture's share of GDP to 21 per cent and a decline in work force employed in agriculture to 57 per cent (1999-2000).

6. As a weight in the index of industrial production.

industrial clusters will receive urgent attention." While this quote directly mentions employment only in the context of the SSI (small scale industry) sector, employment is an area of concern for the UPA government, within the NCMP framework and outside it.

Employment data originate through surveys conducted by NSS (National Sample Survey) and a large NSS survey was last held in 1999-2000 and is therefore somewhat dated now.[7] This shows a labour force of 363.33 million and a workforce of 336.75 million, with an unemployment rate of 7.32 per cent. There is a separate point that with a significant share of the workforce employed in the rural sector, unemployment figures may not reveal much. The problem is more of underemployment. And there are significant variations in unemployment rates across states. For instance, unemployment rates are more than 10 per cent in states like Kerala, Tamil Nadu and West Bengal. What is worrying is that the annual average growth in employment has slowed. While the average annual growth rate in employment was 2.89 per cent between 1983 and 1987-88 and 2.50 per cent between 1987-88 and 1993-94, it was 1.07 per cent between 1993-94 and 1999-2000. This slowing down is largely because in the 1990s agriculture failed to create jobs. However, it is not pure agriculture's business to create jobs. The history of development is one of pulling people out of agriculture, into non-farm activities, into manufacturing and into services, not retaining them there. In that sense, India has witnessed a failed industrial revolution. If 10 million new jobs have to be created a year, manufacturing also has a role to play.

Between 1993-94 and 1999-2000, manufacturing hasn't done that well in creating jobs either. The average annual employment growth in manufacturing during this period was 2.58 per cent, compared to 3.64 per cent between 1982 to 1987-88. Between 1993-94 and 1999-2000, the overall employment elasticity was 0.16. But at 0.33, it was higher for manufacturing. Although the progressive decline in the employment elasticity of manufacturing should cause concern. For instance, this elasticity was 0.59 between 1983 and 1987-88, declining to 0.33 between 1993-94 and 1999-2000. This employment elasticity translates into jobs in the following way. Employment in manufacturing was 40.79 million in 1999-2000. If manufacturing grows at 9 per cent, with an employment elasticity of 0.33, 1.2 million jobs are created in manufacturing a year. But if the employment elasticity is 0.59, as it was between 1983 and 1987-88, with 9 per cent manufacturing growth, 2.2 million jobs are created

---

7. Large NSS surveys are roughly held at five year intervals. Before 1999-2000, the last one was in 1993-94.

a year. And if manufacturing growth increases to 12 per cent, with an elasticity of 0.59, 2.9 million jobs are created a year in manufacturing. There is a target of creating 10 million jobs a year. However, this is for the entire economy and not all of this 10 million is expected to be created in manufacturing. But manufacturing can make its contribution. This is also the right place to mention interstate differences. Most of the demographic dividend, in terms of new entrants into the labour force, is going to occur in central parts of India, leading eastwards. In an era of industrial licensing, manufacturing capacities could be set up in geographical areas where labour forces existed. But industrial licensing is not only impossible now, it is also undesirable. Nor will employment growth primarily happen through the public sector, and it must not be forgotten that many sick public sector units (PSUs) are precisely in these geographical regions and they will eventually be closed down. If one is to avoid tensions over a few jobs in the railways, private sector job creation, including in manufacturing, must compensate. What should be of concern is the declining employment elasticity of manufacturing in the 1990s, compared to say, the 1980s. While labour market rigidities may be partly responsible, these haven't worsened in the 1990s. The answer, therefore, probably lies in restructuring consequent to competition, leading to shedding of surplus jobs, and even a sectoral change in manufacturing sectors that have shown relatively higher rates of growth in the 1990s.

This is also the right place to mention the organised *versus* unorganised sector dichotomy. The figures on work force and labour force given earlier were from 1999-2000, from the NSS. In 2000, the total work force is estimated to be 397.88 million. Of this, 28.15 million, or 7.07 per cent is in the organised sector.[8] The unorganised sector accounts for employment of 369.73 million, or 92.93 per cent. There are indeed three different definitions of organised/unorganised, although they do overlap. First, there is the labour law kind of definition, the Factories Act of 1948 being the obvious example, although this only applies to 'factories'. Registration is required if a factory employs 20 or more people and doesn't use power or if it employs 10 or more people and uses power. Registration is equated with organised and everything else is unorganised. Second, there is a definition of small-scale industry (SSI), in terms of threshold levels of investment in plant and machinery. SSI is often equated with unorganised manufacturing. Third, there is a threshold level of turnover below which, excise doesn't have to be paid. Excise exemption

---

8. *Economic Survey 2004-05* has an organised sector figure of 27 million in 2003, with a breakup of 18.6 million in the public sector and 8.4 million in the private sector.

constitutes yet another definition of unorganised. However, whichever definition of unorganised/organised one uses, the organised sector accounts for less than 8 per cent of the work force. For instance, the 369.73 million work force figure is for 1999-2000. In 2002, the work force is 397 million. And only 27.2 million is employed in the organised sector, constituting 6.9 per cent. 93.1 per cent or 369.6 million is employed in the unorganised sector. Of the total employment of 27.2 million in the organised sector, 18.8 million (69 per cent) is in the public sector. Public sector employment has stagnated in the 1990s. The private sector accounts for 8.4 million employment (31 per cent) in the organised sector. This has increased a bit in the 1990s, but only from 7.6 million in 1990 to 8.4 million in 2002. These figures are of course for total private sector employment. Private sector employment in organised sector manufacturing is 4.9 million in 2002, compared to total manufacturing employment of 40.79 million.[9] Public sector employment in organised sector manufacturing is 1.4 million in 2002. Total employment in organised sector manufacturing is thus 6.3 million, 15.4 per cent of total manufacturing employment. This organised/total ratio may be higher for manufacturing than for overall employment, but is still fairly low.

With reforms, the dichotomy between the organised and unorganised sectors should break down. The organised sector is under the purview of labour laws, which are certainly rigid. Liberalisation will involve making labour market provisions in the organised sector more flexible. However, it should also be noted that the unorganised sector is completely outside the purview of most labour laws, and this includes social security. Liberalisation will also involve extending protection to labour in the unorganised sector. This is indeed the thrust of the recommendations of the Second National Commission on Labour, which submitted a report in 2002.

II. WHAT IS MANUFACTURING?

This section may seem to be irrelevant, but is relevant for purposes of data and statistical systems. The basic classification of all economic activities is the UN system's International Standard Industrial Classification (ISIC).[10] At the 2-digit level, these are also the classifications followed by the CSO (Central

---

9. These figures keep changing. *Economic Survey 2004-05* has a figure of 4.7 million as private sector organised employment in manufacturing in 2003, a slight decline compared to 2002.

10. Revision 3.1. This is not identical with the North American Industrial Classification System (NAICS) used in the CII-McKinsey study, although difference surface at levels of disaggregation far beyond the 2-digit level.

Statistical Organisation). Section D constitutes manufacturing in the industrial classification and the 2-digit codes and descriptions (common to both ISIC and CSO) are given in the Table 16.1. This then constitutes the definition of manufacturing, both for cross-country comparisons and for Indian data. What should be noted is that some of these categories are sometimes not included in data on manufacturing. Examples are codes 22, 36 and 37.

Table 16.1

Industrial Classification and the 2-digit Codes and Discription

ISIC 2-Digit Code	ISIC Description
15	Manufacture of food products and beverages.
16	Manufacture of tobacco products.
17	Manufacture of textiles.
18	Manufacture of wearing apparel; dressing and dyeing of fur.
19	Tanning and dressing of leather; manufacture of luggage, handbags, saddlery, harness and footwear.
20	Manufacture of wood and of products of wood and cork, except furniture; manufacture of articles of straw and plaiting materials.
21	Manufacture of paper and paper products.
22	Publishing, printing and reproduction of recorded media.
23	Manufacture of coke, refined petroleum products and nuclear fuel.
24	Manufacture of chemicals and chemical products.
25	Manufacture of rubber and plastics products.
26	Manufacture of other non-metallic mineral products.
27	Manufacture of basic metals.
28	Manufacture of fabricated metal products, except machinery and equipment.
29	Manufacture of machinery and equipment n.e.c.
30	Manufacture of office, accounting and computing machinery.
31	Manufacture of electrical machinery and apparatus n.e.c.
32	Manufacture of radio, television and communication equipment and apparatus.
33	Manufacture of medical, precision and optical instruments, watches and clocks.
34	Manufacture of motor vehicles, trailers and semi-trailers.
35	Manufacture of other transport equipment.
36	Manufacture of furniture; manufacturing n.e.c.
37	Recycling.

The following longish quote from UNCTAD's explanatory note on manufacturing illustrates the kinds of problems that can arise.

"Manufacturing comprises units engaged in the physical or chemical transformation of materials, substances, or components into new products. The materials, substances, or components transformed are raw materials that are products of agriculture, forestry, fishing, mining or quarrying as well as products of other manufacturing activities. The units in the manufacturing section are often described as plants, factories or mills and characteristically use power-driven machines and materials-handling equipment. However, units that transform materials or substances into new products by hand or in the worker's home and those engaged in selling to the general public products made on the same premises from which they are sold, such as bakeries and custom tailors, are also included in this section. Manufacturing units may process materials or may contract with other units to process their materials for them. Both types of units are included in manufacturing. The new product of a manufacturing unit may be finished in the sense that it is ready for utilisation or consumption, or it may be semi-finished in the sense that it is to become an input for further manufacturing. For example, the product of the alumina refinery is the input used in the primary production of aluminium; primary aluminium is the input to an aluminium wire drawing plant; and aluminium wire is the input for a fabricated wire product manufacturing unit. Assembly of the component parts of manufactured products is considered manufacturing. This includes the assembly of manufactured products from either self-produced or purchased components. Assembly of self-produced prefabricated components of constructions at the construction site is classified as manufacturing when the manufacturing and assembly are integrated activities. When the assembly is performed by separate units, the activity is appropriately classified in division 45 (construction). Therefore, assembly on the site of not self-produced prefabricated, integral parts into bridges, water tanks, storage and warehouse facilities, railroad and elevated rights of way, lift and escalator, plumbing, sprinkler, central heating, ventilating and air conditioning, lighting, electrical and telecommunications wiring systems of buildings, and all kinds of structures, is classified in construction. Assembly and installation of machinery and equipment in mining, manufacturing, commercial or other units, when carried out as a specialised activity, are classified in the same class of manufacturing as manufacture of the item installed. Assembly and installation of machinery and equipment that are performed as a service incidental to the sale of the goods by a unit primarily engaged in manufacturing, wholesale trade or retail trade, are classified with its main activity. Activities of units primarily engaged in maintenance and repair of industrial, commercial and similar machinery and equipment are, in general, classified in the same class of manufacturing as those specialising in manufacturing the goods. However, units engaged in repair of office and computing machinery are classified in class 7250. Units the main activity of which is repair of household appliances, equipment and furnishings, motor vehicles and other consumer goods are, as a general rule, classified in the appropriate class of division 50 (sale, maintenance and repair of motor vehicles and motorcycles; retail sale of automotive fuel) or 52 (retail trade, except of motor vehicles and motorcycles; repair of personal and household goods) in accordance with the kind of goods that are repaired. Substantial alteration, renovation or reconstruction of goods is generally considered to be manufacturing. Manufacture of specialised components and parts of, and accessories and attachments to, machinery and equipment is, as a general rule, classified in the same class as the manufacture of the machinery and equipment for which the parts and accessories are intended. Manufacture of unspecialised components and parts of machinery and equipment, e.g. engines, pistons, electric motors, electrical assemblies, valves, gears, roller bearings, is classified in the appropriate class of manufacturing, without regard to the machinery and equipment in which these items may be included. However, making specialised components and accessories by moulding or extruding plastics materials is included in class 2520. The recycling of waste is also included in manufacturing.

"The boundaries of manufacturing and the other sectors of the classification system can be somewhat blurry. As a general rule, the units in the manufacturing sector are engaged in the transformation of materials into new products. Their output is a new product. However, the definition of what constitutes a new product can be somewhat subjective. As clarification, the following activities are considered manufacturing in ISIC:

- Milk pasteurising and bottling (see 1520).
- Fresh fish processing (oyster shucking, fish filleting), not done on a fishing boat (see 1512).
- Printing and related activities (see 2221, 2222).
- Ready-mixed concrete production (see 2695).
- Leather converting (see 1911).
- Wood preserving (see 2010).

- Electroplating, plating, metal heat treating, and polishing (see 2892).

- Rebuilding or remanufacturing machinery (e.g., automobile engines, see 3410).

- Ship repair and renovation (see 3511).

- Tyre retreading (see 2511).

Conversely, there are activities that though sometimes considered manufacturing, are classified in another section of ISIC (in other words, they are not classified as manufacturing). They include:

- Logging, classified in section A (agriculture, hunting and forestry).

- Beneficiating of ores and other minerals, classified in section C (mining).

- Construction of structures and fabricating operations performed at the site of construction, classified in section F (construction).

- Activities of breaking of bulk and redistribution in smaller lots, including packaging, repackaging, or bottling products, such as liquors or chemicals; the customised assembly of computers; sorting of scrap; mixing paints to customer order; and cutting metals to customer order, produce a modified version of the same product, not a new product, and are classified to section G (wholesale and retail trade)."

Beyond such problems, there are serious issues with CSO's data collection exercises. "The entire manufacturing activities are classified into two broad sectors, *viz.*, manufacturing—'registered' and 'unregistered'. The registered manufacturing sector covers all factories covered under sections 2m (i) and 2m (ii) of the Indian Factories Act (IFA), 1948 which respectively refers to the factories employing 10 or more workers and using power or those employing 20 or more workers but not using power on any day of the preceding 12 months and bidi and cigar establishments registered under *Bidi* and Cigar Workers (Condition of Employment) Act, 1966 and employing 10 or more workers using power or 20 or more workers and not using power."[11] Indeed, factories where a manufacturing process is not carried on are excluded. "The 'manufacturing process' is defined as any process for (i) making, altering, repairing, finishing, packing, oiling, washing, cleaning, breaking-up, demolishing or otherwise treating or adapting any article or substance with a view to its use, sale, transport, delivery or disposal; (ii) pumping oil, water,

---

11. *NAS–Sources and Methods*, CSO, 1989.

sewage or any substance; (iii) generating, transforming or transmitting power; (iv) composing types for printing, printing by letter press, lithography, photogravure or other similar process or book binding; (v) constructing, reconstructing, repairing, refitting, finishing or breaking up of ships or vessels; (vi) preserving or storing any article in cold storage. Factories registered under IFA but not engaged in manufacturing activities are excluded." There is thus a dichotomy between registered manufacturing and unregistered manufacturing. For registered manufacturing, data are collected annually through the Annual Survey of Industries (ASI). This is part survey (sample) and part census. Unregistered manufacturing, which also includes own account enterprises, is covered much less frequently, typically, once every five years.

In 2001, there was a fairly serious critique of the entire Indian statistical system.[12] Although the criticisms were greater for other sectors of the economy, manufacturing data was also criticised—in all the four components of ASI, unregistered manufacturing, small-scale industries (SSI) and the index of industrial production (IIP). For instance, other than time lags and sampling and non-sampling errors, the ASI includes units that shouldn't be included (they have closed down) and excludes units that should be included. Different databases of unregistered (census or survey) manufacturing vary widely, perhaps understandable, because differing concepts and definitions are used. This is compounded by lack of adequate data on SSI and unorganised traditional industries (village and small industries). The National Statistical Commission's report was written much before data on the Third Census of SSIs, undertaken in 2001-02, became available. But this Third Census illustrates the kinds of problems that arise. After the Third Census, for 2001-02, *Economic Survey 2003-04* gives the following figures for the SSI sector—registered units 1.375 million, unregistered units 9.146 million, total units 10.521 million, total production in current prices Rs. 2,82,270 crores and employment 24.909 million. But before the Third Census results became available, *Economic Survey 2002-03* gave the following figures for the SSI sector, also for 2001-02—registered units 2.731 million, unregistered units 0.711 million, total units 3.442 million, total production in current prices Rs. 6,90,316 crores and employment 19.223 million. The discrepancies are remarkable. Finally, other than the problem that the index of industrial production (IIP) represents only 80 per cent of manufacturing, there are problems associated with low response rates, small samples, unsatisfactory

---

12. *Report of the National Statistical Commission,* August 2001.

weights and non-representation of the unorganised sector. As a generalisation, manufacturing data is therefore somewhat satisfactory for registered manufacturing and extremely unsatisfactory for everything else.

III. CROSS-COUNTRY DATA AND MANUFACTURING TARGETS

As was mentioned indirectly earlier, traditional models of development involve a transition from the primary sector to the secondary sector and subsequently, a transition to the tertiary sector. Indeed, many other developing countries have much higher shares of manufacturing in GDP, as compared to India. This is evident from the data in the table, the source being the World Bank[13] and the year being 2003. China's share of 44.5 per cent may be a striking outlier. And the fact that other South Asian countries have shares similar to India's is neither here nor there. There is an obvious correlation with emphasis on import substituting industrialisation. 44.5 per cent may be spectacular. But there is no reason why manufacturing's share in Indian GDP should not be 30 per cent. Notwithstanding the euphoria about services, the expected decline of agriculture's contribution should be mirrored by an increase in manufacturing's share. It isn't the case that manufacturing's share in Indian GDP hasn't increased. But the increase has been very slow. The 15.8 per cent figure in Table 16.2 is from World Bank sources and is for the year 2003. CSO (Central Statistical Organisation) sources show a share of 16.85 per cent in 2001-02 and 17.22 per cent in 2002-03. The share used to be 13.82 per cent in 1980-81. It increased gradually to 17.68 per cent in 1997-98, before declining and then reviving again.

It is possible to play around with numbers to work out future scenarios. Between 1993-94 and 2003-04, the annual average real rates of growth have been 2.66 per cent for agriculture (excluding mining), 5.41 per cent for non-manufacturing industry, 6.92 per cent for manufacturing and 8.03 per cent for services, yielding a real GDP growth rate of 6.24 per cent. As was mentioned earlier, the rough sectoral contributions to GDP are 22 per cent for agriculture and allied activities (excluding mining and quarrying), 51 per cent for services and 27 per cent for industry. Of the 27 per cent industrial contribution, around 9 per cent is non-manufacturing industry (including mining and quarrying). The manufacturing contribution proper is around 18 per cent of GDP. What

---

13. http://web.worldbank.org/WEBSITE/EXTERNAL/COUNTRIES 0,,pagePK:180619~theSitePK:
    136917,00.html.

Table 16.2

Share of the Manufacturing Sector in GDP (Per Cent)

India	15.8[14]
Argentina	23.9
Brazil	11.4[15]
Chile	15.8[16]
Mexico	18.1
South Africa	18.9
China	44.5
Indonesia	25.0
South Korea	23.7
Philippines	22.9
Thailand	34.2
Malaysia	31.1
Pakistan	16.2
Sri Lanka	15.5
Bangladesh	15.8

does it mean to say that manufacturing's share of GDP should be 30 per cent? At one level, one is arguing that historically, manufacturing could have done better and compared to other countries, there is no reason why the share today should not have been 30 per cent, as compared to 8 per cent. This is a valid point to make. But at another level, one is arguing that there should be a game plan to take manufacturing's share to 30 per cent. This is more questionable, more so if it is articulated in terms of manufacturing's share, as opposed to industry's share. Manufacturing's share is a function not only of manufacturing growth, but also of growths in the other sectors. For instance, there is no reason why service sector growth should slow down from that historical trend of 8.03 per cent. Indeed, in the next twenty years, the service sector share in GDP should inch up towards 60 per cent. Nor is there any particular reason why non-manufacturing industrial growth should slow down. And non-manufacturing industry will continue to account for at least 10 per cent of GDP. While agriculture's share in GDP ought to progressively decline, no reasonable projection will assume an agricultural contribution of less than 10 per cent in the next 20 years. That leaves a manufacturing contribution to

---

14. India's share was 16.3 per cent in 1983.
15. Brazil's share was 33.2 per cent in 1983.
16. Chile's share was 21.2 per cent in 1983.

GDP of 20 per cent and no more. Anything more than a 20 or 25 per cent contribution of manufacturing to GDP is extremely implausible. As the historical trend shows, it has taken more than 20 years to increase the manufacturing share by five percentage points to around 18 per cent. Another five percentage points will take another 20 plus years, in a business-as-usual kind of scenario. In a non business-as-usual kind of scenario, the transition will at best be accelerated. If the target is expressed as manufacturing's share in GDP, and the timeframe is the next 10 years, one should at best hope for something like a 23 per cent share in 2015. Not 30 per cent.[17]

Targets are better articulated in terms of manufacturing's growth alone, independent of growth rates in non-manufacturing sectors. Over the last ten years, the trend rate of growth in manufacturing has been 6.9 per cent, say 7 per cent. This is the somewhat pessimistic, business-as-usual kind of target. An aspirational target can be real growth of 9 per cent.[18] This is probably the most likely scenario. A more optimistic target, requiring substantive reforms, will be a growth target of something like 12 per cent. Given manufacturing's present share of 18 per cent of GDP, the difference between 7 per cent and 12 per cent translates into 0.9 per cent additional incremental GDP growth. And the difference between 7 per cent and 9 per cent translates into 0.36 per cent additional incremental GDP growth. As was mentioned earlier, if the employment elasticity increases to 0.59, 9 per cent growth means 2.2 million new jobs a year and 12 per cent growth means 2.9 million new jobs a year. These are figures on direct job creation. Figures on indirect jobs created, as a result of multiplier effects, are impossible to compute.[19]

An overall or aggregate target of 12 per cent growth, or even 9 per cent, is too aggregated for any policy thrust. This needs to be decomposed or disaggregated according to manufacturing sub-sectors. For instance, in the index of industrial production (IIP), there are 17 industry groups at the 2-digit level of classification.[20] This is indicated in the table below and is based on the National Industrial Classification (NIC) and differs from the ISIC 2-digit codes mentioned earlier.

---

17. The CII-McKinsey aspiration is 18-21 per cent share of GDP by 2015.

18. CII-McKinsey has an aspirational target of 8-9 per cent, decomposed into domestic growth of 7-8 per cent and export growth of 15-17 per cent.

19. Although CII-McKinsey suggest two to three times the direct figure.

20. As was mentioned earlier, IIP only covers 80 per cent of manufacturing.

Table 16.3

Seventeen Industry Groups at the 2-digit Level of Classification

NIC 2-Digit Code	Description	Weight in IIP (Per Cent) Growth	Possible Target Growth (Per Cent)	Contribution to Manufacturing
20-21	Food Products	9.1	6	.00546
22	Beverages, Tobacco & Related Products	2.4	10	.0024
23	Cotton Textiles	5.5	8	.0044
24	Wool, Silk & Man-Made Fibre Textiles	2.3	4	.00088
25	Jute & Other Vegetable Fibre Textiles (Except Cotton)	0.6	1	.00006
26	Textile Products (including Wearing Apparel)	2.5	14	.0035
27	Wood & Wood Products, Furniture & Fixtures	2.7	10	.0027
28	Paper & Paper Products & Printing, Publishing & Allied Industries	2.7	20	.0054
29	Leather & Leather & Fur Products	1.1	3	.00033
30	Basic Chemicals & Chemical Products (Except Petroleum & Coal)	14.0	16	.0224
31	Rubber, Plastic, Petroleum & Coal	5.7	7	.00385
32	Non-metallic Mineral Products	4.4	5	.0022
33	Basic Metal & Alloy Industries	7.5	12	.009
34	Metal Products & Parts, except Machinery & Equipment	2.8	7	.00196
35-36	Machinery & Equipment, other than Transport Equipment	9.6	20	.0192
37	Transport Equipment & Parts	4.0	20	.008
38	Other Manufacturing industries	2.6	20	.0052
	Total	100.0[21]		.09694

---

21. There are rounding approximations.

There are two broad ways of identifying sub-sectors for a thrust and it needs to be highlighted that these two methods of identification are not always compatible. The first criterion is in terms of possible employment generation. For instance, if one were to use this yardstick, one would probably pick codes 20-21 through 29 from the above list. The CMP itself mentions some manufacturing industries—food processing, textiles and garments, engineering, consumer goods, pharmaceuticals, capital goods, leather and IT hardware. Although this list is merely illustrative, there is probably an implicit employment criterion in this identification. More explicitly, the budget for 2005-06 mentions the employment criterion and singles out textiles and garments, food processing and IT. To quote from the budget speech, "Sectors with potential for generating employment will receive the highest attention of the government." How this can be operationalised is a separate matter and we will return to that later. The second possible identification of thrust areas is not in terms of employment, but in terms of the weights different sub-sectors have in overall manufacturing growth. These weights are given in the Table 16.3. For instance, as the Table 16.3 shows, basic chemicals (code 30) have a large weight, although its employment potential might not be that large. In general, codes 30 to 37 probably have low employment potentials. The manufacturing sector has performed relatively well in 2003-04 and 2004-05, especially the latter, although nowhere near as well as in 1995-96. Based on the performance in 2003-04 and 2005-06, the Table 16.3 also shows reasonable growth targets for the 17 industry groups. These are not unnecessarily optimistic. Rather, they reflect an aspirational target. As the Table 16.3 shows, 10 per cent growth in manufacturing is within the realm of possibility, provided the growth is uniform across sectors.

IV. WHAT AILS MANUFACTURING?

What are the constraints in pushing up manufacturing growth still further? The constraints themselves suggest the solutions. Some of the constraints are generic in the sense that they cut across all manufacturing sectors. The others are more specific and pertain to specific sectors. Since there will be other papers addressed to specific sectors, in this paper, we only concentrate on the generic problems.

At a very broad level, some indications of competitiveness can be obtained from World Competitiveness Reports. More accurately, there are two such reports—*Global Competitiveness Report (GCR)*, published by World Economic

Forum[22] and the *World Competitiveness Yearbook (WCY)*, published by International Institute for Management Development (IMD).[23] The bifurcation of one initial report into two highlights problems associated with defining competitiveness. While neither report is about manufacturing competitiveness alone, manufacturing does form an integral part of the rankings.

Consider WEF's GCR first. This has a growth competitiveness index (GCI), which captures an economy's capacity to grow in the future. Using a splicing of hard data and subjective perceptions, GCI builds on three pillars of macroeconomic environment, public institutions and technology. There are thus three indices for each of these heads and the three individual indices are aggregated to derive the overall GCI. Quite often, reports about GCI are based on India's relative rank over the years. For instance, India's rank was 45th in 1996 and 55th in 2004. Being 55th means India is wedged between Uruguay (54th) and Morocco (56th). These ranks are however misleading because the number of countries ranked has changed down the years. For example, 50 countries were ranked in 1996 and 104 countries are ranked in 2004. The values of GCI are a better indication of movements than ranks. On the three pillars of macroeconomic environment, public institutions and technology, India obtains a 63rd rank on the technology index, a 52nd rank on the macroeconomic environment index and a 53rd rank on the public institutions index. In addition to the macro and medium-term focus of GCI, GCR also has a shorter term and micro business competitiveness index (BCI). India shows quite a sharp improvement on this, the rank having improved from 37th in 2000 to 30th in 2004. To quote from the 2004 version, "Another low-income country with large improvements is India, up 8 ranks, showing the benefits of increased company sophistication and strengthened clusters."

This is not the place to debate GCR *vis-à-vis* WCY, or even GCI *vis-à-vis* BCI. What is pertinent for our purposes is that companies compete. Countries or economies don't compete. However, government policies provide the environment within which companies compete. These macro policies feed into GCR's GCI through the three intermediary indices of a macroeconomic environment index, a public institutions index and a technology index. And if one scrutinises the heads that go into GCI, one finds eight heads—openness of the economy to international trade and finance, role of the government budget and regulation, development of financial markets, quality of

---

22. Since 1979.
23. Since 1989.

infrastructure, quality of technology, quality of business management, labour market flexibility and quality of judicial and political institutions. However, these macro policies need to be supplemented with other micro variables captured in BCI through two indices of company operations and strategy and quality of the national business environment. To keep the record complete, one should mention that India performs far better on IMD's WCY, the Indian rank having jumped from 50th (out of 60 countries ranked) in 2003 to 34th in 2004. WCY also has a ranking of regions and Maharashtra's rank has jumped from 44th in 2003 to 38th in 2004.

While one can complain about variables included (or excluded) and the methodology used in *GCR* or *WCY*, there ought not to be any great debate about the heads that aid or constrain manufacturing competitiveness. As was mentioned earlier, in this paper, we only concentrate on generic heads. There are indeed sector-specific problems, but we will ignore those. A list of these major heads now follows.

Import Duties

This import duty head has several different strands. First, there is an argument that import duties need to be reduced. This argument is usually advanced when items imported are raw materials and intermediates and not finished goods. The Kelkar Task Force[24] recommended a four-tier import duty (that is, for manufactured goods) structure in 2006-07—5 per cent for basic raw materials (coal, ores and concentrates, xylenes), 8 per cent for intermediate goods (capital goods, basic chemicals, metals), 10 per cent for finished goods other than consumer durables and 20 per cent for consumer durables. Some comments are in order about these recommendations. During the Uruguay Round (1986-94), some of India's manufactured goods were exempt from binding commitments. Consumer goods and non-ferrous metals are examples. The Doha Development Agenda started in 2001 and was certain to have import duty reduction commitments. When there are no bindings, the GATT/WTO system is unclear about the base on which reduction commitments will apply. The base could have been applied rates. Hence, there was a reluctance to unilaterally reduce duties on consumer goods and this was reflected in the Kelkar Task Force's recommendations. But since those recommendations were submitted, there has been a framework agreement in Geneva on August 1, 2004 and this states that, in the absence of bindings, the

---

24. *Report of the Task Force on Indirect Taxes*, Ministry of Finance and Company Affairs, December 2002.

base will be twice the applied MFN (most favoured nation) rate in 2001. Although there are some exemptions for developing countries, this agreement also provides for zero duties on sectoral basis. There are two arguments that follow. First, while there are arguments for reducing import duties on raw materials and intermediates, there is resistance to reducing duties on finished goods, spliced with fears about an appreciating rupee. Within the WTO system, is there any possibility of import duties higher than 5 per cent on raw materials and intermediates and 10 per cent on finished goods, perhaps 10 years down the line? The answer is probably no. Add to that a plethora of FTAs (free trade agreements) outside the WTO system, which invariably involve manufactured products, with eventual zero duties. Second, and this is a policy question, should one even attempt to have a tiered structure of import duties? When developed countries have such tiered structures, developing countries like India invariably argue that this discourages value addition in developing countries. More importantly, it becomes impossible to decide what is a raw material and what is an intermediate. Consequently, as long as variations across sectors continue, trade facilitation will never improve and customs formalities will never have low transaction costs. These discretionary problems are partly evident in the Union Budget for 2005-06. While the peak basic duty has been reduced to 15 per cent, there is no particular reason why duties on some capital goods should be 5 per cent, while they are 10 per cent on others. Stated differently, the policy problem is the following. Should we standardise or should we attempt to differentiate? And as long as we resist reduction of general import duties, the FTA problem will remain. What do we do about rules of origin and value addition requirements? As long as these issues remain, customs formalities will never be eased.

Second, this is the right place to mention customs formalities, highlighted also by the Kelkar Task Force. For example, there are issues like use of EDI (electronic data interchange) and on-line filing of declarations, self-assessment of bills of entry, filing of complete import general manifests before arrival of the cargo, establishment of trade facilitation committees, deadlines for processing of documents, payment of customs duties through cheques and licensing and registration systems for custom house agents.

Third, there is a level playing field kind of argument that goes beyond mere protectionism. At one level, this is about non-imposition or non-enforcement of standards on imported products, or even about testing and certification requirements. There are also arguments about systemic problems in imposing safeguard or anti-dumping duties. But there is also a different kind of duty argument. While the basic customs duty may be zero, imported products should face duties equivalent to domestic indirect taxes paid by domestic manufacturers. The countervailing duty (CVD) is meant to be precisely this, but is presently only equal to central excise. That ignores state-level sales tax and other local levies. The 2005-06 budget has a provision for an additional CVD of 4 per cent, but that is presently restricted to IT products. Unfortunately, this reform gets linked with reform of the domestic indirect tax system.

Domestic Indirect Taxes

Domestic indirect taxes are often singled out as a major reason why Indian manufacturing is uncompetitive. For instance, the CII-McKinsey report argues that total taxes on manufactured goods are 25 to 30 per cent of the retail price in India, compared to 15 per cent in China and indirect taxes contribute 50 per cent to the difference in retail prices between India and China. That the Indian indirect tax structure is cost-cascading and non-transparent is known. It also imposes significant transaction cum compliance costs on business. But conceptually, one must be clear about the argument that is being advanced. Why do high duties *per se* render Indian manufacturing uncompetitive? And where? They shouldn't render Indian manufacturing uncompetitive in export markets, because domestic indirect taxes are supposed to be waived or reimbursed. The argument should then be that these waivers and reimbursements don't work satisfactorily. Nor should high domestic duties render manufacturing uncompetitive in the domestic market, because through the CVD route, importers are also supposed to pay these duties. The argument then becomes that the CVD system doesn't work satisfactorily. The argument about high domestic indirect taxes should therefore be more indirect. High compliance costs impact productivity by pre-empting management time. There is bribery and corruption associated with both excise and sales tax. Lower duties would have boosted the domestic market and permitted synergy (exploitation of economies of scale, attracting FDI) between domestic and export markets.

Reforming indirect taxes is also contingent on reforming direct taxes. In 2004-05, total tax revenue is 10.2 per cent of GDP, if one includes central taxes alone.[25] If one includes state and local level levies, the figure is more like 15 per cent. Given expenditure commitments and demands on the

---

25. *Economic Survey 2004-05.*

government, this ratio probably needs to be 3 per cent more as share of GDP. The Kelkar Task Force on implementation of the FRBM (Fiscal Responsibility and Budget Management) Act also argues that fiscal consolidation will primarily have to occur *via* the revenue route rather than the expenditure contraction route.[26] Central tax revenue as a share of GDP has stagnated at around 10 per cent (sometimes even 9 per cent) of GDP since 1990-91. Kelkar's FRBM projections visualise an increase to 12.96 per cent in 2008-09, provided that tax reforms take place. The stagnation in the tax revenue share in the 1990s however masks an increase in the direct tax contribution from 1.9 per cent of GDP in 1990-91 to 4.5 per cent in 2004-05, neutralised by a decline in the indirect tax contribution from 7.9 per cent of GDP in 1990-91 to 5.7 per cent in 2004-05. This is primarily because of a drop in the customs share, but the share of excise has also declined. On welfare grounds, it is valid to argue that taxation through the direct route is preferable to indirect taxation. However, in a developing country like India, notwithstanding direct tax reform, this argument cannot be pushed too far. Indeed, the Kelkar Report's projections have a 6.46 per cent share of direct taxes in GDP in 2008-09 and an indirect tax share of 6.46 per cent also. The simple point is that the indirect tax contribution to GDP must also increase. The argument for reducing multiplicity and increasing transparency should not be confused with a drop in this share.

The broad shape of indirect tax reform is clear. There should be a combined goods and service tax (GST), with service sector taxation integrated into the VAT framework instead of being a tax on turnover. This will be accompanied by a withdrawal of all other taxes like central excise, central sales tax, octroi, state-level sales tax, entry tax, stamp duties, transportation taxes and so on. The limited VAT, limited in the sense that it is only a unification of state-level sales tax, from April 1, 2005, is uncertain. The complete VAT is a long way off. But three points are pertinent. First, when there is a complete VAT, what is likely to be a VAT rate that is revenue neutral? The state VAT proposed has two basic rates of 4 per cent and 12.5 per cent, with an attempt to push several items to the 4 per cent category. 12.5 per cent is not a revenue neutral rate. A revenue neutral rate, with Central and state VAT both included, is likely to be more like 20 per cent. Indeed, the Kelkar standard rate is 12 per cent for Central VAT and 8 per cent for state-level VAT. Consequently, a figure like the 15 per cent cited for China, is probably impossible. Second, even for

---

26. *Implementation of the Fiscal Responsibility and Budget Management Act, 2003,* Report of the Task Force, July 2004.

something like 20 per cent to work, there has to be an end to discretion. The budget for 2005-06 is a case in point. If there is a standardised rate of 16 per cent for excise, there is a valid argument that cars and aerated soft drinks should also be at this level. But there is an equally valid argument that no items should be below 16 per cent. Why, for instance, should excise be 2 per cent on branded jewellery and 8 per cent on imitation jewellery? Those who push for indirect tax reform should, therefore, simultaneously argue for standardisation and an end to discretionary treatment. Third, and this is an extension of the second argument, indirect tax reform will work only if all exemptions are terminated—product-specific exemptions, SSI exemptions, location-based exemptions. People often quote the CII-McKinsey Report, which argues that indirect taxes in India are unnecessarily high. What they sometimes fail to quote is that this report also argues against removal of exemptions.

Export Incentives/Export Subsidies

There is a conceptual difference between export incentives and export subsidies. Export subsidies involve differential treatment to exports as compared to sales in the domestic market and are in general WTO-incompatible, although there are some exemptions for India. Export incentives are WTO-compatible, as they involve reimbursements (DEPB and duty drawback) or waivers (advance licences) for duties paid in exported products. Problems arise because of the present system of averaging across units in granting waivers. Legitimate export incentives thus become labelled as unwarranted export incentives and are exposed to countervailing duty impositions. This has already arisen in the case of DEPB, but is equally applicable to duty drawback also. In principle, implementation would be easier if one switched over completely to an advance license system. However, given that there are several small exporters, this might not be feasible. Nor should one forget that export procedures continue to be cumbersome because of procedures connected with export incentives/subsidies. If these are not availed of, procedures have become reasonably simple. Implementation of both DEPB and duty drawback will become simpler if there is a complete VAT system. In the absence of a complete VAT, the rates provide for some remission of domestic taxes other than excise and import duties, and because the system is non-transparent, the link becomes difficult to establish. Beyond this conceptual problem, there are also issues connected with procedures, such as delays in reimbursements.

There is yet another conceptual problem for EOUs, SEZs and AEZs. These had a role when there wasn't general liberalisation. But with liberalisation across the board, liberalisation in selected enclaves has become somewhat irrelevant. If customs duties have come down and are going to drop further, what is the added attraction of these schemes, especially if there are going to be restrictions on sales in the domestic tariff area (DTA)? Quite often, debates about SEZs/AEZs *vis-à-vis* EOUs are about equal treatment in sales to the DTA and about concessional customs duties on such DTA sales. With import duties declining, surely one could argue that there should be no restrictions on DTA sales. This might as well be completely freed up. Another argument advanced in favour of SEZs/AEZs is that they involve simplified procedures. That is also a perverse argument. Procedures should be simplified everywhere, not just in SEZs/AEZs. An argument can also be advanced that SEZs/AEZs will have simplified labour laws. We will talk about labour laws later, but given Article 14 of the Constitution, it is doubtful that such an argument can be pushed very hard. This really leaves better infrastructure development in SEZs/AEZs. Stated differently, the argument is no different from the idea of pushing growth in clusters and we will return to this point later.

FDI and Procedures

Foreign investments mean both foreign portfolio investments and foreign direct investments (FDI) and *Economic Survey 2004-05* emphasises FDI in its issues and priorities segment. In a classic sense, FDI has been regarded as desirable because it contributes towards bridging two gaps—the foreign exchange gap and the savings/investment gap. Neither of these is that relevant for India any more, certainly not the first. However, FDI brings better technology and management, access to marketing networks and offers competition, the latter helping Indian companies improve, quite apart from being good for consumers. This efficiency contribution of FDI is much more important. There was a slight problem with Indian FDI definitions, since these didn't conform to IMF guidelines. With the revised definition, FDI inflow figures are 3.40 billion US Dollars in 2001, 3.45 billion in 2002 and 4.27 billion in 2004, there being a gap between approvals and inflows. This is a far cry from China's 53.51 billion in 2003 and the target of annual FDI inflows of 10 billion a year. UNCTAD now has a FDI performance index ranking and a FDI potential index ranking. In 2001-03, India's FDI performance index ranking was 114th out of 140 countries.[27] In a large country like India, FDI as

---

27. *World Investment Report 2004: The Shift Towards Services*, UNCTAD, 2004.

a share of GDP will never be very high. And barring certain sectors, FDI as a share of total investments will also not be very high. But there is no denying that India has underperformed.

Why has India under-performed? The reasons are obvious enough. First, FDI in manufacturing is now completely open, with Press Note No. 18 having been scrapped for new entrants, although there are some restrictions on mergers and acquisitions. Second, the bulk of cross-border FDI inflows are in the services sector and the services sector is still subject to equity caps, not everything having been placed on automatic approval. Third, policies in the infrastructure sector are often not in place. Fourth, there are procedural problems at all three levels of an enterprise's functioning—entry, functioning and exit, although foreign investors often tend to focus on the first. This is not purely a foreign investor issue. Courtesy national treatment, equally cumbersome procedures are also foisted on domestic investors. The expression transaction costs is sometimes used and such an expression also subsumes under it costs associated with inadequate infrastructure. We will talk about infrastructure later. For our purposes, transaction costs mean procedural costs alone. There is no real quantification of the extra cost disadvantage that Indian manufacturing faces because of transaction costs. There are some figures of around 20 per cent, but those include infrastructure costs also. However, a recent World Bank report benchmarks India's transaction costs with some other countries in the world.[28] It takes 89 days to start a business in India, compared to 41 days in China. It takes 67 days to register property in India, compared to 32 days in China. It takes 425 days to enforce contracts in India, compared to 241 days in China. It takes 10 years to complete insolvency proceedings in India, compared to 2.4 years in China. One should remember that many, though not all, of these procedures are at the state government level. Land, labour, water, electricity, environment are examples. This also explains why conversion ratios (percentage of approvals converted to inflows) vary widely across states. Maharashtra, Delhi, Tamil Nadu, Karnataka, Gujarat account for the bulk of FDI approvals under the automatic route.

Interest Rates

High interest rates and availability of credit are often cited as problems, as indeed they are. But one must be careful to separate out the price effect from a non-availability of credit problem. The prime lending rate (PLR) is around

---

28. *Doing Business in 2005*, World Bank, IFC and Oxford University Press.

10.25 per cent now, compared to a deposit rate of around 5.5 per cent. Household financial savings are 11.4 per cent of GDP. If combined, central and state-level deficits are in excess of 10 per cent of GDP, not to speak of artificially high guaranteed rates of return on small savings, there will be upward pressures on interest rates. Whichever index one uses to measure inflation, annual inflation is around 6 per cent now. With a PLR of 10.25 per cent, this means a real rate of interest of 4.25 per cent. In a capital scarce country, real interest rates will never be as low as global interest rates, although this is qualified by the harmonisation that has taken place between global and domestic interest rates. Some parts of the Indian corporate sector are now allowed to borrow globally, though not all. Why are real interest rates still so high? Other than deficits and small savings, one needs to highlight the interest spreads of banks. This masks inefficiencies in the banking system. But it also incorporates elements of priority-sector lending (at pre-determined interest rates) and significant non-performing assets (NPAs). On the latter, it is necessary to recognise that competition means free entry as well as exit. And there is a tendency to prevent exit, notwithstanding the Securitisation and Reconstruction of Financial Assets and Enforcement of Security Interest (SARFAESI) Act. This locks up capital in unproductive sectors and units. There are also special problems with exit in the SSI sector.

Beyond the cost of credit issue, there are problems with availability of capital, not just bank finance, but also through the stock market, and this includes venture capital. As a general proposition, too much capital flows to relatively larger units. There are collateral problems in the SSI sector. But there is also a mindset issue. Even if the risk premiums are not higher, and this need not always be the case, the administrative costs of delivering credit to the SSI sector will be higher. *Ipso facto*, interest rates will be higher, regardless of the euphoria about micro-finance and micro-credit. The argument that credit to the SSI sector will have to be at a few percentage points below PLR then seems to be counter-productive.

Infrastructure

Infrastructure means several different things and there can be no quarrel with the proposition that inadequate infrastructure renders Indian manufacturing uncompetitive. *Economic Survey 2004-05* lists power, telecom, posts, roads, ports (airports and seaports), civil aviation, railways, urban infrastructure and legal infrastructure as infrastructure. As a generalisation, the infrastructure area where there have been visible improvements is telecom, with roads perhaps following as a somewhat distant second. The contours of unbundling, user charges and regulatory agencies are known. The issue is simply one of getting infrastructure reforms implemented and some areas of physical infrastructure are state subjects. From the manufacturing perspective, perhaps the most important infrastructure areas are power, ports and railways, followed by roads. The issues are twofold. First, given scarce government resources, where are these best deployed? Second, again given scarce government resources, what is the scope for private sector involvement?

Labour Laws

Labour law reform is usually equated with Chapter V-B of the Industrial Disputes Act (IDA), but the issues are more complicated. Subject to the caveat that labour is on the concurrent list of the Constitution, there are 45 Central Acts and 16 associated rules that deal directly with labour. There are others that indirectly deal with labour, like the Boilers Act (1923), the Collection of Statistics Act (1953), the Dangerous Machines (Regulations) Act (1983) and the Emigration Act (1983). There is thus an issue of unification and harmonisation, the lack of which contributes to the inspector *raj*. Consider also the time span of the legislation, from the Fatal Accidents Act of 1855 to the Public Liability Insurance Act of 1991. Over a period of time, concepts and definitions have changed. So has the case law, contributing to further confusion. For example, there is lack of unanimity about definitions of wages, workman, employee, factory, industry and child labour. Reforming labour law has many dimensions and issues like reducing state intervention in industrial relations are identified with an exit policy for labour and are therefore controversial. But unification and harmonisation is an issue on which there should be no lack of consensus.

From unification and harmonisation, we now move on to reductions in state intervention, in areas other than industrial relations. Industrial relations will be dealt with later. The Factories Act is a good example of unnecessary government stipulations, sometimes through resultant rules and this includes provisions on over-time. The Shops and Establishments Act of 1954 is yet another example. It is no one's case that welfare provisions should not exist. But are welfare provisions enacted in 1948 or 1954 still relevant? Assuming that they are, is the present government-mandated system with a regime of inspectors the best way to achieve the objective?[29] Each labour legislation has

---

29. A recent FICCI survey (Inspector Raj and Administrative Reforms Required for Indian Manufacturing) mentions an average of 37 annual inspections, with 67 inspections in some cases. In decreasing order of importance, these inspections concern environment, labour, sales tax, excise, provident fund, electricity, ESI and industrial safety and health.

a separate inspector and visits of inspectors are not synchronised across all labour enactments. Barring the Payment of Wages Act, where a maximum period of three years is stipulated, no other labour statute prescribes a maximum period for which records and registers must be maintained. Compliance is thus impossible and visits of inspectors result in bribery and rent-seeking. This system is not distributionally neutral as it tends to hurt the small-scale sector much more than it hurts large-scale industry. That apart, returns under various labour laws are not standardised and inspectors insist on maintenance of manual records and registers. There can be a common format for computerisation of required records. There should be a single inspector for a given area. Some inspections for site and building and site plans or testing equipment can be farmed out to recognised private agencies. With the opening up of insurance, some social security provisions can be farmed out. For example, the Employees' State Insurance (ESI) Act hasn't worked at all well.

We now move on to industrial relations. The three statutes that impinge on industrial relations are the Contract Labour (Regulation and Abolition) Act, the Trade Unions Act and the Industrial Disputes Act. The Contract Labour (Regulation and Abolition) Act was never meant to prohibit contract labour. Section 10 provided the appropriate government the discretion of prohibiting contract labour in selected areas. In fact, in the title of the act, regulation comes before abolition. Contract labour allows flexibility and permits outsourcing. However, a few court judgements have affected this flexibility. There is an argument doing the rounds that the Contract Labour (Regulation and Abolition) Act should be scrapped. This is probably facile. If the 1970 statute is scrapped, decisions on abolition of contract labour will revert from the government to industrial tribunals. To take the Factories Act as an example, industrial tribunals are likely to conclude that since canteens are mandated under Section 46 of the Factories Act, no contract labour can be employed in canteens. It seems to be a better idea to retain the 1970 Act and tighten up Section 10 so that ambiguity about continuance of contract labour and absorption following abolition is removed.

Next one should mention the Trade Unions Act. As a minor point, child labour is not prohibited in India. It is only prohibited in hazardous processes. Yet, under Section 21 of the Trade Unions Act, those under 15 are not allowed to be members of trade unions and under Section 21-A of the Trade Unions Act, those under 18 are prevented from becoming office bearers. But more important are provisions of the Trade Unions Act that lead to multiplicity.

Under Section 4 of the Trade Unions Act, any 7 people can form and register a trade union and these 7 people need not even be workers. There is no cap on office bearers being from outside either. Nor is there any test for representativeness of a trade union, through secret ballots or otherwise. The multiplicity problem impinges on collective bargaining because an agreement with one union is not necessarily binding on others. This is partly due to Section 18(1) of the Industrial Disputes Act, which states, "A settlement arrived at by agreement between the employer and workman otherwise than in the course of conciliation proceeding shall be binding on the parties to the agreement." It is not mandatory on others. Maharashtra and Gujarat are the only states where there are laws requiring recognition of trade unions by employers for purposes of collective bargaining. Following recommendations of the Second Labour Commission, the government has introduced amendments to the Trade Unions Act. The number of persons required for registration of a trade union will change from 7 to 10 per cent of the labour force. Not more than one-third of office bearers (subject to a maximum of five) can be outsiders. And the holding of annual elections and auditing of accounts will be mandatory.

Next one moves on to the Industrial Disputes Act (IDA) and the following is a list of sections where there are problems—Section 9-A, Section 11, Section 11-A, Section 17-B, Sections 22/23 and Chapter V-B/Sections 25-K, 25-L, 25-M, 25-N and 25-0. The argument about Chapter V-B of IDA is indeed a valid one. Labour markets become artificially rigid, employers adopt artificially high capital intensity and circumvent the legislation. An employer-employee relationship ought to be in the nature of a personal contract, with an optional provision of resorting to the government in case of exploitation. However, the provisions of the Industrial Disputes Act make recourse to the government and thus to Labour Commissioners, mandatory. Given the other provisions of labour legislation, the requirement of governmental permission can be dispensed with, without adversely affecting the interests of labour. Unless this rigidity in labour markets is removed, higher growth will not necessarily translate into greater employment. What is involved is not primarily an exit policy for labour. The statute makes it impossible for companies to exit. Competition cannot function without free exit. The NCMP (National Common Minimum Programme) states, "The UPA rejects the idea of automatic hire and fire." Everyone who is against reforming labour markets criticises the government for trying to introduce hire and fire. Everyone who is in favour of reforming labour markets criticises the government for not introducing hire and fire. The recently published *Economic Freedom of the World 2004* is an example. Scores are out of 10 and the higher, the better. India gets an overall score of 6.3. But for flexibility in hiring and firing, the Indian score is 2.0.[30] The point is that this is probably largely perceptional rather than real. And more importantly, while a consensus on Chapter V-B is being rustled up, why not amend the other sections of IDA and implement the other labour law reforms? One should also mention the Second National Commission on Labour, which submitted a report in 2002, the first National Labour Commission having been set up in 1929. If implemented, these recommendations will harmonise labour laws under five heads of industrial relations, wages, social security, safety and welfare and working conditions. While flexibility will improve in the organised labour market, there will simultaneously be better social security provisions in the unorganised one. Implementation of the latter of course remains a problem.

Before concluding this section on labour, one must also mention development of skills, in the absence of which, the demographic dividend will also fail to materialise. No one denies that skill development is important. The issue is, who will deliver these skills? The public sector driven initiative, through the Apprentices Act and ITIs (Industrial Training Institutes) has failed to deliver. The 500 ITIs, promised in the 2004-05 budget, or other forms of vocational training, must be through public-private partnerships, if not outright private sector provisioning, with training authorities delinked from certifying ones.

The Private Sector

The onus for everything mentioned above has implicitly been on the government. But that is only part of the answer. Access to technology, larger investments that drive exploitation of economies of scale and scope, accessing market information and so on are in the private domain, although there is often a tendency to expect the government to provide or subsidise these efforts. But given fiscal and other limitations, there are constraints on what the government can effectively do. And some services, like some areas of physical infrastructure (water treatment is an instance), marketing information or skills development, are not even global public goods. One is not even certain that they are local public goods. They are probably collective private goods. In other

---

30. This is the Fraser Institute's economic freedom index, not the ones brought out by Freedom House or Heritage Foundation (in collaboration with *Wall Street Journal*).

words, once policy-induced entry barriers are removed, it is up to the private sector to deliver these services collectively, with appropriate user charges imposed.

V. WHERE DO WE GO FROM HERE?

A first-best solution is clearly to reform all the above areas. But that's unlikely to happen in a hurry. Despite what was said about enclaves earlier, a second-best solution may be to push growth poles or industrial clusters, mentioned in the PURA (Provision of Urban Amenities in Rural Areas) context, in the 2005-06 budget speech. While general taxation, interest rate or FDI policy problems will remain, it should be possible to have simplified procedures, including on labour laws, in these clusters. It should also be possible to have skill development and focused physical infrastructure initiatives.

There are two related strands that feed into the notion of developing growth poles. First, there is quite a bit of cross-country evidence that shows that small firms thrive and prosper, despite economies of scale and scope and technological advantages associated with large firms. Italy is not the only example. Small firms exhibit flexibilities that large firms are unable to match. Hence, there are also diseconomies of scale. However, small firms also suffer from disadvantages. There are asymmetries in the capital market, imperfect knowledge about demand conditions, lack of marketing information and marketing resources and inadequate access to technology and skills. All these involve fixed costs that are difficult for a small firm to bear alone. But when clusters or hubs develop, there are external economies of both scale and scope and both fixed and variable costs can be spread over a broader base. Small firm flexibilities are thus best exploited when such clusters and hubs develop and UNIDO (United Nations Industrial Development Organization), ILO (International Labour Organization), UNCTAD (United Nations Conference on Trade and Development), UNESCO (United Nations Educational, Social and Cultural Organization), OECD (Organisation of Economic Cooperation and Development), the World Bank and assorted other organisations have all taken an interest in promoting clusters in developing countries in Asia, Africa and Latin America.

The second strand that fits into the growth pole idea is the recognition that rural employment generation has been unsatisfactory in the India of the 1990s. Between 1993-94 and 1999-2000, the two data points for the NSS (National

Sample Survey) large samples, the annual average increase in employment was 1.6 per cent. But this had a break-up of 2.4 per cent for urban India and 1.3 per cent for rural India. As is fairly obvious, unemployment rates mean very little in rural India. However, in the 1990s, there has been slackening growth in agriculture and non-agricultural rural sector employment growth has failed to compensate. Inevitably, this creates a push towards migration into urban areas. Rural growth is also critical to handling the political economy of reforms, with a general impression that liberalisation has thus far had a pro-urban focus and little of the benefits have percolated through to rural India. The National Common Minimum Programme (NCMP) of the government takes explicit cognizance of the rural sector. Both the pull and the push need to be neutralised. However, rural employment cannot conceivably be in the agriculture sector alone. Employment generation will have to be in rural non-farm activities and this includes rural industries, as well as rural services. In both of these, clusters or growth poles can have an important role to play.

The idea of cluster formation isn't new. Ever since the Industrial Policy Resolution of 1948, successive Five Year Plans and promotional schemes have tried to push growth poles. For instance, the First Five Year Plan had the Rural Industrial Estate Programme and the Village Artisan-Oriented Programme. The Second Five Year Plan had the Common Production Programme and the Pilot Project Programme. The Third Five Year Plan had the Rural Industries Project Programme. The Fourth Five Year Plan had the Rural Artisan Programme. The Fifth Five Year Plan had the District Industries Centre Programme and the Backward Area Scheme. The Sixth Five Year Plan had the Growth Centre Programme. The Eighth Five Year Plan had the Integrated Infrastructural Development Programme. And the Ninth Five Year Plan had the National Programme for Rural Industrialisation. That apart, there is the Cluster Development Programme, spearheaded by UNIDO. Specifically, under the National Programme for Rural Industrialisation, there was an objective of setting up 100 rural clusters every year, pushed by KVIC, SIDO, SIDBI and NABARD. Before undertaking a fresh cluster development exercise, one therefore needs to ask, why have earlier attempts not succeeded? And why will new efforts be different? There are two possible reasons for earlier failures. First, there are clusters and clusters. At a conceptual level, there are three kinds of clusters one can visualise—relatively modern, small-firm dominated industrial clusters, that often tend to be located in relatively urban areas; artisan and rural industry based clusters; and clusters that are based on the agro-economy. Arguably, most policy interventions have focussed on the first of the three, rather than the last two. Second, policy interventions and developmental programmes have tended to be *ad hoc*, rather than taking a holistic view of what is necessary. For instance, if infrastructure is not developed and development of skills remains a question mark, it is doubtful that marketing interventions alone will suffice. Stated differently, policy interventions alone won't be sufficient to ensure that clusters develop. Nor should one forget that industrial clusters often tend to be located in the relatively more advanced parts of the country. In contrast, artisan-based or agro-based clusters are more evenly distributed spatially.

There are already some policy initiatives directed towards identifying and promoting cluster development. First, there are the industry clusters proper. UNIDO has identified around 300 industrial clusters across India and is in the process of developing 200 more. As mentioned earlier, these clusters tend to be concentrated in certain geographical regions. UNIDO has identified sectoral cum geographical clusters in leather (Amber), drugs and pharmaceuticals (Ahmedabad), machine tools (Bangalore), hand printing and dyeing (Sanganer and Bagru), food processing (Pune), cotton knitwear (Tirupur) and woolen knitwear (Ludhiana). The S.P. Gupta Committee (the Special Group) on generating employment identified four clusters—the toy industry (Delhi and Mumbai), the stone industry (Rajasthan and Andhra Pradesh), the lock industry (Aligarh and Dindigal) and special purpose machine tools for the lock industry (Aligarh). The 2002-07 Exim Policy recognised three major industrial clusters and towns of export excellence in Tirupur, Panipat and Ludhiana and proposed to extend this identification to 10 clusters. An IDFC-Mckinsey joint study identified high growth potential economic clusters in five broad geographical regions—Mumbai-Pune-Nasik, Delhi-Noida-Gurgaon, Chennai-Pondicherry-Bangalore, Hyderabad-Visakhapatnam and Kolkata and its hinterland. There is a SIDBI identification of clusters that are part geographical and part sectoral and this includes locks (Aligarh), foundry units (Howrah), bicycle/bicycle parts (Ludhiana), scientific instruments (Ambala), salt and salt based chemicals (Saurashtra/Kutch), power loom (Surat/Bhiwandi), machine tools (Rajkot), rubber products (Kottayam), glassware (Firozabad), brass and bell metal (Kantilo), blacksmithy (Mylliem), leather and leather products (Barabanki/Sitapur/Hardoi/Unnao), terracotta (Dhubri), hand tools (Jalandhar), auto-components (Pune), shoe making (Nongstoin). Industry Ministry has a list of 100 clusters identified for development. Such identifications do not have a specific employment focus. For instance, if one were to be interested in pushing employment, one would pick sectors like food processing, textiles and garments, leather and leather products and footwear. Stated differently, if one were to consider the 100 clusters already identified by Industry Ministry and matched them against the employment potential, one would probably pick garments (Rayadurg (Andhra Pradesh), Delhi, Guwahati (Assam), Bellary (Karnataka)); leather (Vijayanagaram, Jammapur, Warangal (all Andhra Pradesh), Gujarat); and food processing [Arunachal Pradesh, Himachal Pradesh, Srinagar, Jharkhand, Shillong (Meghalya)], but not necessarily any of the others.

Second, UNIDO and the government have also identified 1600 artisan clusters, which are not quite the relatively modern industrial clusters. These are spatially distributed much more evenly throughout the country and can also feed into the 15,000 retail outlets that KVIC possesses. If one tracks the 100 clusters already identified by Industry Ministry, one finds that only woodcraft (Jagdalpur (Chhattisgarh), wood packaging (Srinagar), woodcraft (Madhya Pradesh), handlooms (Shillong), handlooms [Aizwal (Mizoram)] and cane and bamboo [Dimapur (Nagaland)] fit the artisan cluster category. One should not forget that the employment potential of the artisan sector is considerable.

Third, one should mention the relatively ignored angle of agro-based clusters, ignored except when there is an attempt to push agro export processing zones (AEPZs), such as pineapples (Jalpaiguri, West Bengal), Gujarat, Chittoor (Andhra Pradesh), Karnataka, Tamil Nadu, Udham Singh Nagar (Uttaranchal) and Nagpur, Amaravati, Ratnagiri, Sindhudurg, Aurangabad (all Maharashtra). But one should also mention the estimated 47,000 *haats* in the country and the estimated 7161 regulated *mandis*. Most of these suffer from inadequate infrastructure and are also characterised by scope of dis-intermediation, which an experiment like ITC's *e-choupal* attempts to tap. There are already 5050 *e-choupals*, covering 29,500 villages and 3.1 million farmers. The target is to reach 100,000 villages and 10 million farmers by 2010. On a smaller scale, there are similar experiments by Pepsi. Tata, EID Parry, Reliance, Bharti, Chambal Fertilisers and Chemicals, Godrej and the Mahindras.

A convenient channel for pushing the cluster idea is the PURA (provision of urban facilities in rural areas) initiative. The PURA scheme envisages four forms of connectivity—road transport and power connectivity, electronic connectivity, knowledge connectivity and market connectivity. Five hundred and four nodal towns have already been identified under PURA. These are pre-determined and there is significant overlap between these identified nodes and the industrial clusters. However, there is a part of PURA that still remains to be identified. Under PURA, each state government has to identify 2 clusters of 10-15 villages every year. These become the spokes that feed into the 504 hubs. Depending on head count ratios (where these are above or below the national average) and the category of the state (special category or not), 826 such clusters have to be identified every year. Over a period of 5 years, this thus adds up to 4130 clusters. While the 504 towns are pre-identified, there is scope for identification of these 826 or 4130 clusters.

The growth pole idea will therefore push all forms of connectivity, using the PURA route. This holistic view distinguishes itself from earlier forms of policy intervention. Road connectivity will be pushed through the Pradhan Mantri Gram Sadak Yojana and bus and truck stands and even rural roads will be developed through centrally sponsored scheme (CSS) funds that are channeled to panchayats. The Rural Electrification Corporation will give priority in offering power connectivity to these growth poles and these poles can also be considered under the decentralised rural power supply programme. Department of Information Technology has a Community Information Centre (CIC) programme for North-Eastern states. This will be broad-based to cover all the growth poles and ensure electronic connectivity. Like the Gyandoot programme in Madhya Pradesh or the Bhoomi project in Karnataka, public services will also be provided through these CICs or cyber kiosks. Knowledge connectivity will be ensured through the Sarva Sikhsha Abhiyan and the additional ITIs that are now proposed to be set up, often through public/private partnerships. Other than cyber kiosks and roads, market connectivity will be ensured by improving infrastructure and processing and cold storage facilities in *haats* and *mandis*, often with *panchayat* involvement.

These growth poles can thus cover all three elements of the cluster approach—industrial clusters, artisan clusters and agro-based clusters. Any pilot scheme has to have a reasonable chance of success, so that its replicability is ensured. Existing industrial agglomerations have demonstrated comparative advantage, at least in a static sense. Focussing on industrial clusters thus enhances chances of success. As a second-best solution, that might be the best way of pushing the cause of Indian manufacturing.

17

Foreign Direct Investment in India

Trends and Issues

R. NAGARAJ

Introduction

Compared to most industrialising economies, India followed a fairly restrictive foreign private investment policy until 1991—relying more on bilateral and multilateral loans with long maturities. Inward foreign direct investment (FDI, or foreign investment, or foreign capital hereafter) was perceived essentially as a means of acquiring industrial technology that was unavailable through licensing agreements and capital goods import. Technology imports were preferred to financial and technical collaborations. Even for technology licensing agreements, there were restrictions on the rates of royalty payment and technical fees. Development banks largely met the external financial needs for importing capital equipment. However, foreign investment was permitted in designated industries, subject to varying conditions on setting up joint ventures with domestic partners, local content clauses, export obligations, promotion of local R&D and so on—broadly similar to those followed in many rapidly industrialising Asian economies.

Foreign Exchange and Regulation Act (FERA), 1974 stipulated foreign firms to have equity holding only up to 40 per cent, exemptions were at the government's discretion. Setting up of branch plants was usually disallowed; foreign subsidiaries were induced to gradually dilute their equity holding to less than 40 per cent in the domestic capital market. The law also prohibited the use of foreign brands, but promoted hybrid domestic brands (Hero-Honda, for instance). However, pragmatism prevailed to ensure stable domestic supply at reasonable prices.

Such a restrictive policy is believed to have retarded domestic technical capability (as reflected in the poor quality of Indian goods); it also meant a loss of export opportunity of labour-intensive manufactures—in contrast to many successful East Asian economies. Moreover, such a policy is said to have encouraged 'rent seeking' by domestic partners on imported technology—with little efforts to improve product quality, undertake innovation, and seek export markets (Ahluwalia, 1985). This popular perception was perhaps best illustrated by the passenger car industry that produced obsolete (and fuel-inefficient) models of the 1950s at very high costs in small numbers.

Without denying some of these arguments and evidence, others have shown that the regulation reduced costs of technology imports (Subramaniam, 1991), and promoted export of goods with relatively stable technologies where domestic firms had the opportunity of 'learning by doing' by catering to the large domestic market—as illustrated by successful firms like TELCO (commercial vehicles) and BHEL (heavy electrical equipment) (Lall, 1982). The recent international achievements of some Indian pharmaceutical firms (Cipla, Ranbaxy, Dr. Reddy's Laboratories, for instance) are also attributed to the regulatory and promotional policies, and the patent laws (Chaudhuri, 1999) that sought to encourage domestic production to reduce drug prices.

However, the 1980s witnessed a gradual relaxation of the foreign investment rules—perhaps best symbolised by the setting up of Maruti, a central government joint venture small car project with Japan's Suzuki Motors in 1982. It was followed by Pepsi's entry in the second half of the decade, to primarily export processed-food products from Punjab, and also to bottle its well known beverages for the domestic market.

Reforms in the 1990s

All this changed since 1991. Foreign investment is now seen as a source of scarce capital, technology and managerial skills that were considered necessary in an open, competitive, world economy. India sought to consciously 'benchmark' its policies against those of the rapidly growing southeast Asian economies to attract a greater share of the world FDI inflows. Over the decade, India not only permitted foreign investment in almost all sectors of the economy (barring agriculture, and, until recently, real estate), but also allowed foreign portfolio investment—thus, practically divorcing foreign investment from the erstwhile technology acquisition effort. Further, laws were changed to provide foreign firms the same standing as the domestic ones.[1]

---

1. For a chronological account of the policy reforms, see appendix of Bajpai and Sachs (2001). For detailed official statements on the policy changes, refer to the Ministry of Industry's annual publication, *Handbook of Industrial Statistics*.

What are the trends in the quantum and composition of the FDI inflow; and what are their benefits and costs to the economy? This paper seeks to provide a preliminary answer for these questions. To do so, we first discuss, very briefly, the recent literature on foreign investment and economic development (Section I). The limitations of the available data to test the propositions following from the analytical literature are discussed in Section II. As a first step in our assessment, Section III describes the trends in FDI in the 1990s. Section IV contains a brief comparison of foreign investment in India and China—an issue that has a bearing on the current policy discussion. Based on the available, limited and preliminary, information, Section V makes an initial assessment of foreign investment by raising some issues for further work, Section VI suggests a more realistic policy on the basis of the analytical discussion and comparative experience. Section VII concludes by summarising the study's main findings.

I. A BRIEF ANALYTICAL REVIEW

Much of the currently held perceptions of foreign investment's role essentially take a macroeconomic view: it is a source of additional external finance (and of risk capital), augmenting fixed investment, potential output and employment.[2] Such a positive view gained currency mainly after the crises in Latin America in the early 1980s, more recently in East Asia, when other forms of capital inflows quickly dried up (or reversed), accentuating the macroeconomic vulnerability of these economies. As against portfolio investment, FDI is also seen as a source of technology and managerial skills, creating tangible (and intangible) assets in the host economy. Foreign firms seek not only the domestic market, but also provide access to external markets by sourcing manufactured products (and services) from domestic firms.

The crux of the policy, therefore, is how the benefits of such investments are distributed between the foreign firms and the host country, as also between the various factors of production within the host country. In other words, the real question is the cost of foreign capital to the host economy: is it too high, compared to the alternative sources of external finance and technology, in the short and the long run?

---

2. There is some evidence to support this view. For instance, using cross-section data for 58 developing countries during 1978-95, Bosworth and Collins (1999) show that a dollar of FDI translates into an equivalent domestic investment, while no such association was found with respect to foreign portfolio investment.

However, in a microeconomic perspective, a different set of questions is usually asked: What does FDI do to the working of the domestic markets, and their effect on output and productivity growth (Caves, 1996). If, as is often the case, the entry of a foreign firm results in the creation of a domestic monopoly, then the benefits of such investment may be limited, unless accompanied by a sound anti-trust law (or competition policy). Similarly, if FDI inflow results in the displacement of domestic monopolies with the foreign ones, then again, social benefits of such investments may be marginal (if any), as any monopolist, regardless of its origin, would maximise profits either by varying price or output (or both). Moreover, the host government may have considerable difficulty in enforcing domestic laws adequately, as foreign firms often seek protection under complicated legal structures.[3]

In industrial organisation literature, from a variety of analytical perspectives, foreign firms are seen as having firm-specific advantages—including significant market power that they seek to exploit in many countries.[4] Availability and costs of these resources for the host economy depend on the relative bargaining strength of the foreign firms *vis-à-vis* the domestic firms (and the host government). While the foreign firms' advantages lie in their size, control over technology and marketing strength worldwide, the host country can use its domestic market, access to cheap labour, location and quality of infrastructure (all of which go to reduce the cost of production to service the international market) to bargain with the foreign firms.

Thus, a social cost benefit approach is perhaps a meaningful method to assess the potential effects of FDI. If such a view is valid, then what countries should do is perhaps not to maximise foreign investment inflow *per se*, but to channel it in the desired directions to maximise long-term returns to the economy. From the development economics perspective, the questions one asks could get even deeper. In a world with unequal resources and technological capabilities (including brand names), how does FDI affect the ownership and control of industrial firms? In the market for industrial technologies that is invariably oligopolistic, does foreign capital inflow

---

3. For a long time developing countries have complained about foreign firms, as they seemed to hide their true operations from the host country rules. But in the recent years under easier capital flow regime, the same legal maze seems to have begun to hurt tax compliance in the developed countries as well. Recently a report in the *New York Times* sought to unveil the legal maze of such operations (Johnston, 2002).

4. Though largely ignored in the mainstream economic writings, much of the literature on the behaviour of international firms builds on Stephen Hymer's (1976) original contribution that focussed on firm-specific characteristic, including their market power.

augment or reduce access to technology and domestic R&D efforts? Does foreign capital improve exports (and export capability) from the host country? What is the cost of FDI over a long period; is it necessarily lower than that of external debt (Helleiner, 1989)?[5]

It is perhaps worth reiterating that markets for industrial technologies continue to be imperfect and probably have got accentuated with the recent international agreements like the TRIPS. Moreover, the experience of the last half a century clearly suggests that countries with liberal FDI and technology import policy are not necessarily the examples of successful industrialisation (Bruton, 1989). They may have become either outposts of foreign firms servicing regional markets (like Singapore), or partners in the international division of labour with limited mastery over production technology and generation of domestic brand names (Brazilian automobile industry, for example).

In the development literature, well reflected in the Indian discourse, there is a wide consensus that regulation reduces costs of imported technology (Lall, 1989). One of the ways to acquire the disembodied technology is to 'unbundle' the package that foreign firms offer, and to buy the technology outright, while providing for capital investment by the domestic financial system. This has been the time-tested method of all the successful late industrialising economies (Amsden, 2001).[6]

II. DATA ON FDI AND THEIR LIMITATIONS

To understand how the recent changes in foreign investment policy have influenced the economy, quantitative information is needed on broad dimensions of the investment (and its distribution) across industries, regions and by size of projects; firm and industry level production accounts, and audited financial statements. However, such information is scarce. The most easily available (and widely used) data in India are on FDI approvals (contracted), by broad industry group (1-digit ISIC), by country of origin, and by states (regions) of destination. This represents mere intentions of

---

5. It has long been held in the development literature that while short-run cost of foreign debt is high, the long-term costs of FDI could be even higher (Lewis, 1953). In fact, it is such a view that prevailed in the successful industrialisation efforts of Japan, Korea and Taiwan that carefully regulated foreign investment inflow.

6. However, some recent literature in mainstream economics has argued that while the state may have succeeded in steering these economies in the past, there is little guarantee that in the developing countries today the state has similar capability to repeat the performance (World Bank, 1993).

investment. The actual (or realised) foreign investment is not available by the same classification, but according to the administrative and institutional channels of the inflow. Therefore, it is not possible to compare the realised with the intentions, in any meaningful manner. Apparently, even the concerned official agency does not seem to know—let alone monitor—how the actual inflows are translated into capital formation, transfer of assets or change in managerial control.

The actual FDI inflow is recorded under five broad heads: (i) Reserve Bank of India's (RBI) automatic approval route for equity holding up to 51 per cent, (ii) Foreign Investment Board's discretionary approval route for larger projects with equity holding greater than 51 per cent, (iii) acquisition of shares route (since 1996), (iv) RBI's non-resident Indian (NRI) schemes, and (v) external commercial borrowings (ADR/GDR route). Reportedly, the Indian definition of FDI differs from that of the IMF, as well as of the UN's *World Investment Report.* IMF's definition includes external commercial borrowings, reinvested earnings and subordinated debt, while the *World Investment Report* excludes external commercial borrowings.[7]

Ideally, FDI inflow should get reflected in (i) capital formation, (ii) formation of new firms and factories, (iii) increase in foreign equity holding in the existing firms, and (iv) mergers and acquisitions of existing firms and factories (or parts of them). However, the availability of information on them depends on their legal status. We know very little about those registered outside the country, and in tax shelters, like Mauritius. For instance, Enron's Dabhol Power Company—the largest foreign investment project yet— is incorporated in India as an unlimited liability company. But it is a shell company that Enron controls through at least six holding companies registered in various offshore locations (Mehta, 1999).[8]

Similarly, fully owned private limited companies of foreign firms (or branch plants) reveal very little information about their investment and output. An increasingly large proportion of foreign firms have set up fully owned subsidiaries that have become manufacturers (and distributors) by acquiring domestic firms. They provide very little audited financial information to assess

---

7. *"Flow of FDI* comprises capital provided (either directly or through other enterprises) by a foreign direct investor to an FDI enterprise or, capital received from an FDI enterprise by a foreign direct investor. There are three components in FDI: equity capital, reinvested earnings, and intra-company loans" (*World Investment Report*, 2001: 275).

8. Apparently, there is a discrepancy in Enron's declaration of its equity holding in the Indian entity. To the US bankruptcy court it has declared that it holds 50 per cent, but here it has declared that it owns 65 per cent equity.

the impact of the firms on the industry, and the corporate sector.[9] Considering these legal problems, many of their operations do not seem to get recorded in the RBI's survey of financial performance of foreign controlled companies—a valuable data source in the earlier times.

Therefore, the assessment of foreign investment reported in this study remains preliminary. However, based on the preceding discussion, the issues raised below can perhaps be taken as working hypotheses for further research.

III. THE TRENDS

FDI Approvals and Its Composition

Approved FDI rose from about Rs. 500 crore in 1992 to about Rs. 55,000 crore in 1997 (*Economic Survey*, 2001-02) (Figure 17.1). Cumulative approved foreign investment during 1991 and 2000, in Dollar terms, is about $ 67bn— at an average exchange rate of Rs. 40 to a Dollar. A fifth of it is from the US (Table 17.1). Mauritius is the second largest source; reportedly a conduit for many US-based firms, as India has a tax avoidance treaty with it since 1982. In Asia, South Korea has emerged as a new source of foreign investment.[10] A

Figure 17.1

FDI into India, 1992-2000

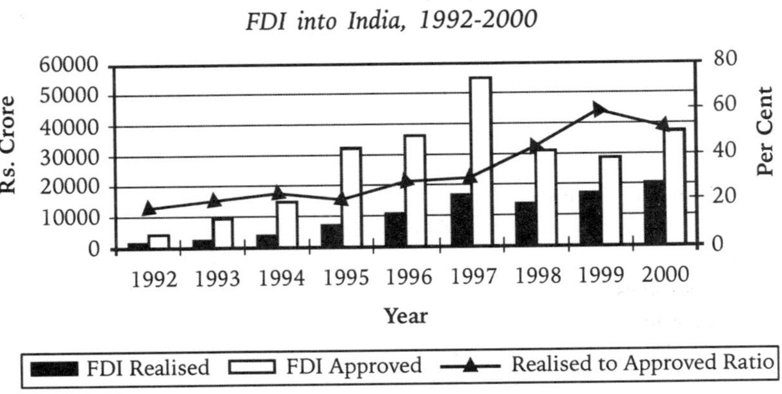

Source: *Economic Survey*, 2001-02.

---

9. The law requires all closely held (private limited) companies to submit their annual audited accounts to the department of company affairs that are, in principle, available to the public. But practice seems different as the law enforcement seems poor.

10. Korean firms have aggressively moved in to India, since they perceive it as their only chance to get into the last unexplored market, to beat their established corporate rival from Japan and the US.

Table 17.1

Top 10 Investing Countries in India, 1991-2000

Country/Region	Share (in per cent)
US	20.4
Mauritius	11.9
UK	6.4
Japan	4.0
South Korea	3.9
Germany	3.4
Australia	2.7
Malaysia	2.3
France	2.1
Netherlands	1.9

Source : *Handbook of Industrial Policy and Statistics, 2001.*

Note : In addition to the countries, external commercial borrowings and non-resident Indians (NRIs) contributed 17.2 and 3.9 per cent of the FDI approvals.

Table 17.2

Sectoral Distribution of FDI Approvals, 1991-2000

Sector	No. of Approvals	Approved Invest-ment (Rs. Billion)	Share (in per cent)
Power and Fuel	541	634531.2	25.7
Telecommunications	579	458845.0	18.5
Services Sector	790	152389.0	6.2
Chemicals (Other than Fertilisers)	809	123016.2	5.0
Food Processing	648	87574.9	3.5
Transport Sector	722	184467.6	7.5
Metallurgical Industries	304	143796.8	5.8
Electrical Equipment (Including Software)	2491	245791.5	10.0
Textiles	548	33617.8	1.4
Paper and Paper Products	111	31580.6	1.3
Industrial Machinery	530	22438.5	0.9
Others	2404	348976.2	14.2
Total	**11965**	**2467025.3**	**100.0**

Source : *Handbook of Industrial Policy and Statistics, 2001.*

Note : Data is for the period, August 1991 to March 1998.

quarter of the approved FDI is for power generation (Table 17.2), followed by telecommunications (mobile phone firms) at 18.5 per cent, and electrical equipment (mainly software) at 10 per cent. While the proportion of projects with investment up to Rs. 5 crore is high, their share is less than 5 per cent in value. At the other end of the distribution, larger projects with Rs. 100 crore and above account for over two-thirds of the total value of approvals (Table 17.3). Evidently, very little of the FDI has gone to augment exports that are mostly from labour-intensive unregistered manufacturing. The economically advanced states of Maharashtra, Delhi, Karnataka, Tamil Nadu and Gujarat have attracted one-half of the approved foreign investment (Table 17.4).

Table 17.3

Distribution of FDI by Size of Investment, 1991-1997

Investment (Rs. Crore)	No. of FDI Approvals		Quantum of FDI Approved	
	Number	*Share (in per cent)*	*Amount*	*Share (in per cent)*
0-1	3040	49.2	919.4	0.9
1-5	1686	27.3	3800.8	3.6
5-25	906	14.7	10046.0	9.5
25-50	212	3.4	7503.5	7.1
50-100	128	2.1	8828.4	8.4
100-500	173	2.8	38699.0	36.6
Over 500	38	0.6	35992.4	34.0

Source : Rao and Murthy (1999).

Note : This distribution is for the approvals during August 1991 and May 1997,

Table 17.4

Top Five Destinations of Approved FDI among the Indian States

State	No. of Financial Collaborations Approved	Approved FDI ($ Million)	Share (in per cent)
Maharashtra	2015	11135.9	16.9
Delhi	1226	9226.7	13.1
Karnataka	1078	5247.1	8.1
Tamil Nadu	1223	5073.8	7.7
Gujarat	458	3129.6	4.5
State Not Indicated	3119	19476.4	27.9

Source : *Handbook of Industrial Policy and Statistics, 2001.*

Table 17.5 provides the actual FDI inflow as estimated by four different agencies, for 1991 to 2000. IMF's and the *World Investment Report's* estimates of the cumulative inflow during the 1990s are roughly the same—at about $ 17bn. The *Economic Survey* estimate is about $ 22bn, while that by RBI is $ 17.3bn. The difference between the last two estimates is mainly on account of ADR/GDR inflows. While the *Economic Survey* classifies them as FDI, RBI records them under foreign portfolio investment.

Table 17.5

Alternative Estimates of the Actual FDI, 1991-2000

Year	Economic Survey (Rs. Crore)	RBI (Rs. Crore)	International Financial Statistics (Million $)	World Investment Report (Million $)
1991	351	316		155
1992	675	965	276.5	261
1993	1787	1836	550.1	586
1994	3289	4126	973.3	947
1995	6820	7172	2143.6	2144
1996	10389	10015	2426.1	2591
1997	16425	13220	3577.3	3613
1998	13340	10358	2634.7	2614
1999	16868	9338	2168.6	2154
2000	19342	10686	2315.1	2315
Total	89286	68034	17065.3	17080

Sources : Economic Survey, various issues; RBI's Handbook of Statistics on Indian Economy, 2001; IMF's International Financial Statistics CD-ROM; UN's World Investment Report, various issues.

As there has been a gradual improvement in the actual inflow from a low base, and a slowdown in the approvals after 1997, there is an increase in the ratio of the actual-to-approved FDI in the last few years. On average, it is a little over one-third in the 1990s (Figure 17.1). India's share in the world foreign investment increased from 0.5 per cent in 1992, to 2.2 per cent in 1997 (Figure 17.2).

Figure 17.3 describes the actual inflow by various routes discussed in the previous section. The FIPB route—representing larger projects requiring the government's discretionary approval—accounts for the bulk of the inflow, though its share is somewhat declining. Automatic approval route *via* RBI meant for smaller sized investments received modest inflow; and the NRI route's share has declined sharply. Proportion of the inflow to acquire shares in the domestic firms, and flotation of ADRs/GDRs have gained in prominence in the second half of the 1990s.

Figure 17.2

India's Share in World FDI

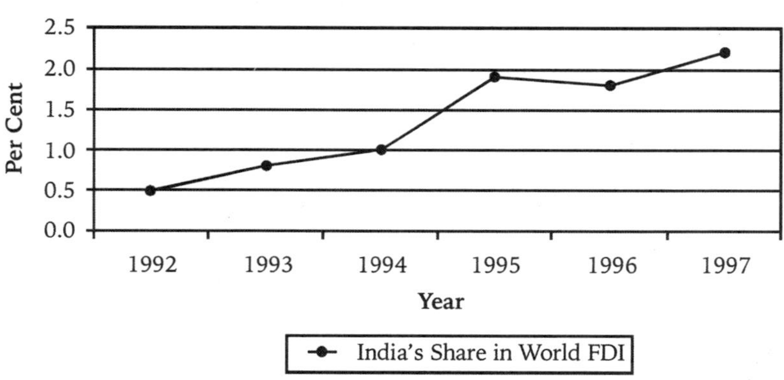

Figure 17.3

Actual FDI by Different Routes

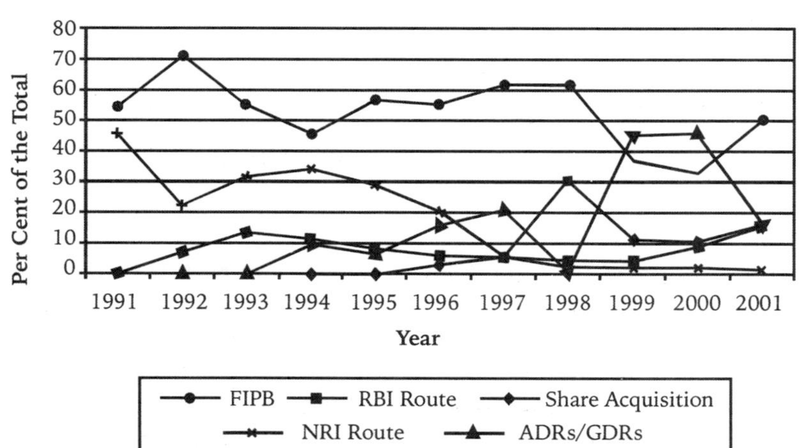

Interpreting the Trends

Though it is not possible to compare the actual with the approved FDI for the reasons discussed earlier, some broad generalisation can perhaps be made based on the available qualitative information. While the bulk of the approvals is for infrastructure, the actual inflow seems to be largely in registered manufacturing—more precisely, in consumer durable goods and automotive industries; very little of it has gone into capital goods industries. The inflow in telecommunication industry is probably to get licences for mobile phone operations, not for manufacturing equipment. The investments in electrical machinery industry are apparently to set up local offices to produce computer software.

Much of the realised FDI has also come in as fully owned subsidiaries (or branch plants) of their parents abroad. Table 17.6 provides an illustrative list of such foreign entities. Most of them have not issued IPOs in the domestic bourses, hence are not quoted companies. Quite contrary to the earlier period, the government has so far not insisted on enforcing its policy in this respect (more about this later).

Table 17.6

An Illustrative List of Foreign Firms Not Listed in the Domestic Stock Market

Product Group	*Foreign Firms*
Automobiles and Allied Products	GM, Ford, Mercedes Benz, Honda, Hyundai, Fiat, Toyota, Volvo, Yamaha, Cummins, Goodyear.
Food and Beverages	Coca-Cola, Cadbury Schweppes, Kellogg, Heinz, Seagram, Hiram Waker, United Distillers, Perfitti, Wrigley, KFC, McDonalds.
Consumer Durable Goods	Daewoo, Samsung, Sony, General Electric, LG Electronics, Black and Decker, Kimberley Clark.
Personal Care Products	Revlon, L'Oreal, Cussons, Unilevers.

Source : Rao, Murthy and Ranganathan (1999).

About 40 per cent of the inflow seems to have been used for acquiring existing industrial assets, and their managerial control (Table 17.7 (i)); and, there seems to be a gradual increase in such merger and acquisitions in the 1990s (Table 17.7 (ii)). Further, Table 17.8 provides an illustrative list of plants (and divisions) of Indian controlled firms acquired by foreign firms in the 1990s. This is also evident from the fact that foreign firms seem to use a larger proportion of their total funds for such acquisition than for capital formation, compared to Indian owned firms in the private corporate sector, the ratio of fixed capital formation to total uses of funds by foreign firms is lower than that by the domestic companies (Nagaraj, 1997).

Table 17.7 (i)

Share of M and A as in FDI Inflows in India

Year	FDI Inflow ($ Million)	M and A Fund ($ Million)	Share of M and A Fund in FDI Inflow (Per Cent)
1997	3200	1300	40.6
1998	2900	1000	34.5
1999 (Jan.-Mar.)	1400	2800	39.4

Source : Kumar (2000: 2852).

Table 17.7 (ii)

Foreign Firms Related M and A in India

Year	Mergers	Acquisitions	Total
1993-94	4	9	13
1994-95	-	7	7
1995-96	-	12	12
1996-97	2	46	48
1997-98	4	61	65
1998-99	2	30	32
1999-2000 (up to Jan. 2000)	5	74	79
Total	**17**	**239**	**256**

Source : Kumar (2000: 2852).

Predominance of acquisitions in India as a route to FDI is similar to the trends in many developing economies. For instance, in Brazil, the ratio is as high as 70 per cent mainly fuelled by privatisation drive in the 1990s.[11] Foreign firms seem to find it a quick and cheaper route to enter a new market, and secure a sizeable market share.

---

11. Assessing the Brazilian reforms, Rocha (2002) said, "Mergers and acquisitions of private firms have been equally central to the restructuring of the Brazilian economy ... A recent study shows that between 1995 and 1999 there were 1,233 mergers and acquisitions in which multinational corporations acquired control or participation in Brazilian industries—the devaluation of the real since 1999 making such purchases cheaper. A KPMG survey reveals that 70 per cent of all acquisitions in Brazil during the same period were undertaken by multinationals, to the tune of some $ 50 billion of FDI inflows" (Rocha, 2002: 23).

Table 17.8

An Illustrative List of Units/Divisions Transferred to Foreign Firms

Units to be Transferred	Remark
Apar Lighting Division	Transferred to the Joint-Venture (JV) GE-Apar Ltd.
Compressor unit of Kirloskar Brothers	Transferred to Kirloskar Copeland
Compressor unit of SIEL and Kelvinator	Taken Over by Tecumseh Venture
Engine Valve Division of Kirloskar Oil Engines	Proposed to be Transferred to a JV with MWP, Subsidiary of Mahel Germany
Halol Plant of Hind Motors	Transferred to a JV with GM, of the US
Hinditron Computers	Acquired by Digital Equipment Corp.
India Linoleum	Transferred to a JV with DLW of Germany
Premier Auto	Taken Over by Fiat
Luxor Pen	Transferred to a JV with Gillette
Electric Meters of VXL Ltd.	Transferred to VXL Landys Gys. Ltd.
Motorcycle Division of Escorts	Transferred to Escorts Yamaha Ltd.
Oral Care Division of Parle	Acquired by Gillette
Refrigerator Division of Godrej & Boyce	Transferred to Godrej-GE Appliances
Specialty Chemicals Division of Max India	Transferred to Max-Atotech
Stabiliser Division of Jan Auto	Taken Over by NHK Jai Suspensions Ltd.
Sugar Machinery Division of KCP Ltd.	Transferred to FCB-KCP Ltd.
Ceat's Two- and Three-Wheeler Tyre Plant	Transferred to South Asia Tyres Ltd. with Goodyear

Source : Rao, Murthy and Ranganathan (1999).

Of late, taking advantage of the changes in the rules governing the stock market listing, in a situation of low share price level, many existing foreign firms are re-purchasing their equity to exit from the domestic bourses. Table 17.9 provides an illustrative list of such firms. This represents a reversal of the positive effect that the foreign firms' domestic listing has had on the development of the primary stock market since the late 1970s (Nagaraj, 1996).

Table 17.9

An Illustrative List of Foreign Firms Moving to De-list from Domestic Bourses

Sl. No.	Company	Acquirer's Current Holding (Per Cent)	Offer Price (Rs.)	Post-offer Holding (Per Cent)
1	Cabot	60	100	92
2	Cadbury	51	500	90
3	Carrier Aircon	51	100	86
4	Centak Chemicals	75	200	93
5	Hoganas	51	100	85
6	Otis	69	280	79
7	Phillips	51	105	83
8	Reckitt & Coleman	51	250	Yet to Open
9	Sandvik	73	850	89

Source : Business India, April 1-14, 2002: 118.

IV. A COMPARISON OF FDI IN INDIA AND CHINA

Though the actual FDI inflow in India in the 1990s increased significantly over the past, it is modest compared to many Asian economies (Figure 17.4); and, it pales into insignificance in comparison to China (Figure 17.5).[12,13] UNCTAD's ranking of countries in terms of foreign investment (relative to the size of the economy) for the period 1998-2000 is 119 for India, and 47 for China. The ranking a decade ago was 121 and 61, respectively (*The New York Times,* August 28, 2002). It shows that even at the start of the reforms, China's ranking was way ahead of India's; China moved up in the ranking much faster than India did in the 1990s.

These statistics are widely seen as an evidence of the failure of India's reforms, since greater inflow of foreign capital in China is believed to be largely responsible for its exceptional growth and export performance. As this perception is much discussed in the current policy discourse, we examine the quality of the Indian and the Chinese estimates, and the evidence on the role of FDI on economic performance in the recent years.

---

12. Data for this graph is from the various issues of the UN's *World Investment Report.*

13. Figure 17.5 is from IFC (2002). In this graph, x-axis represents years, and y-axis measures FDI in million US Dollar.

Figure 17.4

FDI in Selected Asian Economies, 1991-2000

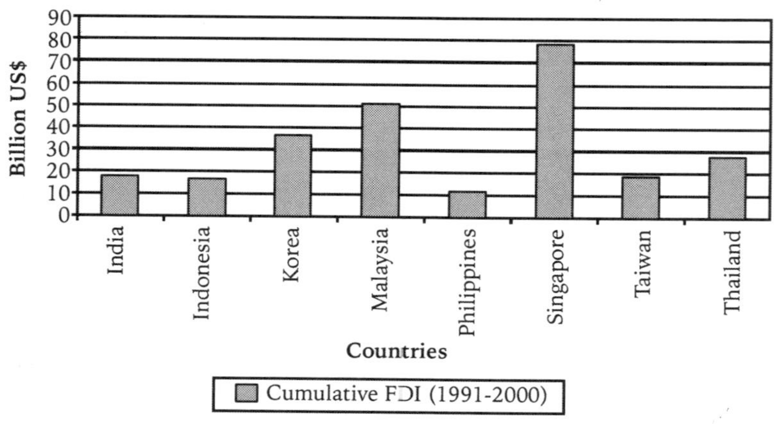

Source : UN's *World Investment Report* (various issues).

Figure 17.5

FDI in India and China

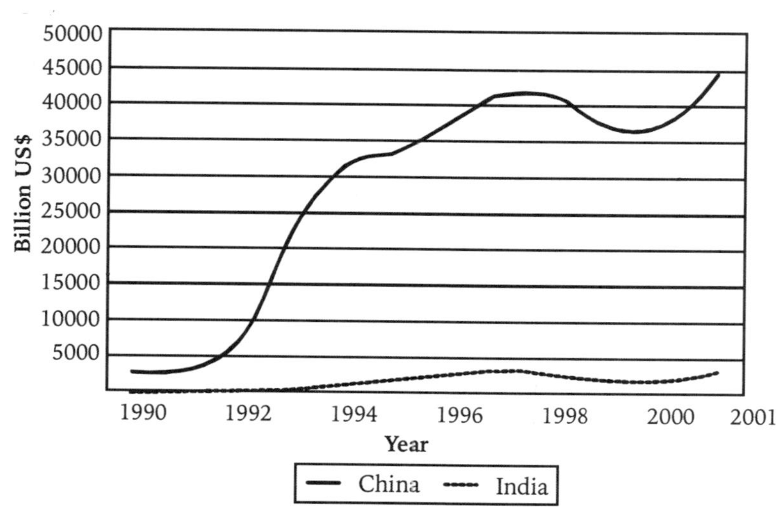

Source : IFC (2002).

According to IFC (2002), India does not follow the standard IMF definition as it excludes: (i) external commercial borrowings, that is ADRs/GDRs,

(ii) reinvested profits, and (iii) subordinated debt.[14] IFC is probably right, but only partially. As noted earlier, the *Economic Survey* estimates include external commercial borrowings, but not the remaining two items. Thus, notwithstanding the underestimation of FDI in the Indian statistics, there is little doubt that foreign investment inflow in India is negligible as compared to China.

However, it is well recognised that a large share of the investment inflow in China represents 'round tripping'—recycling of the domestic saving *via* Hong Kong to take advantage of tax, tariffs and other benefits offered to non-resident Chinese. This is estimated to be in the range of 40-50 per cent of the total FDI (*Global Financial Report, 2002, IFC*).

Further, about a quarter of the inflow in China is invested in real estate (Tseng and Zebregs, 2002). Some of the Chinese coastal cities have attracted considerable speculative capital in this sector in the 1990s after the collapse of the property prices in Hong Kong. It is widely accepted, especially after the east Asian financial crisis, that foreign investment in real estate is inherently problematic, as this sector can easily give rise to financial bubbles, with potentially adverse macroeconomic consequences.

Of the remaining, only a small fraction has gone into large-scale manufacturing that can potentially augment domestic capability and exports. In fact, FDI from the advanced economies that could bring in newer technology and managerial practices are limited, as the Chinese still seem to have a fairly strict regulation on such inflows. Reportedly, in 31 industries China does not allow wholly foreign owned enterprises; and in 32 others, Chinese partners must hold majority share holding.[15]

Based on the foregoing, the International Finance Corporation's study of business environment, in fact, places India marginally ahead of China—from the viewpoint of foreign investors (IFC, 2002). The study also found that the quantum of FDI inflow in China and India, as proportions of their respective GDP, is roughly comparable. Thus, the widely held view of China's ability to attract enormous foreign capital needs to be taken with considerable circumspection.

---

14. I am grateful to Cherian Samuel for providing this unpublished study.

15. Quoting an OECD study, *China in the World Economy*, Srinivasan (2002) reports that majority of Chinese equity holding is mandatory in coal mining, design and manufacture of aircraft, oil and gas, printing and publishing, agricultural production in grains, cotton and oil seeds, domestic commerce, foreign trade, medical instruments and repairs, design and manufacture of ships.

Do countries that attract larger FDI inflow necessarily grow faster? In other words, is there a positive association between foreign investment inflow and GDP growth? Evidence is far from unambiguous. If China's exceptional performance is believed to be largely on account of the foreign capital inflow, then one also has to contend with the recent Brazilian experience that proves the contrary. It has probably attracted the largest FDI from the industrialised economies since 1994. As noted earlier, much of it has gone to acquire domestic assets that were privatised on a large scale. But neither Brazil's growth or its export performance improved in the recent years.

Firm level studies also do not show any evidence that foreign investments improve output and productivity growth (Caves, 1996). There are, however, numerous cross-country studies that provide conflicting evidence on this issue. But, they often suffer from serious methodological problems. A recent study that seeks to address many of the concerns associated with such exercises, seems to find no evidence of a positive association between FDI inflow and output growth (Carkovic and Levine, 2002).[16]

Thus, the quantum of FDI inflow into China, and its positive effect on the economy are perhaps overstated. Without getting into simplistic comparisons, what we need to appreciate from the Chinese experience is perhaps how to take advantage of the openness to investment and trade, to expand domestic capability and get access to external markets for its labour-intensive manufactures.

V. A PRELIMINARY ASSESSMENT

Focus on Domestic Market

As noted earlier, India's seemingly large (and growing) domestic market is probably the main attraction for foreign firms. For instance, international soft drinks producers and fast food chains that were unknown a decade ago have acquired a visible presence in the metropolitan cities, though their quantitative significance may yet be marginal. These firms have brought with them the oligopolistic market structures and firm rivalries that are evident in the developed economies. While such market structures may have some desirable properties, if they lead to tacit collusion to bar new entry, then it may not be a positive development in the long run.

---

16. I am grateful to Edward Graham for this unpublished paper.

Similarly, almost all major international automobile companies have set up assembly and manufacturing facilities in varying extent. The same probably holds true for washing machines, refrigerators and entertainment electronics. Such large-scale entry of firms has resulted in increased price and non-price competition, leading to a greater choice and quality improvement—a desirable outcome for consumers.

Initially, there were considerable apprehensions that international firms with their superior technology, marketing skills and financial strength would wipe out domestic firms (and brand names) in many of these industries. To some extent this has indeed happened—in the aerated drink market, for instance. The same is partly true in the automotive industry as well: Fiat gradually acquired Premier Auto (its erstwhile licensee); Hindustan Motors (an erstwhile GM licensee) has largely become a sub-contractor for GM and Ford, producing engines and transmission equipment.

But many technologically strong and financially sound domestic firms seem to have withstood the growing competition—at least so far. In some cases, domestic firms have severed their ties with their foreign collaborators to assert their managerial independence after some years of association, though such cases are only a few.[17] Further, contrary to many early apprehensions, bulk of the domestic firms (and brand names) have not been displaced from the market. Dominant domestic firms have sough to protect their market shares by expanding capacity and distribution networks, contributing, among other factors, to the boom in fixed investment in registered manufacturing in the 1990s (Nagaraj, 2002).

Though foreign firms have acquired a visible presence in consumer durable goods industries, by and large, it has apparently not been an easy entry for them. While, again, no definitive estimates are available, popular reports suggest many of them overestimated the size (and the growth) of the domestic market, and the appeal of international brands, and thus now suffer from excess capacity and poor profits (*Financial Times*, April 25, 2002). Foreign firms seem to have realised the smallness of the domestic market, and price

---

17. For instance, in the two-wheeler industry, TVS, Kinetic and LML have terminated their technical and/ or financial collaboration with Suzuki, Honda and Piaggio, respectively, to introduce indigenously developed motorcycle/scooter models that have been well received in the market. Bajaj has stopped making motorcycles in joint brand name with Kawasaki for the domestic market, to introduce its own brand of motorcycles. In consumer products, Godrej, a leading domestic firm, terminated its comprehensive ties with Proctor and Gamble, and repromoted own brands to regain its lost market share. In wristwatch industry, Titan industries ceased its collaboration with Timex to expand internationally.

sensitivity of its consumers.[18] Reportedly, a few foreign firms have left India, while many others have staggered their investment and expansion plans.[19]

However, realising the narrowness of the domestic market, many foreign firms are discovering the way out is to indigenise production to reduce costs and secure economies of scale. Moreover, there seems to be a growing appreciation of the cost advantage of domestic manufacturing for exports. For instance, discovering that their car was too expensive for the domestic market, Ford has now found it profitable to use its Indian facilities for the external market. Reportedly, it has exported 30,000 CKD kits to China and South Africa last year (*Business World,* December 2, 2002). Samsonite is apparently expanding its Indian operations for exports, while closing down its Europe plants. There are similar reports from ABB (electrical equipment manufacturer) and Cummnis (Diesel engine manufacturer) as well. If such a tendency gathers momentum, India could possibly emerge as a competitive manufacturing base in these firms' global production networks.

Problems with Infrastructure Investment

Foreign investment in power generation that attracted the largest approved FDI was predicated on securing a high and assured rate of return on invested capital—modelled after Enron's DPC. It was the first of its kind, offering exchange rate guaranteed 16 per cent rate of return on investment on power purchase by the Maharashtra State Electricity Board. The agreement was not based on competitive bidding, violating many established norms of investment planning for a project of that size and scope. This was apparently done in the early years of the reforms to signal India's eagerness to invite foreign investment.

Most of these power projects did not fructify, as they were based on unrealistic assumptions regarding the profitability and the market size. Moreover, as the Enron's Indian saga unravelled, most foreign firms discovered the state governments' inability to ensure the guaranteed return, hence cancelled their investment plans. The speed and secrecy, with which the Enron project was launched, ignoring the checks and balances in public decision-

---

18. External liberalisation was predicated on the proposition that India has a core of about 200 million consumers with purchasing power close to that in the developed economies. After a decade's experience, many market research agencies have reportedly pruned the estimate to a quarter of the original.

19. For instance, BMW (motorcycles), Piaggio (scooters), Nine Gold (broadcasting), Kokna and Haier (Chinese electronics firms), Roche, Merck (pharmaceuticals), Blue Bunnies (ice cream) and so on have left India (*Business Standard,* October 28, 2002).

making, invoked considerable debate in the press, parliament and academia. In retrospect, many of the criticisms seem valid, denting foreign investment's popular image (and the credibility of its exponents).

However, there are probably other reasons as well. Much of the projected demand for power that formed the basis for inviting such a large FDI in this sector was apparently inflated.[20] After the industrial slowdown since the mid-1990s, the demand-supply gap was found to be relatively modest (Nagaraj, 2002). Moreover, cost of production of the thermal power plants of many state electricity boards using domestic raw material and capital equipment were found to be lower than that of the proposed FDI (invariably using imported feedstock). With hindsight—consistent with much of what the critics maintained—the problem with the power sector was not so much the inefficiency of generation, but pricing and recovery of the user charges. Despite the much publicised reforms in the 1990s, the average revenue-to-cost ratio in the power sector has not improved.

Net Foreign Exchange Inflow

For long it has been held that foreign firms bring in limited net resources in the host economy, as they usually take a large surplus out of the country as dividends and royalties (Chandra, 1991). This, to some extent, is probably true of what happened in India in the early 1990s, though it may be hard to substantiate. One of the earliest changes in the foreign investment rules after the reforms was to remove the restriction on the foreign equity holding in the existing foreign firms—reversing the policy initiatives of the earlier period. Foreign firms were quick to seize the opportunity to issue large equity to themselves at a fraction of the market prices (when the stock market was booming). This meant, in principle, a substantial FDI inflow in the book of accounts during 1991-94, but in reality it was simply a book transfer without any fresh capital inflow. With a larger proportion of equity held by the parent firms, it is now possible for them to take out an ever-larger share of surplus in perpetuity.[21] Table 17.10 provides an illustrative list of the foreign firms that followed such a practice, and their gains due to the discount on the issue price of the fresh equity.

---

20. During the earlier policy regime, the Central Electricity Authority—an autonomous body—was responsible for looking into the techno-economic feasibility keeping in view the network externality of power generation and distribution system. Apparently after the deregulation, such official scrutiny was largely ignored in the belief that, 'markets know the best'. Hence, based on power demand projections drawn up by private consultants, large numbers of projects were approved.

21. Admittedly, the share of foreign controlled firms in the private corporate sector is, by most reckoning, small. However, they account for a substantial share of total profits and dividend in this sector.

Table 17.10

An Illustrative List of Foreign Companies that Issued to Themselves Shares at a Concession

Sl. No.	Company	No. of Shares Allotted (In Million)	Preferential Issue Price (In Rupees)	Market Price on Allotment Date (Rupees)	Gain to the Company (In Million Rupees)
1	Colgate	11.3	60	700	7227.5
2	Castrol	3.5	110	1050	3325.7
3	Sesa Goa	3.3	120	1025	2968.4
4	Asean Brown Boveri	4.8	60	325	1260.0
5	Bata	4.7	35	325	936.7
6	Coats Viyella	7.5	65	260	1444.7
7	Alfa Lavel	3.4	73	290	738.8
8	Nestlé	4.8	70	285	1021.6
9	Glaxo	4.5	75	255	808.0
10	Hoechst	2.2	70	370	645.3
11	Lipton	3.5	105	380	972.4
12	Procter & Gamble	4.8	70	285	1021.6
13	Procter & Gamble	1.9	225	340	223.1
14	Phillips	7.7	40	205	340.0
15	Reckitt & Coleman	3.0	100	380	848.4
	Total Gain to the Foreign Firms				24737.0

Source : Jain (2001: 219).

It only goes to show how sensitive foreign firms are about the managerial control. In the absence of suitable regulations, they would like to retain an absolute control that may not be desirable for the host country. However, it is often argued that majority equity holding is necessary for international firms to be assured enough to bring in the latest technology that could potentially have positive spillover in the host economy. This view seems suspect. There is some evidence to show it is not the majority control, but the market structure that determines innovation and the introduction of new technology. Mani (1983), in a case study, showed that in the 1970s when the world's leading firms dominated the Indian automotive tyre industry, it was the new Indian entrants like Apollo and Vikrant Tyres that introduced innovations, and not the incumbent firms. Faced with such a threat, foreign firms quickly followed suit to protect their market shares.

Technology Spillovers

As noted earlier, one of the argument in favour of FDI is the potential positive externality of technology into the host economy. However, in reality, the process may not be that simple. We have seen, that foreign investment does not necessarily lead to fixed capital formation; moreover, technical spillovers depend on the extent of value addition that is carried out in the host economy. For instance, assembly operations or production of simple consumer products is likely to have marginal externality.

For instance, most automobile firms—barring Hyundai and to a less extent Ford—have essentially set up minimal facility to assemble and paint their imported CKD kits, leading to a proliferation of firms and models with modest rise in domestic production and technological capability.[22,23]

In other durable goods industries too, foreign firms have acquired dormant domestic firms and/or resorted to contract manufacturing with the existing firms rather than set up green field plants.[24] While these may be efficient strategies for the firms concerned, the social benefit of such arrangements may remain modest. Our contention is consistent with Richard Caves's observation:

> "... While productivity spillovers from foreign subsidiaries to local firms are apparently widespread, they are neither ubiquitous nor independent of firms' market ambient structure ... Spillovers may be a justification for LDC government policies to encourage flow of foreign direct investment ... . Justification is likely to be conditional on the country's state of development and the structure of particular industries in which foreign subsidiaries might alight" (1999: 17).

Decline in Competition

FDI, in principle, brings in greater market discipline on the incumbent firms by increasing competition. But, as we have seen, foreign firms often acquired dominant positions by taking over domestic firms (and brands). This,

---

22. In fact, considering the fragmented nature of the market, many automotive firms view their Indian operations as mainly distribution and 'brand building' exercises, rather than manufacturing ones. Therefore, it is hard to expect such operations to have significant positive spillovers.

23. According to knowledgeable sources, the Indian auto industry now is as fragmented as the Brazilian industry was when it liberalised its industry some 30 years ago. While Brazil failed to climb up the technology ladder, it was strategic technology importing countries like Japan and Korea that produced world-class automotive manufactures. If the present trend persists it seems likely that India will follow the Brazilian path, rather than the Japanese and the Korean one.

24. To illustrate, Hyderabad Allwyn, acquired by Voltas, after privatisation, has been engaged in contract manufacturing for the Korean firm Samsung (*Business Standard*, November 11, 2002).

again, is best illustrated by Coca Cola's acquisition of the dominant domestic competitor, Thums Up; and Hindustan Lever's—Indian subsidiary of Unilever—acquisition of its largest domestic rival, and the second largest firm in the industry, TOMCO, and the largest cosmetics firm, Lakme.

In principle, in a well-functioning market economy such acquisitions would have attracted the provisions of the competition law. But they went unchallenged in India as the MRTP Act—the anti-trust law—was practically abolished as part of the economic reforms. Further, the government ignored the public and academic criticisms of such acquisitions, as it was keen to signal a positive outlook towards FDI. Thus, our examples show, the widely held view of foreign investment *per se* leading to greater competition needs to be taken with caution.

Foreign Exchange Earnings

One of the common apprehensions against foreign investment is the net drain of foreign exchange in the host countries. Many countries seek to overcome this problem by imposing foreign exchange neutrality clauses. Reportedly even the UK applied such a clause while permitting Japanese automotive firms in the early years of conservative reforms in late 1970s and the early 1980s. Many states in the US apply conditions of job creation while offering incentives for Japanese automotive firms. Though, we do not have data to examine net foreign exchange outgo on account of foreign firms that came into India in the 1990s, the government, reportedly, has been lax in enforcing this clause or has diluted it.[25] This could be a serious matter, especially with many automotive firms that have set up largely limited assembly plants.

Brand Names

In consumer goods industries intangible assets like brand names matter most; and, it takes a long time and effort to create them. A large home market is widely accepted to be advantageous in building such assets before 'exporting' them. India followed a prudent policy in this respect up to the 1980s. However, in the 1990s, as mentioned earlier, in soft drink industry, Coca Cola bought rival brand Thums Up; Gold Spot and Limca; Pepsi purchased Mangola, Dukes, and so on. The foreign firms destroyed many of the purchased brands that competed with their international ones. Coca Cola

---

25. Reportedly, Coca Cola has repeatedly refused to comply with the law in diluting its equity in the domestic capital market for the past six years (Guha, 2002).

'killed' all competing brands except Thums Up, as it was too uneconomical to do so. Reportedly, even now, this Cola drink sells four times as much as the worldwide brand of Coke. It only seems to show how 'path dependent' brand loyalty can be in consumer goods. Therefore, there seems to be considerable merit in promoting indigenous brands that have the potential to compete in the world market. Such hasty policy changes could prove a costly mistake in the long run for India, as consumer goods are nothing, but their brand names.[26]

Loss of Bargaining Power in the Technology Market

It is well accepted that dominant international firms have substantial market power, and many developed countries widely intervene in the technology market to protect and promote interests of their firms.[27] Indian policy, after the reforms, practically ceased to intervene in the technology market, significantly weakening domestic firms' bargaining position.

With the increasing role of financial collaborations, foreign technical agreements as a source of technology have steadily dwindled in the 1990s—both in absolute and relative terms (Figure 17.6), (*Economic Survey, 2001-02*). Evidently, foreign firms do not want to part with their technology, as they can now come into India without a domestic partner.

Considering their superior financial and technical strengths, many foreign firms in the capital goods industry seem to have wrested managerial control in the existing joint ventures in the 1990s. For example, Caterpillar bought out Birla's stake in their joint venture manufacturing earthmoving equipment although the firm was doing well in the market. Many automotive firms started as joint ventures, but gradually foreign partners increased their financial stake by buying out domestic partners, as Indian partners were unable to bring in the resources to make up for the losses in the early years of the firms' operations. This happened at a time when the domestic interest rates were higher than the international rates. Foreign partners found it an inexpensive way to acquire a greater managerial control, especially as the currency was steadily depreciating.

---

26. Apparently, the US tax laws provide tax credit for promotion of American brands abroad. We do not have evidence to substantiate this claim.

27. The US protection of the super computers manufacturer, Cray, despite competing products by Japan's Hitachi and Fijitsu being much cheaper is a well known case. Recently when, for the first time, the US department of agriculture bought a Fujitsu super computer, *The New York Times* considered the decision news worthy to report it (June 14, 2002).

Figure 17.6

Decline in Technical Collaborations Agreements

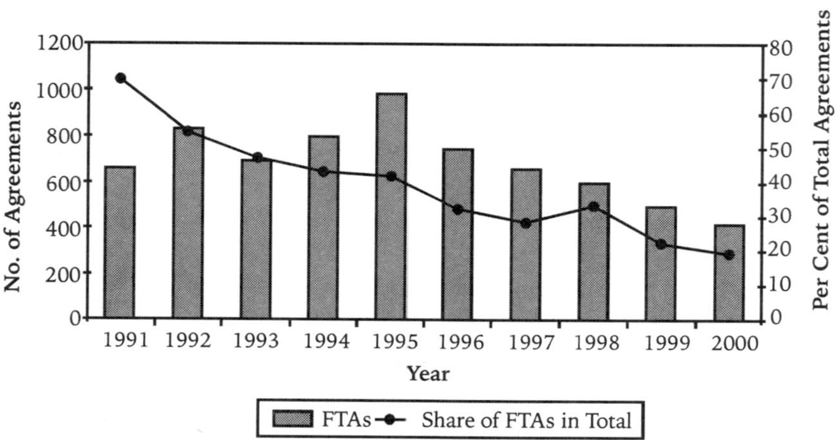

Source : Economic Survey, 2001-02.

For instance, Honda bought out the Sriram group, and Ford acquired Mahindra's stake in their joint venture car projects. However, more recently, there are instances of the converse, where Indian firms have bought out their foreign partners; for instance, TVS Motors and Suzuki, Kinetic motors and Honda, and LML and Piaggio. But such instances seem far fewer.

Arguably, the above examples illustrate the virtues of a market- driven process for corporate control that is best left to it. Such a benign view may not necessarily favour developing countries and their consumers in the long run. For instance, the demise of Spanish automotive firms with its integration in the European Union, and the lack of technological and market dynamism in the Brazilian auto industry—despite substantial investment and output growth—probably suggests that strategic intervention to support domestic firms and industry are not incompatible with securing dynamic comparative advantage and export competitiveness.

In sum, while the entry of foreign firms has increased competition and improved the variety and quality of consumer goods, there are some disturbing signals. Foreign investment in infrastructure is a failure. Gradual loss of managerial control in many industrial firms, decline in competition in some industries, extinction of some leading domestic brand names and limited improvement in domestic production capability seem to be signs of concern.

VI. TOWARDS A REALISTIC FDI POLICY

It is widely believed that India has not done enough of policy reforms to attract substantially more foreign investment. Moreover, it is not the financial incentives but the lack of adequate infrastructure, bureaucratic delays and above all, the rigid industrial labour laws that have come in the way of attracting more investments (Bajpai and Sachs, 2001). This view seems to have many limitations. For instance, there is no evidence of a positive association between the extent of market-oriented reforms and FDI inflows across developing economies (Easterly, 2001). Moreover, as discussed earlier, greater foreign investment inflow does not necessarily mean faster output and export growth. What, then, should guide India's foreign investment policy?

If history is any guide, foreign investment in infrastructure is potentially problematic. Latin America witnessed a wave of foreign infrastructure investment from the US in the 1930s, only to leave with the bitter experience of nationalisations in a couple of decades. It bears repetition that infrastructure is inherently capital-intensive with long gestation lags, and low (but stable) returns over a long period. Market failures are ubiquitous in these industries, with considerable network economies necessarily inviting wide and deep state intervention. In a world consisting of politically independent nations with a growing number of democracies, the pricing of infrastructure is bound to be a political decision. Foreign firms with short pay-back periods invariably find it hard to stay on, as it conflicts with the goals of developing economies caught in an increasingly uncertain world economy.[28]

There are also perhaps some India specific factors for the relatively small foreign capital inflow. It seems worth reiterating that India is still largely an agrarian economy, with land productivity being a third of China's, where the average disposable income after meeting food and clothing (wage goods) requirement is still relatively small. Price-income-ratio of most consumer goods that foreign firms usually sell is high by domestic standards, accentuated perhaps by cultural factors and regional heterogeneity of markets (*Financial Times*, April 25, 2002).

In infrastructure industries, the rupee cost of electricity supply by foreign firms seems high. Given India's fairly diversified industrial capability, and low labour costs, foreign firms may not have a cost advantage over the domestic

---

28. Writing at the height of the foreign infrastructure investment boom in the 'emerging markets' in the mid-1990s, Wells and Gleason (1995) cautioned the American businessman against rushing into such investment precisely on the above arguments.

producers—especially with the currency depreciating in nominal terms. This is perhaps best illustrated, again, by the Enron's DPC. With imported capital goods and fuel, and high operating cost due to international norms of costing, Enron's cost of production was found to be higher than the comparable new plants using domestic capital equipment (Morris, 1996).

At the same time, Hyundai's large investment with consciously built-in high domestic content secured through economies of scale has succeeded in producing a small car that seems competitive both in price and quality. Reportedly, Hyundai proposes to use its Indian plant as a global hub for its small car (*The Economic Times*, January 2, 2003). Thus, the key to increasing FDI inflow seems to lie in industries (and products) with relatively high technology that have large economies of scale, with substantial domestic content.

However, the foregoing reasoning still does not explain why foreign investment does not come to use cheap labour and skills for export of labour-intensive manufactures—as it has happened in China. We are inclined to believe that the foreign investment policy lacks a clear focus. Unlike China, India has not invested in export infrastructure. In fact, as is widely accepted now, the share of infrastructure in fixed capital formation has declined sharply for nearly one and half decade now (Nagaraj, 1997). Further, what is needed is perhaps not large investment but suitable inducement to international marketers—trading houses and retail chains—to set up purchase offices and testing facilities to tap the potential of the domestic manufacturers.[29] It is widely acknowledged that China's export success largely lies in marrying its low cost manufacturing capability in Town and Village Enterprises (TVEs) with Hong Kong's highly developed trading houses and other long-established commercial organisations catering to international trade. While it is out of question for India to replicate the locational and historical advantage of Hong Kong for China, investment in export infrastructure in strategic locations and carefully tailored incentives to international trading houses (and retailers) merit a serious consideration. Similarly, such investments are perhaps equally necessary to tap the growing potential for using India's labour cost advantage for doing back office jobs—business processes outsourcing—for international firms (*The Economist*, May 5, 2001).

Realistically, what is it that India expects from foreign investment, and how to secure it? In principle, openness to foreign investment should be strategic,

---

29. In fact, it was Mrinal Datta Chaudhuri (1981) who long ago emphasised the role of large domestic and international trading houses as market institutions in promoting manufactured exports from Korea and Taiwan.

not passive (or unilateral). History does not seem to support such an uncritical international integration as a proven route to growth and efficiency. If the recent experience is any guide, foreign capital is far from a major provider of external savings for rapid industrialisation of any large economy. It can only supplement the domestic resources, wherever they necessarily come bundled with technology, and access to international production and distribution networks. The terms of foreign investment will depend on the relative bargaining power of the foreign firm *vis-à-vis* domestic firms, backed by the state. Indian advantages are the availability of skilled workforce, cheap labour, and the size of the domestic market, which it should leverage as most successful countries have done. A telling instance of it is perhaps Korea's big leap in semi-conductor and telecom equipment manufacturing in the recent years, as it seems to have tied liberalisation of domestic market to sharing of production technology.

If this view has any value, then how should we go about inviting FDI that is consistent with the economy's long-term interests? Foreign investment should be allowed mainly in manufacturing to acquire technology, and to establish international trading channels for promoting labour-intensive exports.

VII. SUMMARY AND CONCLUSION

Ending its long held restrictive foreign investment policy in 1991, India sought to compete with the successful Asian economies to get a greater share of the world's FDI. Cumulative approved foreign investment since then is about $67bn, but the realised amount is about a third of it—the ratio roughly comparable to China's. While the foreign investment inflow represents a substantial jump over the 1980s, it is modest compared to many rapidly growing Asian economies, and minuscule compared to China. While the bulk of the approved FDI is for infrastructure, the realised investment is largely in manufacture of consumer durable goods and the automotive industry seeking India's seemingly large and growing domestic market. Foreign investment in telecom and software industries has also been significant. Approved FDI has largely gone to a few developed states—similar to its concentration in the southern coastal provinces in China. A sizeable part of the foreign investment seems to represent a gradual increase in foreign firms' equity holding (hence managerial control) in the existing firms, and acquisition of industrial assets (and brand names).

China's ability to attract a phenomenal amount of foreign investment is a puzzle for many. About 40-50 per cent of China's FDI represents its domestic saving recycled as foreign investment *via* Hong Kong to take advantage of economic incentives—popularly called the 'round tripping'. Another 25 per cent or so, seems to represent investment in real estate by overseas Chinese that is potentially problematic, as such investments could easily give rise to property bubbles. Thus, the quantum of foreign investment from the advanced economies that could improve domestic production capability is perhaps not very different from that in India, in relation to its domestic output. Contrary to the popular belief, China's foreign investment regime is said to be more restrictive than India's. Therefore, what India should be concerned about is not so much the absolute quantum of the inflow, but how effectively it uses its external openness to augment the domestic capability, and access foreign markets for its labour-intensive manufactures.

For a careful economic analysis of the effects of foreign investment, considerable detailed statistical information is required—both at the aggregate and at the firm or industry level. In their absence, much of our analysis is indicative in nature, raising questions for further enquiry.

As the 1990s experience shows, quite contrary to the popular perception, the size of India's domestic market is relatively small, given the low levels of per capita income. After meeting the needs of food and clothing (wage goods), income let for spending on products that most foreign firms offer seems small; their price-income ratio too high for Indian consumers. Therefore, many of them seem to be making efforts to indigenise production to reduce costs and secure economies of scale. In this process, many foreign firms are discovering the potential of low cost of manufacturing for exports.

Much of the approved FDI in infrastructure did not fructify, as the rupee cost of electricity supply by foreign firms is too much high for Indian consumers. This seems true for two reasons: one, prices of goods like electricity are widely subsidised, and cannot be increased without inviting public opposition; second, India produces much of these services at lower cost using domestic raw material and capital equipment.

Foreign investment in consumer goods industries has increased domestic competition, resulting in greater choice and quality improvement. While FDI inflow displaced some domestic firms (and brand names), the bulk of them have—at least yet—largely been able to withstand the competition by making large capital investment, and in expanding distribution networks.

However, in industrial goods there have probably been sizeable acquisitions of domestic firms (and factories) whole details are not known. There are many instances of foreign firms gradually acquiring controlling interests, edging out domestic partners. Whether these firm-level changes get reflected in industrial efficiency in the aggregate—as many expected—is a moot point.

What should be done to increase foreign investment? It is popularly believed that a more liberal policy regime, industrial labour market reforms, and infrastructure investment are needed. While infrastructure improvement surely merits a close attention, one is not so sure if the extent of the reforms and the quantum of foreign investment inflow are positively related. Moreover, there is little evidence that greater FDI inflow ensures faster output and export growth. Such simplistic associations, usually based on cross-country analysis, seem to have support neither in principle nor in comparative experience.

What is needed is a strategic view of foreign investment as a means of enhancing domestic production and technological capability, and so also to access the external market for labour-intensive manufactures—as China has precisely done. It seems valuable to reiterate what K.N. Raj, a perceptive observer of comparative economic development, noted early on in China's liberalisation drive, "It is certainly not without good reason that China has chosen to be hospitable even to multinationals with worldwide ramifications like IBM, evidently in the expectation of securing the know-how for building up semi-conductor industry of its own. Those who do not realise the implications of all this for India are living in a dream world of their own..." (Raj, 1986).

Such interventions need selectivity, and strategic intent. Comparative experience seems to clearly favour such a policy stance.

References

Ahluwalia, Isher (1985). *Industrial Growth in India—Stagnation Since the Mid-Sixties*, Oxford University Press, Delhi.

Amsden, Alice (2001). *The Rise of 'The Rest': Challenges to the West From Late-Industrialising Economies*, Oxford University Press, New York.

Bajpai, Nirupam and Jeffery D. Sachs (2001). "Foreign Direct Investment in India: Issues and Problems", HIID, *Development Discussion Paper* No. 759, March.

Bosworth, Barry P. and Susan M. Collins (1999). "Capital Flows to Developing Countries: Implications for Savings and Investment", *Brooking Papers on Economic Activity*, No. 1.

Bruton, Henry (1989). "Import Substitution" in *Handbook of Development Economics*, Vol. 2, edited by Hollis Chenery and T.N. Srinivasan, North Holland, London.

Carkovic, Maria and Ross Levine (2002). *Does Foreign Investment Accelerate Economic Growth?*, Finance Department, University of Minnesota, *mimeo*.

Caves, Richard E. (1999). "Spillovers from Multinationals in Developing Countries: The Mechanisms at Work", *Working Paper* No. 247, Department of Economics, Harvard University.

————. (1996). *Multinational Enterprise and Economic Analysis*, 2nd Edition, Cambridge University Press, London.

Chandra, Nirmal (1991). "Growth of Foreign Capital and Importance in Indian Manufacturing", *Economic and Political Weekly*, Vol. 26, Nos. 11-12.

Chaudhuri, Sudip (1999). "Growth and Structural Change in the Pharmaceutical Industry in India", *Working Paper* No. 356/99, Indian Institute of Management, Calcutta.

Datta Chaudhuri, M.K. (1981). "Industrialisation and Foreign Trade: The Development Experiences of South Korea and Philippines" in E. Lee (ed.), *Export-led Industrialisation and Development*, ILO, Geneva.

Easterly, William (2001). "The Lost Decades: Developing Countries Stagnation in spite of Policy Reforms 1980-1998", *Journal of Economic Growth*, Vol. 6, June.

Guha Thakurta, Paranjoy (2002). "Coke: Arrogance of a Multinational", *www.rediff.com*, July 20.

Helleiner, G.K. (1989). "Transnational Corporations and Direct Foreign Investment" in H. Chenery and T.N. Srinivasan (eds.) *Handbook of Development Economics*, Vol. 2, Elsevier Science Publishers B.V.

Hymer, Stephen (1976). *The International Operations of National Firms: A Study of Foreign Direct Investment*, MIT Press, Massachusetts.

International Finance Corporation (2002). "Business Environment and Surveys", *mimeo*, Washington, DC.

Jain, Virendra (2001). *Investors Beware*, Macmillan India, Delhi.

Johnston, David Cay (2002). "Tax Treaties with Small Nations Turn into a New Shield for Profit", *The New York Times*, April 16.

Kumar, Nagesh (2000). "Mergers and Acquisitions by MNEs: Patterns and Implications", *Economic and Political Weekly*, August 5.

Lall, Sanjaya (1989). *Learning to Industrialise*, Macmillan, London.

————. (1982). *Developing Countries as Exporters of Technology*, Macmillan, London.

Lewis, W. Arthur (1953). *Aspects of Industrialisation*. Bank of Egypt, Cairo.

Mani, Sunil (1983). *Industrial Concentration and Economic Behaviour: Case Study of Indian Tyre Industry*, Centre for Development Studies, Trivandrum.

Mehta, Abhy (1999). *Power Play: A Study of the Enron Project*, Orient Longman, Hyderabad.

Morris, Sebastian (1996). "Political Economy of Electric Power in India", *Economic and Political Weekly*, Vol. 31, No. 21, May 25.

Nagaraj, R. (2002). "Performance-of India's Manufacturing Sector in the 1990s: Some Tentative Findings" in Shuji Uchikawa (ed.) *Economic Reforms and Industrial Structure in India*, Manohar, Delhi.

————. (1997). "What has Happened Since 1991? Assessment of India's Econmic Reforms", *Economic and Political Weekly*, Vol. 32, No. 44-45.

————. (1996). "India's Capital Market Growth: Trends, Explanations and Evidence", *Economic and Political Weekly*, Vol. 31, Nos. 35-37 (Special Number).

Raj, K.N. (1986). *New Economic Policy*, Oxford University Press, Delhi.

Rao, K.S. Chalapati, M.R. Murthy and K.V.K. Ranganathan (1999). "Foreign Direct Investment in the Post-Liberalisation Period: An Overview", *Journal of Indian School of Political Economy*, Vol. 11, No. 3, July-September.

Rao, Chalapati K.S. and M.R. Murthy (1999). "Foreign Direct Investment" in *Alternataive Economic Survey, 1991-98: Seven Years of Structural Adjustment*, Alternative Survey Group, New Delhi.

Reserve Bank of India (2001). *Handbook of Statistics on Indian Economy*, Mumbai

Rocha, Geisa Maria (2002). "Neo-Dependency in Brazil", *New Left Review*, No. 16, July-August.

Srinivasan, G. (2002). "Secret of China's FDI Riches", *Business Line*, December 6, 2002.

Subramaniam, K.K. (1991). "Technological Capability under Economic Liberalism: Experience of Indian Industry in the Eighties", *Economic and Political Weekly*, Vol. 26, No. 35, August 31.

Tseng, Wanda and Harm Zebregs (2002). "Foreign Direct Investment in China: Some Lessons for other Countries", *IMF Policy Discussion Paper* (PDP/02/03), Washington, DC.

Wells, Louis, T. and Eric, S. Gleason (1995). "Is Foreign Infrastructure Investment Still too Risky?", *Harvard Business Review*, September-October.

World Bank (1993). *The East Asian Miracle: Economic Growth And Public Policy*, Oxford University Press, New York.

18

Financial Stability: Some Analytical Issues

C. RANGARAJAN

Abstract

Serious financial crises that have gripped several countries in the last two decades have brought to the fore the issue of financial stability. The key element of a financial crisis is the disruption that is caused to the financial system and the consequent loss in real output. Stability applies to both institutions and markets. A question that is being increasingly asked is whether the financial sector today is inherently more volatile and vulnerable than before. Close inter-dependencies among markets and market participants have increased the potential for contagion. The approach to regulating financial markets as distinct from institutions, has been somewhat unclear and ambiguous.

Regulations are aimed at ensuring the 'soundness and safety' of the financial system. The oversight over financial institutions have three components: (i) setting standards, (ii) assessing risk and internal controls, and (iii) supervision. Each of these elements has several subcomponents. The capital adequacy ratio has emerged as a primary instrument of financial regulation. Despite its widespread adoption, this indicator is not without its shortcomings. There is now a greater emphasis on the assessment of risk and Basle-II seeks to encourage banks to go for a balanced portfolio and reduce the overall risk exposure. An important development in the supervisory system is the move from an inspection which is transaction based to a framework that emphasises on the implementation of effective risk management systems. An 'incentive-compatible' financial regulation is also being contemplated to use market forces to supplement the regulatory system. Another improvement in

An earlier version of this paper was presented as the R.S. Bhatt Memorial Lecture delivered in Mumbai, June 2004. I am grateful to Ms. Shyamala Gopinath and Ms. Usha Thorat for their help in writing this paper. I am thankful to Mr. S.S. Tarapore for his suggestions for improving the text. I must also thank Dr. A. Prasad and Dr. A. Samantaraya for the assistance provided by them.

the supervisory process has been the introduction of macro-prudential indicators to assess the vulnerability of the financial system. With the emergence of financial institution providing multiple services, the issue of single *versus* multiple regulators has assumed importance.

In a broad sense, financial stability is very much an objective of monetary policy. In this context, two questions arise. First, how can a central bank identify the situation when it has to intervene from the point of view of financial stability? Second, can any action that is called for from the angle of avoiding financial instability come into conflict with other objectives? Anticipation regarding financial instability needs to be taken into account in one way or the other, while deciding monetary action. Following the pattern adopted by several central banks in recent periods, there is some advantage in the Reserve Bank of India bringing out separately every quarter, an Inflation Report and semi-annually a Financial Stability Report.

Serious financial crises that have rocked several countries particularly in the last two decades have brought to the fore the issues of financial stability. These bouts of financial instability within individual countries and across countries have compelled policy makers and analysts to pay attention to the problem of predicting, avoiding and managing financial crises. Fundamental to all these prescriptions is a clear understanding of the causes of the crises.

In the 60s and 70s of the last century, the major concern in relation to the financial sector was how to avoid 'financial repression'. It was felt that the administered structure of interest rates combined with various other direct controls by the central banks had inhibited the growth of financial sector in many countries. These controls, it has been argued, had the effect of diluting the operational and allocative efficiency of the financial institutions. By and large the emphasis was on the developmental role of the financial sector. Deepening and widening of the financial system was a major concern of public policy. However, attention has recently shifted to stability because of the frequency of financial crises and the costs they have imposed. Besides causing a significant loss to private wealth, they have imposed a substantial burden on the public finance because of the need to re-capitalise financial institutions and restore public confidence. 'Resolution Costs' in several countries have been estimated to exceed 10 per cent of gross domestic product (GDP). One estimate puts the average fiscal costs of banking resolution alone across countries at 16 per cent of GDP (Hoggarth and Saporta, 2001).

Defining Financial Stability

It is difficult to define the term 'financial stability'. There is no universally accepted definition. The term 'stability' or 'instability' refers to the behaviour of the system rather than to individual institutions. However, one cannot rule out that failure of a single financial institution can trigger significant financial turmoil. Nevertheless, the key element of a financial crisis is the disruption that is caused to the financial system and the resultant cost to real output. Stability applies to both institutions and markets. Crockett (1997) writes "Stability requires (i) the key institutions in the financial system are stable, in that there is a high degree of confidence that they can continue to meet their contractual obligations without interruption or outside assistance, and (ii) that the key markets are stable, in that participants can confidently transact in them at prices that reflect fundamental forces and that do not vary substantially over short periods when there have been no changes in fundamentals." Alternatively, instability implies inability of institutions to meet their obligations on their own. Markets are said to be unstable when prices in financial markets are volatile and moved by amounts not justified by changes in fundamentals. Like unstable equilibrium, instability implies inability to correct itself on its own. Instability, if it persists, turns into a crisis. It is this potential for full blown crisis, involving bankruptcy of institutions and loss of wealth by individuals, that compels regulators and other policy makers to take action to contain instability. In the past, financial crises tended to occur in two areas, (i) banking, and (ii) foreign exchange market. While over extended loan portfolio and imprudent lending were usually the major causes of banking crises, exchange rate crises were the outcome of the pressures developing in foreign exchange markets supplemented by actions of speculators to force a depreciation of the currency. However, crisis in one market can lead to a crisis in another. For example, the currency crisis can lead to a banking crisis which, in turn, can lead to a financial sector crisis with damaging effects on the real sector. The East Asian crisis of 1997 is a typical example of this sequence. However, in the East Asian episode, given the fragility of the financial sector, the crisis could very well have originated in the banking arena and later spread to the currency market. With increasing interdependence of markets, instability in one market can lead to instability in another.

Instability Bias

Anyone can recognise the very fast growth of the financial sector in almost all countries, both developed and developing. A question that is being asked increasingly is whether the financial sector today is inherently more fragile and vulnerable than before. The very factors that have contributed to the growth of the financial sector may well have contributed to the increased fragility. Financial institutions have become more sophisticated; the volume of transactions has increased phenomenally and competitive pressures have grown. As a result of very rapid increase in telecommunications and computer-based technologies, a dramatic expansion in financial flows both cross-border and within countries has emerged. Along with these changes, consolidation, increased geographic spread of banks and other financial service providers, and the blurring of the distinctions between various financial institutions have also occurred. Developments in technology and in the pricing of assets have enabled innovations and financial instruments that allowed risks to be separated and allocated to parties most willing and able to bear them. Thus, the menu of financial products has expanded enormously. For example, in the case of debt instruments, investors can now choose among structured notes, syndicated loans, coupon strips and bonds secured by pool of other debt instruments. Another dramatic development is the growing use of financial derivatives. All these changes have undoubtedly created new opportunities, but they have also magnified risks. In fact, it has been remarked that the increased complexity of new instruments makes it harder to understand the risks to which the institutions concerned are exposed. Close inter-dependencies among markets and market participants have increased the potential for adverse events to spread quickly. They have increased significantly the scope for and speed of contagion.

Apart from these factors, sometimes a fear is expressed that the financial system may be prone to instability because of its inherently pro-cyclical character (Berger and Udell, 2003; Borio, 2004). Asset prices move procyclically. So too is the ratio of credit to GDP. However, if these normal behavioural patterns reach abnormal proportions, they become the cause of financial distress. For example, asset price booms in property markets when they come to an end cause serious distortions since they constitute the collateral for various loans. Hence, the old adage "Bad loans are sown in good times." The financial system may not always be able to build sufficient cushions in good times which can act as effective shock absorbers in bad times. Therefore, the search for early warning signals of financial imbalances. The critical thing to identify is the timing of when 'exuberance' turns into 'irrational exuberance', so that imbalances do not build up.

Regulating Institutions and Markets

It is well understood, that if financial stability is to be achieved, it must relate to both institutions and markets. However, much of the discussions and regulatory measures focus primarily on institutions. The case for public intervention in relation to financial institutions is well understood and, has indeed, a long history. Financial institutions and, more particularly, banks have been subjected to a number of regulatory measures for a long time even though in recent years, there has seen a significant tightening. Vulnerability and contagion have been the major reasons for advocating public intervention. Vulnerability of financial institutions to pressures comes from the maturity mismatch between liabilities and assets. This mismatch particularly is stark in the case of banks. A good part of the liabilities of banks is redeemable on demand while their assets have a much longer maturity. While this mismatch may not cause any problem in the normal circumstances, any loss of confidence can lead to destabilisation. The vulnerability of banks to 'runs' has always been recognised. The other major reason is contagion. The failure of a financial institution, such as a bank, causes losses not only to its depositors and owners but also to all the institutions with which it is interlinked. This exposure to other institutions and individuals is extremely high in the case of banks because of the role they play in the payments system. It is this possibility of negative externality that has resulted in financial institutions to be brought under regulatory regimes (Stiglitz, 1994). The multiplicity of financial products and more particularly derivative products has tended to heighten the contagion factor. To take care of the changing environment in which financial institutions operate and the new types of pressures that they are subjected to, the regulatory mechanism relating to financial institution has undergone a change. These issues are discussed at a later stage.

The approach to regulating financial markets as distinct from institutions has, however, been somewhat unclear and ambiguous. Regulation of asset price runs into problems because there is no easy way of determining what the appropriate or equilibrium price is. However, one can perceive certain differences in approach with respect to various markets. In the foreign exchange markets, central banks do intervene to offset tendencies that are not considered desirable. Even in countries where currencies are not pegged, central banks make a distinction between interfering with fundamental factors and correcting volatile or disorderly conditions in the market and are willing to intervene to maintain orderly conditions. That foreign exchange markets tend to overshoot is well known. With technology facilitating speedy transfer of funds and with the free movement of funds across countries, exchange rates no longer reflect the behaviour of the current account of balance of payments.

Thus, intervention is resorted to in one way or the other by several central banks in the foreign exchange markets. However, most central banks, at least in the developed countries, would in normal times, prefer to let the markets determine the price. But the need to watch over the foreign exchange markets is accepted and intervention is not ruled out.

However, in relation to equity markets, bond markets or real estate markets, there is much less emphasis on direct public intervention to alter the asset prices. Instability in stock markets can have serious consequences not only for the investors in these markets, but also for the rest of the financial system as well as the real economy. However, there is no direct attempt at influencing prices in these markets. The regulatory approach has been to ensure investor protection, prevention of manipulation and establishing transparency. Nevertheless, the question of assessing, when these markets are 'overpriced' and when they are misaligned with fundamentals, is critically important both for monetary authorities and regulators of financial markets. In fact, an issue that is being debated now is how central banks should take into account factors relating to financial stability in the conduct of monetary policy. This has implications both for the timing and specifics of monetary policy.

Components of Regulation

The need to regulate financial institutions, particularly banks, from the point of view of system stability, has been long understood. In fact, it has even been argued that there exist some forms of government intervention that will not only make the institutions function better but also improve the performance of the economy (Stiglitz, 1994).

The early regulations in banking related to licensing. But, countries like the US initially had adopted a liberal policy, with different authorities entrusted with the power of licensing. However, in the US there were certain preventive measures such as activity restraints as under the Glass-Steagel Act and restrictions on branch banking, mergers and acquisitions. Nowadays, regulations are aimed at ensuring, to use a cliché, the 'soundness and safety' of the financial system. The broad oversight over financial institutions can be viewed from several angles. For example, one can classify the elements of oversight into three components:

(i)   Setting standards.

(ii) Assessing risk and internal controls.

(iii) Supervision.

Each of these elements has several sub-components. These have been discussed at length in international fora. In fact, the regulations have become more complex, raising questions of compliance costs. The 'Dense regulatory style', to borrow an expression from Greenspan, has come in for some criticism.

Setting Standards

Standards can be interpreted in a number of ways. Narrowly interpreted, they refer to norms with respect to some performance or activity indicator. Capital adequacy ratio is a classic example of this. Broadly viewed, standards can be applied to diverse areas such as accounting, transparency and legal framework including bankruptcy legislations. Much work has been done at both levels in recent years. Starting with the Core Principles for Effective Banking Supervision initiated by the Basle Committee on Banking Supervision in 1988, the move to establish standards has extended to other areas such as securities trading and insurance. The internationalisation of standards has become necessary to avoid 'regulatory arbitrage', i.e., an attempt by multinational financial corporations from moving the centers of activities to less and loosely regulated areas.

The evolution of prudential norms was a major development in the 1990s. While capital adequacy ratio has emerged as a primary instrument of financial regulation, the prudential norms cover other important areas such as income recognition, provisioning for bad and doubtful debts and the classification of assets into performing and non-performing. Capital adequacy ratio tries to ensure that the banks maintain a minimum amount of own funds in relation to the credit risks they face. The availability of adequate equity capital is a basic requirement for stability in a market economy. This is all the more so in the case of banks, given their high degree of leverage. Risk weighted capital adequacy requirement which was the result of the 1998 Basle Capital Accord is one of the main pillars of the present regulatory regime in banks. The risk weighted capital adequacy framework (Basle-1) required banks to hold different categories of capital against both on-balance sheet assets and off-balance sheet asset items with different risk weights assigned to counterparties. There is no doubt that the capital held by banks should be appropriately related to the size and nature of the risk they run. The adequacy ratio was originally related only to credit risk. However, an expanded system of capital adequacy ratio incorporating market risks was introduced in 1996.

While the capital adequacy ratio has been adopted by more than 100 countries including India, it is not without shortcomings (Nachane *et al.*, 2000). One can think in terms of three sets of issues which need to be resolved. The first concerns how much capital banks should be required to hold. The second concerns the relationship between the level of capital and the economic cycle. And the third concerns the specific question of how to measure the risks against which capital is to be held and fix the weights.

The very simplicity of the formula relating to capital adequacy ratio carries with it many problems. Though what the Accord prescribed was a minimum capital ratio, very often it was assumed to be the most appropriate, leading on occasions to regulatory forbearance. This may have also led to depositors taking less interest in monitoring banks' activities. Minimum capital ratio has to be distinguished from 'maximum insolvency probability'. If the regulators had to adopt the latter criterion, the required capital would be much higher. This may, however, impose undue burden. There were two other drawbacks. First, the capital adequacy ratio did not take into account explicitly risks other than market and credit risks. Increasingly, there is greater stress on 'operational risk'. Second, the Accord treated all assets falling into a certain risk category as carrying the same weight. It ignored the fact that assets in the same risk class can have widely varying quality. The degree of concentration or diversification of a portfolio, which is an important determinant of risk, was ignored.

While the prescription of a minimum capital linked to riskiness of assets was an important first step, the changing financial scenario comprising of advancement in technology and telecommunications, innovations in financial products and services and the increasing globalisation of the markets calls for more sophisticated systems of assessment of risk (Caruana, 2004). Banks have evolved, on their own, various techniques to measure and manage risk. The Basle Accord-II, which is under discussion and which is to be adopted by 2006, takes note of the need to link capital adequacy to risk management.

It may be pointed out at this stage, that capital adequacy ratio as a regulatory measure suffers from some analytical shortcomings (Stiglitz, 2003). It may pose a 'moral hazard' problem. The maintenance of the soundness of the system cannot be achieved by continuously raising the ratio. This may make the banks to go in for more risky assets within a certain risk bracket in order to earn a higher return. The regulatory system must encourage the banks to go for a balanced portfolio and reduce the overall risk exposure. Forward-looking provisioning for non-performing assets (NPAs) should be encouraged in good times. The capital-adequacy ratio can also cut the other way. In an effort to maintain the ratio consistent with the available capital, banks may cut down their asset portfolios. While on occasions, this may be welcome, this may not be desirable, if resorted to by a large number of banks at a time when credit expansion is needed.

Assessing Risk and Internal Controls

Financial institutions face a wide range of risks. These include credit, interest rate, foreign exchange, liquidity and operational risks. While these risks could analytically be separated, they are highly interdependent and events that affect one area of risk can have implications for other risk categories. As a consequence, increasingly various types of risk evaluation tools including value at risk models and stress tests are being used to assess risks. These models provide continuous information for the management and Basle-II seeks to build on these developments. With the move towards Basle II, banks would be encouraged to go for a balanced portfolio, reduce the overall risk exposure and enable maintenance of adequate capital. The new Basle Accord rests on the assumption that an internal assessment of risk by a financial institution will be a better measure than an externally imposed formula. However, much will depend on the model used by individual institutions and this will require external validation.

There are three pillars to Accord-II (BIS, 2003 and Nachane, 2003). These are: (i) minimum capital requirement, (ii) supervisory review, and (iii) market discipline.

Basle II—Pillar I: Minimum Capital Requirements

With respect to minimum capital requirement, the new Accord has made substantial changes to the treatment of credit risk relative to the current Accord. It has also introduced an explicit treatment of operational risk. Deviating from the earlier one-size-fits-all approach, the new Accord allows banks a certain latitude in determining their own capital requirements based on internal models. With respect to the assessment of credit risk, there are two approaches. One is a standardised approach and the other is the internal rating based approach (IRB). The standardised approach is very similar to the present

Accord except that the risk weights are revised depending upon the rating of the counter-parties by external credit rating agencies. There is also greater differentiation across risk categories. In the IRB approach, banks calculate their own risk exposures through internal models and these exposures are converted into a single numerical component of risk-weighted assets in a prescribed manner.

Regarding the first pillar, several reservations have been expressed. With respect to the standard approach to credit risk, a major objection has been to the involvement of external rating agencies in the regulatory process. Many developing countries iincluding India have taken objections to this. This shows a certain lack of faith in the rating agencies. Besides, in a country like India, only a small fraction of even the large borrowers is rated. In fact some of the rating agencies themselves are not in favour of their ratings to become part of the regulatory regime. This could be from the fear that such an involvement could lead to the ratings of the raters. On the other hand, the implementation of the IRB approach will involve substantial upgradation of the management information systems and risk management systems within the banks. A bank would need several core inputs for each credit facility such as the probability of default and the expected loss rate given a default. Apart from the complexity of the models that would be required to assess and measure risk, the possibility of manipulating the internal models by the banks to their own advantage cannot also be ruled out. Perhaps in the Indian situation, the best option would be to adopt a modification of the standard approach with the exclusion of the intervention of external agencies in determining risk weights. This is basically Basle I plus capital for operational risk. However, this should not preclude or underestimate the need for banks and other financial institutions to evolve and put in place appropriate risk assessment models. Supervisors should encourage banks and possibly even lay down a time table for at least the significant banks' to adopt the internal ratings based approach.

Basle II—Pillar II: Supervisory Review Process

The supervisory review, as envisaged under the Basle-II, points to the need for banks to assess their capital adequacy positions relative to their overall risks including those for which no capital is maintained and for supervisors to review and take appropriate action in response to those assessments. Supervisors are required to take a comprehensive view on how banks handle the risk management and internal capital allocation process. On such a review, supervisors could require banks to hold higher than the minimum regulatory capital. The supervisory review process in the Indian context is critical given the longer transition required to move to more sophisticated risk management approaches under Pillar I. This review will enable supervisors to assess banks' economic capital and not just the regulatory capital.

Basle II—Pillar III: Market Discipline

The potential of market discipline to complement capital regulation depends on the disclosure of reliable and timely information that would allow market participants to access key information about a bank's risk profile and level of capitalisation. Underpinning meaningful disclosures is use of sound accounting and valuation standards. The information which should be disclosed has been classified under six categories. The disclosures envisaged are to be made available on a semi-annual basis. In India, the disclosures are mostly quantitative and it is now opportune to introduce more qualitative disclosures such as risk management policies.

Supervision

The supervisory system is an integral part of the oversight over financial institutions. It is as part of the effort to strengthen the supervisory system, the prudential norms evolved. They formed part of what the Basle Committee called 'Core Principles for Effective Banking Supervision'. Supervision over the different segments of the financial system has always existed. Central Banks, the world over had regarded supervision of banks as a key function, even though there is some shift in thinking in recent times. In the case of banks, the main objectives of supervision are enshrined in the acronym CAMELS. For maintaining the safety and soundness of banks, supervision looks at six important dimensions of the functioning of banks. These are: capital adequacy, asset quality, management soundness, earnings and profitability, liquidity and sensitivity to market risk. In relation to each of these dimensions, there are several prescribed norms and bank supervisors try to see how far banks conform to these standards.

Process and Mechanism

The mechanism of supervision varies from country to country. In India, as in many other countries, on-site inspection is an important part of the supervisory process. However, it is based on historical data and is in a sense backward looking. It is also transaction based. While these are important and need to be pursued, if not as elaborately as before, on-site inspection has to be supplemented by off-site surveillance which has the advantage that it helps to continuously monitor the functioning of the institutions. The results of on-site analysis can be fine-tuned with the latest off-site data. By helping to monitor continuously the behaviour of several ratios, off-site surveillance becomes a better check on the efficiency and adequacy of management practices in banks.

An important development in the supervisory process is the move from an inspection which is transaction based and directed towards verifying compliance with prudential norms to supervisory framework that puts a greater emphasis on the accountability of bank boards and top management to formulate and implement effective risk management system. Such a shift in approach pre-supposes that banks have established the required risk management practices and controls. The Reserve Bank of India (RBI) in line with many other central banks had also issued risk management guidelines to banks. A full-fledged risk management system besides assessing and measuring risk must also include effective internal controls for prompt housekeeping and preventive measures against frauds. In countries which have moved to risk based supervision, the supervisory imposition and punishments are severe even for small violations. In the present stage, in the evolution of the banking system in developing countries like India, risk based supervision can only supplement on-site inspection and off-site surveillance, both of which are required to ensure compliance with prudential norms and to prevent individual transgressions. Needless to say, the implementation of risk based supervision would also require upgrading the technology support as well as skills of the supervisory staff in the central banks.

Increasingly another issue that is being debated is how far market forces can be used to supplement the regulatory system. The third pillar of Basle-II talks of market discipline as aiding regulation of banks. This is sought to be achieved by making available to all information relating to the functioning of banks. The BIS had identified six sets of information that should be made available to all. Such a transparency is expected to compel individual institutions to manage their affairs prudently and their counter-parties to exercise appropriate discipline. This has sometimes been described as 'incentive-compatible financial regulation'. However, there are very few countries which depend exclusively on market forces to achieve the supervisory ends. Perhaps New Zealand is the only country which has gone the farthest in using the market discipline. Self-regulatory organisations which have a long history in relation to capital markets have not been of much success in regulating the capital market. At best the availability of information can play only a supplementary role. An interesting issue that arises in this context is how much of the information that comes into the possession of central banks should be revealed to the public. The central banks through inspection reports and direct contacts have access to a wide variety of information about individual banks. So too other regulators with respect to their respective institutions over which they have control. Sometimes, regulators also send certain warning signals to individual institutions. A complete silence on all of these will be inappropriate. At the same time, the central banks or any other regulator should not precipitate the very crisis they want to avoid. The timing of the release of the information is critically important. There is as yet no consensus on this. But the RBI has to take a lead to determine how far it will go.

Macro-Prudential Indicators

Another improvement in the supervisory process has been the introduction of macro prudential indicators to assess the soundness and vulnerability of the financial system. The emphasis here is on assessing the system rather than the individual institutions. These macro prudential indicators comprise of (a) aggregated micro-prudential indicators on the health of individual financial institutions, and (b) macroeconomic variables associated with the financial system soundness (Evans *et al.*, 2000). The indicators of financial soundness developed in relation to individual financial institutions have been referred to earlier. These indicators relate to six dimensions of supervisory oversight. While some of the financial soundness indicators measure the capacity of the system to absorb loss, others monitor vulnerability. A question that is relevant is whether an aggregation of financial soundness indicators is needed, if in relation to each individual institution, these indicators are at appropriate levels. Is there any additional information that comes out of aggregation? It is quite possible to envisage situations when the aggregated picture reveals vulnerability which may not be thrown up by looking at the ratios of individual institutions separately. For example, when we aggregate capital adequacy ratios, the aggregated picture includes not only the average of the ratios but also their dispersion. The frequency distribution of the ratio will throw additional light. While examining sectoral credit concentration under asset quality, the aggregated picture alone will reveal the vulnerability. Once again, it is the aggregation of the credit provided by all banks which will reveal how far the credit system is stretched. Thus, the supervisors gain by looking at the aggregated picture.

The operation of financial system depends on the overall economic activity and, therefore, the behaviour of certain macroeconomic variables need to be watched as part of the supervisory process. Macro-prudential indicators, therefore, include several macroeconomic variables such as those relating to economic growth, balance of payments, inflation, interest and exchange rates and lending and asset price behaviour. Macro-prudential analysis should therefore include stress tests and scenario analysis to determine the sensitivity of the financial sector to macroeconomic shocks. Some of the macroeconomic indicators can signal imbalance that may affect the financial system and, therefore, serve as lead indicators. Many research studies have been undertaken to understand the relationship between macroeconomic variables and financial crisis.

An analysis of the key relationships among financial soundness indicators is necessary to assess the impact of the shocks to financial soundness. A change in one indicator can affect another. For example, an increase in non-performing loans could lead to additional provisioning and thereby reducing the available capital. It is also necessary to monitor risks to financial system stability on account of developments in the corporate and household sector or exposure to non-banking financial intermediaries and real estate markets.

Single versus Multiple Regulators

Another issue in the system of supervision relates to the regulation of financial institutions such as banks whose activities are no longer confined to the provision of a single financial service. In recent years, market forces have led to the formation of financial groups that provide a range of financial services—banking, securities and insurance—across jurisdictions. Diversified financial groups are thus becoming the dominant institutional structure in the financial services industry, including in India. Diversification through ownership linkages, raises additional supervisory concerns, the principal of which are contagion, transparency, regulatory arbitrage and conflicts of interest. In response, financial sector supervisors have supplemented their traditional approach of supervising individual group entities on a 'solo-basis' with 'consolidated supervision'. Consolidated supervision may be broadly defined as a quantitative and qualitative evaluation of the strength of a financial group. It allows financial sector supervisors to better understand the relationship among the different group entities and assess the potential for adverse developments in one part of the group affecting the operation of others. Prudential regulations such as capital adequacy, large exposures and risk concentration are assessed on group basis. However, so long as there are different regulators overseeing different financial services, a single institution or group offering more than one service will come under the supervisory review of several authorities. It is in this context, the concept of a 'lead regulator' has emerged. Under such circumstances, coordination among the authorities is required both at the policy and operational levels. There has to be an extensive exchange of information including inspection reports among the authorities.

Given the emergence of conglomerates, some countries are moving towards a single regulatory authority for all financial services. The creation of the Financial Supervisory Authority (FSA) in the United Kingdom, announced in May 1997, provided an enormous impetus for the establishment of single regulators in many other countries, given the role of London as one of the leading financial centres around the globe. There were several teething problems in setting up the single authority in the UK. However, it is understood that the system is functioning more smoothly now. Under a single regulatory authority regime, the focus of supervision may get blurred, since the supervisory objective varies from one type of institution to another. It has been argued that in the case of banks, there are some special advantages in vesting the supervision of banks in the central bank (Goodhart, 2000). The disadvantage of a single authority is that it becomes unwieldy. Because of the enormity of the work involved, effective supervision of the various components may become difficult. Such a system can function efficiently only in countries where the various individual regulatory authorities had already achieved certain levels of maturity in terms of supervision. In India, we have at the present moment, a coordinating mechanism among the regulators which operate primarily at the policy level and through technical committees at the operational level. While for the present, this arrangement of independent authorities may be the most workable scheme, eventually, we would also have to move towards a single authority supervising over the various financial service providers. Also in the meanwhile, the coordinating mechanism has to be further strengthened at the operational level through exchange of information.

Regulating Payment and Settlement Systems

Payment and settlement mechanism is a crucial component of any financial system and ensuring the integrity of the payment systems is a key central banking function. The efficiency with which the finance flows and the security and stability of these flows ultimately determine the impact of intermediation process on economic performance. They also affect the liquidity in the system and in the process impinge upon the transmission mechanism of monetary policy. The objective of an efficient payment and settlement system is to secure final settlement of all transactions in order to remove an important source of uncertainty in the financial system.

Payment systems may propagate disturbances because problems with one member are likely to have direct and rapid effects on other members. It can lead to unexpected financial exposures for members. Payment obligations generated in a particular market, if not honoured on time, will affect not only the financial entities in that market but also the liquidity and stability of other markets. Thus the robustness of the payment system is critical for financial stability.

Macroeconomic Stability

As already indicated, the functioning of the financial system rests on the functioning of the real sector. Therefore, financial stability can be achieved only if they operate in a suitable environment. Every economy needs to grow. However, this must happen without causing serious upheavals. Growth with stability is not a contradiction in terms. Stability here refers to modest rates of inflation, acceptable level of fiscal deficit and orderly conditions in the foreign exchange market. Many of the problems faced by the financial system in the 1970s and 1980s were due to high and fluctuating rate of inflation. The need for hedges against inflation became necessary. Again, disorderly conditions in the foreign exchange market can lead to disturbing changes in the balance sheets of financial institutions. While markets have evolved products to provide cover for foreign exchange rate and interest rate fluctuations, for the system, as a whole, there is no escape. Thus, a policy framework relating to inflation and exchange rate management has a key role to play in ensuring financial stability.

As indicated earlier, the two sectors with which the financial system is closely associated are the household and corporate sectors. In developing countries like India, the household sector is a surplus sector. The corporate sector is the main borrower and, therefore, what affects the corporate sector has an immediate affect on the financial system. The standards maintained by the corporate sectors are, therefore, of relevance to the financial system. While lending institutions themselves compel the corporate sector entities to conform to certain standards, the recent revelations in several countries of the manipulation of accounts by well known corporates have brought to the fore issues of corporate governance. The need for accountability on the part of the management to various stakeholders including the shareholders, the public and the financial institutions has assumed importance. The accounting profession has also come in for severe criticism. Market discipline requires that the market is supplied with information that is credible and can be depended upon. This has become all the more important in the context of the changing structure of financial system with capital markets and traded securities playing a greater role in the allocation of capital. Thus, stability in the financial sector requires not only norms and standards to be maintained by the financial institutions but also corporate entities who borrow heavily from the financial system and the general public.

Crisis Prevention and Crisis Management

The purpose of regulation is to keep the volatility in check. Nevertheless, the authorities must know how to act when a crisis is brewing and when it actually hits the system. There has been a considerable discussion on crisis prevention and crisis management measures at home and abroad in recent times. In a broad sense, all the standards that are prescribed and the supervisory mechanism that is in place are intended to prevent crisis. In fact, recognising the fact that financial soundness indicators may show deterioration in individual institutions, several regulatory authorities have initiated what is known as 'prompt corrective action' programme. Under such a system when norms fall below a level, action is triggered and the central banks intervene through a set of mandatory actions to stem further deterioration in the health of the banks showing signs of weakness. In India, the RBI instead of placing reliance on a single trigger point such as capital adequacy, have set two more trigger points which serve as early warning signals. However, certain specific issues need to be tackled when signs of a crisis make their appearance. It is here that the roles of 'safety nets' and 'lender of last resort' (LOLR) come into picture. The most classic example of a 'safety net' is deposit insurance which protects depositors up to a limit in case of failure by a bank. The existence of a safety net ensures continued confidence in a bank. However, there is a 'moral hazard' problem. The potential for imprudent behaviour increases when such a cover exists. Several proposals have been made to limit the 'moral hazard' problem. Similarly 'the lender of last resort' function which has always been recognised as an integral part of the functions of a central bank since the days of Bagetrot, is meant to provide support to banks in times of need. The 'need' in normal times is different from 'need' in extraordinary circumstances. In the former situation, central banks have less difficulty in providing support. In the latter situation, support may be needed by several banks at the same time. As these safety nets provide liquidity, an imminent crisis can be averted only if the problem is one of liquidity. Timely action through the use of 'safety nets' can prevent contagion and limit the spread of a difficulty faced by a single institution from becoming a systemic problem. Although, in the case of LOLR, a distinction is made between illiquidity and insolvency, it is not easy to determine the problem in practical terms. There is also a moral hazard problem of too big to fail syndrome. Nevertheless every regulatory authority should have a policy towards safety nets which should include a well designed set of procedures to deal with demands of liquidity.

The same set of issues is faced more intensely, when a crisis actually hits. The first concern of authorities must be to prevent the contagion spreading. This, however, poses a dilemma. If a central bank or a regulatory authority takes extraordinary steps to bail out a single institution to avert contagion, it can invite criticism. The criticism will be louder, if the effort ultimately fails. The protection of the integrity of the payment system can become a dominant objective at times of crisis. Public sector intervention should be kept to the minimum compatible with addressing the crisis. Not all situations of crisis arise purely out of liquidity needs. Disturbances in foreign exchange market can occur for a variety of reasons, some of which can be due to inappropriate policy stances. Therefore, some policy corrections may be called for. Also at the policy level, some conflicts can arise between other objectives and financial stability objective. A balance will have to be struck by policy makers. This takes us to an important issue relating to monetary policy.

Monetary Policy and Financial Stability

In a broad sense, financial stability is very much an objective of monetary policy. Monetary authorities influence the economy through changes in the cost and availability of credit and money. The effectiveness of monetary policy actions depends upon the financial infrastructure in the country. Imperfections in the financial system can defeat or dilute the intentions of monetary authorities. A network of well functioning banks and other financial institutions is a necessary prerequisite for the efficient conduct of monetary policy. A stable financial system is, therefore, an important concern of monetary authorities. The objective of price stability which has become a dominant concern of most central banks facilitates financial stability. Financial institutions grow faster in a stable price environment which promotes savings and investment. As already noted, financial instability if it leads to a real crisis involves heavy cost both in terms of fiscal burden and output loss. There is, therefore, a strong ground to treat financial stability as part of the objectives of monetary policy. This raises two questions. How can a central bank identify the situation when it has to intervene from the point of view of financial stability? Second, can any action that is called for from the angle of financial instability come into conflict with other objectives? (Laker, 1999). As for the identification of the appropriate time to intervene, the central bank faces the same dilemmas as it does in relation to other objectives. For example, the timing of the change in interest rate or money supply to correct the 'overheating' of the economy has always been a difficult decision. Monetary authorities have often been criticised for having acted 'too late' or 'too early'. However, central banks do decide when to intervene taking into account a wide variety of factors. With respect to financial stability what the central banks need to prevent is the excessive build up and the subsequent unwinding of imbalances. The authorities must be willing to tighten policy, when they perceive excessive build up of financial imbalances. Much effort is called for to identify the nature of imbalances and to determine when they are excessive. Judging asset price behaviour particularly in the stock market, is a difficult task. Nevertheless, regulators including the central bank need to evolve appropriate indicators which can reveal persistent deviation from the fundamentals. ·

The second issue of conflict with other objectives may arise not because of fundamental concerns but because of indicators showing contradictory signals. For example, a serious imbalance may be building up in the stock market. Stock prices may be booming. However, at the same time, the inflation situation may be benign. The question is whether monetary authorities should tighten policy, even though near term inflation pressures are not apparent. For one thing, such a contradiction arises because the price indices normally used do not include asset prices such as those of stock and real estate. A situation where conventional price index is subdued but asset prices are rising has been aptly described as 'disguised overheating'. Of course, a central bank tightening monetary policy when near-term inflation prospects are low, can be accused of aborting real growth. However, this will be true only by taking a very short term view. If the financial imbalances have to be wound up later, it can cause a much greater output loss. All these are difficult judgment calls. At an analytical level, what can be said is that anticipations regarding financial instability need to be taken into account while deciding monetary action.

Many central banks bring out an 'Inflation Report' at periodic intervals. Some central banks in recent years also bring out semi-annually financial stability reports. The Norwegian Central Bank in its Financial Stability Report focuses on three aspects: (a) macroeconomic developments of particular importance for financial stability such as developments in debt, assets prices and the debt servicing capacity of borrowers, (b) Banks' earning and financial strength and the risk picture banks face, and (c) Developments in financial institutions other than banks. At the end, an overall qualitative assessment of risk magnitude is made. It also indicates the direction risk has moved since the previous report. The inflation report should not be confined to a discussion of the sectoral trends. It must deal with aggregate demand pressures in relation to aggregate supply and point to the possibility of achieving any goal set. The Financial Stability Report, besides analysing the trends in different markets, must make some assessment of the risk profile and pressures faced by the different segments of the financial system.

The RBI brings out several publications at periodic intervals. Apart from the Annual Report, there is the Report on Currency and Finance which now focuses on a specific theme each time and the Report on Trend and Progress of Banking in India. Besides, there are bi-annual monetary and credit policy statements. While in a sense, these reports in totality do bring out substantial set of information and perceptions on the financial system, there is some advantage in RBI brining out separately every quarter an Inflation Report and at least initially semi-annually, a Financial Stability Report.

The purpose of this paper is to highlight some of the analytical issues relating to financial stability. The objective of banking sector reform in this country has been to improve the productivity of the system. The paper has, however, not addressed the international dimensions of the problem. The need for the creation of an appropriate international financial architecture to deal with the problem of contagion has been discussed extensively in the literature. Returning to banking reform in this country, the focus was on efficiency, as stability was not perceived as an issue or concern. In the period since 1991, there have been a number of disruptions to the financial system in India. These episodes of financial distress point to the need for: (a) enlarging the legal framework of regulation to include all segments of the financial system, (b) moving towards internationally accepted prudential norms and other standards of transparency and disclosure, and (c) strengthening the supervisory system to take effective preventive actions. A number of significant steps have been taken in all these areas. Worldwide also, these have been the trends. While the regulatory system lays down the rules, it is the supervisory system that ensures their implementation. A regulatory system is only as good as its implementation. What is needed is to evolve a system that will improve the ability to detect sources of vulnerability and to take timely corrective measures. That will pave the way for financial stability.

References

Bank for International Settlements (2003). *Consultative Document—The New Basel Capital Accord*, April.

Bean, Charles (2004). "Asset Prices, Monetary Policy and Financial Stability: A Central Banker's View", paper presented at the AEA Conference, San Diego.

Berger, Allen N. and Gregory F. Udell (2003). "The Institutional Memory Hypothesis and the Procyclicality of Bank Lending Behaviour", *BIS Working Papers* No. 125, January.

Borio, Claudio (2004). "The Elusive Search for Monetary and Financial Stability", inaugural Keynote Address of the Sixth Money and Finance Conference organised by IGIDR at Mumbai, March 25-27.

Caruana, Jaime (2004). "Basel II—A New Approach to Banking Supervision", *BIS Review* 33, pp. 1-9.

Craig, Sean and V. Sundarajan (2003). "Using Financial Soundness Indicators to Assess Risks to Financial Stability", *mimeo*.

Crockett, Andrew (1997). "Why is Financial Stability a Goal of Public Policy?", paper presented at the Federal Reserve Bank of Kansas City's 1997 Symposium, *"Maintaining Financial Stability in a Global Economy"*, in Jackson Hole, Wyoming, August 28-30.

———. (2002). "Strengthening the International Financial Architecture", lecture delivered at ASCII, Hyderabad, January 28.

Das, Udaibir S. *et al.* (2004). "Does Regulatory Governance Matter for Financial System Stability? An Empirical Analysis", *IMF Working Paper* No. 04/89, May.

Evans, Owen *et al.* (2000). "Macroprudential Indicators of Financial System Soundness", *IMF Occasional Paper* No. 192, International Monetary Fund, Washington, DC.

Goodhart, Charles A.E. (2000). "Whither Central Banking?", *Eleventh C.D. Deshmukh Memorial Lecture*, organised by Reserve Bank of India at Mumbai, December 7.

Hemming, Richard *et al.* (2003). "Fiscal Vulnerability and Financial Crises in Emerging Market Economies", *IMF Occasional Paper* No. 218, International Monetary Fund, Washington, DC.

Hoggarth, Glenn and Victoria Saporta (2001). "Costs of Banking System Instability: Some Empirical Evidence", *Financial Stability Review*, June, Bank of England, pp. 148-165.

Laker, J.F. (1999). "Monitoring Financial System Stability", *Reserve Bank of Australia Bulletin*, October, Reserve Bank of Australia, pp. 1-13.

Nachane, D.M. *et al.* (2000). "Capital Adequacy Requirements and the Behaviour of Commercial Banks in India: An Analytical and Empirical Study", *RBI Development Research Group Study* No. 22, Reserve Bank of India, Mumbai.

Nachane, D.M. (2003). "Basel Accord II: Implications for the Indian Banking System", *Bank Quest*, October-December, pp. 47-54.

Norges Bank (2003). *Financial Stability*, 2/2003, November.

Rangarajan, C. (2001). "Financial Reforms and Stability: Systemic Issues", speech at the Asian Regional Seminar on *Financial Sector Reforms and Stability* at ASCII, Hyderabad, March 29.

Reddy, Y.V. (2002). "Choice between Single and Multiple Regulators of the Financial System", in *Lectures on Economic and Financial Sector Reforms in India*, OUP, New Delhi.

Stiglitz, Joseph E. (1994). "The Role of the State in Financial Markets", proceedings of the World Bank Annual Conference on Development Economics 1993, IBRD/World Bank.

Stiglitz, Joseph and Bruce Greenwald (2003). *Towards a New Paradigm in Monetary Economics*, Cambridge University Press.

19

The Emerging Configuration in the Financial Sector

S.S. TARAPORE

It is now over 10 years, since the financial sector reforms were launched. The time is now apposite to undertake a transparent and realistic stocktaking essentially to ensure enduring and sustainable reforms. It would only be fair to acknowledge that a lot has been achieved over the past decade and if the visible problems of the financial sector today appear more daunting than a decade ago, it is not as if nothing has been achieved. All that has happened is that the regulatory standards have been made more exacting and the system is-revealing more of the truth. Banks and non-bank financial intermediaries are facing challenges in that competition is intensifying while barriers between different segments of the financial system are breaking down. In this context, all segments have to recognise that there is a paradigm shift which is putting into trail certain basic and irreversible changes. The watchword is going to be efficiency of operations and the bottom line would be the ultimate test of performance. The course of developments in the financial sector will also depend on the macro perspective and the legislative framework. For any meaningful assessment of the likely financial sector developments we need to make some reasonable assumptions and forecasts of developments in the economy.

Macro-Perspective

A realistic assumption for the next five years should be that the real rate of growth will average in the 6-7 per cent range and this should be considered as a very good performance. This would be dubbed as pessimistic but when dealing with the financial sector, we need to be hard-nosed and eschew from any sentimental dreams and aspirations which are not backed up by the necessary pre-requisites. We should also recognise that over the next five years, there would not be any material improvement in the fisc. It is not as if one is assuming that there would not be any attempts at fiscal rectitude. All that is implied is that any efforts made in the ensuing period are unlikely to yield any positive results in the next 3-5 years. Translated into the impact on the financial sector, it could be assumed that the already large and rising government borrowing programme would continue to have an overarching impact on the financial sector. It would be dangerous if the financial sector were to pay heed to the cheer squads calling for a 10 per cent real growth rate. With the unleashing of strong consumerist forces and the repeated assaults in recent years on savers, there is absolutely no possibility of an increase in the household sector savings—income ratio. Thus, a sharp increase in the real rate of growth is nothing but a pipe dream.

Legislative Progress

Given the political configuration, legislation relating to the financial sector is not going to have easy passage through the Parliamentary process. The enactment of the Fiscal Responsibility Bill, the amendment of the banking laws, the IDBI corporatisation and the abrogation of the UTI Act are all unlikely to reach the stage of enactment. One would fervently hope that this assessment is totally wrong and that all these salutary legislative changes will be put through successfully—but the ground realities are very different. The likelihood is that these enactments just will not take place or, if enacted, they would be significantly watered down.

The Securitisation and Reconstruction of Financial Assets and Enforcement of Security Interest Ordinance, 2002 has been repromulgated. This is indeed a laudatory effort by the government but there are fears that vested interests will ensure that it is checkmated in the parliamentary process. After decades, when the legal system was stacked against the lenders, the ordinance attempts to bring about a semblance of order in the financial system. In terms of protection of legitimate lender rights, the ordinance does try to rectify the fundamental flaws in the system. In no other country can a defaulter simply walk away after incurring a large liability without facing the consequences. Borrowers must realise that the financial system has been damaged by the nonchalant attitude of borrowers and in the ultimate analysis, borrowers have irreparably hurt the interests of the mass of savers who have entrusted their hard-earned savings to bank and non-bank intermediaries. While borrowers can use their muscle power to prevent the proposed legislative from being enacted, savers can revolt, and equally financial intermediaries can be sticky when it comes to lending. As such, borrowers would be well advised to limit their articulation to a few legitimate safeguards rather than attempting a total stalling of the proposed legislation. It is not the divine right of borrowers to access funds from the financial system and it is not obligatory on the part of banks and institutions to lend to borrowers who are not credit-worthy.

The problem of the Indian system, is that entrepreneurs have got habituated to unsustainable large borrowing with minimal owned funds. Any successful entrepreneur must realise that borrowing should only be the icing on the cake and internal generation should form the predominant element. Thus, the question which needs to be posed is not how to stimulate the flow of funds from intermediaries to industry but how industry can become self-financing. Making interest rates too attractive and credit too easy to obtain is a sure path to disaster.

In the recent period, good initiatives have been taken to set up Asset Reconstruction Companies (ARCs). The first of these has gone beyond the drawing boards. While these initiatives need to be encouraged, a drawback is that primary lenders have taken the lead in setting up the ARC and the consanguinity does give considerable discomfort. It would be best to have ARCs promoted by institution which are not primary lenders.

How Really Large is the Financial Sector Hole?

If the numbers are to be believed, the scheduled commercial banks non performing assets (NPAs) as a percentage of advances in March 2001 were 11.4 per cent (gross) and 6.2 per cent (net). Increasingly it is being recognised that these numbers lack creditability. Transparency and good corporate governance are the new *mantras* and we all swear that our numbers tell the truth and nothing but the truth. It is time this charade is called for what it is and we recognise that our norms do still have a considerable element of softness and the truth serum has not really been applied to the financial sector. There are large tracts of NPAs tucked away in the standard assets. There is a conspiracy of silence to which borrowers, financial intermediaries and the supervisors are a party. I am well aware that such a statement will cause apoplexy in many circles but the time has come to remove the *purdah* from NPAs.

It is not as if the banks are the only ones with NPAs. In all probability, the non-bank financial intermediaries carry an even larger burden of NPAs. In the first flush of revealing the NPAs, the government provided about Rs. 20,000 crore by way of bank recapitalisation. Recapitalising banks, which in turn invested in government paper, was initially considered as fiscally neutral. It is now increasingly recognised that all this arrangement provided is a deferred fiscal liability. From 1998-2001, the government stoutly defended the stance that it would no longer bail-out the financial system. In the wake of the problems of the Unit Trust of India (UTI), the Industrial Finance Corporation of India (IFCI) the Industrial Development Bank of India (IDBI) and the co-operative banks, it has no longer been possible for the government to keep its earlier resolve not to come to the aid of the financial sector. From an outside assessment, it would appear that the government would have to provide a minimum of Rs. 30,000 crore to ease the pain of the financial sector. This appears to be a gross underestimate and the eventual burden over the next three to four years could be significantly higher. It is necessary to undertake a holistic assessment of the burden on the fisc. It is only after a transparent assessment that the options can be meaningfully assessed by the government. The concept of closure is not something which is countenanced in the Indian system and we are too easily intimidated by the costs and consequences of closure and, therefore, give in too easily to artificial props from the government. In such a situation, there will be repeated and unending bouts of recapitalisation of financial intermediaries and the fisc, which is already weak, will bleed. I am well aware that the figure of Rs. 30,000 crore will be competently rubbished by the authorities. Admittedly, the government support would be staggered and it would be argued that support for different types of institutions cannot be clubbed. But the fact remains that the fisc is one and it cannot pass the buck. While there is considerable euphoria that in 2001-02 all banks, which were earlier in the red have shown substantial improvement, it is clear that this is largely attributed to the bonanza on investments in government paper. This cannot repeat and in 2002-03 a number of banks will be back in the red and would turn to the government for *largesse*.

The Future Configuration of the Financial Sector

While it is difficult to portend the future there are some parameters which would point to the directional changes in the configuration of the Indian financial system in the next few years.

Public Sector Banks

The public sector banks are still predominant in the Indian financial sector and will continue to do so in the next five years. The constraint on their growth would be that internal generation would not be adequate and fresh injection of capital would face a major roadblock. The government would be bleeding providing funds to bail-out weaker banks and institutions and thus be unable to provide additional capital to the performing banks. At the same time, the government is unlikely to be able to put through legislative changes reducing the public sector holding to a minimum of 33 per cent. Thus, there would be a constraint on the growth of public sector banks but, nonetheless, these banks would continue to account for the predominant share of financial activity. What then should their strategy be? These banks should concentrate on quality business and eschew their so called social role, wherein they have become the repository of all the ills of the Indian economy. These banks should not show extra zeal in mobilising relatively high cost deposits as their fund-based activity would give way to non-fund activity thereby altering their asset-liability profile. This may sound an extremely pessimistic assessment but if the public sector banks are to avoid endemic sickness, consolidation rather than growth should be their objective.

Issues of corporate governance and board accountability would come to the fore. Boards of public sector banks need to recognise that the current milieu is not sustainable wherein the invisible hand dictates board decisions when the going in good and the accusative finger points to board members when the going gets tough. Boards of banks now do not have a choice; they must stand up and be counted. The boards should push at the limits to make these banks essentially board-run banks and the Chief Executive Officer (CEO) should be genuinely accountable to the board. This is easier said than done, but the Ganguly Report does provide a basis for credible action.

Private Sector Banks

The stronger private sector banks would continue to grow but even after another five years, these banks would still account for a small segment of the financial sector. Privatisation is often claimed to be a panacea but a sobering thought for the government is that ultimately, when bail-outs have to be worked out in the financial sector, the experience the world over is that governments have to bail-out both public and private sector financial organisations.

Foreign Banks

Although limits for foreign direct investment and foreign institutional investment are quite liberal in the Indian financial sector, the real constraint on the growth of foreign banks is the 15 per cent cap on total market share. So long as this limit remains effective, foreign banks will remain minor players in the Indian financial sector. Given the constraints on providing capital to public sector banks and the clear limitations of Indian private sector banks—the few strong Indian private sector banks would no doubt continue to grow rapidly—there is no choice but to gradually raise the ceiling of foreign banks share of business from the present level of 15 per cent.

Financial Institutions (FIs)

There has been much talk about the future of FIs. In the ultimate analysis, the Narasimham Committee II dictum will prevail; FIs have to either become banks or non-bank financial companies—there is no third way.

Non-Bank Financial Companies (NBFCs)

An unusual feature of the Indian financial sector is that NBFCs also raise deposits. This is a historical aberration and sooner or later, an end would need to be put to this practice. In the first instance, all NBFCs of over Rs. 1,000 crore of deposits need to be given a definite time frame within which to convert themselves into banks and if they fail to do so their deposit taking activity would need to be curtailed. I am aware that the NBFCs would be up in arms but the time has come to effectively deal with the soft under-belly of the Indian financial system. The continued existence of Residuary Non-Banking Companies (RNBCs) is an outrage and RNBCs above a certain size, say Rs. 100 crore, should be required to fall in line with the regulatory framework for NBFCs. It is unconscionable that an RNBC, essentially a very weak NBFC, is allowed to accept unlimited deposits. An *amicus curiae* has to appeal to the Supreme Court to reconsider its 1987 verdict in today's milieu.

Cooperative Banks

The cooperative banks are quite clearly in shambles and the situation is far worse than the authorities and these banks would care to admit. There is little point in picking bones with the regulator/supervisor. The polity clearly stands indicted. I do not tire of repeating Alan Greenspan's dictum that "A financial system is as strong as its weakest link." If, in the next few years, the Indian financial system is to strengthen, it will have to distance itself from the cooperative banks. Hard decisions have to be taken. The issue whether cooperative banks should be allowed to be part of the payments/settlement system needs to be considered. The raising of this issue would no doubt create protests but that does not make the problem go away. A bank is a bank and 'cooperative' is only a form of ownership; and all banks must be subject to the same regulatory framework. The sooner this issue is headed off the better for the financial system.

Issues in Regulation and Supervision

In the past few years, there have been significant improvements in regulation and supervision. Regulation has moved away from the minutia of controls while supervision has become relatively more effective. Nonetheless, these improvements have just not been enough to meet the emerging situation.

The RBI had set out in some details, almost three years ago, an extremely sound framework for Prompt Connective Action (PCA) but this framework has yet to be fully operationalised. It is necessary that the PCA should be put in place immediately. What the PCA framework does is that corrective measures are put in place as soon as incipient signs of deterioration are observed in the financial sector. If such a process is actually put into practice, the authorities would not be faced with devastated institutions.

As a corollary to this, there is a need for full disclosures. The absence of adequate disclosures are an endemic problem the world over but, unfortunately, this drawback is even more accentuated in India. Any bank or non-bank financial institution, while raising resources from the public must be made to display, in simple terms understandable by the public, the performance of the organisation in relation to key parameters laid down by the RBI. All the transparency relating to the balance sheet is of little relevance as the general public does not have access to it and even when access is provided, the general public cannot comprehend the intricacies of the balance sheet. Regulators/supervisors often argue that if the public really comprehends the performance of the weaker elements in the financial sector, there would be an exodus of funds from these organisations. Far from fearing such repercussions, the regulator/supervisor should welcome such developments. The fear of loss of public confidence is the best adverse action and meaningful disclosures would be the most effective corrective action. To ensure this, no display or advertisement soliciting resources should be allowed without revealing of the performance of the organisation. For instance, juxtaposed to any soliciting of resources from the public should be disclosures on capital adequacy, losses if any, the extent of NPAs and adverse action by the regulator/supervisor.

When adverse action is taken by the regulator/supervisor, it should be contemporaneous to the violation. A system should evolve of pay and then talk and once the adverse action is confirmed the authorities should give wide publicity to the violation and the penalty thereon. It is the right of the regulator/supervisor to name and shame the perpetrator of the violation and to impose a cease and desist order. It is unfortunate that, in India, the authorities are reluctant to reveal to the public the adverse action taken by them. The fears of a panic in the financial system are unfounded. In fact, such an approach will give teeth to the regulator/supervisor and by virtue of that require only mild but timely adverse action.

Concluding Observations

The fact that this presentation focuses largely on problem areas and issues which have defied solutions should not be viewed as a negative approach. Identifying the problems in an open and transparent manner would contribute to their resolution. We cannot move forward unless we take decisive action to tackle the present problems.

Address delivered at Financial Sector Round Table organised by Economist Corporate Network and International Market Assessment India Pvt. Ltd.. Mumbai, August 28, 2002.

Economic Developments in India, Vol. 57.

20

Managing India's External Sector

Overcoming Challenges in a Globalising Economy

Y.V. REDDY

Merchandise Trade

A key objective of structural reforms instituted in the aftermath of the crisis of 1991 was to correct for the implicit anti-export bias built up during the first three and a half decades of planning and to reap the competitiveness and efficiency gains for the economy from a more open trade regime. What were the major elements of the reforms?

First, arrangements were put in place for the move towards a market determined exchange rate. Second, since 1992 the trade policy imbibed a medium-term perspective. Third, a key aspect of the trade reforms has been a substantial reduction in import tariff rates and a drastic rationalisation of the tariff structure, including their dispersion. Fourth, concerted efforts have been made to dismantle the panoply of non-tariff barriers that was predicated upon the balance of payments reasons under the GATT. Fifth, the Reserve Bank of India has undertaken several measures to ensure adequate and timely availability of bank credit for trade finance at competitive interest rates. Sixth, there has been a policy thrust for creating appropriate institutional arrangements for supporting a vigorous export drive. These include export processing zones, special economic zones, overseas banking units and technology parks.

India has engaged herself, constructively in multilateral trade negotiations under the WTO. Within its multilateral commitments, India has forcefully articulated its position which reflects the concerns of the developing countries. In tune with the worldwide spread of regional trading arrangements and our belief that such arrangements act as prelude to progressive multilateral trade liberalisation, India has entered into several preferential trade agreements.

These reforms in the trade policy regime have unlocked entrepreneurial energies. India's merchandise exports have been rising at a rate of over 20 per cent per annum, in US dollar terms, in recent years. As a result, the secular decline in India's share in world exports from 2 per cent in 1950 to 0.5 per cent in the 1980s has been halted. This share began rising in the 1990s and is currently at 0.8 per cent. The export strategy envisages a doubling of India's share in the world merchandise trade by 2008-09.

Services

Trade policy reforms undertaken since the 1990s have shed their traditional focus on merchandise trade and encompassed a wide range of tradable services, reflecting India's competitive advantage in business services, technical and professional services. The EXIM policies of recent years have selected services for special focus. India accepted the obligations under Article VIII of the IMF's Articles of Agreement and instituted current account convertibility in 1994. Besides, there has been a progressive liberalisation of the exchange control regime. Foreign direct investment (FDI) has been permitted in a host of services in order to take advantage of modern technology, with some restrictions on financial services, taking into account the current stage of development and openness. Further, increasing availability of speedier and cost-effective money transfer arrangements through the banking channels and post offices has resulted in significant increase in the use of formal channels for remittance transfers.

Exports of services have risen consistently, by over 20 per cent per annum in recent years. Within services exports, software and IT-enabled services have been growing at an average rate of 46 per cent annually since the mid-1990s. Over the years, skill content of Indian labour has been rising and the traditional markets of the Middle East have given way to the US, Europe and other industrialised countries. For the external sector, this natural advantage has translated into significant inflows in the form of remittances from Indians working abroad. Workers' remittances are nearly four per cent of India's GDP now and have provided considerable and sustained support to India's balance of payments.

Trade and Current Account

A discussion on the recent trends in trade and current account will perhaps be in order. A distinguishing feature of India's external sector developments during the fiscal year 2004-05 was the expansion of the merchandise trade deficit to more than five per cent of GDP from an average of a little below three per cent of GDP during 1990-2004. Underlying this expansion in the trade deficit was a surge in oil imports on the back of the soaring international crude oil prices and the pick up in investment demand as well as the growing strength of domestic industrial activity. This trend in imports may continue in view of the possible strengthening of upturn of activity in the economy. However, an intrinsic link between merchandise imports and exports has emerged and become entrenched so that the large expansion in imports is also spurring vigorous export growth. Given the recent experience, this order of the trade deficit appears to be manageable at this stage and is consistent with our growth aspirations.

Despite the large trade deficit, the current account recorded only a modest deficit of less than one per cent of GDP in 2004-05 after a continuous run of surpluses over the three-year period, 2001-2004. The high trade deficit during 2004-05 was to a large extent accommodated by the net invisible surplus at five per cent of GDP, supported by buoyant services exports and sustained remittances from migrant workers overseas. In fact, invisible surpluses have traditionally provided valuable support to India' s balance of payments and in recent years, they have taken on the character of a permanent component in the current account. It is in this context that we believe that the current account deficit is sustainable with enough headroom available for accommodating even higher levels of investment activity.

From a cross-country perspective, the Indian experience with managing the current account reveals some unique features. First, the lessons of the 1991 crisis brought forth policies which ensured a low current account deficit in the ensuing years. This approach stood us in good stead in warding off the contagion from the Asian crisis of 1997-98. Second, the sustainability of the current account was ensured by a policy choice for non-debt flows and emphasis on the consolidation and reduction of external debt. Third, the low current account deficit was underpinned by shifts in international competitiveness favouring software, IT exports and workers' remittances over traditional exports. Fourth, although the fiscal deficit remained somewhat inflexible, it was not allowed to spill over into the current account. Finally, the current account deficit, being the mirror image of the absorptive capacity, is best assessed over the business cycle rather than at discrete points.

Capital Account

Since the initiation of gradual liberalisation of the capital account in 1991, capital flows have been in excess of current account deficit (CAD) except, in

1992-93 and 1995-96, adding to the reserves. It is interesting to note that the stock of external debt came down steeply from 28.7 per cent of GDP at the end of March 1991 to 17.4 per cent by March 2005. The decline in debt reflected the policy-induced shift in the composition of the capital account in favour of non-debt flows. The level of short-term debt continues to be low at US$ 7.5 billion as at the end of March 2005. As regards the composition of capital flows, there is, of late, almost a total shift in favour of private flows. The foreign direct investment increased from less than one per cent of net capital flows in the 1980s to 20 per cent of net capital flows in 2004-05. Total portfolio investment flows on account of FIIs, GDRs and others were US$ 8.9 billion in 2004-05 on top of net inflows of US$ 11.4 billion in the preceding year.

In brief, given the adverse international experience with unfettered capital account liberalisation, we have been risk averse and have adopted a policy of active management of the capital account. The compositional shifts in the capital account have been consistent with the policy framework, imparting stability to the balance of payments. The sustainability of the current account is increasingly viewed as consistent with the volume of normal capital flows. The substitution of debt by non-debt flows also gives us room for manoeuvre since debt levels, particularly, external commercial borrowings, have been moderate and can be raised in the event of a sustained pick up in the demand for external resources. There is also the cushion available from the foreign exchange reserves.

Since non-debt creating flows are dominating, the emphasis is on encouraging inflows through foreign direct investment, and enhancing the quality of portfolio flows by strict adherence to what may be described as 'know your investor' principle. Further, in view of entrepreneurial skills in India and evolving synergies in a global economy, overseas investment by Indian corporates has been receiving a positive response. Further, prudential regulations over financial intermediaries, especially over banks, in respect of their foreign exchange exposures and transactions are a dynamic component of management of capital account as well as financial supervision.

Reserve Management

The adequacy of foreign exchange reserves is a relevant consideration in the management of the capital account. First, adequacy has to be viewed not only in terms of trade needs but also other short-term liabilities. Second, it is not merely the long-term or short-term debt in terms of original maturity that is relevant for reserves, but the profile of external debt in terms of residual maturity. A trade-related debt which is in the nature of collateralised debt may be less severe on reserve requirements. Third, any addition to portfolio flows may warrant comfort through some additions to reserves. In fact, there is merit in presuming that the flows are temporary till there is reason to judge them to be permanent. Fourth, it is necessary to recognise that reserves provide cushion to manage real and external sector shocks like oil prices. Fifth, there is usually an opportunity cost of maintaining foreign exchange reserves, but this must be weighed against the financial and non-financial costs associated with volatile and adverse exchange rate movements. Finally, while the optimal level of reserves is difficult to quantify, attention to level of reserves as a means of self-insurance is essential. In the final analysis, the adequacy of reserves needs to be assessed in terms of a medium-term perspective taking into account the possible levels of the current account deficits, the composition of capital flows, the level of international confidence in the ability of the country's payment position and pace and quality of growth. Viewed from all these perspectives, the current level of reserves continues to be comfortable.

The essence of portfolio management of reserves by the RBI is to ensure safety, liquidity and optimisation of returns. The reserve management strategies are periodically reviewed by the RBI in consultation with the government. In deploying reserves, attention is paid to the currency composition, duration and selection of instruments. While there is no set formula to meet all situations, the RBI applies sound portfolio management principles and risk management.

Exchange Rate Management

A major success in external sector management has been the transition from an administered exchange rate regime to a more flexible, market-based system. Under the new arrangements instituted in early 1993, the day-to-day movements in exchange rates are market determined. India's current exchange rate policy focusses on management of volatility without a fixed target, while allowing the underlying demand and supply conditions to determine the exchange rate movements over a period, in an orderly way. To this end, the RBI monitors closely the developments in the financial markets at home and abroad, and takes such monetary, regulatory and other measures as considered necessary from time to time.

The conduct of exchange rate policy is guided by three major purposes: first, to reduce excessive volatility in exchange rates, while ensuring that the movements are orderly; second, to help maintain an adequate level of foreign exchange reserves and third, to help eliminate market constraints with a view to developing a deep and liquid foreign exchange market. The policy is aimed at preventing destabilising speculation in the market while facilitating foreign exchange transactions at market rates for all permissible purposes.

There is a wide consensus that India's exchange rate policy has stood the test of time, despite several domestic and external developments, including the severe currency crises which characterised the 1990s. Recent international research on viable exchange rate strategies in emerging markets has lent considerable support to the exchange rate policy followed by India.

Global Economy and India

The debate in India has customarily been on the contours of the public policy in the context of increasing global economic integration. More recently, however, a debate in the rest of the world has been in evidence on the challenges likely to be faced by the global economy on account of progressively increasing global integration of the Indian economy. Hence, there is merit in looking at, perhaps illustratively, some of the global challenges of our integration while we move forward in this regard.

Over the next half-century, the population of the world will age faster than during the past half-century as fertility rates decline and life expectancy rises. In Europe, the demographic profile is already tilted towards the higher age group and by 2050, this is projected to accelerate. Projections suggest a turning point between 2010 and 2030 when the European Union, North America and Japan will experience a substantial decline in savings rate relative to investment which may be reflected in large current account deficits. Most of the high performers of East Asia and China are in the second stage of the demographic cycle. Elderly dependency is expected to double in these countries by 2025. Their working age populations will increase modestly first and then shrink. These projections suggest that East Asia could increasingly become an important supplier of global savings up to 2025; however, rapid population ageing thereafter would reinforce, rather than mitigate, the inexorable decline of global savings. India is entering the second stage of demographic cycle and over the next half-century, a significant increase in both savings rate and share of working age population is expected. The share of the labour force in population in India is expected to overtake the rest of Asia, including China, by 2030. Looking ahead, the rest of the world may increasingly rely on China and India for supplies of both labour and capital and this could significantly influence the evolution of the global economy. It is evident that China and India will have to give high priority to generating employment and both are poised for substantial increases in productivity.

The global economy will have to contend with the implications of these developments on prices, exchange rates, wages and structures of employment in industrialised countries. Over the medium term, it is felt that outsourcing will grow rapidly and may also cover high-end research and development activities. In manufacturing, China has emerged as a leader and India is catching up rapidly. Though agriculture is heavily subsidised in major industrialised countries, such subsidisation would be difficult to sustain from a fiscal point of view, since many of the countries concerned are poised to meet the mounting pension liabilities, not to speak of burgeoning health care costs of maintaining the deteriorating demographics. One sector where the industrialised economies continue to show considerable strength and dominance is the financial sector, partly attributable to the confidence factor in financial markets that favours the industrialised economies and traditional international financial centres. It is essential for India to carefully monitor the developments in both real and financial sectors, and to frame the policies in tandem with the global developments so that global integration continues to be a positive sum game for all countries.

Financial Integration

On the path of integrating the Indian financial markets with the global financial system, we have chosen to proceed cautiously and in a gradual manner, calibrating the pace of capital account liberalisation with underlying macroeconomic developments, the state of readiness of the domestic financial system and the dynamics of international financial markets.

Unlike in the case of trade integration, where benefits to all countries are demonstrable, in case of financial integration, a 'threshold' in terms of preparedness and resilience of the economy is important for a country to get full benefits. A judgmental view needs to be taken whether and when a country has reached the 'threshold' and the financial integration should be approached cautiously, preferably within the framework of a plausible roadmap that is drawn up by embodying the country-specific context and institutional features. In India, we have been adhering to a cautious and sure-footed approach in our reforms so far and there is merit in doing so since it enables us to avoid policy reversals on the one hand and build on the past strengths on the other.

The experience of the 1990s has shown that our approach to financial integration has stood the test of time. Even as we have embarked on a measured pace of financial liberalisation, we have ensured that we have a well-capitalised financial system by international standards, with low levels of loan delinquency. Our financial markets are orderly and smoothly functioning and the ability of our financial intermediaries to deal in various segments of the financial market spectrum is improving almost continuously.

The optimism generated by the recent gains in macroeconomic performance, warrants a balanced consideration of further financial liberalisation. Undoubtedly, it contributes to growth through enhancement of allocative efficiency in the use of resources, by promoting financial deepening and by expanding the volume of resource flow to the economy. At the same time, it is important to recognise the risks to the financial system emanating from stressed macroeconomic fundamentals such as those associated with fiscal deficit, inflation and uncertainties in international financial markets. Turbulence in the domestic financial systems tends to amplify related distortions and generates undesirable fluctuations in economic activities. Further, it also exposes the economy to external shocks and fluctuations in international business cycles. There could, therefore, be a trade-off in the initial stages while considering financial liberalisation and in policy terms, the trade-off takes the form of a choice between measured and premature financial liberalisation as also appropriate sequencing, the choice being contextual and often judgmental. In general, the downside of a premature financial liberalisation would be in the form of financial instability and associated social costs of disruption, which are significantly higher for a developing economy like India.

India has made significant progress in financial liberalisation since the institution of financial sector reforms in 1992 and this has been recognised internationally. External financial liberalisation, in particular, has expanded at a fairly rapid pace. At this stage, the optimism generated by impressive macroeconomic performance accompanied with stability, has given rise to pressures for significantly accelerating the pace of external financial liberalisation. It is essential to take into account the risks associated with it while resetting an accelerated pace of a gradualist approach.

First, India's public debt and fiscal deficit as a proportion of GDP is currently among the highest in the world, but it has been financed almost entirely from domestic savings. There is a commitment to fiscal consolidation in the medium term with the implementation of the Fiscal Responsibility and

Budget Management Act, 2003. In the interim, however, before embarking on any faster pace of external financial liberalisation, the possible spill-over effects of fiscal deficits into external sector need to be carefully evaluated.

Second, it is widely recognised that financial instability can lead to high variability in real activity and, as the Asian financial crisis has tellingly demonstrated, even cause interruptions in the growth process. Financial distress has resulted in macroeconomic and welfare losses. Resilience and flexibility in the real sector of the economy are essential to deal with surges of capital flows, large reversals and associated fluctuations in financial prices that become inevitable with accelerated liberalisation of financial sector. At present, some inflexibilities in pricing policies and restrictions on domestic trade constrain the response of the real sector. In general, therefore, low level of system flexibility, at the current juncture, is a major constraint on economic agents and financial market participants in responding to highly accelerated financial liberalisation and dealing with its downside risks.

Third, the adequacy of foreign exchange reserves is often cited as a consideration for significantly accelerating the pace of financial liberalisation. Foreign exchange reserves are, in the final analysis, a cushion to withstand both cyclical and unanticipated shocks. Therefore, reserve adequacy may be a necessary condition but not a sufficient one for speeding up financial liberalisation. There is a clearer recognition today that the net benefits from financial liberalisation in respect of any developing country would be enhanced only if complementary policies in non-financial sectors are followed.

Finally, the existing international financial architecture is not adequate to prevent or mitigate the domestic and external effects of financial crisis in large economies like India. The impact of instability in times of crisis appears largely to be borne by the home or domestic public sector rather than the global private sector. The issue of setting the pace of financial liberalisation revisits the issue of trade-off between sustained growth and a growth rate that could potentially turn volatile and unstable. While it is necessary to add to the pace of growth, it is also equally important to minimise the risks of instability and experience shows that more than desirable pace of financial liberalisation was often followed by financial instability and crises.

Thus, the recent experience in many countries shows that periods of impressive macroeconomic performance generate pressures for speedier financial liberalisation since everyone appears to be a gainer from further liberalisation, but the costs of instability that may get generated are borne by the country, the government and the poorer sections. Avoiding crises is ultimately a national responsibility. The approach to managing the external sector, the choice of instruments and the timing and sequencing of policies are matters of informed judgment, given the imponderables.

Conclusion

Over the years, India's commercial and financial linkages with the rest of the world have been increasing with trade liberalisation and openness on the capital account. This is reflected in the transmission of international impulses to the real sector and domestic financial markets. Trends in international prices have now significant influence on domestic prices. Indian corporates and institutions are increasingly accessing international markets with consequent diversification benefits. While this process has provided important opportunities, it has also brought in new challenges and risks, necessitating fine-tuning of macro policies in a much broader canvass and context. India is, thus, moving from a focus on managing external sector to implementing an optimal integration of domestic and external sectors, with the global economy.

Lecture delivered at the India Programme of The Foreign Policy Centre, London, June 23, 2005. *Economic Developments in India*, Vol. 90.

Index

A

access to
    a minimum level of education 103
    food 238, 243
    foreign technology 173
    irrigation 120
    sanitation 155
accountability 53, 156, 159, 165
    lack of 252
accounting standards 173
Acharya, Shankar 23, 24
administration, good 152
administrative efficiency 53
AEZs 285
affirmative action 127
    policies 123
Africa 169
Agarwal, Bina 125, 248
agricultural
    diversification 180
    employment 121
    growth 97, 187, 217, 222
        and diversification 216
    modernisation 181
    policies 25, 211, 217, 229
    price policy 251
    products, value addition in 188
    research 26
        and development 218
        and extension 180

agricultural
    sector 215
        opening up the 181
        slowdown in the 188
    subsidies 216
    technology 119
    trade liberalisation 225
agriculture 26, 180
    diversification of 188
    dynamic 242
    role of 188
    subsidisation of 181
    value added in 217
agro-based clusters 295, 296
agro-climatic regional plans 132
Ahluwalia, Montek S. 23, 58, 119
AICC 99
Allen, Lindsay 215
allocative efficiency 53
anaemia, incidence of 213
anaemia, Iron deficiency 213
Andersen, Per Pinstrup 25
Anglo-Saxon model 47
Annapurna programme 240
anti-dumping duties 152
anti-globalisation 20, 86
    policies 83
anti-market 20, 86
Antoydaya 238
    programme 240

Arab countries 148
artisan clusters 295, 296
Asian countries 31
Asian Development Bank 222
Asian economic crisis 215
assets, acquisition of 132
Asset Reconstruction Companies 355
aviation 45
Ayodhya 143, 150

B

Babri masjid 143
backward states 57, 58
balance of payments 22, 148, 151
    crisis in 1991 173
balance of power 152
BALCO 48
Bangalore 58, 144
bank credit 361
bank deposits 47
bank nationalisation 102
banking sector reform 29
Bardhan, P.K. 101, 125
basic minimum needs 102
Basle Capital Accord 337
    II 338
Basle Committee on Banking
    Supervision 337
Basu, Priya 48
Bengal famine of 1943 143
Berger, Allen N. 334
Berkoff, D.J.W. 256
Bhagwati, Jagdish 19, 20
Bhalla, Surjit 101
Bhalla, G.S. 211
Bhardwaj, Gautam 48
Bhatty, I.Z. 115
BIMARU states 53, 57
biotechnology 224, 251

bipartisan support 41
BJP 83, 165
black market 145
board accountability 357
Bombay 58, 144
Bombay University 147
BoP crisis 40
Borio, Claudio 334
Borlaug, Norman 221
brand names, domestic 322
Brazil 23, 170
breakpoint 36
Brewer, J. 253
BRIC 28, 263
Brihanmaharashtra College of
    Commerce 143
British 143
    capital 146
    managing agents 146
    rule 146
    treasury 144
broad-based growth 98
BSE 47
buffer stocks 243
buoyancy, export 40
bureaucrats 158
bureaucracy, role of the 138
Burki, S.J. 101
business environment 172
Business World 316

C

Calcutta 144
California 44
calorie deficiency 231, 234
calorie deprivation 234
calorie intake, mean 107
Calvo, A. Guillermo 38
capabilities 106

capital account 43
    active management of the 364
    liberalisation 194
capital adequacy 338
    ratio 337, 338
capital, availability of 171, 201
capital controls 43
capital flows 363
capital formation 302
capital-adequacy ratio 339
capital-intensive choice of techniques 83
Caruana 338
casualties of the mass riots of 1947 and 1948 143
central banks 350
Central Statistical Organisation 274
central tax revenue 283
CGIAR 251
Chambers, Robert 124
Chandigarh 58
Chandra, Nirmal 317
Chaudhuri, Sudip 298
Chaudhuri, Mrinal Datta 324
cheap money 145
checks and balances 20
child labour 289
child malnutrition 213, 219
China 23, 29, 70, 89, 159, 170
China's foreign investment regime 326
Chinese 60
Chopra, Kanchan 254
Chowdhury, Nuimmudin 225
CII-McKinsey Report 284
Cipla, Ranbaxy 298
civic amenities 68
civic groups 20, 69
civil servants 161
civil society 158

civilisation, ancient 93
civilised society 26
closed economies 24
cluster approach 296
cluster development 294
cluster formation 293
CMC 48
co-operative banks 356
coalition dharma 64
coalition governments 41
cold storage 188
communication technology 202
communism, collapse of 169
communist 165
community kitchens 95
comparative advantage 43, 200
competition 69
competition, domestic 326
competitive economy 74
competitiveness 278
    in the world economy 211
    of the agricultural sector 188
    of the Indian industry 185
computers, application of 173
computer technology 152
Conference on Millennium Goals 26, 231
Congress 150, 165
    led coalition 183
    Party 99
connectivity 107
    improving 243
conservation 180
Constitution 77
Constitutional Amendments 180
constraints 278
consumer goods 215
consumption habits 151
    diversification of 22

consumption patterns 106, 123
contagion effect 56
contemporary policy makers 92
contract labour 289
Contract Labour (Regulation and
    Abolition) Act 289
convergence, process of 55
convergence, forces of 58
conversion ratios 286
cooperative banks 358
corporate governance 357
    better 172
corporate practices in a globalising world
    173
corruption 128, 130, 152
cost-effectiveness 153
counter-cyclical fiscal policy 50
countervailing duty 282
countervailing power 20
    creation of 69
credit and marketing, support
    institutions in 242
credit, availability of 286
crisis of 1991, The 150
crisis management 347
crop specific inputs 188
crop varieties 251
cropping pattern 188
crowding out 87
    private investment 50
currency depreciation 40
currency flexibility 38
current account 43, 151, 362, 363
    surpluses in the 187
customs rate, peak 43

D

dairy sector 226
Dandekar, V.M. 101

de-reservation 189
Debroy, Bibek 28
debt capital 47
debt sustainability 50
Deccan Gymkhana 143
decontrol 70
defence expenditures 51
deflator 105
Delhi 144
Delhi Cloth Mills 148
Delhi School of Economics 87
delicensing 70
delivery systems 255
Delong, J. Bradford 36
demand surplus, effective 92
democracy 22, 149, 156
democracy, functioning 177
democratic decentralisation 135
democratic framework 19, 40, 64
democratic institutions, creation of 137
democratic institutions 42
democratic polity 183
democratic society 67
demographic dividend 60, 64, 263, 267
demographic dynamics 195
demographic pressure on land 119
demographic profile 366
demographic transition 19, 60, 65
demographics 62
dependency ratio 60, 171
deprivations, nature of 231
Desai, Ashok 19, 21, 22
Desai, Gunvant 120
determinants of rural poverty 121
developed countries 227
developing countries 36, 148, 228
development 166
    creative 67
    indicators 108

development, paradigm of 67
    planning process 90
    policy, ingredients of 89
Dharam Vira Commission 78
Dhawan, B.D. 255
Diaz-Bonilla 225
direct taxes 52
Directive Principles of State Policy 99
disinvestment 147
DMK 147
Doha Development Agenda 280
domestic market, narrowness of the 316
Dr. Reddy's Laboratories 298
Dréze, Jean 124, 214
drought prone 131
    areas 248
DWACRA 127

E

East Asia 56, 181
East Asian countries 173, 178
East Asian crisis of 1997 333
East Asian growth 62
Easterly, William 37
Eastern Europe 169
eastern parts 57
economic
    activity 67
        location of 144
    agents 68
    constraints 150
    development 67
    freedom index 291
    growth 19, 61, 197, 211
    incentives 69
    laws 70
    opportunities 81, 86, 107
    performance 174
    policies 99, 172, 177, 236

economic
    policy reforms 215, 217
    power, dispersing 69
    reforms 23, 46, 82, 86, 172, 179
        in agriculture 227
        process 42, 173
    strategy 20, 82
    theory 69
Economic Times, The 324
Economist, The 324
education, basic 107
educational status 117
efficiency, quest for 153
e-governance, promotion of 260
Eighth Five Year Plan 293
elderly dependency 366
Election Commission 165
electoral reform 78
electoral success of Congress Party 102
electorate 166
electricity 45
Electricity Act 46
Eleventh Plan 92
emergency 21, 148
emerging market countries 169, 170
Employees State Insurance 289
Employment Assurance Scheme 96
employment cess 96
employment elasticity 266
employment expansion 92, 94
employment, gainful 81
employment generation 278
employment growth in manufacturing 266
Employment Guarantee Act 180
employment guarantee programme 244
Employment Guarantee Scheme 233
employment in agriculture 188
employment, insufficient growth in 177

employment opportunities 120
employment schemes 132
empowerment 86
    of citizens 20, 69
    of poor 214
    of women 58
energy conservation measures 192
energy deficiency, chronic 235
energy prices 215
Enron's DPC 316, 324
entrepreneurial ability 171
entrepreneurship 19, 67
environmental externalities 74
environmental impact 217
environment protection, better 53
EOUs 285
equalising differences 54, 55
equity 53
    derivatives trading 47
    markets 336
ethnic 40, 41
exchange control 146
exchange rates, flexible 38
exchange rate, market determined 175, 361
exchange rate policy, conduct of 365
exchange rate regime, administered 365
exchange rate systems, rigid 38
executives 164
exogenous shocks 185, 198
export incentives 284
export subsidies 284
export-oriented services production 39
exportable surpluses 26
exports of services 362
extension services 251
external commercial borrowings 302, 312
external debt, stock of 364

external finance 299
external food aid 211
external liberalisation 174, 316
    gradual process of 173
external sector 40
    liberalisation 197
    policies 193
    resilient 187
external shocks 38, 215
externalities 73, 74
externality of technology 319

F

factor markets 70
factor mobility 54
factor productivity accelerators 65
fairness 156, 158, 165
family planning 102
FAO 212, 222, 233
farming 26
fastest growing economies of the world 197
FCI 92
FDI 158, 299
    approvals 303
    inflow 299, 302, 314
    performance index 285
    policy 323
fertility rates 366
fertiliser, subsidy on 150
Fifth Five Year Plan 102, 293
Film Institute 143
finance ministry 150
financial allocations 103
financial collaborations 321
financial crises 29, 331, 332
financial independence 151
financial institutions 97, 331, 336
    vulnerability of 335
financial integration, approach to 368

financial investors 158

financial liberalisation 195

    premature 368

financial sector 25, 47, 49, 334, 369

    reforms 48, 97, 186, 353

        process of 173

financial sector, strong 187

financial stability 25, 29, 30, 186, 332, 333, 335, 348, 351

financial supervisory authority 345

financial system 331, 334, 344

Financial Times 315

FIPB route 306

fiscal balance 183

fiscal consolidation 51, 52, 53

    issues 49

fiscal deficit 49, 73, 368

    consolidated 49

fiscal policy, prudent 191

Fiscal Responsibility Act 52

Fiscal Responsibility and Budget Management (FRBM) 191, 283

    Act 41, 183

Fiscal Responsibility Bill 354

fiscal transfers 55

Five Year Plans 81

    documents 99

Food and Agriculture Organization of the United Nations (FAO) 25, 212

food availability 25, 212

Food Corporation of India 90, 91, 96, 219, 255

food delivery mechanism 93

Food for Work Programme 76, 94, 96, 180

food, availability of 236

food basket, commodity composition of 105

food, entitlement to 237

food insecurity 214, 231

food intake levels 124

food management policy 89

food management, muddle-headedness of 93

food policy, muddle-headed 91

food processing industries 180

food, right to 96

food security 25, 26, 91, 92, 93, 129, 217, 231

food self-sufficiency 26

food subsidies 92, 239

food supply, flow of 237

foodgrain production 147

foodgrain self-sufficiency 216

foodgrain shortages 145

foodgrains, stock of 92

foodgrains, surplus of 151

Ford 322

foreign aid 151

foreign banks 357

foreign currency debt 40

foreign currency reserves 40

foreign direct investment 25, 155, 285, 362

    a positive outlook towards 320

    opening of 189

foreign equity holding 302

Foreign Exchange and Regulation Act 297

foreign exchange constraint 175

foreign exchange reserves 91, 364

foreign institutional investors (FIIs) 175

foreign investment 171, 285

    in consumer goods 326

    policy 301, 325

    rules 317

foreign investment, direct 83

    effects of 326

    terms of 325

foreign portfolio investments 285

Fourth Five Year Plan 100, 129, 293
FRBM 283
Friedrich List 144

G

Gaiha, Raghav 118, 124
Gandhi, Indira 102, 148, 149
Gandhi, Mahatma 81, 82, 155, 157
Gandhi, Rajiv 150, 173
Gandhi, Sanjay 148
GATT 361
GATT/WTO system 280
GDP growth 35, 89
    acceleration in India's 20, 36, 82
    higher 92
    low volatility of 35
    per capita 42, 101
    rates 61, 274
    real 185
    volatility 37
    ratio 50, 56, 192
    sectoral composition 28, 264, 265
gender and group disparities 107
gender development index 24
gender discrimination 110
gender disparities 125
Germany 151
Gillespie, Stuart 215
global competition 158
Global Competitiveness Report 278
global
    economic integration 366
        increasing 193
    economy 195, 196, 367, 370
    growth 185
    integration 196
        of the Indian economy 193
    mobility of capital 201
    ranking 35
    world 155

globalisation 23, 25, 43, 49, 82, 155,
    169, 199, 225, 229, 252
    challenge of 24, 183, 199
    compulsions of 23
    impact of 170
    indicator of 24, 200
globaliser, hesitant 43
globaliser, willing 64
globalising 170
    world 23, 170, 171, 172
Golden Quadrilateral 94
Gopinath, Shyamala 331
governance, deterioration of 67
governance, good 69, 89, 91, 96, 97
governance procedures, heterogeneity of
    56
governing system, effective 156
government, downsizing 50
government failure 19, 67, 252
government intervention 74
government, role of 71
governmental functions, decentralisation
    of 69
gradualism 176
gradualist process 183
Graham, Edward 314
Gram Panchayats 96
green revolution 217, 249, 250, 251
growth 84, 86
    decentralised and broad-based 89
    golden age of 64
    in the manufacturing sector 190
    miracles 31, 60
        rates 64
    of cities in postwar India 144
    of international trade 39
    of labour force 120
    of services exports 39
    performance 86
    rate in agriculture 180

growth
    resilience of 38
    strategy 20
Guerra, L.C. 253
Gulati, Ashok 211
Gurgaon 58

H
Hashim, S.R. 252
Hazari, R.K. 101
Hazell, Peter 217, 220, 222
health facilities 102
health indicators 178
health status 117
healthcare facilities 107
high growth economies of Asia 31
high growth trajectory 89, 93
high yielding varieties 242
Hindu rate of growth 21, 36, 83, 150
Hoda, Anwarul 216, 226
Honda 322
horticultural products 252
horticulture 180
household sector savings—income ratio
    354
human capital accumulation 19, 64, 65
human capital, quality of 171
Human Development Index 24, 155
hunger, elimination of 94
Hyderabad 58
Hyundai 324
HYV 73
    package 73

I
ICAR 255
ICICI 146
ICRISAT 109, 123
ICT-based community service centres
    260

IFPRI, Research at 219
illiteracy 100
import duties 280
improving productivity, process of 176
import licensing 150
import-substituting industrialisation
    146
incentive distorting laws 68
incentive structures 65, 68
    in government 71
incentives 42, 81, 161
independence movement 146
India 23, 158, 170
India Shining 177
India-specific situation 89
Indian agriculture 180, 211
Indian Council of Agricultural Research
    223
Indian economy, dynamism to the 178,
    185
Indian economy, opening up of the 185
Indian food policy 211
Indian Institutes of Management 172
Indian Institutes of Technology 172
Indian Labour Conference, The 15th 99
Indian manufacturing 282
Indian National Congress 82
Indian pharmaceutical firms 298
Indian Space Research Organisation 260
Indian statistical system 108, 273
India's
    balance of payments 148, 186
    exchange rate policy 366
    external sector 30, 185
    federal system 214
    financial sector 29
    financial system 47
    growth prospects 23, 170
    macroeconomic parameters 183
    manufacturing strategy 25

India's
    potential growth rate 170
    share in world 185
      trade 199
indigenous knowledge 223
indirect tax reform 283, 284
indirect taxes 282
industrial boom 22, 150, 151
industrial clusters 296
industrial countries 36
Industrial Development Bank of India
    146, 356
Industrial Disputes Act 288, 290
Industrial Finance Corporation of India
    356
industrial growth 176
industrial licensing, lifting of 151
industrial licensing, removal of 189
Industrial Policy Resolution of 1948
    293
industrial relations 289
industrial revolution 201
industrial sector 189
industry-led growth 146
inefficient implementation 128
inequalities 115
    in income distribution 101
    of income, reducing 100
inflation 37, 143, 186
    stable 191
    volatility in the 192
information technology 186, 191, 215
infrastructure 26, 44, 49, 176
    development 181
    hard 174, 177
    major initiatives in the area of 183
    sector 44
innovation 20, 67, 69
input intensification 251
input subsidies 216

institutional architecture 48
institutional credit 131
institutional infrastructure 19, 64
institutional support 251
institutions 172, 173
    of conflict management 41
Integrated Child Development Scheme
    (ICDS) 238, 240
Integrated Child Development Services
    214
integrated pest management 222
integrated regional resource planning
    132
Integrated Rural Development, IRDP
    102
intellectual property rights 224
interest payments 51, 52
interest rates 37, 286
International
    agencies 170
    capital flows 200
    competitiveness 175, 226
    Crop Research Institute 224
    crude oil prices 186, 192
    debts 148
    Finance Corporation 313
    financial crises 38
    oil prices 185
    sanctions 38
    trade liberalisation 215
International Food Policy Research
    Institute (IFPRI) 211
International Institute for Management
    Development 279
International Monetary Fund 151
International Water Management
    Institute (IWMI) 247, 256
Internet 44
    connected ICT centres 260
intervention 336

Investment 242
    choices 48
    in agricultural research 219
    in health infrastructure 53
Inward foreign direct investment 297
IRDP 127, 130, 131
irrigation 180, 242
    efficiency 27
    management, participatory 248, 253
    management transfer 27, 253
    subsidies 216
    water, productivity of 251
issue prices 91, 92
IT enabled services 177
IT-enabled sector 191
IT-enabled services exports 58

J
Jalan, Bimal 23, 24
Janta Party 149
Jawahar Rojgar Yojana 133
Joint Parliamentary Committee 150
judiciary 164
    independent 41, 173
jute mills 146

K
Kansal 110
Kelkar Task Force 280, 281, 283
Kelkar, Vijay L. 19
Kenya 146
Keynes, John Maynard 144
Kerr, John 223
Kidwai, Rafi Ahmed 145
Kinetic 322
kitchen garden movement 245
knowledge centre, every village a 28
knowledge connectivity 259

knowledge, diffusion of 63
knowledge-based services 202
Kochi 182
Korean War 145
Koreans 60
Krishna, Raj 83
Krishnaji, N. 127
Krishnan, T.N. 127
Krugman, Paul 59, 62
Kumar, Gopala Krishna 125, 309
KVIC 293

L
labour
    constraint 264
    cost advantage 263
        low 58
    force, quality of 24, 60
    law reform 288
    market 41
        flexibility of the 54
    mobility 84
    intensive manufactures 29
    intensive unregistered manufacturing 305
Laffer curve 52
Lakdawala Committee 105, 117
Laker 349
land access for the landless 95
land reforms 100, 131
land-saving technologies 249
landless labour 103, 244
late comer's advantage 31
latent social conflict 40
Latin America 169
Law Commission 78
leadership 156
    effective 157

legal institutions 173
legislature 164
length of the reference period 114
Leviathan 67
    government 71
liberalisation 156
    of agricultural trade 227
    of capital markets 169
    of direct foreign investment 215
    of exchange control 151
    of the industrial sector 226
    of the telecommunications sector 191
life expectancy 101, 155, 241, 366
    low 107
Lipton 118, 124, 125
literacy 85, 101, 107, 189
    adult 155, 179
living environment 117
living wage 99
LML 322
Lohia, Ram Manohar 100

M

macro prudential indicators 343
macroeconomic environment, benign 37
macroeconomic management 185, 186
macroeconomic performance 195
macroeconomic stability 183, 346
Madras 58, 144
Mahalanobis Committee 101
Mahalanobis, P.C. 146, 201
Maharashtra Employment Guarantee Scheme 127, 214
malnourishment 100
malnutrition 91, 212, 231
    incidence of 234
manufacturing 270
    boundaries of 271
    growth 275, 276, 278

manufacturing
    off-shoring of 28, 264
    process 272
    sector 189
marginal farmers 244
Marilou, Uy 48
market
    discipline 341
    domestic 314
    economics 54, 169, 173
    failure 19, 67, 69, 74, 253
    freeing of 169
    goods 70
    infrastructure 243
    mechanism 159
    oriented agricultural policy 221
    oriented reforms 41
    theologists 91
Maruti 48
maternal mortality 189
McKinsey 264
media 164
Mehta, Abhy 302
Mellor, John 120
merchandise trade 362
mergers and acquisitions 302
meso-economic reforms 42, 63
micro-enterprises 21, 93, 98
micro-level planning 188
micro-nutrient malnutrition 214
microcredit institutions 21, 98
mid-day meal programme 240
mid-day meals scheme 94, 238
middle income status 184
Minhas, B.S. 110, 121
minimum living 21, 126
    standard 103, 107
minimum needs programme 102
minimum standards of social amenities 106

minimum standards, norms of 130
minimum support price 242
Mishra, Lalit Narayan 149
Mission 2007 260
mobile phones 45
modern agricultural biotechnology 223
modern agricultural technology 211
modern agro-processing 180
modern economics, insights of 68
Mohan, Rakesh 23, 121
monetary policy 191
    objective of 348
monetary stability 191
monopoly 69
mortality rates 107
most favoured nation 281
MRTP Act 320
Mujumdar, N.A. 19, 20, 21
multilateral agencies 158
multilateral trade negotiations under the
    WTO 361
Murthy, M.R. 308, 310
Murthy, N.R. Narayana 19, 22

N
NABARD 96, 97, 260, 293
Nachane, D.M. 339
nagar palikas 75
Nagaraj, R. 25, 29
Nair, P.R.G. 124
Naoroji, Dadabhai 81
Narayan, Sudha 216
NAS estimate of consumption 113
NASSCOM 191
nation building 158
national alliance 259
national boundaries 201
National Commission for Integrated
    Water Resource 27, 247
National Commission on Farmers 27,
    260

National Common Minimum
    Programme (NCMP) 183, 260, 265
National Council of Applied Economics
    Research 109
National Family Health Survey 109, 234
National Highways Development Project
    94
National Nutrition Monitoring Board 109
National Nutritional Monitoring Bureau
    234
National Planning Committee 82, 99
National Rural Health Mission 179, 261
National Sample Survey 108, 266
National Sample Survey Organisation 232
natural monopolies 69
natural resource degradation 217
natural resource management 221
natural resources, sustainable use of 26
NCAER 61, 115, 118
NCMP 291
negative externalities 73
Nehru, Jawaharlal 81, 82, 99, 147, 157,
    184
Nehruvian Socialism 21, 145, 147
network externalities 42
network industries 19, 65
new agricultural technology 223
new development paradigm 19
new technology 120
    diffusion of 19, 65
New York Times, The 321
NGOs 20, 21, 98, 135, 138, 181, 243
Ninth Five Year Plan 176, 293
nitrogenous fertiliser subsidies 151
Njobe-Mbuli 223
Nohria, K.K. 157
Noida 58
non performing assets 355
non-agricultural activities 118
non-alignment 215

non-bank financial companies 358
non-economic factors 44
non-excludability 73
non-farm employment 95, 244
non-government organisations 71, 134
non-performing assets 46
non-rivalry 73
non-sampling errors 113
non-tariff barriers 361
North India 58
NRI schemes 302
NS surveys 232
NSE 47
NSS 114
    consumption surveys 111
    rankings of states 115
nuclear weapons 151
nutritional 101
    and health status 107
    norm 105
    security 235
    status 26, 123, 124, 245
        of the population 117

O

OECD 292
    countries 227
oil crisis 21, 148, 149
oilseeds processing 220
operational holdings 120
organic farming 95
organised sector 93, 268
organised *versus* unorganised sector 267

P

Paarlberg, Robert L. 222, 223, 224
Panagariya, Arvind 39
Panchayati Raj 57
Panchayati Raj Institutions 21, 75, 98, 138
Panchayats 95, 256

paradigm shift 30
Parliament 164
Patil, Balasaheb Vikhe 150
Pawar, Sharad 151
payment and settlement mechanism 345
Payment of Wages Act 289
payment systems 346
payments crisis of 1991 149
PDS 239
    outlets 245
peak rate, drop in the 43
pension sector 48
pension system 48
Perry, C.J. 253, 254
perspective planning division 100
pest resistant crop varieties 222
philanthropy 152
Piaggio 322
PL 480 programme 89
plan holiday 147
planning 100
Planning Commission 82, 100, 117
planning, inception of 89
pluralist and participative democracy 176
policies, eliminating protective 220
policy imbibed 361
policy innovations 56
policy reform 183
    process 215
political institutions 41
political leadership 165
political parties 22, 127, 149, 170
political sustainability 176
political system 41
politicians 149
politics 149
Poona 58, 144
poor, headcount of the 41
poor population, composition of the 117

population 100
    densities 217
    growth 249
    working 60, 64
        age 366
portfolio investment 155, 158
portfolio management of reserves 365
ports 45
post-independence experience 41
poultry 180
poverty 20, 41, 82, 85, 88, 103, 115, 214
    alleviation 20, 90, 211, 220, 234
        allocation for 130
        programmes 103, 126, 129, 130
    definition of the 109
    eradication 90
        progress towards 107
    estimates 113, 114
        methodology of 110
    high incidence of 90
    in India 101
    incidence 101, 116, 122
        and its trends 109
        trends in 101, 110, 118
    line 21, 103, 233
        national level 105
        proportion of population below the 107
    measurement of 103
    ratio 187
    reduction 81, 89, 90, 93
        basic approach to 89, 92
    report, state of 117
    studies 121
    temporal variations in urban 122
    trends in 92
    urban 121
        reduction 122
    worsening of 102

power, demand-supply gap in the availability of 190
power utilities 182
Prasad, A. 331
price flexibility 39
primary education 178, 179
primary health centres 76
primary sector 28
private entrepreneurship 172
private investment 50
private sector 158
    banks 357
privatisation 48, 49, 82, 87, 147
    of government services 67
    of irrigation 253
    of the infrastructure sector 63
privy purses, abolition of 102
pro-public-enterprise 20, 86
processing industry, domestic 221
procurement 237
    policy 255
productivity increases 62
profits, remittance of 146
prompt connective action 359
proper marketing infrastructure 188
property rights 252
protectionist 152
prudential norms 337
public accountability 134
public debt 368
public distribution system 91, 128, 238
    targeted 214
public expenditure on health 189
public good 73
    and services, basic 20
    provision of 73
public governance 22, 156, 158
    effective 157
    system 158, 159, 164
public health facilities, minimum 102

public investment 248
public ownership 100
public savings 171
public sector banks 356
public sector employment 268
public sector enterprises 83
public securities market 47
public tele-information centres 261
PURA (Provision of Urban Amenities in Rural Areas) 292, 295
purchasing power parity 155

Q
QRs, elimination of 43
quality of life 198
quantitative restrictions 43
quantum 299
quasi-public 71
questionnaire design 114
quinquennial surveys 113

R
rainfed areas 216
rainwater 95
    conservation 95
    harvesting 95
Raj, K.N. 327
Rajagopalan, V. 211
Raju, K.V. 254
Ramanna, Anitha 224
Ramasamy, C. 211
Ranganathan, K.V.K. 308, 310
Rangarajan, C. 25, 29
Rangarajan Committee, 1993 193
Rao, C.H.H. 25, 27, 254, 308, 310
Rao, Narasimha 151
Rath, Nealkanth 101
rationing 145
    of foodgrains 143
ravines 143

real sector 346
Reddy, V. Ratna 254
Reddy, Y.V. 25, 30
reference periods 114
    changing 114
reforms after 1991, intensification of 174
regional balance 177
regional disparities 49, 54
regional equity 59
regional imbalances in growth 177
regional inequalities 57
regional role models 56
regular elections 41
regulation 359
    of financial institutions 344
regulators 72
regulatory functions, transfer of 69
regulatory systems, appropriate 72
Reinhart, Carmen M. 38
religious diversity 41
rent seeking 298
Repeal of the Essential Commodities Act 219
Report of the High Level Committee on Balance of Payments 193
Report of the National Statistical Commission 273
Reserve Bank of India 302, 332
resilience to shocks 37
resource allocation, improved 59
resource availability 171
returns to scale, increasing 42
reverse leasing 120
Right to Information Act (2005) 261
right-sizing of government 20, 69, 71
rising expectations 138
roads 45
Robinson, Sherman 225
Rodrik, Dani 36, 40, 41

Rogoff, Kenneth S. 38
rolling window growth 36
rule of law 173
rules of the game 44
rural administration 96
rural artisan programme 293
rural development 25
    programmes 96
    projects 133
rural electrification 103
rural employment 95
    schemes 102
rural industrialisation 293
rural infrastructure 73, 188
Rural Infrastructure Development Fund
    96, 260
rural population living below the poverty
    118
rural poverty, debate on 120
rural poverty incidence 119
rural roads 180
rural sector, flow of credit to the 188
Russia 23, 169, 170
Ryan, James 125

S

Sachs, Goldman 23, 170, 263
safety net programmes 221
safety nets 347
Sahn, David E. 124
Samantaraya, A. 331
sampling 114
    error 113
Samuel, Cherian 313
Samyukta Maharashtra agitation 147
savings, domestic 171, 187
savings, household 50, 62
scale economies 48
scarcity of land 249
school enrolment 107

science and technology 221
Seckler, David 252
Second Five Year Plan 293
Second National Commission on Labour
    268, 290
Second World War 145
secondary sector 28
security environment 19, 65
security tensions 38
self employed 118
self-help groups 21, 76, 95, 96, 98
self-reliance 215
semi-arid tropical zones 223
semi-starvation 91
semi-starving India 92
semi-starving population 94
Sen, A.K. 106, 214
Sen, Abhijit 101, 122, 124, 125, 214
services, conventional view of 202
service tax 51
services revolution 201, 202
services sector 186, 191
SEZs 285
Shah, Ajay 47
Shah Bano judgment of the Supreme
    Court 148
Shastri, Lal Bahadur 147
Shenoy, B.R. 146
Shiv Sena 147
Shome, Partho 49
shortages 143
Shy, Oz 63
SIDBI 293
SIDO 293
Singh, Manmohan 82, 88, 173
Singh, V.P. 150
single regulatory authority 345
Sixth Five Year Plan 293
small and medium enterprises 190
social agendas 85

social cost benefit approach 300
social equity 95
social over-head capital 95
social safety net 89
social sector indicators 188
social sectors 76
social security mechanisms, informal 125
social welfare 73, 74
   expenditure 100
socialist experiment 147
socioeconomic deprivation 123
socioeconomic pyramid 116
soft infrastructure 174
software boom 151
software industry 173
software sector 191
soil conservation approach 95
South Asian countries 274
South Asian infants 213
South East Asia, tiger economies of 60
South Korea 160
spatial allocation, criteria for 134
spatial targeting 133
special area programmes 130
   rationale for 132
special skills, acquisition of 69
sprinkler methods of irrigation 255
Srinivasan, T.N. 101
Sriram group 322
SSI reservation 70
stakeholders 158
standard deviation 35
   of GDP 36
starvation, prevent 159
state finances 191
state intervention 126
state monopolies 70
state power, sale of 149
state, role of the 169
state-specific price indices 105

sterilisation campaign 148
Stewart, Frances 125
Stiglitz, Joseph 46, 338
stock exchanges, functioning 173
stock market listing 310
Streeten, Paul 101
structural reforms 185, 197, 361
Sub-Saharan Africa 212
Subramanian, Arvind 36, 298
subsidiary occupations 92
subsidies 51, 72
   reduction in 51, 52
      input 219
Sukhatme, P.V. 152, 233
Sundaram, K. 119, 121
supervision 359
supply response 86
supportive policies 188
Susan Collins 62
sustainable development, quest for 90
sustainability 82
sustained growth 85
   high 35
Suzuki 322
Swaminathan, M.S. 25, 27, 127, 221
Swatantra party 146
Sydenham College 151, 153
systemic stability 65

T

Tamil Nadu Integrated Nutrition
   Programme 214
Tamil Nadu's Mid-day Meals Programme
   127
Tarapore, S.S. 25
targeting 133
tax administration, reform of 183
tax/GDP ratio, stagnation in the 49
tax revenues 51
   structure of 51

tax system, rational 51
taxation, progressive 100
technology, level of 171
technology market 321
telecom 45
telecommunication industry 308
teledensity 45
Tendulkar, S.D. 119, 121
tensions 177
Tenth Five Year Plan 25, 90, 93, 95, 176, 187, 264
terms of trade 226
    shocks 38
tertiary sector 28
TFP growth 62
    annual 63
poverty rate, rural 217
Third Five Year Plan 293
Thomas Malthus 249
Thomas, Susan 47
Thorat, S. 211, 222
Thorat, Usha 331
Thottan, Pushpa 121
thrift 69
tiger economies of South East Asia 60
Times of India, The 91
TOMCO 320
total factor productivity 19
town and village Enterprises 324
trade flows, gross 39
trade integration with the world economy 43
trade liberalisation 189, 370
trade policy 243
    regime, reforms in the 194, 362
Trade Unions Act 289, 290
trade-distorting policies 229
trade/GDP ratio 43
transactions costs 48
transparency 53, 156, 158, 165

transport costs 144
transport, lack of 144
transportation facilities 188
TRIPS 301
TRYSEM 127
Tseng, Wanda 313
turnpike 35
TVS Motors 322

U

Udell, Gregory F. 334
unconventional approach 89
UNCTAD 285, 292, 311
UNDP 91
unemployment 93, 100
    backlog of 93
    growing 102
    rate for the economy 188, 293
UNESCO 292
UNIDO 294
undernutrition, chronic 214
unilateral trade liberalisation 43
Unit Trust of India 356
United Kingdom 345
United Nations 26
United Nations Human Development Reports 108
United States 158
unorganised sector 268
UPA government, The 265
Urban Employment Guarantee Programme 244
urban infrastructure 190
urban poverty 121
    reduction 122
urban poor, characteristics of the 122
US tax laws 321
user charges 52
UTI 146
Uttar Pradesh, western parts of 57

Uttaranchal 57

V

Vaidyanathan, A. 19, 20, 21, 110, 124, 125, 129
Vajpayee, A.B. 83
value system 158
variations across states 118
VAT 52, 183, 283
        system 183
village level infrastructure projects 96
Virmani, Arvind 19, 20
Visaria, Pravin 118
VKC 261
voluntary organisations 138
VSAT 152
VSNL 48
vulnerable groups 245
Vyas, V.S. 25

W

wage employment 96
wage labourers 120
wage-goods 97
Walker, Thomas S. 125
warabandi system 256
wastelands, utilisation of 95
water institutions 256
water losses 252
water management 180
water pollution 74, 249
water productivity 251
water resources 247
water supplies, usable 247

Water Users Associations 27, 248, 253, 256
water-intensive crops 252
water-use-efficiency 249, 251
watershed development 132, 248
        programmes, micro 94
watershed plus 95
wealth generation 69
well-being 107, 108
wells 323
white elephants 83
white revolution 220
wisdom, conventional 92
white-collar workers 146
World Bank 56, 108, 274, 292
World Competitiveness Reports 278
World Competitiveness Yearbook 279
World Economic Forum 278
World Food Conference 26, 231
World Investment Report 306
world market 89
World Summit on the Information Society 259
WTO 224, 225, 227, 228, 264
        agreement 227
        negotiations 181
        process 43
        rules 228
        system 281

Y

Yadav, Sharad 90

Z

Zebregs, Harm 313